W9-AVK-615

AMERICAN BATTLES & CAMPAIGNS

AMERICAN BATTLES & CAMPAIGNS

A CHRONICLE
FROM 1622 – PRESENT

THOMAS DUNNE BOOKS
ST. MARTIN'S PRESS NEW YORK

THOMAS DUNNE BOOKS
An imprint of St. Martin's Press

For information, address St. Martin's Press, 175 Fifth Avenue,
New York, N.Y. 10010.

www.thomasdunnebooks.com
www.stmartins.com

Library of Congress Cataloging-in-Publication Data
on file at the Library of Congress

ISBN: 978-1-250-10114-3 (hardcover)
ISBN: 978-1-250-10115-0 (e-book)

Editorial and design by
Amber Books Ltd
74–77 White Lion Street
London N1 9PF
United Kingdom
www.amberbooks.co.uk

Project Editor: Michael Spilling
Designer: Jerry Williams
Picture Research: Terry Forshaw

Printed in China

First U.S. Edition: November 2016
10 9 8 7 6 5 4 3 2 1

PICTURE CREDITS

Library of Congress: 14/15, 20/21, 24/25, 52/53, 55, 76/77, 80/81, 97, 102/103, 106/107, 130/131
Photos.com: 6/7
U.S. Department of Defense: 64/65, 140/141, 146/147, 156/157, 162/163, 165, 166/167,
170/171, 192/193, 206/207, 210/211, 218/219

Contents

Colonial Wars and the War of Independence, 1622–1783

North America became a battleground for European colonial ambitions during the 17th and 18th centuries, with Britain and France fighting a series of bloody wars against each other, and against the native peoples. But it was the War of Independence that came to redefine the political identity of the continent, with the Declaration of Independence of 4 July 1776 announcing the creation of a new nation: the United States of America.

Left: 'Siège de Yorktown' (1836) by Auguste Couder. Generals Rochambeau and Washington giving their last orders before the assault on Yorktown in 1781. The future American president stands in the centre of the group of officers, with French surveyors and engineers to the right.

American Colonies/French and Indian War 1622–1774

■ Virginia Colony, 1622

The commercial success of tobacco cultivation at Jamestown resulted in the rapid expansion of the English plantations into surrounding Indian territory, provoking a large-scale attack and the massacre of 350 colonists by the Powhatan tribe.

■ Kalingo (Kalinago), 1626

Upon arriving at the British island of St Kitts, French settlers found the native Caribs resisting, with 4000 of the Kalingo tribe in arms. The French joined forces with the British to butcher them.

■ Pequot War, 1634–38

The expanding Massachusetts colony ground into the expanding Pequot tribe with bloody results. After the murder of an English trader by some of the tribe, indemnity negotiations broke down. Further incidents led to colonial punitive expeditions burning villages. Indian counter-attacks led to the co-operation of Connecticut with Massachusetts against a Pequot-Narragansett alliance. An amphibious assault upon two Pequot stockaded towns devastated the tribe, making the English dominant in New England.

■ Iroquois Wars, 1640–98

These were struggles between the Great Lakes tribes for control of the trade for European goods. The Iroquois Confederation combined the powerful Cayuga, Mohawk, Oneida, Onondaga and Seneca tribes into a formidable body. The Iroquois desired control of the trade routes with the English settlements in New York and to increase their power and numbers decimated by multiple epidemics. The initial attacks were upon native rivals in the fur trade, which expanded to a full-scale attack upon the Hurons, through whose lands the trade went. Using European-supplied weapons, the Iroquois defeated the Hurons and went on to fight the Susquehannocks, who resisted successfully with weapons purchased

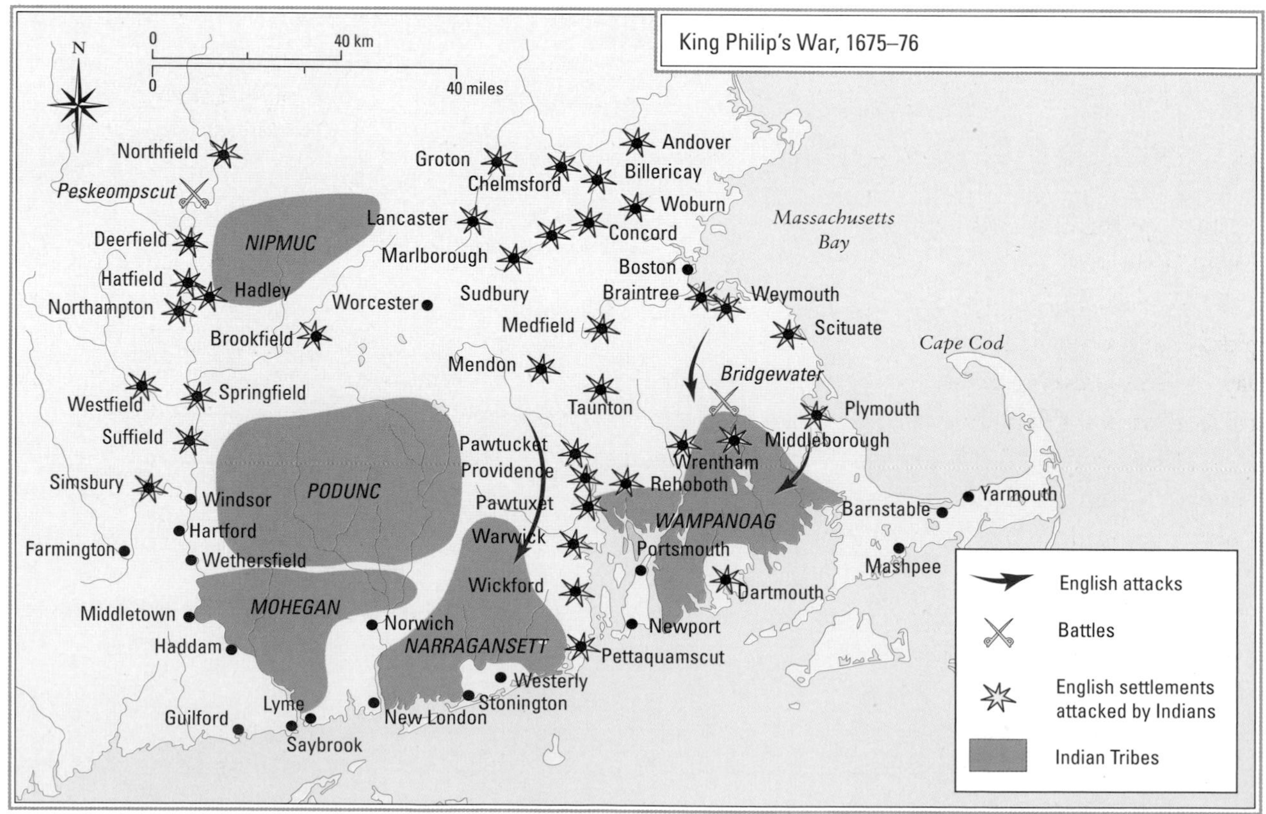

from the Swedish along the Hudson and with the support of the English in Maryland and Delaware. Surrounded by hostile tribes, the Iroquois finally ceased their expansion.

■ Kieft's War, 1643–45

The Dutch Governor Willem Kieft turned a theft of pigs on Staten Island into warfare with previously friendly tribes. Reprisals on both sides led to widespread slaughter, ending when the Dutch imported English mercenaries and negotiated.

■ Long Sault, 1660

The Iroquois stormed this unprepared French fort at a strategic portage on the Ottawa River. Joined by some 200 friendly Hurons, Adam Dollard and 54 French unsuccessfully resisted a powerful Iroquois force coming down the river.

■ King Philip's War, 1675–76

In terms of proportional casualties, this conflict remains North America's bloodiest Indian war. Alliance with the Pilgrims and subsequent Puritan settlements in and around Boston had made the Wampanoag tribe the most powerful in New England, but upon assuming leadership, Metacom, christened 'King Philip' by the Pilgrims, realized that English expansion would include his tribe's lands. Colonial efforts to disarm his tribe exasperated Metacom's fears and prompted his alliance with the Nipmuck and Narragansett tribes. The Wampanoags began killing English spies and raiding outlying farms, while the Massachusetts Bay Colony raised a militia and established new tribal alliances, slaughters taking place on both sides. By the time a powerful colonial force had reduced the last of Metacom's strongholds and set Metacom's head on a pike, at least 2500 colonists plus an unknown, but larger number of Indians had perished.

■ Bacon's Rebellion, 1676

Virginia Governor Berkeley's policy of Indian conciliation provoked a strong reaction by planter Nathaniel Bacon, who led colonial attacks upon the Susquehannocks and Pamunkey tribes. Bacon lost support when he burned the capital at Jamestown.

■ Lachine Massacre, 5 August 1689

With England suddenly at war with France, the allied Iroquois sacked this French village with 1500 warriors under cover of a hailstorm. The village's three blockhouses could not prevent the death or capture of 114 inhabitants.

■ Leisler's Rebellion, 1689

After the Glorious Revolution, protestant Jacob Leisler seized power in New York, seeking royal authorization for his measures against Catholics and Indians. Leisler's plan backfired and he was hanged after the return of British government and his enemies to power.

■ Port Royal, 19 May 1690

This French bastion and naval base in Acadia became a target of the English colonists in King William's War. Sir William Phips led a Massachusetts regiment by sea against the town, which Governor Meneval surrendered.

■ Apalachee Massacre, 25–26 January 1704

During the War of the Spanish Succession, Governor James Moore of British Carolina attacked the allied Apalachee tribe in Florida with colonists and native allies. The 1000 surviving Apalachees were taken as slaves back to Carolina.

■ Deerfield, 29 February 1704

The French and allied Indians attacked this western Massachusetts town, killing 41 villagers and taking 112 for ransom to Canada. The attackers scaled the ungarrisoned town's stockades at night and captured the village's houses individually.

■ Cary's Rebellion, 1707–11

Thomas Cary, governor of Carolina, disputed the claim of Edward Hyde to be his appointed successor. Sporadic fighting between associated religious factions ended when Royal Marines entered the capital, with Cary eventually acquitted of treason charges.

■ Bloody Creek, 1711

Acadian French and Abenaki Indians successfully ambushed 70 Massachusetts militia in three boats moving up the Annapolis River. The ambush killed 16 in the first boat and wounded nine of the others, capturing the surrendering survivors.

■ **Quebec Expedition, 1711**

Buoyed by success in Nova Scotia, the Massachusetts colony sent 12,000 sailors and soldiers under Sir Hovenden Walker against French Canada. Eight transports in the Gulf of St. Lawrence grounded with 900 dead, Walker abandoning the campaign.

■ **Nicholson Expedition, 22 August 1711**

Col Francis Nicholson led 2000 militia overland from Albany against French Canada, intending to rendezvous with Sir Hovenden Walker's forces sailing up the St. Lawrence. The troops from three colonies turned back when Walker retreated.

■ **Fort Neoheroka, 1713**

Governor James Moore of British Carolina advanced into Florida, attacking Tuscarora Indians retaliating for British incursions into their tribal lands. Moore's taking of this fort killed many, some Tuscaroras fleeing north to join the Iroquois.

■ **Villasur Expedition, 1720**

Along with a mixed force of Spanish and allied Indians, Pedro Villasur moved from New Mexico up the Platte River to assert Spanish authority. French traders and their Indian allies attacked and killed Villasur in Nebraska.

■ **Chickasaw Campaign, 1736–40**

The French and allied Choctaws had defeated the Chickasaws, Natchez and their British allies in the Natchez Rebellion of 1729. The French, lacking resources to maintain their extensive claims in the Mississippi drainage, did not authorize the Choctaws to launch a surprise attack against the Chickasaws in 1734. A French gunpowder convoy opened fire upon encountering a large force of Natchez and Chickasaw, prisoners and the gunpowder ending up in the Indians' hands. Abandoning diplomatic settlement, Louisiana governor Jean-Baptiste Le Moyne de Bienville ordered the construction of Fort Tombeché in Alabama and employed mercenaries in invasions of the Chickasaws' lands.

Warfare with the Chickasaws by both the French and Choctaws proved difficult, because of both the Chickasaw's acquisition and skilled use of European muskets and their tradition of living in hilltop forts of considerable defensive strength. The Chickasaws also proved adept at throwing French grenades back at the Europeans in the gap between ignition and detonation.

Pierre d'Artaguette led a force of French and Indian allies into ambush attacking the Chickasaw village of Ogoula Tchetoka, with the Chickasaws burning the survivors. Meanwhile, Bienville, with a European-style column, assaulted a prepared Chickasaw position at Ackia (modern Tupelo). Efforts to employ siege equipment proved futile, and the French scorned the advice of the Choctaws witnessing their attack. The resulting disaster infuriated the Choctaws, who became increasingly disaffected at French ineptitude and disdainful of them as allies. The French withdrew, Bienville leaving his governorship in 1740. They then supplied their Choctaw allies with weaponry while securing passage for their Mississippi trade from the Chickasaws. French prestige among the Indians and, consequently, influence, entered into irreversible decline.

■ **Stono Rebellion, 1739**

Twenty colonists and 40 slaves perished in this uprising in South Carolina. A Spanish proclamation of emancipation for slaves escaping to their territory combined with a Yellow Fever outbreak to spark the revolt, which was soon crushed.

■ **Gully Hole Creek, 18 July 1742**

The Spanish launched one major assault against the Georgia colonists, who were well prepared, with a fort and an ambush with allied Indians here. Fort Fredrica holding, the Spanish lost the resulting battle of Bloody Marsh.

■ **Kathio, 1750**

The Chippewa attacked this large Lakota village, in retaliation (so Chippewa legends say) for the murder of four Chippewa travellers. Purchasing muskets and ammunition, the Chippewa mustered at Fond du Lac and drove out the Lakota.

■ Pima Indian Revolt, 1751–52

Efforts to Christianize south-western tribes conflicted with Spanish colonization and Indian resistance to wholesale changes in daily life. Pima resistance was sporadic and largely unfocused, complicating Spanish efforts at repression. In 1751, secular Spanish resentment of the Church's lands and efforts to protect the natives' land flared up when Oacpicagigua began killing Spanish settlers. The Spanish response was crushing and the revolt and the mission system in the area both collapsed from lack of support.

American Colonies/French and Indian War 1754–1774

As each nation's colonists expanded influence over North America, the inevitable conflict began between French fur traders and English farmers. French wiles and Indian alliances could not overcome superior British resources thrown into the fray.

■ Fort Necessity, 3 July 1754

Maj George Washington led 150 Virginia militia to investigate accurate reports of French entry into Trans-Allegheny Virginia. Seneca allies led Washington to a French encampment. In the resulting skirmish, the Indians butchered all but 20 of what turned out to have been a diplomatic mission, including the surrendering Ensign Jumonville. Washington began building Fort Necessity in expectation of the French counter-attack, soon receiving 350 reinforcements and constructing a military road. French soldiers numbering 600 plus 100 Indians soon reached the uncompleted fort, which could not contain Washington's entire force. Their weapons and spirits soaked in two days' worth of heavy rain, the Virginians offered only 10 hours of resistance to the French, who offered lenient terms that included Washington's unknowing admission that he had ordered Jumonville's death. The entire affair sparked a war raging for seven years from Canada to India.

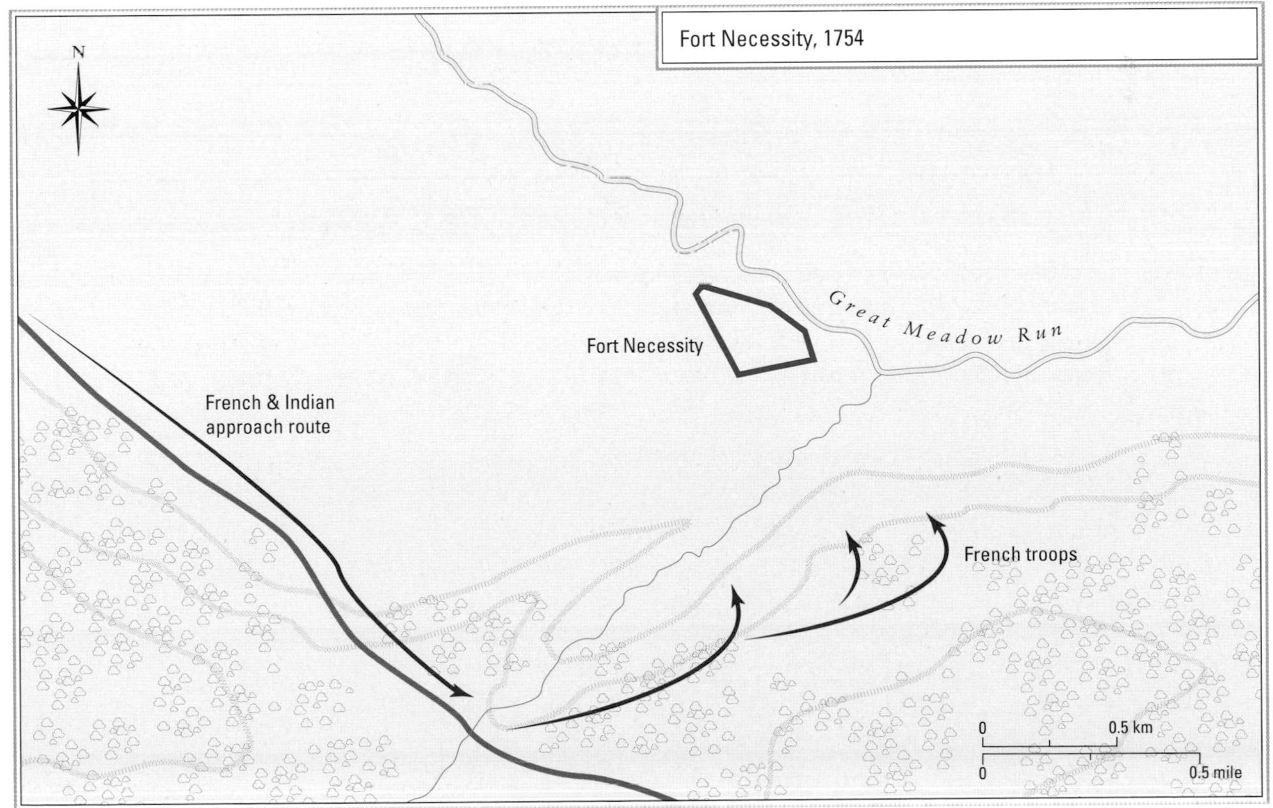

■ **Beauséjour, 3–16 June 1755**

The Micmacs and French built this pentagonal stone bastion across the Missaquash River from British Fort Thomas in Acadian territory. With a traitor's aid, the British and colonials launched a strong siege, which the fort surrendered to.

■ **Monongahela River, 1755**

Gen Edward Braddock refused to recognize the differing nature of colonial warfare as he led a powerful column against the French forts in the Ohio valley. With a large supply train, the 2200 British regulars and militia moved slowly, road-building as they went, giving the French time to collect Indian allies and ambush Braddock at the crossing of the Monongahela River. Braddock and two-thirds of his command perished in the rout.

■ **Crown Point Expeditions, 1755**

Crown Point was a staging point for invasions south into British areas of North America. Gen W Johnson led several columns into the area, constructing a road and Fort William Henry.

■ **Lake George, 8 September 1755**

Gen William Johnson with 2000 militia and 200 Indian allies dug in to interdict a French invasion route. French Col Ludwig Dieskau routed a supply column, then attacked the fort without Indian support and fell captive.

■ **Taliwa, 1755**

Expanding their territory southwards, the Cherokee (under Oconostota) invaded the territory of their long-term enemies, the Creeks. The outnumbered Cherokee defeated the Creek war-party and secured the territory north of the Chattahoochee.

■ **Oswego, 10–14 August 1756**

Advancing against French Fort Niagara, which controlled the portage-way around the namesake falls, Governor William Shirley of Massachusetts and British Gen William Pepperell ended their march at Fort Oswego, which they further fortified with a post – Fort Ontario – and garrisoned with 1600 men. The column's retreat that winter left Forts Ontario and Oswego insufficiently defended

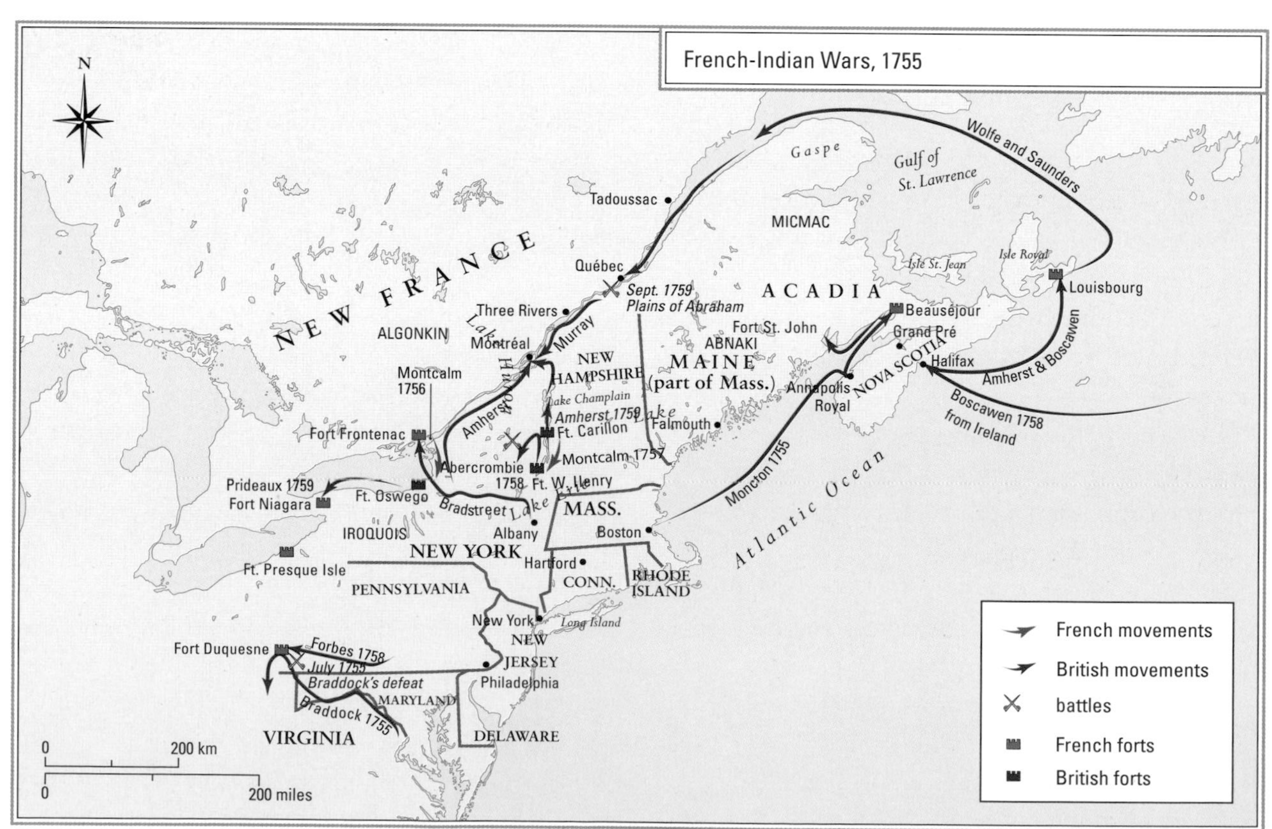

against French Gen Montcalm's advance and siege train, Ontario's fall leaving Oswego indefensible and having to surrender.

■ **Fort Bull, 27 March 1757**

The French followed up their victory at Fort Oswego by their winter attack on this small post further down the supply road from British territory. A total of 362 French, Canadians and Indians overwhelmed a colonial garrison of 60.

■ **Fort William Henry, 3–9 August 1757**

The French Marquis de Montcalm continued his policy of reducing the unsupported chain of British outposts meant to forestall French counter-thrusts down from Canada. A previous attack and difficulties in transport had left Fort William Henry damaged and with smaller artillery than those possessed by the French siege-train, which included mortars. LCol George Monro commanded 1500 regular and colonial garrison with 18 guns in the fort's defence.

Montcalm's forces included 6000 French and 2000 allied Indians, lured on by promises of glory and plunder. The fort's strength prompted Montcalm to begin a classic European-style siege of trenches and traverses as his artillery weakened the fort's walls and defenders, while allowing a message that reinforcements would not be forthcoming to reach Monro. Such tactics left Montcalm's Indians bored and angry as the siege wore on for six days. In keeping with European tradition, Monro asked for terms when the French created a breach in the fort's walls.

Montcalm granted honours of war and safe passage to British territory to the British, with the French retaining the fort and its stores. Indians out to profit from the campaign proceeded to do so on the night of the surrender, by taking the scalps of the British wounded left behind and, for the following two days, attacking and slaughtering as many as 184 of the departing garrison as they sought loot, scalps and prisoners to be held for profitable ransom. French efforts to stop the Indians proved ineffective, the massacre provoking

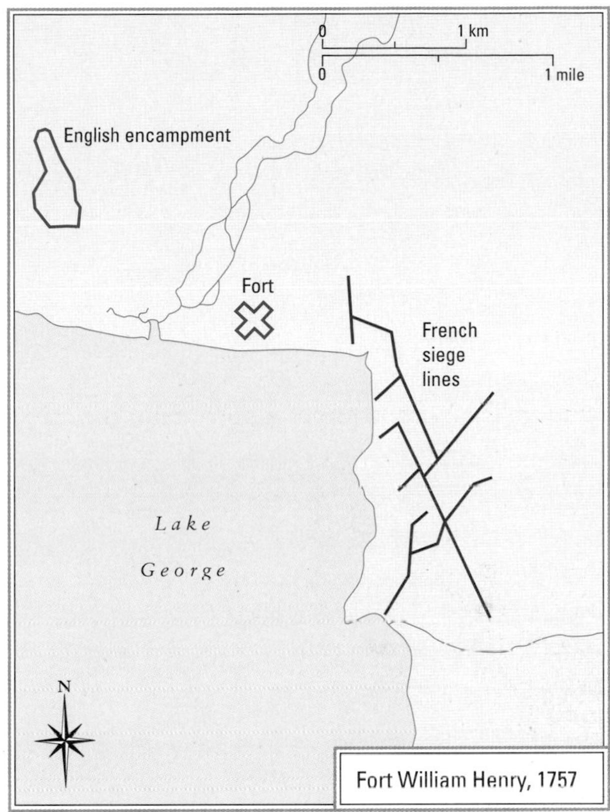

Fort William Henry, 1757

an enduring storm of resentment among the English and colonists, since celebrated in literature. Montcalm burned the fort and retreated back into Canada, while the British began preparations for a massive counter-thrust.

■ **Sabbath Day Point, 23 July 1757**

British MGen Daniel Webb probed for Montcalm's advancing siege column in ignorance of the French numbers. Col John Parker lost 250 killed or captive when 450 French fired on his boats. Webb retreated.

■ **Fort Carillon, 6–8 July 1758**

Gen James Abercromby led a waterborne British thrust towards the French forts along Lake Champlain towards this strong stone bastion, later Fort Ticonderoga. Both a reconnaissance and six subsequent assaults failed with heavy casualties. Abercromby withdrew.

■ **Louisbourg, 8 June–26 July 1758**

Having survived previous attacks, this French fortified port fell after a large-scale assault by 39

Native American warriors prepare to ambush General Braddock's mixed British and colonial force at Monongahela River in 1755.

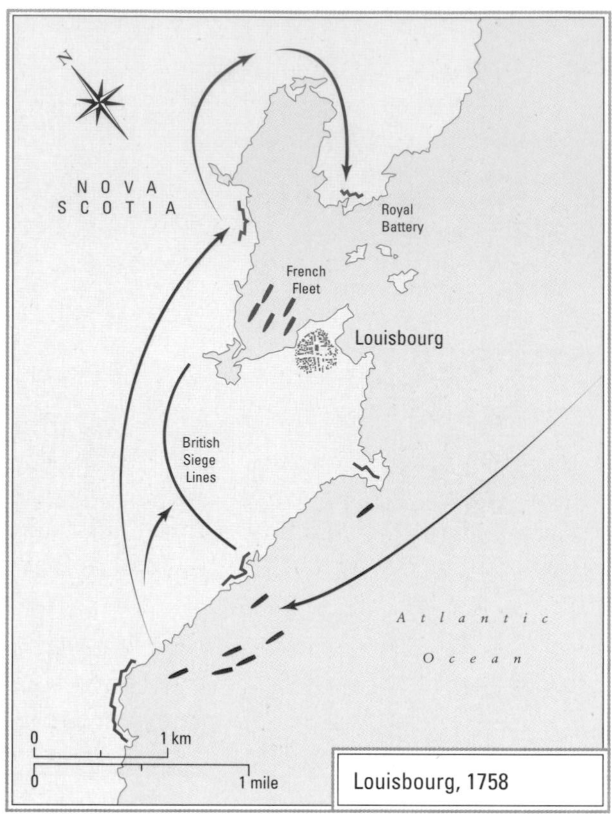

Louisbourg, 1758

British ships and landings by 13,200 troops under Gen Jeffrey Amherst. Hard fighting by both arms finally carried the town.

■ **Fort Frontenac, 26–28 August 1758**
From the site of burned Fort Oswego, LCol John Bradstreet launched a successful amphibious attack against this vital French stone fort. Landing stealthily with 3000 men, Bradstreet's gunners' bombardment startled the French into surrender.

■ **Fort Duquesne, 26–28 August 1758**
Gen John Forbes led a British force of 1600 regulars with several thousand Colonials against this southernmost French bastion (modern Pittsburgh), suddenly isolated by Fort Frontenac's fall. Forbes moved slowly, rebuilding Braddock's military road in preparation for British Prime Minister Pitt's planned powerful thrust into Canada. Forbes carefully wooed the surrounding Indians away from their French alliances. With supplies and living conditions eroding rapidly, the French finally burned the post and retreated north.

■ **Fort Ligonier, 12 October 1758**
This strong wooden stockade served as a supply depot for the British column moving against Fort Duquesne. Col James Burd and his garrison repelled an attack by 1200 French with Indian support, resulting in heavy losses.

■ **Fort Ticonderoga, 26–27 July 1759**
Using his secured line of communications southwards, Gen Jeffrey Amherst followed up previous inroads into Canadian French defenses with a build-up at the southern end of Lake George, his forces numbering 7000 soldiers. Taking forces and siege artillery up the lake, Amherst landed and positioned his cannon, the French taking advantage of the interval to evacuate the fort and fire its magazine, delaying further invasion of the Fort.

■ **Fort Niagara, 6–26 July 1759**
Capt Pierre Pouchot sent most of his garrison south against the British advance before Gen John Prideaux's army attacked. Pouchot surrendered after the British defeated a relieving column at the battle of La Belle Famille.

■ **Beauport, 31 July 1759**
The British found this village the most strongly defended of the French positions around Quebec. Montcalm had anticipated a landing on the rising ground and Wolfe's men suffered badly before retreating back into the river.

■ **Quebec, 13 September 1759**
Just as the Fort William Henry Massacre had steeled British resolve to take Canada, it also had made Marquis de Montcalm nervous about relying on Indian allies, weakening his ability to resist Prime Minister William Pitt's large-scale invasion of Canada. Both sides considered strongly fortified Quebec on its promontory the most likely site for a final decisive battle. Pitt's choice of command was Gen James Wolfe, who had distinguished himself in earlier battles.

The British sailed up the St Lawrence, where they established a heavy battery across the river and bombarded the city for seven weeks. In turn, the

French tried fireships in vain against the British. Wolfe launched probing attacks after landings at Beaupre and Beauport, which failed. The length of the siege and intelligence that the French were expecting a supply train allowed Wolfe to employ pioneers to scale a height overlooking a cove near the city, where they dispatched Montcalm's sentries. Wolfe then secretly landed half of his force before advancing toward the city's walls.

■ **Plains of Abraham, 13 September 1759**

After seven weeks of siege, Gen James Wolfe sent pioneers to scale cliffs overlooking this open area outside Quebec's walls to remove sentries placed there by the Marquis de Montcalm, in expectation of an attempt to resupply his city. Surprise achieved, Wolfe moved 4500 men onto these plains and drew them up in view of the French with the support of two cannon.

It is difficult to understand Montcalm's decision to lead only 4000 men outside his defences against Wolfe's smaller force (his superiority in numbers or fear of the British fleet starving his city are both explanations). The approaching onset of winter favoured the French. Wolfe took the time to entrench his men and position artillery as the French advanced towards them across the Plains of Abraham.

Montcalm put militia and allied Indians on his flanks and opened a bombardment on the British with three field guns. The French line, however, lost formation charging the British, while the British maximized shock with volleys of double-shotted muskets. When the French broke, the British artillery inflicted still further casualties, fatally wounding Montcalm while Wolfe, struck three times by musket fire, died shortly after securing his victory.

■ **Sainte-Foy, 28 April 1760**

With Wolfe dead, the defences breached and only Gen James Murray and 7300 men left to secure captured Quebec, escaping French forces rallied under Gen François-Gaston de Lévis

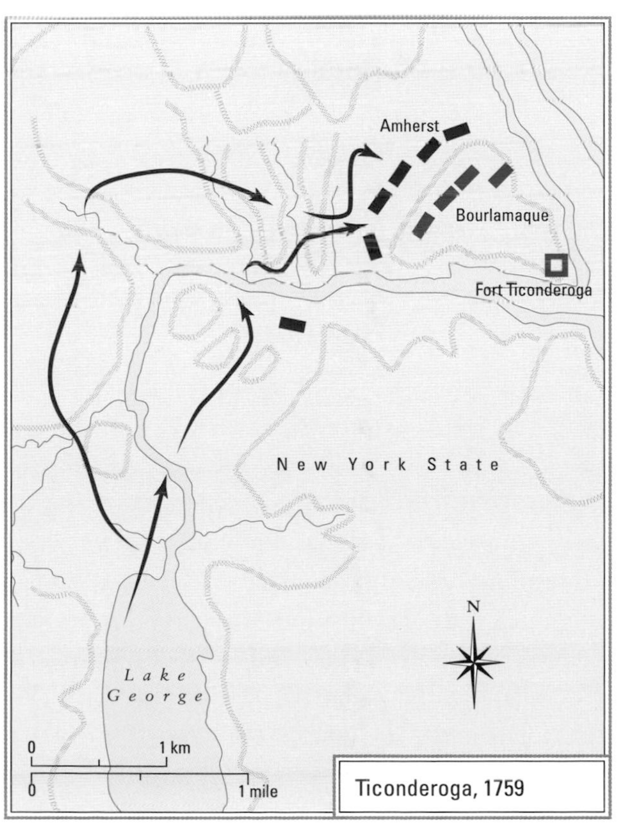

Ticonderoga, 1759

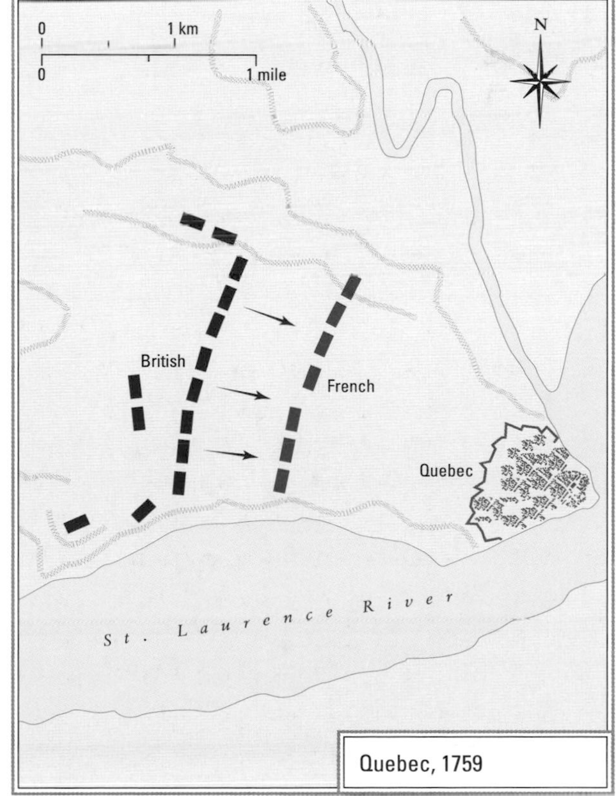

Quebec, 1759

and got ready to retake the city as the British garrison dwindled over a winter of scurvy and hunger. Lighter French ships could move in the St Lawrence before the British fleet escaped the frozen harbour. These ships landed 7000 French soldiers, militia and allied Indians upon this spot on Quebec's promontory near the Plains of Abraham. Murray led out the 3800 men still fit to bear arms, the French prevailing on this occasion when their superior numbers overwhelmed the British. Murray retreated into the city's remaining defences, which he held until the British fleet drove off the French and resupplied him. Lévis retreated to Montreal, where converging British armies forced his surrender.

■ **Restigouche, 3–8 July 1760**

After Prime Minister Pitt's renewal of the blockade of Canada and with spring allowing movement in the St Lawrence, the British fleet bombarded French positions along the river and destroyed the French flotilla in this bay.

■ **Thousand Islands, 16–24 August 1760**

The final stages of the British control of forts and regions captured during Prime Minister William Pitt's large-scale invasion of Canada depended upon the ability of the British navy to transport men and supplies up the St Lawrence River. Gen François-Gaston de Lévis nearly recaptured Quebec before the British could resupply the city's starving garrison. The French enjoyed some advantage in that their smaller river craft regained their mobility in the spring thaw before the ocean-worthy British vessels could move. Capt Pierre Pouchot with 400 men and two gunboats held a fortified position here in the St Lawrence archipelago. An arriving British fleet cleared the river and bombarded Pouchot's fort, reducing it after two days.

■ **Tacky's War, 1760**

Jamaican slaves rose against their British masters under the leadership of Takyi, an enslaved Ghanaian war chief intending to conquer the island. Several plantations fell before the authorities could organize and slaughter the rebel slaves.

■ **Havana, 6 June–13 August 1762**

Spain's new king renewed an alliance with France, prompting the descent by a powerful British and colonial amphibious force upon this slackly defended port. The city fell, later to be exchanged by the British for Florida.

■ **Signal Hill, 15 September 1762**

The French sought to secure a negotiating advantage with a landing and occupation of St Johns on Newfoundland. French and Irish infantry began systematically pillaging the island. A British force here ejected the raiders, with the French securing fishing rights.

■ **Louisiana Rebellion, 1768**

The 1762 Treaty of Fontainebleu ceded French Eastern Louisiana to Spain in compensation for Spain's alliance in the Seven Years' War. Spanish governor Antonio de Ulloa found his effort to regulate New Orleans's trade opposed.

■ **Boston Massacre, 1770**

Increasing resentment against British troops quartered in Boston culminated in the deaths of five colonists. Harassment of a sentry at the State House escalated into eight British soldiers firing their muskets into the large rock-throwing crowd. Five protesters were killed.

■ **Dunmore's War, 1774**

After the conclusion of hostilities in the French and Indian War, the British Crown issued the Proclamation of 1763 forbidding the colonists from further westward settlement, with the view of avoiding further expensive conflict with the powerful Trans-Appalachian tribes, such as the Mingos and Shawnee. With claims extending to the Pacific Ocean, the Western colonies reacted with fury and conflict between encroaching whites and responding Indians finally erupted into open warfare in 1774. The inability of the Iroquois Confederacy to compel non-conferated tribes to honour treaty obligations complicated the situation. With atrocities fuelling both sides' militancy, Virginia governor Lord Dunmore began sending strong forces into Ohio, striking at Shawnee and Mingo villages. The Shawnee-Mingo counter-attack upon Dunmore's camp at Point Pleasant collapsed and both tribes eventually ceded land and made terms. Dunmore's army suffered about 215 casualties, of whom 75 were killed. Further British efforts to limit conflict provoked colonial resentment.

War of Independence 1775–83

■ **Boston, April 1775–May 1776**
With cannon captured from Ticonderoga posed on the surrounding heights, the British under Gen Thomas Gage made the rational decision to evacuate by sea, the Americans sparing the British and the city by withholding bombardment.

■ **Lexington and Concord, 19 April 1775**
With both sides already poised on the brink of hostilities, Gen Thomas Gage sought to arrest colonial leaders John Hancock and Samuel Adams and to seize an American depot of weapons and ammunition at Concord, outside of Boston. Previous British forays had prompted the Americans to establish an early warning system that alerted the surrounding countryside to the departure by sea of LCol Francis Smith of the 10th Regiment and Maj John Pitcairn of the Royal Marines with 700 men from Boston. At Lexington Common, Capt John Parker with 130 'Minute Men' stood in line before the British column. An exchange of fire began hostilities, with the British meeting much fiercer resistance at Concord Bridge and retreating under continuous attack with losses by land back to Boston. The American leaders escaped and the British failed to find the sought-for cannon.

■ **Fort Ticonderoga, 10 May 1775**
Left useless since the French surrender in 1763, this post still contained 90 cannon and stores. At the commencement of hostilities, Ethan Allen and his Vermont militia surprised the garrison of 42 men. As George Washington and the Continental Army surrounded the British in Boston, Washington dispatched bookseller-turned-artillerist Henry Knox to Fort Ticonderoga to move the cannon south. Knox's brilliant improvisations in transporting the guns forced the British to withdraw.

■ **Chelsea Creek, 27–28 May 1775**
Hostilities commenced and the British raided islands in Boston harbour for livestock. Around 600 colonials sought to remove the animals across this creek, while 400 British regulars and the schooner *Diana* engaged the Americans, suffering casualties, including *Diana*, which was destroyed.

■ **Machias, 11–12 June 1775**
HMS *Margaretta* escorted two sloops loading timber for barracks at this Maine town as hostilities commenced. Patriots seized a sloop, sailing out and engaging *Margaretta*, taking her after a short pursuit and a sharp fight.

■ **Bunker (Breed's) Hill, 17 June 1775**
At the commencement of open warfare, 20,000 New England militia mustered under Gen Artemis Ward and surrounded Boston. The Americans learned through spies that British governor and Gen Thomas Gage intended to occupy the Charlestown peninsula and strategic heights overlooking Boston. Two days before Gage's move, on the advice of Gen Israel Putnam, 1000 colonials under William Prescott and Richard Gridley with two small cannon constructed at night a redoubt on Breed's Hill. The position north of Boston lay in the line of the planned British advance and directly under British observation, the covert and necessarily hasty establishment of the position limiting the amount of food and ammunition the Americans had on hand. British ships commenced an ineffective bombardment at daylight, Gage and his generals deciding upon an immediate attack before the Americans could link the new fortification with their others. Tides, wind, shallows and the height elevation hampered the British Royal Navy's efforts to assist the army's attack. The first British difficulty

Captain John Parker and the local militia exchange fire with British regulars at Lexington Common, 19 April 1775, firing the first shots of the War of Independence.

in launching an infantry assault upon the position was in securing enough water transport to land Gage's allotted force of 2600 men, the first British wave of 1000 troops digging in and prompting Ward to reinforce the American position to 1400 men, while Prescott frantically tried to firm up the resolution of his green troops and anchor his line on the Mystic River. The British failed to scout the line of their planned attack, which was crossed with stony ridges, long grass and fences. Gen Putnam did his best to solidify the American defenders, who wavered in some cases between fleeing before the attack or attacking outside of the defences.

Additional British forces landing in Charlestown came under American fire and retaliated by burning the town. The British plan, followed repeatedly in the course of the ensuing war, was to flank the Americans out of their position; in this case the British right found fences and a well-designed American position pouring an effective fire into their advance despite the British artillery bombardment. With the flanking movement failing, Charlestown in conflagration and evening approaching, Gage ordered his entire force into a headlong attack uphill.

The celebrated American order was, 'Don't fire 'til you see the whites of their eyes' and, with breastworks, walls and fences to steady them, the Americans obeyed it, maximizing the effectiveness of their minimal ammunition supplies. As the British force drew back with casualties, Gen Henry Clinton moved through burning Charlestown and launched another attack upon the American left, victorious so far, but now searching the fallen for ammunition.

British artillery finally cleared the American defenders and the British finally rolled up the American flank. Both sides resorted to the bayonet as the Americans slowly withdrew, suffering 310 casualties and 30 prisoners, having inflicted 1053 British casualties. Despite the efforts of the British light infantry to exploit the Americans' withdrawal, sufficient resistance and reinforcements remained to halt further advance, leading to stalemate on the peninsula upon which the battle had been fought.

Both sides considered the engagement a classic 'Pyrrhic' victory, one not worth the costs to the victorious British side. The Americans found a battle cry and a sense of confidence from the clash, in which untried numbers had faced, fought and bloodied one of the finest armies in the world. The stage was set for more long years of sanguinary struggle.

■ **Fort Johnson, July 1775**

As revolution erupted, 100 patriots in Charleston launched an attack across the harbour and surrounding mudflats to seize this fort at the mouth of the harbour. The surrendering British had already removed the fort's cannon.

■ **Gloucester, August 1775**

HMS *Falcon* under John Linzee seized a schooner returning to this port from the West Indies. A 'cutting out' expedition failed, Americans retook the prize, and Falcon withdrew after a desultory bombardment.

■ **Saint Johns, 17 Sep–3 Nov 1775**

Anticipating the American invasion, British, Canadian and allied Indian land and water forces collected at this post, with about 1000 defenders wearing down Gen Richard Montgomery's 2000. The starving British surrendered after lengthy fierce fighting.

■ **Longue Pointe, 25 September 1775**

Rapid action having secured him Fort Ticonderoga, Col Ethan Allen of the Vermont militia pressed swiftly up into Canada with 110 men, hoping to take Quebec unprepared. Surrounded here by some 250 defenders, Allen surrendered.

■ **Falmouth, 18 October 1775**

Adm Samuel Graves made an example of this Maine town, retaliating for patriot attacks along the New England seaboard. After a warning, Capt Henry Mowat and a small squadron burned the town, infuriating the colonies.

■ **Kemp's Landing, 15 November 1775**
Moving out of Norfolk, Virginia governor Lord Dunmore led a series of raids against patriot storehouses and posts. At this location, Dunmore's regulars routed 170 green militia, seizing the town and proclaiming Virginia in revolt.

■ **Great Bridge, 9 December 1775**
Virginia governor Lord Dunmore tried to seize the militia's stores of arms and ammunition as revolt loomed. Retreating to Norfolk, he offered freedom to slaves supporting the crown and raised the first loyalist forces, which defended Norfolk at this bridge with a wooden stockade. Col William Woodford took 900 men and established a position at the Virginia side of the bridge. The loyalists and regulars attacked, retreating with casualties.

■ **Quebec, 31 December 1775**
With the British withdrawing from Boston and the Americans hoping for a Continental revolution, a force moved northwards under Gen Philip Schuyler and Col Benedict Arnold to drive the British out of their last stronghold of Quebec. Gen Richard Montgomery's 3000 men were to converge with Arnold's 1050 at Quebec after Montgomery reduced intervening British forts and captured Montreal. Matters progressed slowly, Arnold's depleted column rendezvousing with Montgomery's as winter started. The British and Canadians spotted Arnold's column and put the city into a state of defence. Arnold crossed the river and sought in vain to lure the British from the defences as Montgomery's force moved up and began a formal siege. Disease and cold weather reduced the Americans to 1700 against a 1200-strong British and Canadian garrison and a complicated American assault collapsed disastrously.

■ **Norfolk, 1 January 1776**
Great Bridge convinced Lord Dunmore and loyalist families in Norfolk to withdraw to the crowded British ships in the roadstead. As the Americans occupied the town, the British ships opened fire and the city burned.

■ **Moore's Creek Bridge, 27 February 1776**
Americans who remained loyal to the crown, 'Tories' to the patriots' 'Whigs', sought to support royal control of North Carolina. British Gen Donald MacDonald organized 1600 loyalists into a force of 'Highlanders', which encountered Col James Moore with 1100 patriot militia at this location. Charging across the defended bridge with bagpipes and broadswords, the loyalists collapsed under withering fire, losing 30 dead and 850 captured, along with vital military stores.

■ **Rice Boats, 2–3 March 1776**
Under threat of the city's destruction, a British fleet landed at this Georgia port to collect supplies for the war in the north while patriot forces mustered in response. Roughly 500 patriot militia moved the sought-for supplies on rice boats upriver to Hutchinson's Island. A British landing party of 300 secured 10 boats before the patriots ignited two with fire ships and forced the British to retreat with their haul.

■ **Nassau, 3–4 March 1776**
Capt Esek Hopkins with two ships, two brigs and a sloop led the Continental navy's first overseas descent upon this island city in the Bahamas, where the islanders turned over British cannon and stores bloodlessly.

■ **Saint-Pierre, 25 March 1776**
French Canadians joined both patriot and British armies during the American invasion of Canada and siege of Quebec. Alerted patriots, numbering 230, surprised and captured 46 loyalists here near Quebec after the American invasion faltered.

■ **The Cedars, 18–27 May 1776**
As the patriot invasion of Canada collapsed, the British counter-attack under Gens Carleton and Burgoyne, with a force of 13,000 troops, followed up on the Americans' retreat from the areas around Quebec and Montreal. Indians allied to the British located a party of 400 patriots in this location west of Montreal, the British capturing both these troops and another 100 sent in a relief column before Gen Benedict Arnold arrived with the main patriot force.

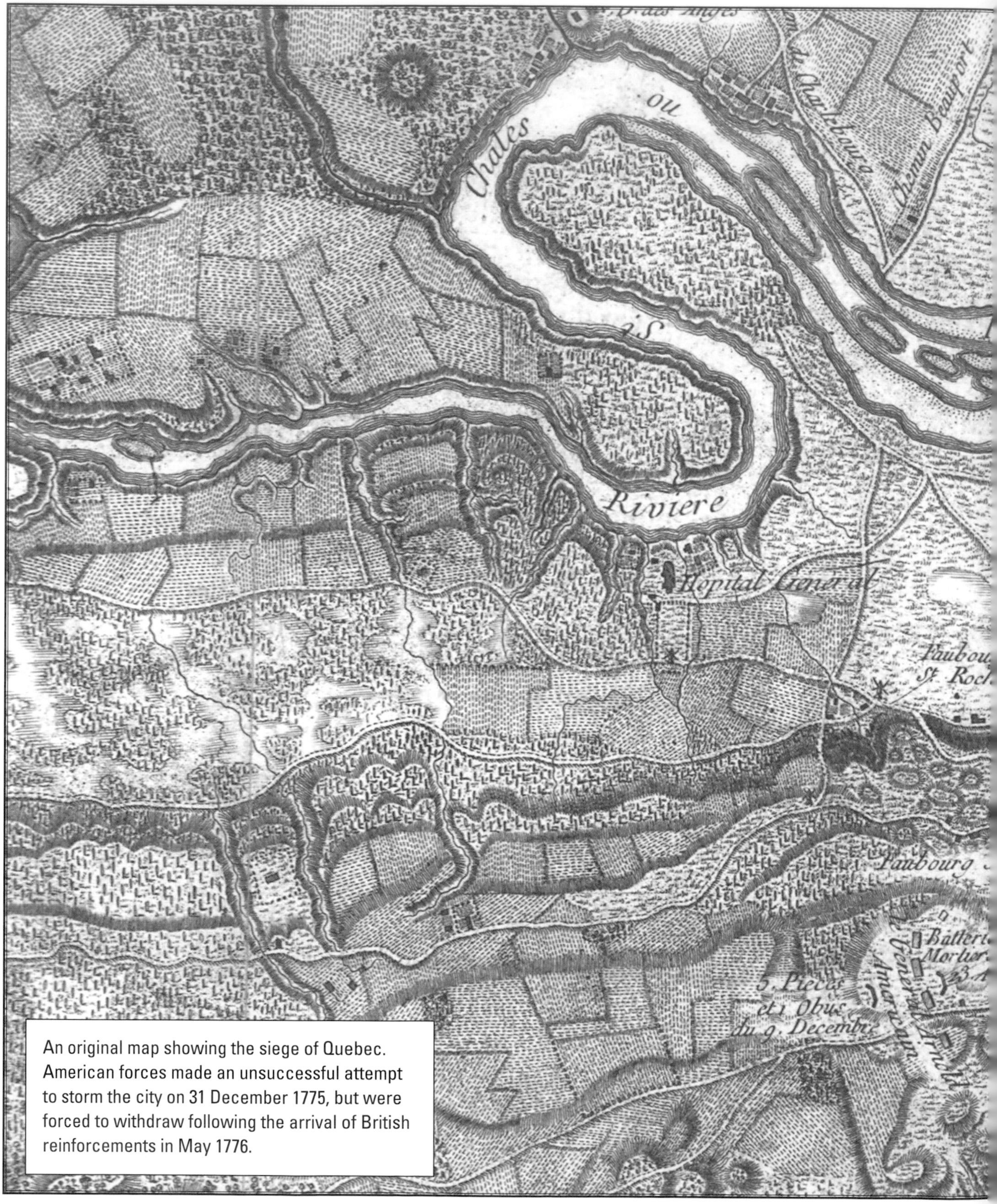

An original map showing the siege of Quebec. American forces made an unsuccessful attempt to storm the city on 31 December 1775, but were forced to withdraw following the arrival of British reinforcements in May 1776.

Environs
DE QUEBEC.
Bloque.
par les Americains
du 8. Decembre 1775.
au 13. Mai 1776.
A Paris
Chez le Rouge rue des grands Augustins.
1777.

a. Bastion Diamant.
b. .... Glaciere.
c. .... St. Louis.
d. .... Ste. Ursule
e. .... St. Jean.
f. .... Potasse.
g. Porte du Palais.
h. Gouvernement et Citadelle.
i. Eglise de la Basse Ville.
k. Congregation.
l. Attaque du Général Montgomery le 31. Decembre entre 4. et 5. heures du matin.
m. Sault du Matelot. attaque du Colonel Arnold le 31. 10.bre
o. Cazernes.
p. Porte St. Jean.
q. Porte St. Louis.
r. Jesuites.
s. Ursulines.
t. Recolets.
u. Seminaire.
x. Port.
y. Cavalier.

■ Trois-Rivieres, 8 June 1776

Gen William Thompson reconnoitered this region with 2000 men as the Americans withdrew from Canada. Led into a swamp, the Americans took fire from British vessels and infantry, losing Thompson, 235 prisoners and 40 dead.

■ Charleston I, 28 June 1776

A British fleet from Ireland combined with troops from New York to attack the southern port. Patriot defences and a botched landing on a tidal island produced a British debacle and retreat to New York.

■ Fort Moultrie (Sullivan), 28 June 1776

William Moultrie commanded Fort Sullivan (walled with logs) with 435 men and 31 cannon protecting the mouth of Charleston harbour when a British fleet and landing force assailed the vital port. Supported by 750 infantry on Sullivan's island, the garrison survived a 10-hour bombardment by the British fleet, the soft logs and sand of their palisade absorbing British shot, while their own careful gunnery killed 225 British before the attackers withdrew.

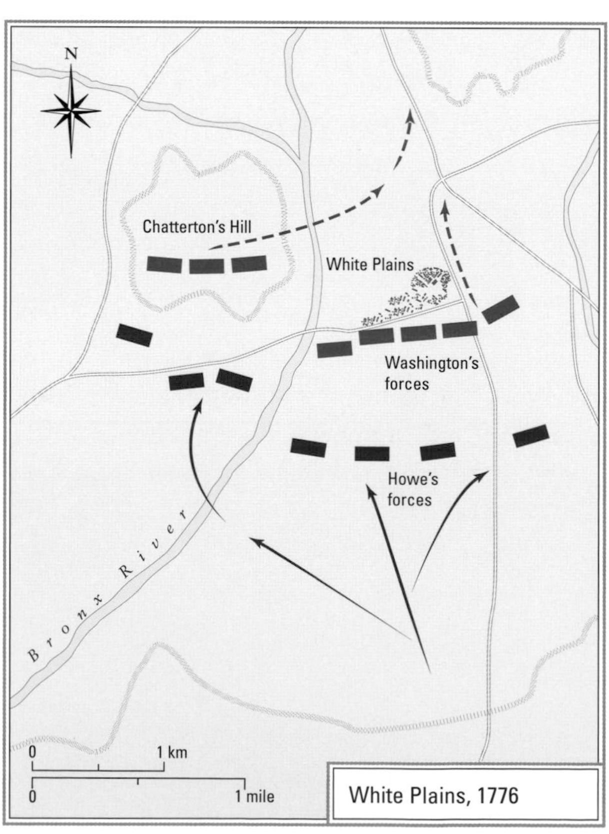

White Plains, 1776

■ Long Island, 27 August 1776

Howe's coordinated invasion of New York began with a fleet-supported landing here opposite Manhattan. A total of 15,000 British troops repeatedly outflanked 9000 patriots, who, by stubborn fighting, kept their retreating army intact and escaped to Manhattan.

■ Harlem Heights, 16 September 1776

As the British Army and Royal Navy advanced out of lower Manhattan, Washington made his first stand, allowing his force of 2000 to collect their numbers and supplies. The Americans withdrew after bloodying the British advance guard.

■ Fort Hill/Lookout Place, 1776

Gen William and Adm Richard Howe established this bastion on Staten Island, where arriving fleets collected 30,000 men including loyalists and supplies for the British assault upon New York City and the 23,000 patriot defenders.

■ Valcour Island/Bay, 11 October 1776

Gen Benedict Arnold fought and lost this three-day fleet action on Lake Champlain with 15 small vessels against 23 heavier British craft. Despite the loss of his flotilla, Arnold successfully delayed Gen John Burgoyne's invasion.

■ Pell's Point/Pelham, 18 October 1776

British and Hessian troops, numbering 4000, landed here against a strong delaying action fought by Col John Glover and 750 Continentals, who by retreating slowly and firing from multiple defensible lines safeguarded Washington's retreat from Manhattan.

■ White Plains, 28 October 1776

The patriot army of 14,500 – disordered and demoralized by the reverses at Long Island and Harlem Heights – along with Israel Putnam and William Heath, sought to draw up a defensible line across the Bronx River from which they could bloody the advancing British. Sir William Howe advanced with 13,500, including Hessians. The British succeeded in forcing Washington's

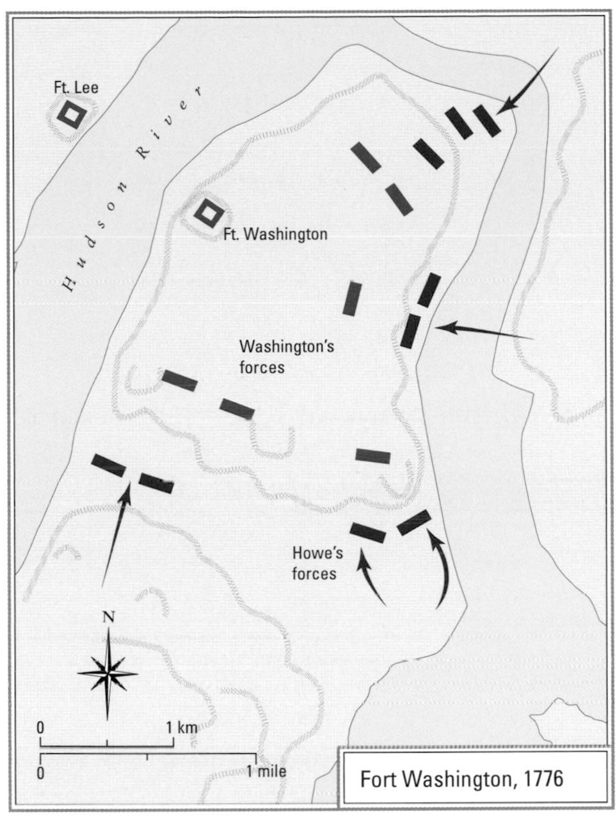

Fort Washington, 1776

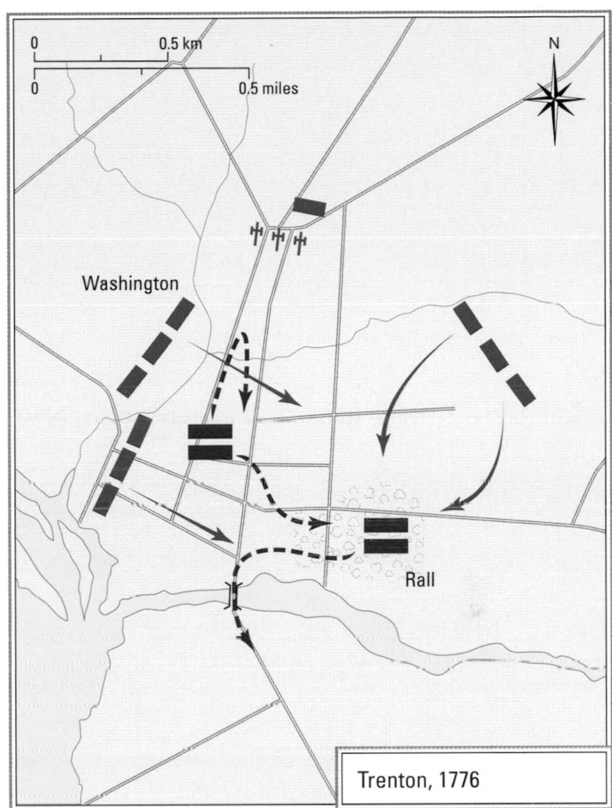

Trenton, 1776

withdrawal through a series of flanking movements, the patriots retreating in good order.

■ **Fort Cumberland, 10–29 November 1776**
Nova Scotia nearly joined the patriot cause when Col Jonathan Eddy and 400 militia attacked this post and 200 defenders under the British commander Joseph Goreham. Support from the locals prompted British retaliation when the patriots withdrew.

■ **Fort Washington, 16 November 1776**
Against its namesake's wishes, the garrison of 2800 held this Manhattan earthwork against the British Army and Royal Navy. Howe attacked with 11,000 men and captured the fort and defenders before they could be reinforced or withdrawn.

■ **Fort Lee, 20 November 1776**
The American earthwork guarding the New Jersey side of the Hudson lasted until November, when Gen Charles Cornwallis and 4000 men attacked across the river. The Americans had sufficient warning for the garrison to escape.

■ **Iron Works Hill, 22–23 December 1776**
Col Samuel Griffin, with 600 New Jersey militia, raided New Jersey, drawing Hessian Col Carl von Donop and 1500 men away from Trenton. The brief clash resulted in few casualties on either side.

■ **Trenton, 26 December 1776**
A characteristic of Washington's generalship was that he always left his army opportunities either to withdraw or attack. Winter's onset added to the misery of the patriots' retreat into Pennsylvania with depleted numbers after multiple defeats in the unsuccessful defence of New York City. Washington's ability to flee or menace the British forces received tremendously valuable assistance from the general's own intelligence network of spies and observers. Through these channels came the news across the Delaware that Col Johann Rall and 1600 Hessians held Trenton on the river's far bank as part of a chain of outlying posts screening the British continental beachhead in Manhattan. Some 6000 men remained to Washington, who

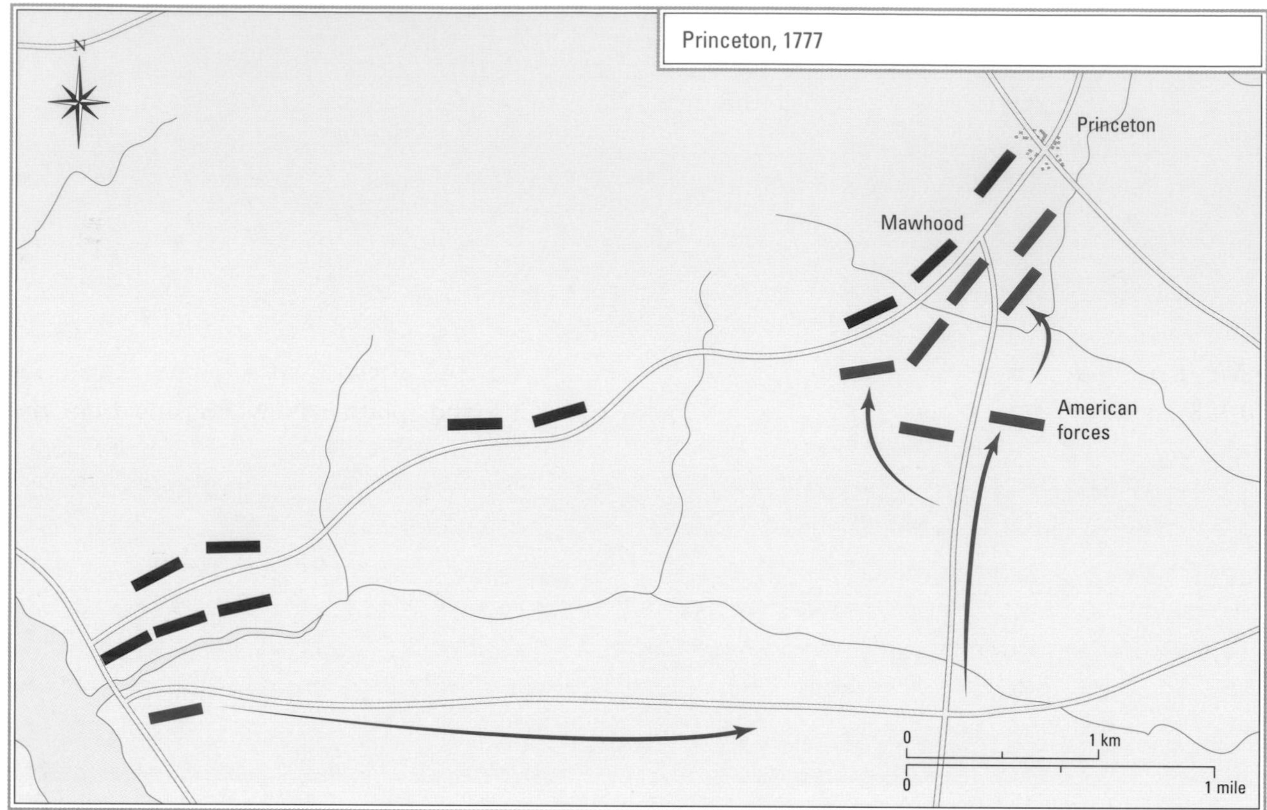

felt any hope of prolonging the war rested upon a demonstration that the Continental Army could still prevail. The British had their own reports that Washington intended to attack New Jersey, but long quiescence and the previous defeats lulled Rall and his superiors into celebration of Christmas and their victories. Washington gathered boats capable of crossing the nearly frozen river and awaited his opportunity.

A snowstorm blinded Hessian sentries and chilled Washington's 2400 tattered soldiers as they crossed the Delaware. They sent out screening forces around Trenton and drew up in line before the barracks where the Hessians were digesting their Christmas dinner. Rall was killed trying to rally his befuddled men with a final spy's warning left unread in his vest pocket. Of the Hessians, 900 surrendered and 106 died. Two colonials were wounded. Not the least reward of the victory were the warm winter uniforms of the captured Germans, but the resulting legend raised patriot spirits and forced the British to forfeit control of the New Jersey countryside.

■ Second Trenton/Assunpink Creek, 2 January 1777

After the successful surprise attack, Washington again moved his forces to Trenton, withdrawing before the advance of British Gen Charles Cornwallis and his 5000 regulars and inflicting heavy casualties here on the road from Princeton.

■ Princeton, 3 January 1777

The British withdrawal of the scattered units, such as the Hessians Washington had overwhelmed at Trenton, convinced Washington to re-cross the Delaware and link up forces already operating in New Jersey. In response, Gen Charles Cornwallis and 8000 British and Hessian troops advanced from Princeton towards Trenton, where Washington and 5000 Continentals were dug in. Expecting to crush Washington the following day, Cornwallis prepared his assault only to find that the Continental Army had decamped and moved around his flank to attack his rear guard of 1700 back in Princeton. Valiant fighting by LCol Charles Mawhood and a retreat through the university prevented collapse, but the British suffered some 130 captured, 28 killed and 58 wounded, while the American casualties totalled 44. Washington went into winter quarters at Morristown, from which he further weakened British control of New Jersey.

■ **MILLSTONE/SOMERSET COURTHOUSE, 20 JANUARY 1777**

Gen Philemon Dickinson, harassing the British, with 500 Jersey militia successfully attacked a British foraging party on the patriot side of the Millstone River, capturing 40 wagons and 100 horses before the regulars retreated.

■ **BOUND BROOK, 13 APRIL 1777**

Gen Benjamin Lincoln avoided an American Trenton by leading 500 men out of an attack by 4000 Hessian Jaegers against his outlying camp. The Americans reoccupied the New Jersey post before Washington withdrew them.

■ **DANBURY, APRIL 1777**

Gen William Tryon and 1800 seaborne troops sought to capture a patriot arsenal here. The materiel there having been moved, Tryon's battered troops destroyed other supplies and escaped through Continental forces attempting to trap them.

■ **RIDGEFIELD, 27 APRIL 1777**

Gen William Tryon and 1800 regulars landed to destroy patriot stores in Connecticut, finding here Gen Benedict Arnold and 500 colonial militia across their line of retreat. The British outflanked the Americans and resumed their retreat.

■ **THOMAS CREEK, 17 MAY 1777**

Georgia militia cavalry under Col Samuel Elbert moved towards the British and Indians based at St Augustine, Florida. Planned naval support collapsing, the Americans fell into a costly ambush, losing some 30 taken captive and killed.

■ **SHORT HILLS, 26 JUNE 1777**

Gen William Howe sought a decisive battle with Washington's forces in New Jersey. At this place, his army attacked Lord Stirling's command, the Americans retreating into Washington's nearby army. Their flanks endangered, the British retreated.

■ **FORT TICONDEROGA II, 2–6 JULY 1777**

The British counter-attack out of Canada took the form of an invasion southwards along Lake Champlain with 8500 men under Gen John Burgoyne, planning to link with a force under Gen Charles Cornwallis moving up out of New York City and splitting New England from the rest of the colonies. The naval battle of Valcour Island delayed, but did not stop, the movement southward. Gen Arthur St. Clair and 3100 men garrisoned the stone fort blocking Burgoyne's route into New England. Ticonderoga had changed sides several times over its existence. In previous sieges, attackers had mounted siege cannon on Mount Defiance, a neighbouring height, which St Clair had neglected to defend. Burgoyne having followed that precedent, St Clair and his men abandoned the fort by night, following another precedent of the fort's past defenders. St Clair faced and survived a court martial.

■ **HUBBARDTON, 7 JULY 1777**

Burgoyne's advance guard of 1750 men overtook the retreating St Clair's exhausted rearguard of 1300 recovering bivouacked at this town. The British captured 200 Americans after a bitter fight that allowed St Clair's withdrawal.

■ **FORT ANNE, 8 JULY 1777**

British Gen John Burgoyne's advance guard of 190 moved towards this fort – in between Lake Champlain and the Hudson – into an ambush by its 550 militia garrison. The Americans then burned the fort and retreated.

■ **FORT STANWIX, 2–22 AUGUST 1777**

Col Barry St Leger led 1600 of Burgoyne's force through the Mohawk valley at this bastion, against Col Peter Gansevoort's 750 men. St Leger's allied Indians forced him to abandon his siege after losses.

■ **ORISKANY, 6 AUGUST 1777**

Gen Nicholas Herkimer led 800 men in a relief

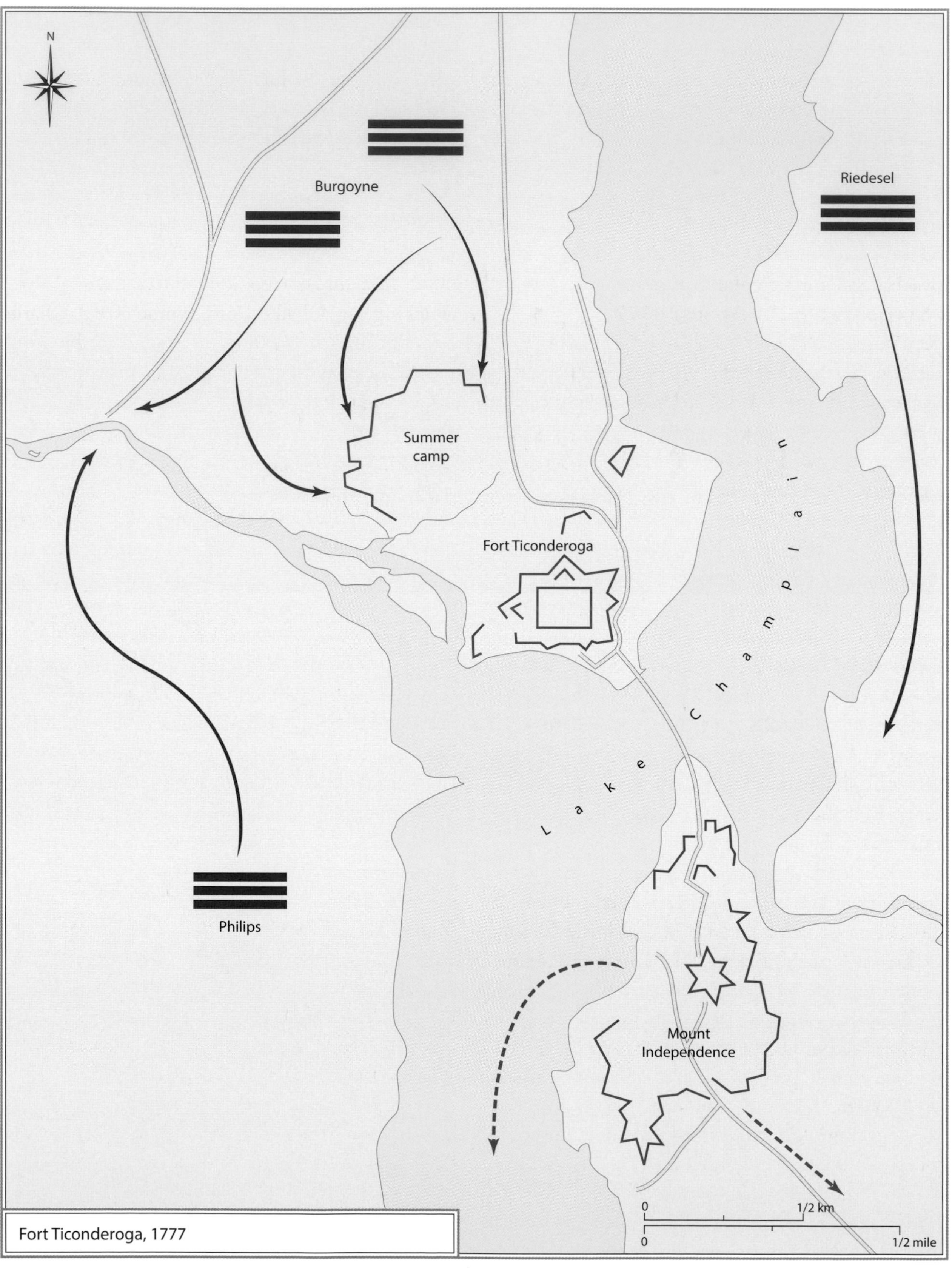

Fort Ticonderoga, 1777

column for Fort Stanwix into an ambush by British Col Barry St Leger's Indians. A thunderstorm allowed the patriots to withdraw. St. Leger's advance completely stalled.

■ **Bennington, 16 August 1777**

LCol Friedrich Baum led 1200 Hessians and Loyalists screened by Indians into Vermont, seeking horses for Burgoyne's invasion. Gen John Stark of Vermont collected 2000 militia and engulfed the invaders and a relief column.

■ **Staten Island, 22 August 1777**

Gen John Sullivan led 1000 militia from New Jersey in a raid upon this British base. Achieving surprise and some initial success against Tory forces, the Americans retreated before two British regiments, suffering 172 captured.

■ **Freeman's Farm (First Saratoga), 1 September 1777**

American resistance and several lost actions on the periphery of his advance had slowed, but not halted, Gen John Burgoyne's advance into New York from Canada. With 5500 regulars and 800 Tories and Indians, Burgoyne moved towards American Gen Horatio Gates's heavily fortified camp where 7000 Continentals prepared to resist him. In the namesake farm's fields, Burgoyne's army eventually prevailed with heavy losses against American attacks through the surrounding woods.

■ **Cooch's Bridge, 3 September 1777**

As the British moved to capture Philadelphia, Washington marched to Delaware, where a 700-strong screening force blocked the British advance at Cooch's Bridge. The British flanked the American force several times before Washington withdrew into Pennsylvania.

■ **Brandywine Creek, 11 September 1777**

With the help of the newly arrived Marquis de Lafayette, Washington and the Continental Army ventured open battle to prevent Gen William Howe's thrust up from the Chesapeake to seize the American capital of Philadelphia. British forces numbered 13,000 men against Washington's 15,000, making this action the largest battle on the North American continent before the American Civil War.

American light infantry shadowed the British Army's approach to Washington's line across Chad's Ford through the namesake creek. Finding the Americans prepared to receive him, Howe dispatched light units and received intelligence from the local loyalists about the American positions. Howe decided upon a holding attack, with 5000 men under Gen Wilhelm von Knyphausen attacking at Chad's Ford, while Gen Charles Cornwallis took 8000 troops around Washington's right flank. The British forced the crossing, while Washington received a growing trickle of reports about a second British force to the north.

Washington sent troops to reinforce his right and ordered a defensive line prepared on Birmingham Meeting House, a half-mile to his rear. With both American flanks slowly yielding to his attacks, Howe launched a bayonet charge into the American centre that collapsed Washington's

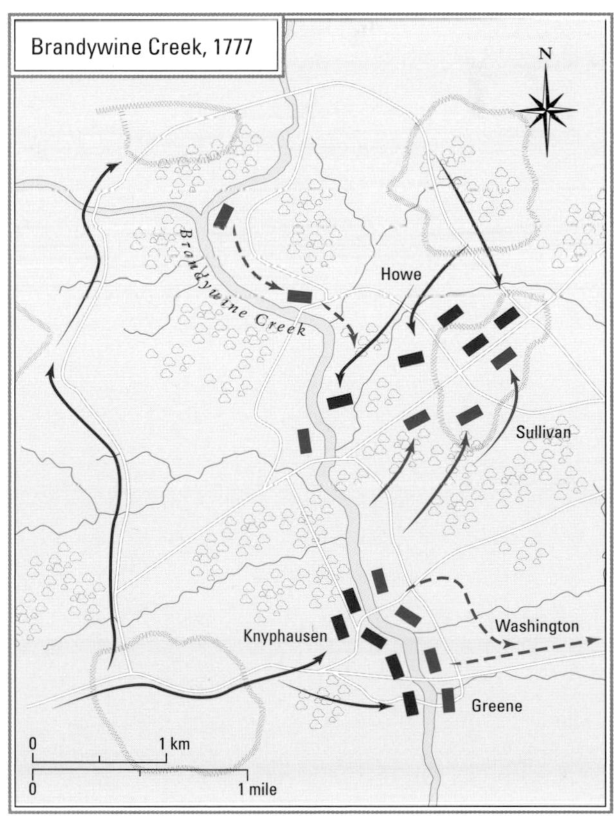

line as other British units attacked frontally. Isolated American units slowed the British as the day drew on, while Gen Nathaniel Greene's command's determined resistance retreating from Birmingham Meeting House to Battle Hill frustrated British attempts to turn the defeat into a rout. Howe had cleared the way to Philadelphia, but his primary objective of Washington's army survived with 300 killed, 600 wounded and 400 captured against the British losses of 100 dead and some 400 wounded. The grimness of American resistance signalled a fundamental shift in the war.

■ The Clouds/White Horse Tavern, 16 September 1777

After Brandywine, Washington positioned his army between the White Horse and Admiral Warren taverns in the Pennsylvania countryside. British Gen William Howe hoped to trap and destroy the Continentals before severe rain allowed Washington's retreat.

■ Paoli, 20 September 1777

Gen 'Mad Anthony' Wayne's command of 1500 men in bivouac at this Pennsylvania town suffered 350 casualties before fleeing a night attack by British Gen Charles Grey and 5000 regulars. The British employed their bayonets heavily.

■ Germantown, 4 October 1777

With the British now occupying Philadelphia, Washington with 11,000 men launched a four-part attack from the north of the city. Confusion, the plan's complexity and unexpectedly stiff British resistance eventually frustrated the assault.

■ Second Saratoga, Sep–Oct 1777

British plans to sever New England by an invasion south along Lake Champlain finally collapsed along with Gen John Burgoyne's army in the second most decisive battle of the American Revolution. Foraging and scouting parties repeatedly fell foul of American militia drawn to the line of his advance, the defeats at Bennington and Oriskany breaking off significant portions of Burgoyne's army and reducing his ability to receive supplies and information. Meanwhile, American generals Horatio Gates, Philip Schuyler, Daniel Morgan and Benedict Arnold were becoming used to Burgoyne's tactics and capabilities as the British advance got ever further from reinforcement or safe retreat. Burgoyne continued southwards in the hope of linking up with a force of some 3000 under Gen Henry Clinton marching up from occupied New York City, which had met and overcome American resistance at forts Clinton and Montgomery and when attempting to close the Hudson.

As the British advance down the Hudson neared the namesake town, Gates collected all available forces in a large camp expertly fortified by Thaddeus Kosciuszko as Burgoyne's advance ground to a halt around 5km away. Burgoyne's probe towards Gates's fortifications ran into attacks by Morgan's troops from the surrounding woods, with generals Friedrich von Riedesel, Simon Fraser and James Hamilton's troops holding the battlefield at Freeman's Farm. However, they were outnumbered and still some distance from the American camp on Bemis Heights. Burgoyne chose to rest his troops in trenches on the Freeman's Farm battlefield while the Americans brought up additional supplies of ammunition and constructed fortifications in the direction of Clinton's advance. Meanwhile, Burgoyne fortified posts near the Hudson to help the delivery of vital supplies from New York as his men went onto reduced rations. The stalemate lasted for three weeks, Burgoyne's forces dwindling to 5000.

Burgoyne broke out of his trenches and probed the Continental left on 7 October with 2100 men, the regulars and loyalists finding three American columns marching in response more than powerful enough to halt their advance and pressure the British on both flanks before the British withdrew. Fraser was mortally wounded and Benedict Arnold was wounded in the attack that broke the British centre. British casualties were some 400 men.

Arnold pressed the attack back upon Burgoyne's own fortifications constructed during the intervening weeks, carrying the strongest with 700 Hessians killed or captured against 150 Continental losses, the 1000 total casualties and silence from Clinton convincing Burgoyne to abandon his advance and retreat back to Fort Ticonderoga. Rains and mud slowed the speed of the disengagement, with Burgoyne finally constructing a camp overlooking the town of Saratoga, inviting Gates's attack. Instead, Gates was content to leave the British starving as further troops arrived, swelling Continental numbers to some 20,000, while additional militia blocked Burgoyne's retreat. Clinton, who had relieved Gen William Howe in command of the war, had abandoned his advance after burning the town of Kingston in New York and declined to send reinforcements. Burgoyne now found his army trapped by the Americans, starvation and the Hudson River, with no hope of rescue. On 17 October, he surrendered 5895 men and himself to Gates and the Continental Army.

The consequences of the debacle extended beyond Howe's relief by Clinton and unpleasant political repercussions for Lord North's ministry in London. American resistance at Brandywine, Germantown and the victory at Saratoga had combined with Benjamin Franklin's canny diplomacy to secure an alliance between the American colonists and Louis XVI's France, which brought additional supplies, a potent navy and international consequences into the war.

■ **Fort Clinton/Fort Montgomery, 6 October 1777**

These two unfinished American bastions protected a chain across the Hudson river intended to prevent British forces supplying Burgoyne's invasion from Canada. Gen Henry Clinton's river-borne forces stormed and captured both and destroyed the chain.

■ **Bemis Heights, 7 October 1777**

Polish engineer Thaddeus Kosciuszko fortified this camp overlooking the endpoint of the British advance, where American Gen Horatio Gates collected troops and dispatched forces defeated at Freeman's Farm and victorious at Saratoga.

■ **Fort Mercer/Fort Mifflin, Oct 1777**

Fort Mercer in New Jersey and Fort Mifflin, a Pennsylvania stone fort, blocked the Delaware even after British forces had seized Philadelphia. Bombarded by siege artillery and warships, Fort Mifflin's stubborn defenders succeeded in burning HMS *Augusta* and a brig before finally abandoning the ruins. Col Carl von Donop with 2400 Hessians failed to storm Fort Mercer, with 400 falling due to the abatis, ditch and resolute defenders who later evacuated the post.

■ **Whitemarsh, 5–8 December 1777**

British Gen William Howe launched a probing night attack towards Washington's first winter camp at this Pennsylvania town, encountering screening forces that resisted and fired as they retreated. Advised, Washington's strong position prompted Howe's retreat.

■ **Matson's Ford, 11 December 1777**

British Gen Charles Cornwallis and 3500 regulars left Philadelphia seeking livestock for Gen William Howe's army. Pennsylvania militia repeatedly fought Cornwallis before the British advance, while Washington's army avoided engagement by crossing the Schuylkill elsewhere.

■ **Valley Forge, Winter 1777**

Washington set his winter quarters 40km from occupied Philadelphia, menacing the British and having the distance to respond to a surprise attack. Supplies unexpectedly lacking, Gen Friedrich von Steuben's drills hardened Washington's cold and hunger-tested troops.

■ ***Randolph* vs. *Yarmouth*, 7 March 1778**

Continental Capt Nicholas Biddle had taken prizes in the frigate *Randolph*. HMS *Yarmouth*, twice *Randolph*'s size, demanded surrender and received a close hot action until *Randolph* suddenly exploded, killing Biddle and nearly all the *Randolph*'s crew.

■ **Quinton's Bridge, 18 March 1778**

A powerful British scouting party received

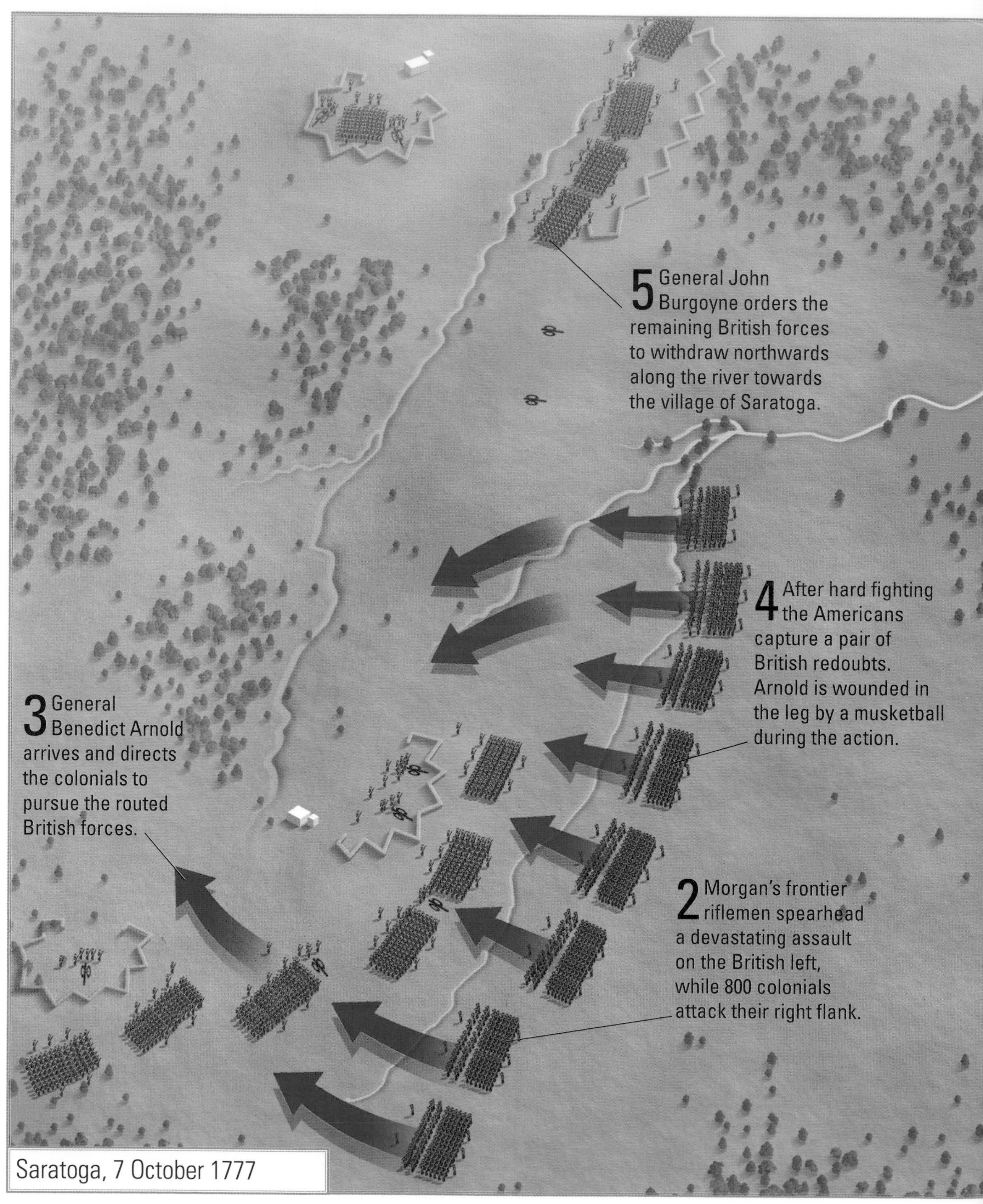

Saratoga, 7 October 1777

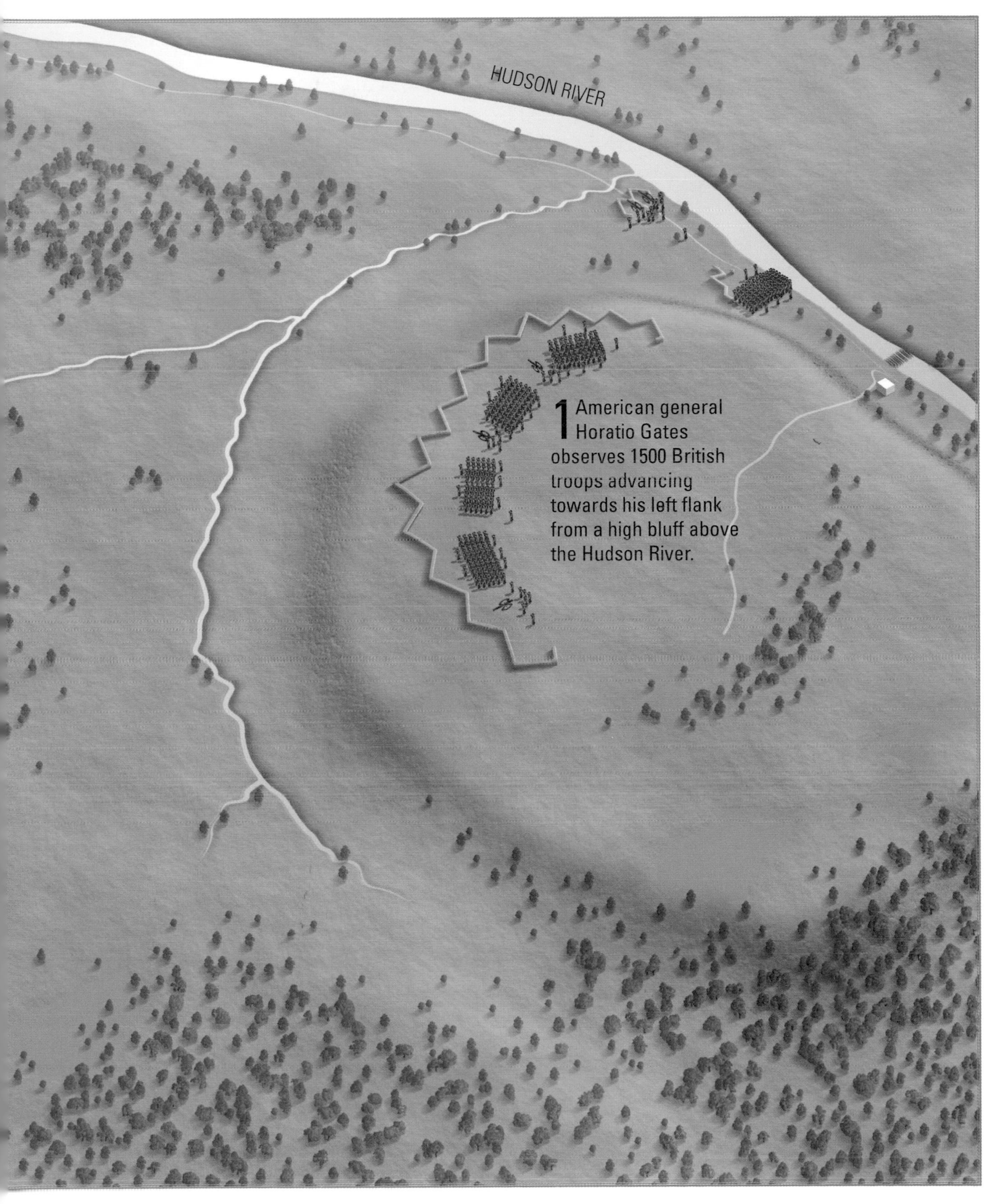
HUDSON RIVER
1 American general Horatio Gates observes 1500 British troops advancing towards his left flank from a high bluff above the Hudson River.

word from New Jersey loyalists of an American detachment 300-strong guarding this bridge some distance away. Col Charles Mawhood allowed a portion of his command to be seen by the Americans after placing the rest of his force in concealment and trapping Americans crossing in pursuit. The arrival of reinforcements allowed the Americans to fall back from the British ambush with light casualties.

■ **Hancock's Bridge, 21 March 1778**

British Col Charles Mawhood announced that he would leave New Jersey if the militia disbanded. If they did not, he would attack militia leaders. Mawhood lived up to his threat by massacring a household full of civilians here.

■ **Frederica, 19 April 1778**

Col Samuel Elbert discovered a British frigate, sloop and two supply vessels anchored in this Florida river. Four galleys of the Georgia navy attacked the becalmed ships at ebb tide, capturing all but the frigate.

■ **Raid on Whitehaven, 22 April 1778**

John Paul Jones took the sloop *Ranger* to raid this familiar English port, retaliating for British depredations along the American coast. British reaction to the raid was vastly disproportionate to the slight amount of damage inflicted.

■ **North Channel/*Ranger* vs. *Drake*, 24 April 1778**

After the raid at Whitehaven, John Paul Jones, along with *Ranger*, greatly compounded British consternation by taking HMS *Drake* after a short, sharp, ship-to-ship combat. Jones' escape greatly embarrassed the Royal Navy in its home waters.

■ **Crooked Billett, 1 May 1778**

Repeating the tactics of Paoli, 850 British troops surprised and drove off the bivouacked three regiments of Gen John Lacey in disorder, inflicting some 92 casualties before the Americans escaped, with reports of atrocities against the wounded.

■ **Freetown, 25 May 1778**

A British landing from Newport at this Massachusetts town encountered unexpected resistance from local patriots, British marines and barges responding with grapeshot to patriot challenges and musket shot. The British set some fires and withdrew.

■ **Cobleskill, 30 May 1778**

With the support of the Iroquois and British in Quebec, loyalist Joseph Brant and other Indians attacked and destroyed much of this small town in upstate New York, after routing and scattering the outnumbered defenders.

■ **Monmouth, 28 June 1778**

Gen Henry Clinton, relieving William Howe as ground commander in the colonies, had to evacuate Philadelphia after France's open entry into the war on behalf of the patriots. Moving his wounded and endangered loyalists by sea and his army by land, Clinton and the rest of the army moved out of Philadelphia. Washington chose to shadow the British march and wait for a favourable opportunity to bring them to battle. With the British tired from the march to Monmouth

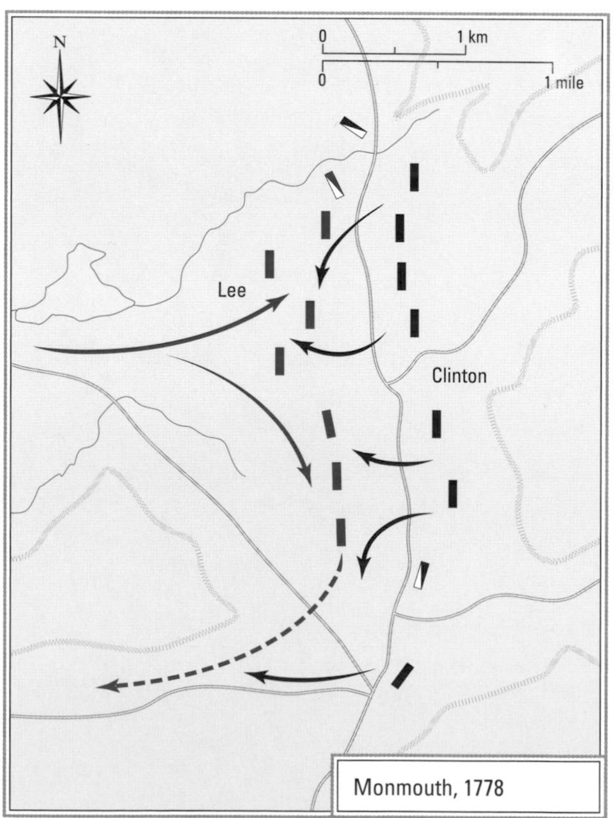

Monmouth, 1778

Courthouse, Washington engaged, ordering Gen Charles Lee to attack the British rear, while the bulk of the Continental army blocked the British advance. Lee's wavering delayed his attack, allowing the British to concentrate on the forces ahead. Washington and more decisive generals firmed up the Continental line, Clinton deciding to break off the engagement and complete his march towards New York.

■ Alligator Creek (Swamp), 30 June 1778

American Gen Richard Howe led 3000 Continentals south against the British in Florida. Loyalist Col Thomas Brown's Rangers fled to the British fort here, the patriots retreating with casualties. The invasion was soon abandoned.

■ Great Runaway, July 1778

The Iroquois Confederation imploded as Oneidas attacked loyalist Mohawks in the aftermath of Oriskany. Fighting between the Indians and loyalists urged on by the British in Quebec prompted this wholescale flight of the region's settlers.

■ Illinois Campaign, July 1778–Feb 1782

George Rogers Clark launched an expedition into Kentucky against British outposts, encouraging the local tribes to attack patriot towns and settlements. Clark used intelligent diplomacy towards the Indian tribes. British LGov Henry Hamilton moved from Detroit to counter Rogers' efforts, but Rogers countered the British occupation ofVincennes and efforts to court the powerful Shawnee tribe. Clark's activities largely neutralized British efforts in the Trans-Appalachian west.

■ Wyoming Massacre (Wilkes-Barre), 3 July 1778

Loyalist John Butler and allied Seneca fell upon this Pennsylvania village and surrounding region for five days, burning eight forts and 1000 houses, killing 227 men and executing some prisoners, while securing cattle for British Fort Niagara.

■ Newport, 29 August 1778

The British occupied this Rhode Island town as a fleet anchorage. The French fleet and army intended to clear the British in a combined assault with American Gen Philip Sullivan's army, stormy weather producing a debacle.

■ Rhode Island, 29 August 1778

The smallest colony held disproportionate laurels and action due to its vital ports and brave soldiers, both of which drew the attention of the British, who occupied the important port of Newport for three years from 1776. After the French alliance, Gen Philip Sullivan led 10,000 Continentals, with the Comte de Rochambeau landing 4000 French with the goal of retaking the city. The British successfully counter-attacked during bad weather.

■ Boonesborough, 7–8 September 1778

A French-Canadian engineer and Shawnee Indians sought to reduce Daniel Boone's namesake fortified town in Kentucky. The siege collapsed after determined resistance by the settlers and the collapse of a sapping tunnel due to rain.

■ German Flatts, 17 September 1778

A combined force of Loyalists and Iroquois under Joseph Brant ravaged this town in upstate New York. A scout's warning allowed the inhabitants to shelter in two forts, while the raiders sacked and burned the town.

■ Tappen Massacre, 27 September 1778

Col George Baylor and his dragoons, bivouacked away from the main Continental force, fell victim to a Loyalist-guided British night surprise attack. Gen Charles Grey could not or did not spare many, bayoneting the surrendering Americans.

■ Chestnut Neck (Mincock Island), 6 October 1778

American privateers operating from New Jersey's Little Egg harbour provoked a British landing here, which burned several ships, but failed to destroy a neighbouring ironworks. Col Patrick Ferguson's night attack upon houses produced several atrocity reports.

■ Carleton's Raid, 24 Oct–14 Nov 1778

Capt Christopher Carleton with soldiers, two warships and smaller craft destroyed patriot supplies, boats and mills, and arrested male civilians

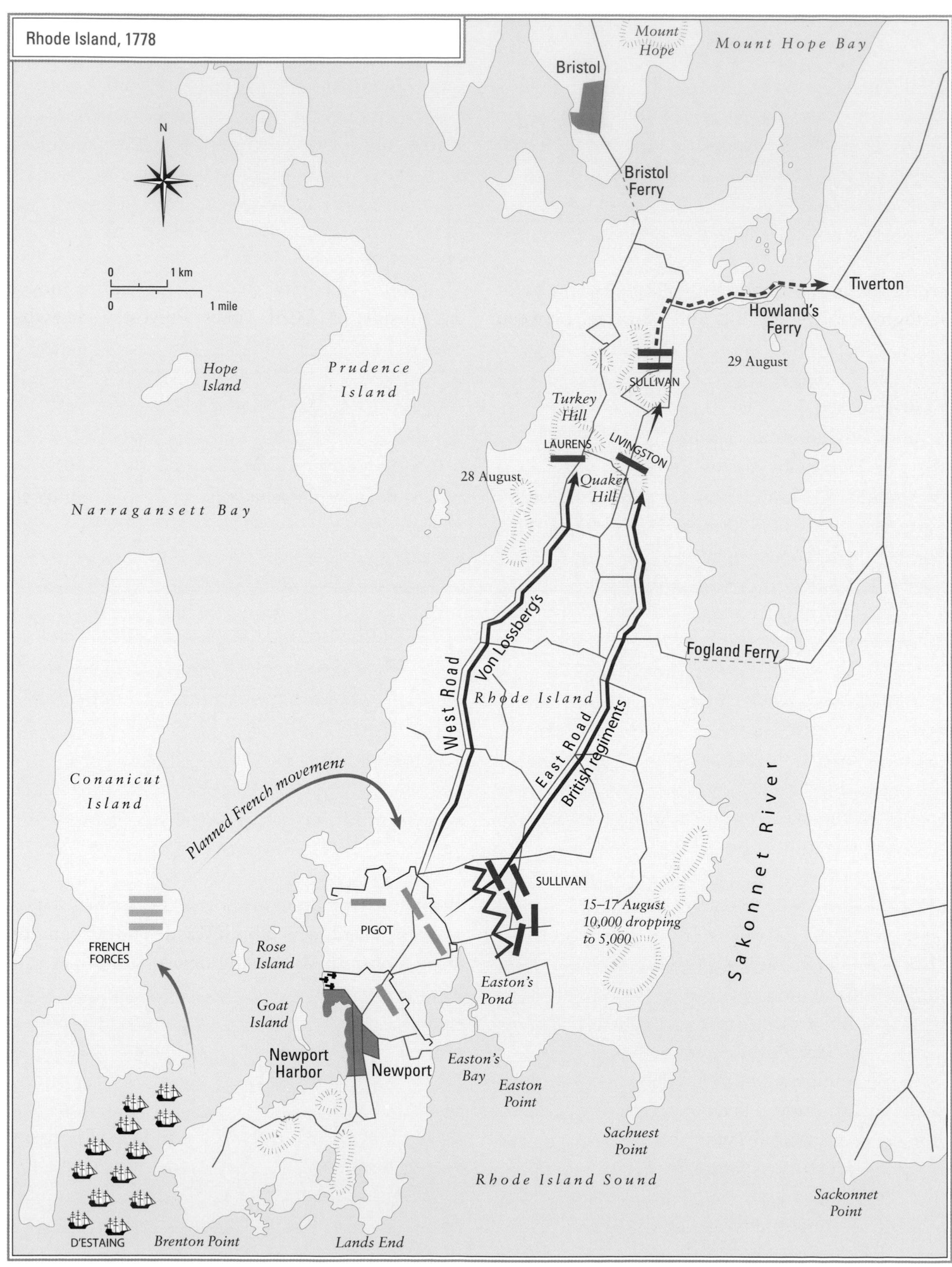

Rhode Island, 1778
Mount Hope
Mount Hope Bay
Bristol
N
Bristol Ferry
0 1 km
0 1 mile
Tiverton
Howland's Ferry
29 August
Hope Island
Prudence Island
SULLIVAN
Turkey Hill
LAURENS
LIVINGSTON
28 August
Quaker Hill
Narragansett Bay
Von Lossberg's
West Road
Fogland Ferry
Rhode Island
East Road
British regiments
Conanicut Island
Planned French movement
Sakonnet River
SULLIVAN
15–17 August
10,000 dropping to 5,000
FRENCH FORCES
PIGOT
Rose Island
Easton's Pond
Goat Island
Newport Harbor
Newport
Easton's Bay
Easton Point
Sachuest Point
Rhode Island Sound
Sackonnet Point
D'ESTAING
Brenton Point
Lands End

along the coast of Lake Champlain. Driving off his captives' families, Carleton met little resistance.

■ Cherry Valley Massacre, 11 Nov 1778

Col Walter Butler and Mohawk Joseph Brandt led 250 loyalists and 400 Iroquois against Fort Alden here. The Iroquois burned the town, killing 15 soldiers and 32 civilians. The fort held.

■ Savannah I, 29 December 1778

In an early effort at a 'Southern Strategy,' the British seized this important Georgia port, assisted by fugitive slaves, loyalists and a quarrel between the governor, John Houstoun, and the garrison commander, Gen Richard Howe.

■ Port Royal Island/Beaufort, 3 Feb 1779

A force of 200 regulars and loyalists moved to disrupt Continental supply routes at this South Carolina port. Col William Moultrie moved with 300 men in response, putting up sufficient resistance to send the British back to Savannah.

■ Kettle Creek, 14 February 1779

LCol Archibald Campbell moved with 3000 men in the South Carolina backcountry in the hope of rallying Loyalists. Around 500 Loyalists were encamped here when Andrew Pickens led 300 militia from surrounding colonies to attack the loyalist bivouac from three sides, killing the leaders and scattering the loyalists after initial resistance. This dramatic failure of the 'Southern Strategy' of reasserting British control in the south did not yet discourage the British.

■ Vincennes, 23–25 February 1779

George Rogers Clark's Illinois expedition had taken this French trading town and protecting fort the previous summer, only to see them recaptured by a British expedition from Detroit, led by Col Henry Hamilton, named 'the Hair Buyer', from his employment of the Indians against the patriots. Clark moved back along the rivers with a stronger force, skilfully using his own knowledge of Indian mores to dissuade them from support of the British, and also playing upon the French population's resentment of British control. With good intelligence about the size of Hamilton's force at Vincennes, Clark attacked, carefully keeping the British unaware of his actual numbers and Hamilton's French-Canadian militia informed of his support among their brethren. Caught at a loss, the British surrendered, Clark capturing Hamilton and making reprisals upon the captured Indians, greatly damaging Britain's control of the Trans-Appalachian west.

■ Briar Creek, 3 March 1779

Gen John Ashe with 2000 colonial militia moved in pursuit of LCol James Prevost's somewhat smaller force of Highlanders and Loyalists in upper Georgia, while the British at Savannah proclaimed the colony under royal control. Prevost used 900 men to launch a holding attack on Ashe's encamped force, which collapsed when the balance of Prevost's men attacked from the rear, solidifying British control of that part of the colony.

■ Stono Ferry, 20 June 1779

Continental Gen Benjamin Lincoln sent 1200 of his command to flush out 900 Scots and Hessians at the redoubt British Gen Augustine Prevost constructed here. Unexpectedly tough resistance allowed the British to retreat unmolested further.

■ Stony Point, 16 July 1779

The British established outposts to maintain their grip along the lower Hudson River valley. Getting control of Washington's elite force of Continental Light Infantry, Gen 'Mad Anthony' Wayne secured Washington's permission to use 1200 of these in a surprise assault upon the northernmost British post at Stony Point, which both Wayne and Washington had reconnoitred. Landing upriver, the Americans advanced through the British ditch and abatis under darkness with strict (and obeyed) orders not to fire. The Americans succeeded in catching the 500-strong garrison between the two prongs of their attack and overrunning the fortification, delivering an implicit rebuke to British conduct of previous similar operations by maintaining discipline and granting quarter to the surrendering enemy, despite Wayne himself being wounded. Taking prisoners, ordinance and supplies, the Americans levelled the post and withdrew before the British could respond.

■ **Penobscot, 24 July 24–12 August 1779**
Capt Dudley Saltonstall had to scuttle 46 Continental ships with 500 casualties after the British Royal Navy trapped his force and marines in the Penobscot River, when the colonials tried to dislodge a landing in Maine.

■ **Paulus Hook, 19 August 1779**
Emulating the raid on Stony Point, Maj Henry 'Light-horse Harry' Lee launched a attack on this British post directly across from Manhattan. Mistaken for Loyalist foragers, Lee and his men withdrew almost unscathed with 158 prisoners.

■ **Newtown, 29 August 1779**
Gen John Sullivan and 5000 Continentals attacked the Iroquois in response to depredations in the Wyoming valley. Mohawk Joseph Brandt and loyalist William Butler with 700 Indians and loyalists failed to stop Sullivan's expedition here.

■ **Boyd and Parker Ambush, 13 Sep 1779**
Little Beard and his Seneca ambushed a scout of 23 men under Lt Thomas Boyd with Sgt Michael Parker. The Indians tortured and killed Boyd and Parker; seven colonials escaped.

■ **Baton Rouge, 12–21 September 1779**
The Spanish, entering the war, immediately attacked and overwhelmed this British fort on the border between West Florida and previously ceded French Louisiana. Spanish governor Bernardo de Gálvez with 1000 Spanish, militia and allied Indians captured this and two other forts. Gálvez paroled the garrisons after heavily fortified Baton Rouge collapsed under a large-scale bombardment scientifically applied by Gálvez's large artillery train. The British defeats let Spain control the lower Mississippi valley.

■ **Flamborough Head, 23 September 1779**
John Paul Jones with an old Indiaman he named *Bonhomme Richard*, plus the ships *Alliance* and *Pallas,* encountered HMS *Serapis* under Capt Richard

Stony Point, 1779

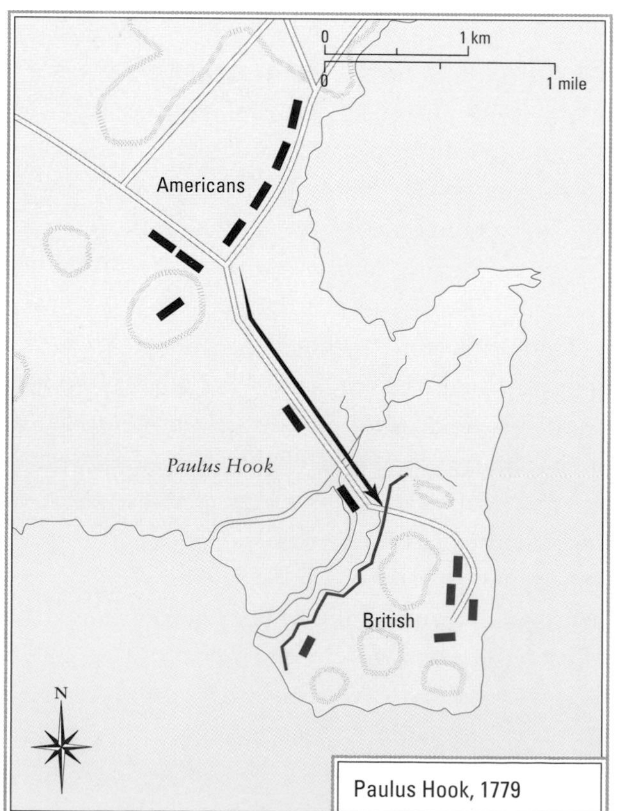

Paulus Hook, 1779

Pearson and *Countess of Scarborough* escorting the Baltic convoy off the north coast of England. The convoy scattered when *Bonhomme Richard* hotly engaged *Serapis*, while *Alliance* periodically attacked both ships. French *Pallas* captured *Scarborough* while Jones' sheer determination and heroic crew captured his second prize within sight of England, *Bonhomme Richard* sinking afterwards.

■ Savannah II, 16 Sep–20 Oct 1779

Gen Benjamin Lincoln and the Continental Army, supported by the French fleet and marines of French Adm Jean Baptiste d'Estaing, bloodily failed to dislodge the British Army fortified here due to difficulties co-ordinating repeated attacks.

■ Young's House, 3 February 1780

Col Joseph Thompson with 250 Continentals sheltered here during a winter storm north of New York City. A force of 450 British, Hessian and Loyalist infantry, plus 100 dragoons learned of their location and killed 14, capturing 73.

■ Fort Charlotte, 2–14 March 1780

Marching eastwards, Spanish governor of Louisiana Bernardo de Gálvez continued his policy of reducing British outposts, this large brick fort with 300 garrison and the village of Mobile soon falling to 2000 Spanish troops and artillery.

■ Charleston II, 29 March–12 May 1780

Gen Benjamin Lincoln, with 5200 Continentals and militia and four Continental warships, defended this port against a second British attack by Gen Augustine Prevost with 10,000 troops, supported by the Royal Navy. The British bypassed the city's defending forts and launched a punishing bombardment that the Americans, weakened by illness, proved unable to endure. The British captured the garrison, port and ships. Much of South Carolina returned to British control.

■ Monck's Corner, 14 April 1780

British LCol Banastre Tarleton defeated Gen Isaac Huger and 500 men here north of Charleston along the city's route of supply. Tarleton's dawn attack captured a Patriot wagon train and scattered Huger's command.

■ Lenud's Ferry, 6 May 1780

Continental Col Anthony White with 300 men captured a British foraging party during the siege of Charleston. LCol Banastre Tarleton, alerted by a Loyalist, scattered White's command here with 150 dragoons, freeing the captives.

■ St. Louis/Fort San Carlos, 25 May 1780

Spanish Louisiana's LGov Fernando de Leyba built a large stone tower that protected the town from an attack by British-allied Indians, prompted by British fur traders eager to gain control of the upper Mississippi.

■ Waxhaw Creek/Buford's Massacre, 29 May 1780

Continental Col Abraham Buford with some 350 men withdrew north after the fall of Charleston. LCol Banastre Tarleton moved in pursuit with 270 loyalist cavalry, overtaking Buford and killed 113, inflicting 203 further casualties.

■ Connecticut Farms, 7 June 1780

Hessian Gen Wilhelm von Knyphausen marched with 5000 men against this New Jersey town near Washington's winter quarters. Militia engaged Knyphausen in the village, while Washington brought up the main army, forcing a British retreat.

■ Mobley's (Gibson's) Meeting House, 8 June 1780

Despite British orders to disband, loyalists in South Carolina fought their own war against the patriots in the aftermath of Charleston. Patriot Maj Richard Winn rallied 100 scattered militia and dispersed a Loyalist concentration here.

■ Ramseur's Mill, 20 June 1780

With British money and success, Col John Moore rallied 1300 South Carolina loyalists here. Col Francis Locke, with 400 Patriot infantry and horses, defeated the loyalists in a pitched battle, both sides suffering 70 killed.

■ Springfield, 23 June 1780

Hessian Gen Wilhelm von Knyphausen's 5000 British here in New Jersey engaged Gen Nathaniel Greene's 1500 Continental regulars and militia, while Washington counter-marched. Greene slowly retreated to defensible heights and held out, prompting Knyphausen's retreat.

■ Huck's Defeat/Williamson's Plantation, 12 July 1780

Loyalist Capt Christian Huck favoured reprisals against Patriots' homes in South Carolina. During one such attack, a girl escaped to alert Patriot militia, who attacked from two directions, killing Huck and some 40 of his men.

■ Colson's Mill, 21 July 1780

Col William Davidson rallied North Carolina militia and assaulted 400 loyalists mustering here seeking to surprise the encampment with his 250 patriot partisans. Despite Davidson's wound early in the fight, his men scattered the Loyalists.

■ Rocky Mount, 1 August 1780

LCol George Turnbull with 300 New York and South Carolina loyalists held off three assaults by Gen Thomas Sumter with 500 men, who then ambushed a loyalist relief column, inflicting 60 casualties before withdrawing.

■ Hanging Rock, 6 August 1780

The British consolidated their hold on South Carolina with scattered outposts. Gen Thomas Sumter attacked this one with 800 militia and inflicted 200 casualties on the British defending force of 500 men, with much less loss.

■ Camden, 16 August 1780

Taking command in the south after Charleston, Gen Horatio Gates led 3000 Continentals against what Thomas Sumter had told him were 700 British. Lincoln's hasty march starved and weakened his army, while British Gen Charles Cornwallis reinforced Camden with 2400 men. Learning too late of Cornwallis's arrival, Gates' army fought desperately, but eventually disintegrated, with Gates and the survivors hounded by LCol Banastre Tarleton's loyalist cavalry.

■ Fishing Creek, 18 August 1780

British LCol Banastre Tarleton with 160 dragoons and double-riding infantry caught Gen Thomas Sumter's command of 500 partisans unprepared, inflicting 150 casualties and capturing 300. Tarleton also recaptured 44 supply wagons and 100 prisoners.

■ Musgrove Hill, 18 August 1780

South Carolina patriots rallied after Camden to lure a loyalist force into a prepared ambush behind previously constructed breastworks prepared here. Patriot cavalry drew on loyalist infantry who suffered 63 dead, 90 wounded and 170 prisoners.

■ Blue Licks, 19 August 1780

The powerful Shawnee tribe, led by Tory captain William Caldwell and loyalist renegade Simon Girty, dealt Patriot settlers in Kentucky a severe blow in an ambush here. A total of 77 colonists died; Girty burned seven alive.

■ Black Mingo, 14 September 1780

Loyalist numbers swelling after Continental defeats, Continental Gen Francis Marion, the 'Swamp Fox', rallied remaining Patriot militia and, at this creek, defeated a Loyalist force under John Ball, some 50 men fighting on each side.

■ Wahab's Plantation, 21 September 1780

Col William R. Davie with 150 cavalry and infantry surprised 300 loyalists here in North Carolina, with the infantry engaging, while the cavalry charged from the rear. The patriots killed 20 men, capturing 96 furnished horses.

■ Charlotte, 26 September 1780

Col William R. Davie sought here with 120 militia to impede British Gen Charles Cornwallis's advance into North Carolina, where Cornwallis sought to rally loyalists. Driven back with 30 casualties, Davie and his men inflicted 15 on the British.

■ King's Mountain, 7 October 1780

British Maj Patrick Ferguson led 1000 picked loyalists into the North Carolina mountain country in an effort to force the locals to cease rebellion. When Ferguson threatened reprisals against intransigents, Isaac Shelby and John Sevier rallied angry highlanders, their ranks soon joined by militia from other states as they prepared to engage Ferguson and his force. Possessed of superb Pennsylvania rifles, many of the highlanders were superlative shots. Ferguson moved south, seeking to overtake a retreating Georgia patriot band. Ferguson occupied the ridge of King's Mountain upon learning that patriot bands were converging on him from all directions. Rifle fire from surrounding trees cut down Ferguson and any British officer trying to lead a charge. Loyalists numbering 400 fell before the Patriots accepted the surrender of the surviving 600, some of those later executed after this blow to British prestige.

■ **Royalton Raid, 16 October 1780**
After Burgoyne's defeat, the British and allied Indians ravaged New England to forestall Patriot attacks upon Canada. Lt Houghton, with 300 Mohawks, launched a raid in which they escaped with 26 captives and much property.

■ **Fishdam Ford, 9 November 1780**
British Maj James Wemyss sought to kill Gen Thomas Sumter with a night attack upon his encampment. However, Wemyss was wounded with his men when silhouetted by the light of picket fires surrounded by alert, rifle-equipped sentries.

■ **Blackstock's Ford, 20 November 1780**
Patriot Gen Thomas Sumter with 1000 militia prepared defences here against LCol Banastre Tarleton's onrushing 250 dragoons. Sumter attacked with horsemen when Tarleton hesitated, inflicting some 200 casualties on Tarleton's force, despite Sumter's wound.

■ **Jersey, 6 January 1781**
The Channel Islands had become a nest of British privateers, against which the French sent a landing force of 1000 marines. Forces of 2000 regulars and island militia overwhelmed these, both the British and French commanders perishing.

■ **Mobile Village, 7 January 1781**
A small post here guarded the supply route to the Spanish occupying captured Mobile. Indian attacks having failed, the Spanish then resisted a British assault, sheltering with 40 casualties in a wooden blockhouse, inflicting 20 wounded.

■ **Cowpens, 17 January 1781**
Gen Nathaniel Greene moved the Continental army back into South Carolina, dispatching Gen Daniel Morgan to rally militia and threaten British outposts. LCol Banastre Tarleton with 1250 British regulars and loyalists moved in pursuit, while Morgan gathered forage and militia forces around his Continentals. Upon hearing of Tarleton's pursuit, Morgan consolidated his forces at this battlefield, which offered opportunities for both forage and retreat. Tarleton exhausted his own men in a rapid approach that failed to catch Morgan off guard. As more militia arrived, Morgan made the decision to engage the dreaded commander. Morgan had about 2000 men to face Tarleton's picked body.

Placing riflemen in the trees on his flanks, Morgan put his militia in the crescent front line facing Tarleton's advance with his Continentals behind them, exacting from the former a promise to fire three volleys before they ran, with the

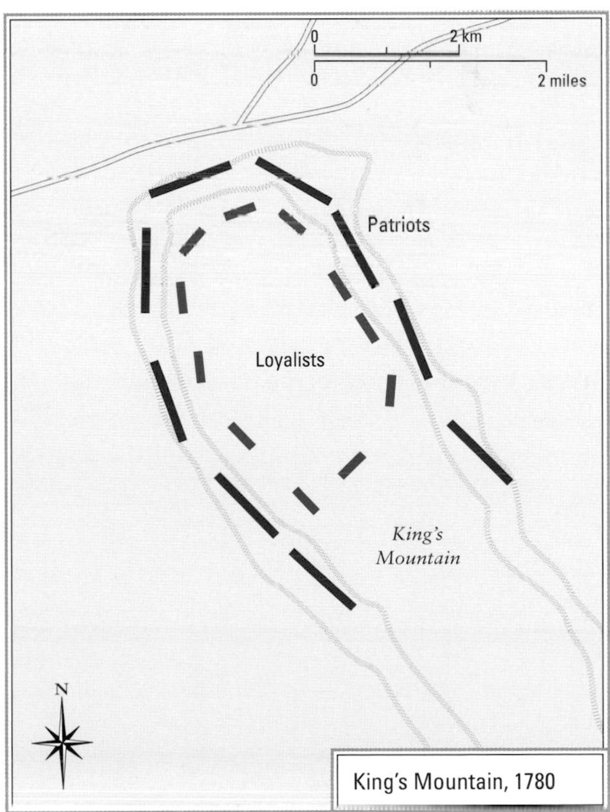

King's Mountain, 1780

Continentals ready to enforce that guarantee. Too worn out for elaborate flanking manoeuvres, Tarleton's men marched forward as Continental riflemen picked off their officers. British efforts to flank or re-form collapsed under attack by Col William Washington's more numerous cavalry. The British line narrowed under pressure, while the Americans retreated before it, firing volleys as they fell back and re-formed. British artillery supporting the advance fell to a swift American rush. Washington's cavalry charged again as the British line collapsed, capturing guns, wagons and supplies. Tarleton suffered 800 casualties to 25 Americans killed and 125 wounded.

■ **Haw River/Pyle's Defeat, 25 Feb 1781**

Col John Pyle with 400 mounted loyalists mistook Cols Henry Lee and Andrew Pickens with 900 cavalry for British troops under Banastre Tarleton, who wore similar uniforms. The American ruse resulted in 240 loyalist casualties.

■ **Wetzell's Mill, 6 March 1781**

Continental Gen Otho Williams with 1000 cavalry and infantry avoided British Gen Charles Cornwallis's effort to trap them between parts of the British Army by a fighting retreat in stages across the Reedy Fork here.

■ **Pensacola, 9 March–8 May 1781**

Spanish governor Bernardo de Gálvez completed evicting the British from the Gulf of Mexico, this port attacked by an army from New Orleans and a Cuban fleet. Bombardment exploding Fort George's magazine, the British surrendered.

■ **Guilford Courthouse, 15 March 1781**

The defeats at King's Mountain and Cowpens galvanized British Gen Charles Cornwallis into launching a full-strength effort with 1900 troops against the resurgent patriot cause in the Carolinas. Gen Nathaniel Greene's brilliant strategy of allowing the British to chase his Continentals and alienate populations throughout the south had left Cornwallis with only brute force as a means to reassert British sovereignty. With his own forces elevated in numbers and morale, Greene carefully selected this battlefield and made ready for Cornwallis's assault, setting up his 4440 Continentals and militia in three independent lines in the face of the British advance. Fighting began with an inconclusive cavalry skirmish between Col Henry Lee's Legion and British LCol Banastre Tarleton's British Legion. The British line fanned out from the road, while light artillery supported their advance from the centre and heavier guns replied from the American third line. Cornwallis' line moved straight ahead, shifting sideways as the terrain necessitated and crumbled the North Carolina militia in Greene's first line, patriots retreating back to the flanks of their second line. The Virginia militia there held out longer, the British taking a steady amount of casualties as they advanced, their own artillery blasting both sides in the middle. Despite the collapse of the third line's Marylanders soon afterwards, Greene's forces withdrew 16km in good order and largely re-formed. American casualties were 79 killed, 260 wounded; British 93 dead, 213 wounded, a Pyrrhic victory.

■ **Fort Watson, 15–23 April 1781**

Riflemen in a wooden 'Maham Tower' allowed Gen Francis Marion and LCol Henry Lee's 400 Continentals and militia to reduce this South Carolina palisade and capture its 114-man garrison of regulars and loyalists.

■ **Hobkirk's Hill, 25 April 1781**

Ignoring Gen Charles Cornwallis' march into Virginia after Guilford Courthouse, Continental Gen Nathaniel Greene moved into South Carolina with 1550 Continentals, most of his militia returning home. LCol Francis Rawdon raised 900 regulars and loyalists, the latter certain of reprisals if the Continentals retook the South. Attacking Greene's army at the namesake hill, Rawdon's regulars and loyalists succeeded in throwing the Continentals into disorder, but not stopping Greene's advance.

■ **Blandford, 25 April 1781**

Gen William Philips arrived with 2500 regulars and loyalists from New York to raid Virginia.

Continental Gen Friedrich von Steuben and 1000 militia here fought a delaying action, reducing the damage of the British raid.

■ **Fort Royal, 29–30 April 1781**

British Adm Samuel Hood, with 18 ships, sought to intercept French forces at sea meant for North America. The French Adm Comte de Grasse had 20 warships in escort of the supply ships and transports, the British appearing off the island of Martinique. De Grasse put out to sea with his convoy en route to this port. Hood tried to close, failed and, after an exchange of fire, withdrew.

■ **Fort Motte, 8–12 May 1781**

Mrs Rebecca Brewton Motte's disapproval of British use of her South Carolina house as a supply depot extended to supplying Continental Gen Francis Marion with a bow to launch flaming arrows to burn the fort and her home, resulting in the British surrendering.

■ **Fort Augusta/Fort Cornwallis, 22 May–6 June 1781**

LCol Henry Lee continued Continental Gen Nathaniel Greene's policy of reducing isolated British outposts, this one in Georgia having changed hands repeatedly. A brisk two-week assault finally prompted the stubborn garrison to surrender.

■ **Ninety Six, 22 May–19 June 1781**

With less than 1000 men in his army, Continental Gen Nathaniel Greene employed it in reducing British outposts in South Carolina. The defences of this outpost and Col John Harris Cruger withstood a formal siege.

■ **Tobago, 24 May–2 June 1781**

At the outbreak of hostilities with the Dutch, the British occupied this West Indies' island. The French Marquis de Bouillé recaptured the island with an amphibious force at the cost of 50 wounded and 50 dead.

■ **Charlottesville, 1 June 1781**

When British Gen Charles Cornwallis moved his army into Virginia, LCol Banastre Tarleton launched a two-pronged raid on the provisional Virginia capital here, burning stores and capturing seven of the legislature, the rest escaping.

■ **Spencer's Ordinary, 26 June 1781**

Having fought British Gen Charles Cornwallis's vanguard, Continental Gens Lafayette and Anthony Wayne attempted his rearguard here as Cornwallis's army occupied Williamsburg. Gen Richard Butler led an indecisive attack against an improvised British palisade.

■ **Green Spring, 6 July 1781**

The vanguard of British Gen Charles Cornwallis's army and LCol Banastre Tarleton's cavalry caught Continental Gen Anthony Wayne's 500 with 3000 regulars. Wayne retreated until darkness; swamps and the Marquis de Lafayette saved him.

■ **Francisco's Fight, 9–24 July 1781**

By his own account in this unconfirmed rumour, Continental soldier Peter Francisco seized a sabre from one of British LCol Banastre Tarleton's raiders stealing his shoe buckles, killing three and dispersing the surviving six. Tarleton admitted to casualties.

■ **Lochry Massacre, 24 August 1781**

Traveling to join Clarke's expedition in the Ohio valley, Col Archibald Lochry and some 100 Pennsylvania militia fell into Mohawk Joseph Brant's ambush, the Indians killing 40 after Lochry surrendered, the rest were held in Canada.

■ **Chesapeake Bay, 5 September 1781**

The supervisors of the French Navy had, from long experience of being beaten by the British fleet, raised their own level of ship design and armaments and, in some cases, achieved more than parity with their traditional rivals. The improvement of French technology and signaling came to fruition at this battle. Adm François de Grasse positioned 28 ships of the line across the mouth of Chesapeake Bay, having frightened off British Adm Samuel Hood with 14 ships seeking to preserve Gen Charles Cornwallis's army's route of evacuation or supply from the Yorktown peninsula. British Adm Thomas Graves with 19 ships moved to break the French

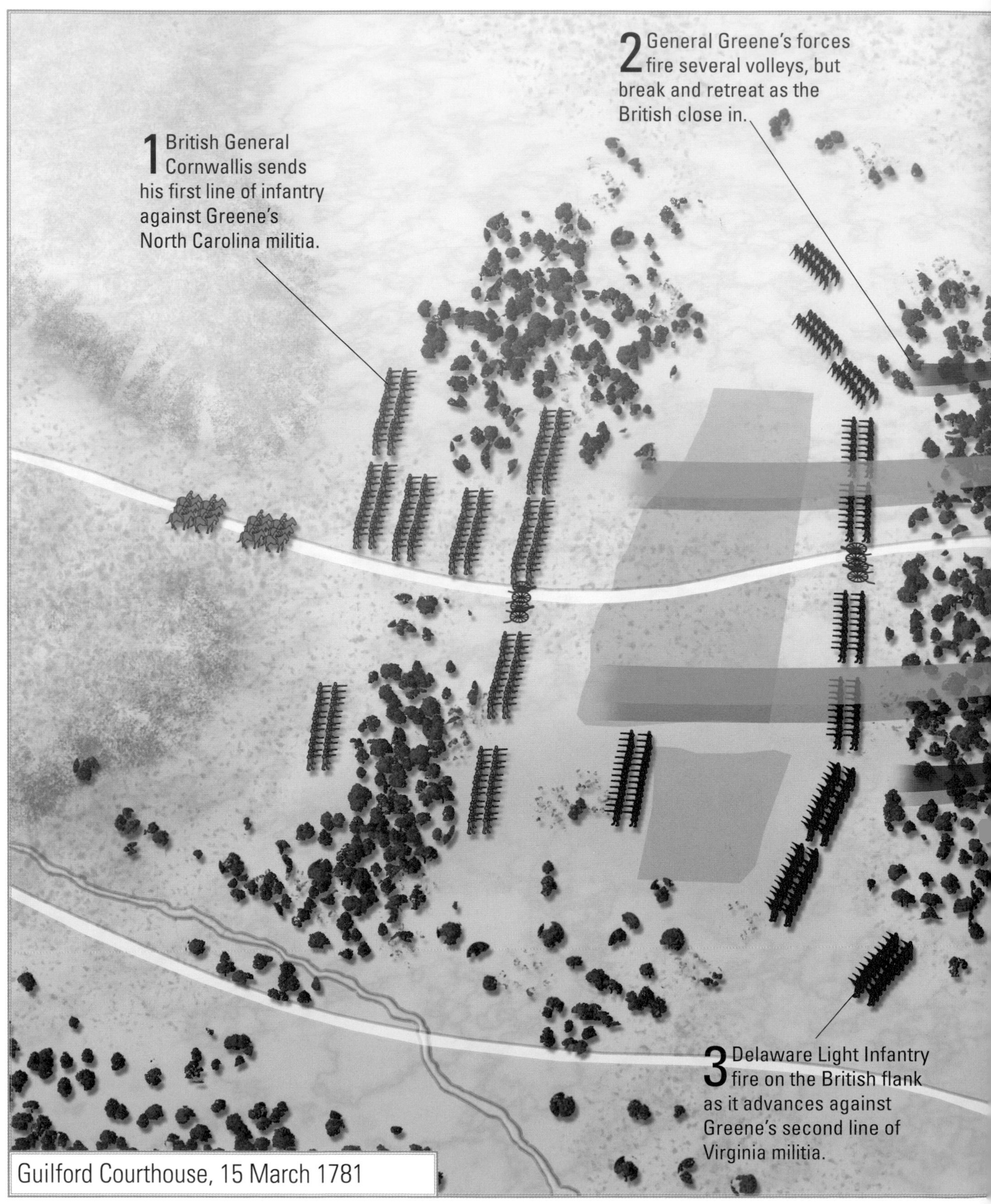

Guilford Courthouse, 15 March 1781

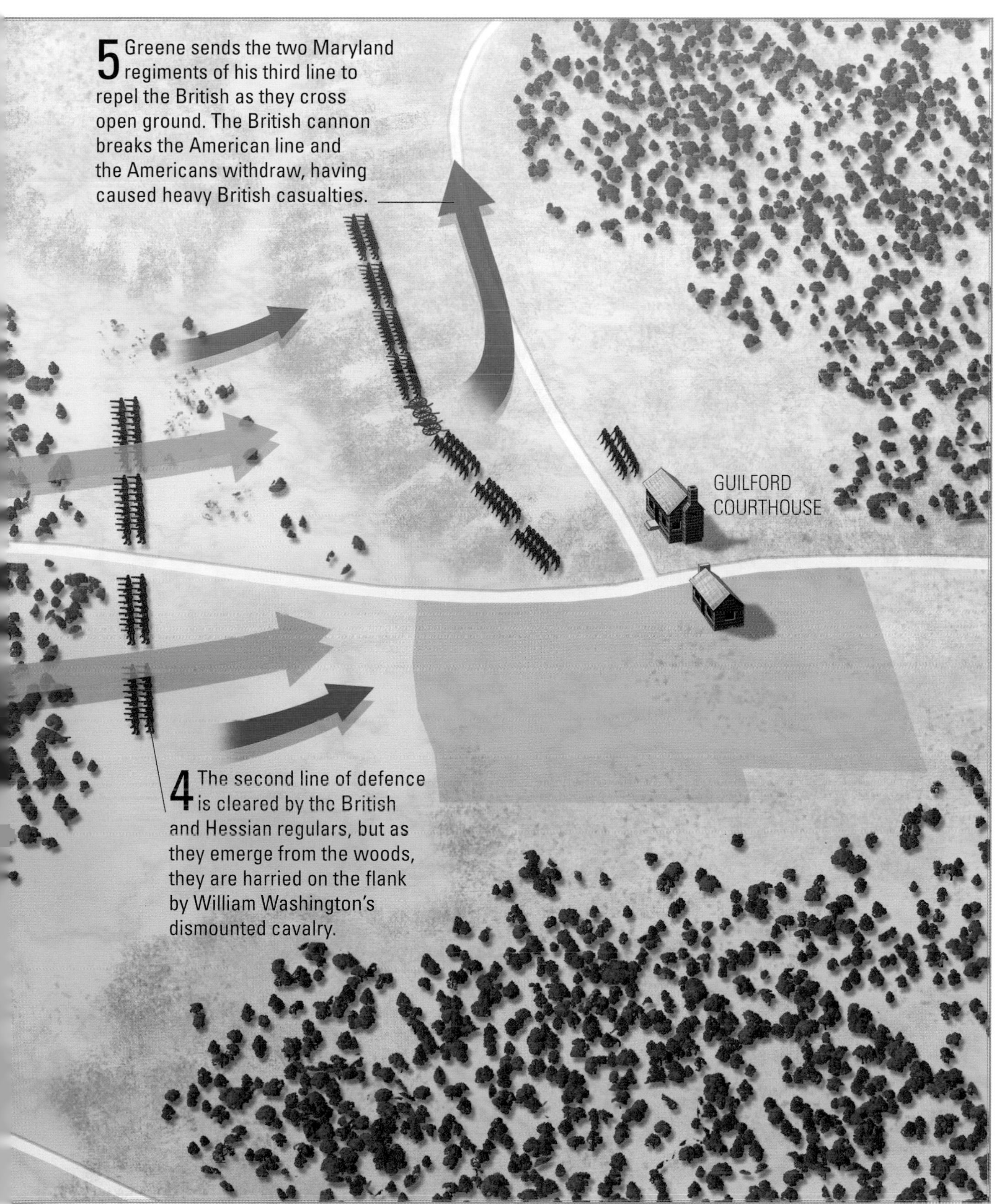
5 Greene sends the two Maryland regiments of his third line to repel the British as they cross open ground. The British cannon breaks the American line and the Americans withdraw, having caused heavy British casualties.
GUILFORD COURTHOUSE
4 The second line of defence is cleared by the British and Hessian regulars, but as they emerge from the woods, they are harried on the flank by William Washington's dismounted cavalry.

blockade. De Grasse moved out to offer battle, both fleets having difficulties of coordination, but the British retreated when unable to penetrate De Grasse's formation. Cornwallis's trapped army was doomed.

■ New London, 6 September 1781

Former Continental Gen Benedict Arnold accepted a loyalist brigade and launched a destructive raid in 1780 up the James River, burning Colonial ships and barely failing to capture Virginia governor Thomas Jefferson. In 1781, Arnold turned against his native Connecticut with 1700 troops. Arnold's force sailed from New York and burned New London and Groton, overwhelming and butchering 80 of the 215 garrison of Fort Griswold near Groton before withdrawing.

■ Eutaw Springs, 8 September 1781

Continental Gen Nathaniel Greene with 2400 men sought decisive battle here with Col Alexander Stewart's 2000 men, worried that peace negotiations might leave the British with the Carolinas. Greene trusting to his cavalry to prevent a rout, his militia stiffly withstood British fire, both sides erring as the costly battle progressed. The British remained when Greene withdrew, but themselves retreated two days later to defensible positions, leaving the Carolinas to Greene.

■ Yorktown, 28 Sep–19 Oct 1781

The final decisive major battle of the war, Yorktown established both the collapse of the British 'Southern Strategy' and Prime Minister Lord North's ability to prosecute the war further. After a series of reverses and costly battles in the Carolinas, plus the hoped-for masses of loyalists not flocking in vast numbers to his army, British Gen Charles Cornwallis shifted his 7000 remaining troops into Virginia, having sent 2000 to the New York area in response to George Washington's plans to assault the main British foothold in the colonies.

Meanwhile, the French general dispatched to assist in the war, the Comte de Rochambeau, demurred at that objective, but offered the 7000 troops under his command to support operations against Cornwallis in Virginia. Washington had 2000 of his troops combined with the Marquis de Lafayette's 2000 Continentals in Virginia before British Gen Henry Clinton in New York was aware of their departure.

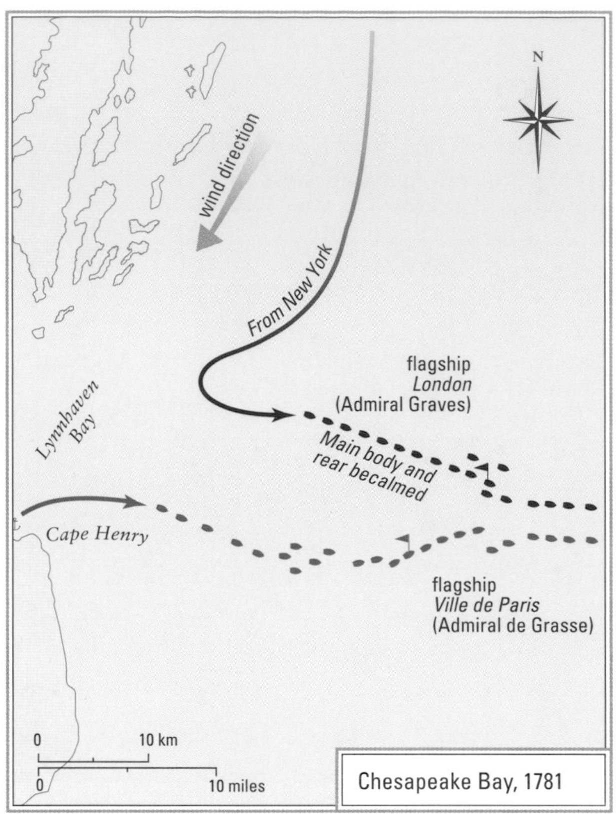

Chesapeake Bay, 1781

Cornwallis added the then British Gen Benedict Arnold's command to his own and moved the combined force into the Yorktown peninsula, a magnificent defensive position, in the reasonable assumption that the Royal Navy would maintain command of the sea. Across the peninsula's neck, Cornwallis employed his artillerymen and engineers in erecting a series of trenches and redoubts, with which he felt confident of repelling any conceivable Franco-American attack. Having forfeited the initiative, Cornwallis could only watch as Patriot troops clustered before his lines and French ships in the James River landed thousands of troops and, significantly, siege artillery. His entire strategy predicated upon the idea of support or evacuation by sea, Cornwallis found himself bereft of both when the French fleet under Adm François de Grasse drove off a British relieving squadron in the battle of the Chesapeake Capes.

Washington and Rochambeau's combined forces numbered some 7000 Continentals, 4000 militia and 3100 French marines with 5000 regulars. Cornwallis' 65 cannon found themselves under the close-range fire of 92 guns under the expert command of Gen Henry Knox. The besiegers moved their lines to within 730m of the British and opened fire. Cornwallis gradually contracted his perimeter in the vain hope of yet another relief force from New York by sea, the allies pressing in each time and further limiting British opportunities for escape or forage. British sapping parties did at times capture or disable Allied batteries and positions, only to see them recaptured the next day by overwhelming counter-attacks that also began to capture the British redoubts. Smallpox and starvation joined the ranks of Cornwallis's enemies, even a simple lack of ammunition limiting his offensive ability.

An attempt to evacuate part of Cornwallis's army via boats to the neighbouring Gloucester peninsula collapsed under a sudden storm with severe losses. After a siege of some three weeks, Cornwallis offered to begin negotiating his surrender. Terms concluded upon the same day that Clinton finally arrived with 25 ships and 7000 relieving troops, which returned to New York at the news of Cornwallis' surrender. Slaves promised their freedom in the British lines returned to their masters' control, while 8041 British and Hessian troops stacked arms. A total of 660 British had died and 478 of the allies. With the surrender and the transfer of the British and Hessian troops to prisoner camps, land combat in North America essentially ceased, while British Prime Minister Lord North finally resigned upon the news of a second large-scale surrender in the Colonies.

■ **JOHNSTOWN, 25 OCTOBER 1781**

A force of 670 loyalists, regulars and allied Indians from Canada raided this upstate New York town. Col Marinus Willett, leading 400 militia, engaged a small force attacking from the raiders' rear, prompting their withdrawal.

■ **JERSEYFIELD, 30 OCTOBER 1781**

Col Marinus Willett with 460 militia and Oneidas pursued 1000 British regulars, loyalists and Indians, led by Walter Butler, retreating to Canada from their raid upon Johnstown, New York. Butler died and the other raiders escaped.

Other Colonial Wars, 1782

■ **GNADENHUTTEN MASSACRE, 8 MARCH 1782**

The peaceful Moravian Christian Delawares of this settlement perished, caught between suspicious tribesmen and militia vengeful for other tribes' attacks. Despite their having offered no resistance, colonial militia butchered 96 and burned their settlement.

■ **LITTLE MOUNTAIN/ESTILL'S DEFEAT, 22 MARCH 1782**

Kentucky Capt James Estill died in a bloody combat, having pursued a Wyandot raiding party discouraged from attacking Estill's Station by Monk, a captured slave, later freed. One of the bloodiest fights of the Kentucky frontier, seven of the 25 militia died, along with 17 Wyandots.

■ **CRAWFORD EXPEDITION, MAY–JUNE 1782**

Col William Crawford led 485 mounted militia into the Ohio River valley, shadowed by 200 Wyandot and Delaware tribesman enraged by past attacks and reinforced by 240 loyalists, including the infamous Simon Girty and two cannon. Brought to battle near the Sandusky, Crawford's command ran low on ammunition after refusing Girty's offer of quarter. Most of the expedition fought their way out; Crawford was captured and tortured to death.

■ **PIQUA, 8 AUGUST 1782**

After the Blue Licks disaster, George Rogers Clark led 1050 militia and a vengeful Daniel Boone in burning five Shawnee villages and a British trading post in Ohio.

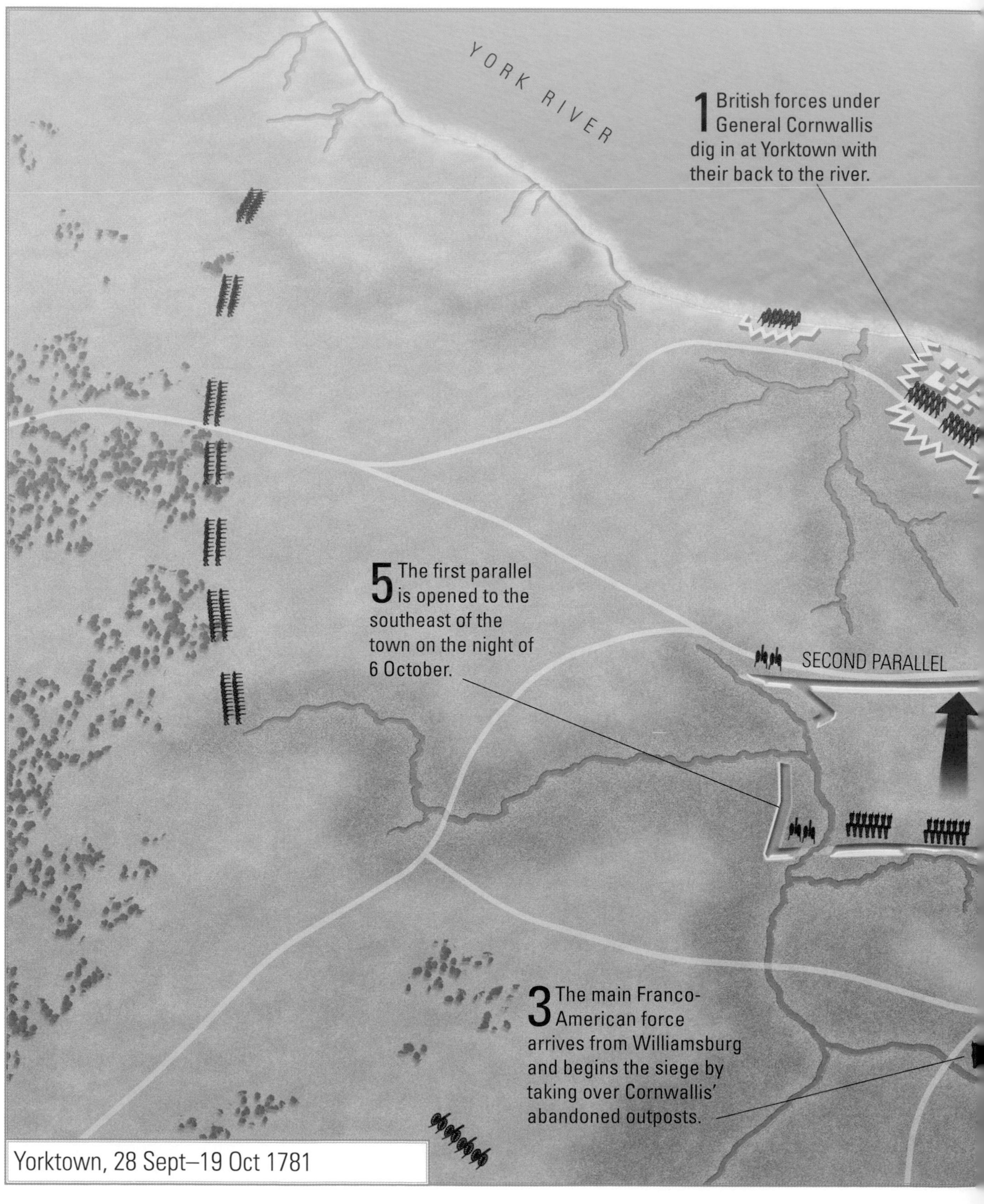

Yorktown, 28 Sept–19 Oct 1781

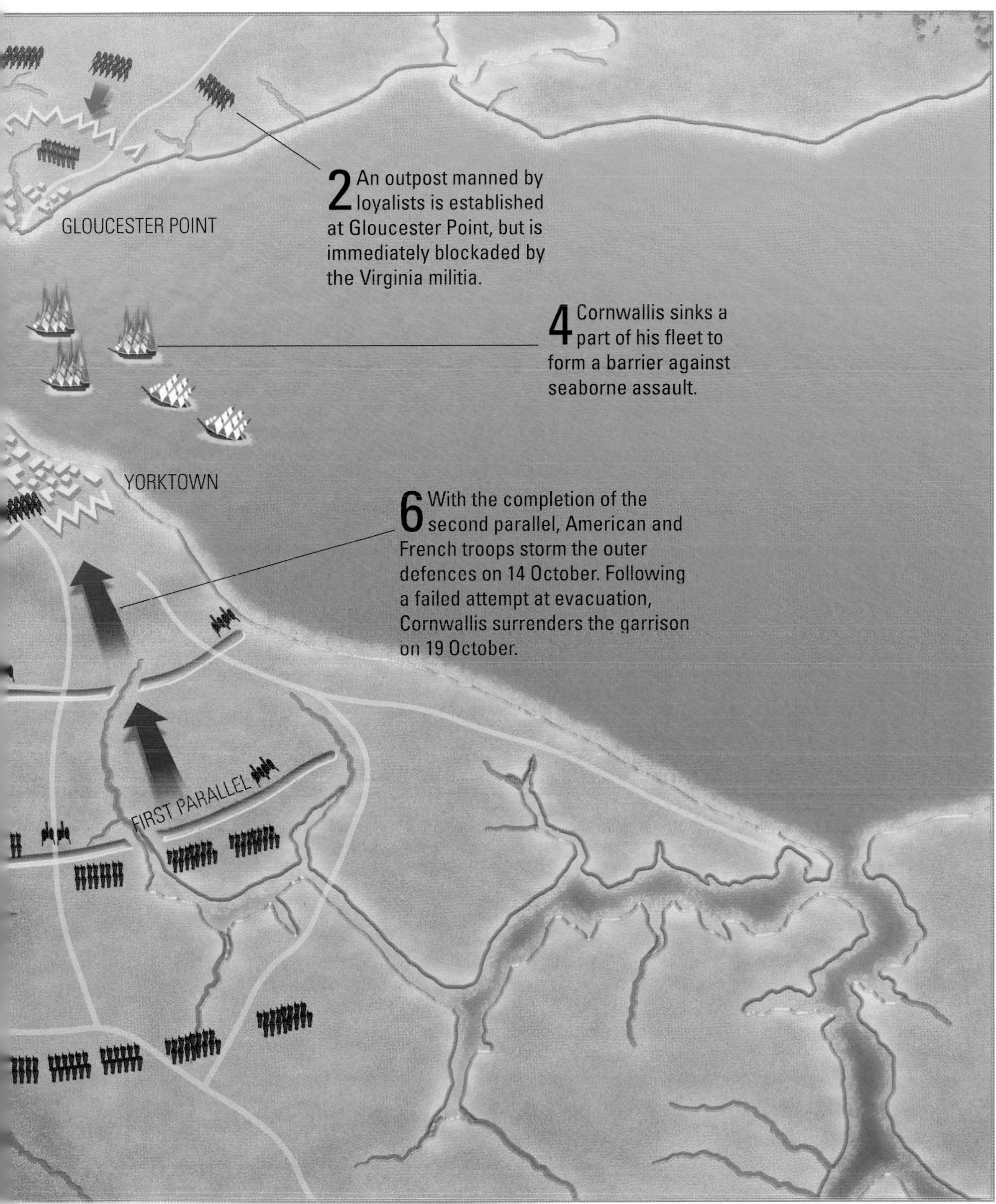
2 An outpost manned by loyalists is established at Gloucester Point, but is immediately blockaded by the Virginia militia.
GLOUCESTER POINT
4 Cornwallis sinks a part of his fleet to form a barrier against seaborne assault.
YORKTOWN
6 With the completion of the second parallel, American and French troops storm the outer defences on 14 October. Following a failed attempt at evacuation, Cornwallis surrenders the garrison on 19 October.
FIRST PARALLEL

Early 19th Century Wars, 1798–1848

The new nation of the United States of America soon became embroiled in conflicts with its former imperial masters, fighting both the French (Franco-American War) and British (War of 1812). As American settlers moved westwards, the United States soon came into conflict with Mexico over disputed territories. Texans fought for their independence in the Texas Revolution, while a decisive victory in the American-Mexican War (1846–48) gained the United States vast new territories stretching from the Mississippi delta to the Pacific Ocean.

Left: Texans defend the Alamo mission station in this imagining of the 1836 battle by painter Percy Moran. Heavily outnumbered, the Texan defenders eventually succumbed to overwhelming odds.

Franco-American War (The Quasi-War) 1798–1800

US presidents George Washington and John Adams considered the alliance with France terminated on Louis XVI's execution. The Directory authorized privateers to seize US ships and the US Navy engaged French warships.

■ ***La Croyable*, 7 July 1798**

USS *Delaware* under the command of Stephen Decatur captured this French privateer schooner of 12 guns operating off New Jersey. She became USS *Retaliation*, later recaptured, then taken for good by the US.

■ ***Constellation* vs. *Vengeance*, 1 Feb 1800**

Secretary of War Henry Knox had urged the construction of frigates capable of outrunning what they could not outfight. One of these, *Constellation*, under Capt Thomas Truxtun, found French frigate *Vengeance* about to return to France off Guadalupe. *Vengeance* surrendered after a fierce 12-hour battle. The escaped French ship became an American prize, but when *Constellation*'s mainmast collapsed, *Vengeance* absconded under cover of darkness and limped back to France.

■ **Santo Domingo Raid, May 1800**

Toussaint L'Ouverture became LGov of French Saint-Domingue as invading British and Spanish freed and armed French slaves, after which the French abolished slavery. Using fellow freed slaves, he conquered Spanish Santo Domingo without French authorization.

■ **USS *Boston* vs. *Le Berceau*, 12 October 1800**

USS *Boston*, under Capt George Little, overhauled French ship *Le Berceau*, under Cdr Louis André Senes. The battle lasted until sunset, both ships damaged and losing manoeuvrability. *Boston* captured *Le Berceau* upon making repairs.

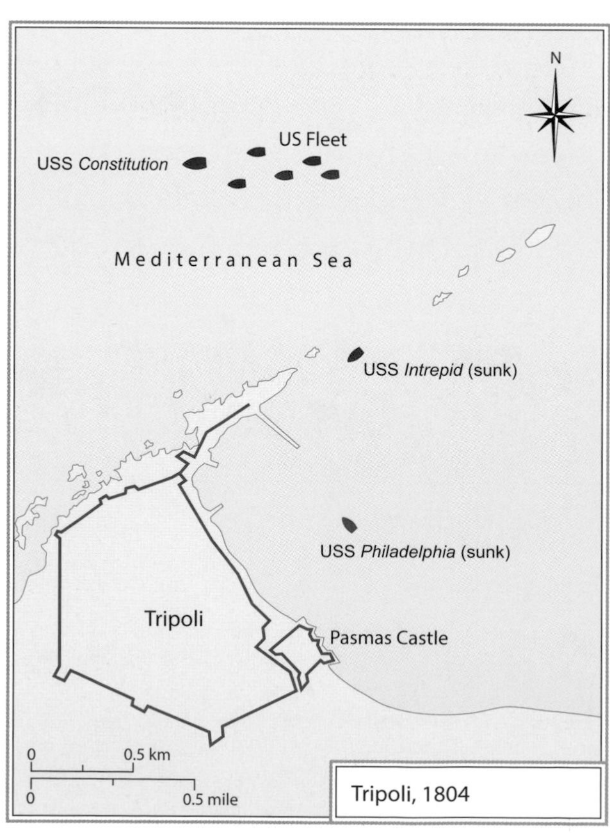

First Barbary War 1801–05

■ **Tripoli Harbour, 1804**

Cdre Edward Preble assumed command of the US Mediterranean Squadron in 1803 and blockaded Tripoli harbour to prevent raids by the Barbary pirates. The first significant action of the blockade came on 31 October, when the 36-gun frigate USS *Philadelphia* ran aground on an uncharted reef and was captured by Tripolitan gunboats together with its crew and Capt William Bainbridge. Although the frigate was unfit for sea, it was anchored in the harbour as a floating battery.

If the *Philadelphia* could be repaired, it would become the Barbary pirates' most powerful naval unit and its destruction was Preble's top priority. The defences of Tripoli harbour ruled out a conventional naval attack and it was decided that a night raid offered the best chance of success. On the night of 16 February 1804, a captured Tripolitan ketch renamed USS *Intrepid* disguised as a local merchant vessel sailed into the harbour under the command of Lt Stephen Decatur, Jr. He bluffed his way alongside the *Philadelphia*, allowing

Lieutenant Stephen Decatur and Midshipman Thomas Macdonough board an enemy gunboat during the attack on Tripoli under Commodore Preble, August 1804.

his detachment of marines hidden below decks to board the frigate and set her on fire. Despite heavy fire from the shore batteries, Decatur and his men successfully escaped in *Intrepid*.

In August 1804, *Intrepid* was converted into a 'floating volcano' to be sent into the harbour and blown up in the midst of the corsair fleet. The vessel was loaded with 100 barrels of powder and 150 shells, with their fuses set to burn for 15 minutes. On the evening of 4 September, *Intrepid* sailed into the harbour commanded by Master Commandant Richard Somers, but was hit by fire from shore batteries and blew up with the loss of all hands before reaching the enemy fleet.

■ Derna, 27 April–13 May 1805

Six months after failing to destroy the pirate fleet at Tripoli, American forces turned against Derna, which was attacked by a force from Alexandria, comprising a small detachment of US Marines and 500 Arab and Greek mercenaries under Capt William Eaton, Marine Lt Preston O'Bannon and the deposed Tripolitan ruler Hamet Karamanli. The USS *Nautilus*, the USS *Hornet* and the USS *Argus* were detailed to supply the force and provide naval gunfire support. On 27 April, the three vessels bombarded the defences of Derna, and Eaton's force successfully stormed the city, whose garrison fled after a short fight. The Pasha of Tripolitania, Yusuf Karamanli, had sent reinforcements to Derna, which arrived too late to prevent its capture. They made several attempts to retake the city, all of which were beaten off with the loss of 2000 men.

German Coast Uprising, 1811

■ German Coast Uprising, 8–10 Jan 1811

The German Coast region near New Orleans had a complex political situation, with French and Spanish influences and a large free black population in addition to a high proportion of slaves working the sugar plantations. Discontent among the latter resulted in a revolt that began in January 1811 after a period of plotting among the slave populations. Although the rising was violent, with considerable destruction of property, only two white people were killed. The rebels armed themselves as best they could, but had few firearms and were joined by only a small proportion of the slave population on the plantations they passed. They were met by militia and federal troops, and a short and one-sided battle ensued. The rebels, whose numbers have been postulated at anywhere between 200 and 500, suffered heavy casualties and scattered. The survivors were hunted down and recaptured.

Pre-war of 1812

■ *Chesapeake-Leopard* Affair, 22 June 1807

As US frigate *Chesapeake* (36 guns), under Cdre James Barron, left Virginia, British frigate *Leopard* (50), under Capt Salusbury Humphreys, ordered her to allow the British to search for deserters. Upon Barron's refusal, *Leopard* fired for 10 minutes at the completely unprepared Americans, *Chesapeake* surrendering. The British boarded and took four accused deserters, having killed three Americans and wounded 18.

War of 1812 (1812–15)

■ Mackinac Island I, 17 July 1812

British Capt Charles Roberts caught Lt Porter Hanks unaware that war had broken out with British artillery in position and his fort surrounded. Fearing that the British-allied Indians might massacre his command, Roberts surrendered.

■ Brownstown, 5 August 1812

US Maj Thomas van Horne set out to escort a supply column to Hull in Detroit. Tecumseh had rallied the local Indians to support the British and ambushed van Horne here, capturing dispatches, frightening Hull.

■ Maguaga, 9 August 1812

US Gen William Hull sent 600 men under LCol James Miller to bring supplies to Detroit. Tecumseh

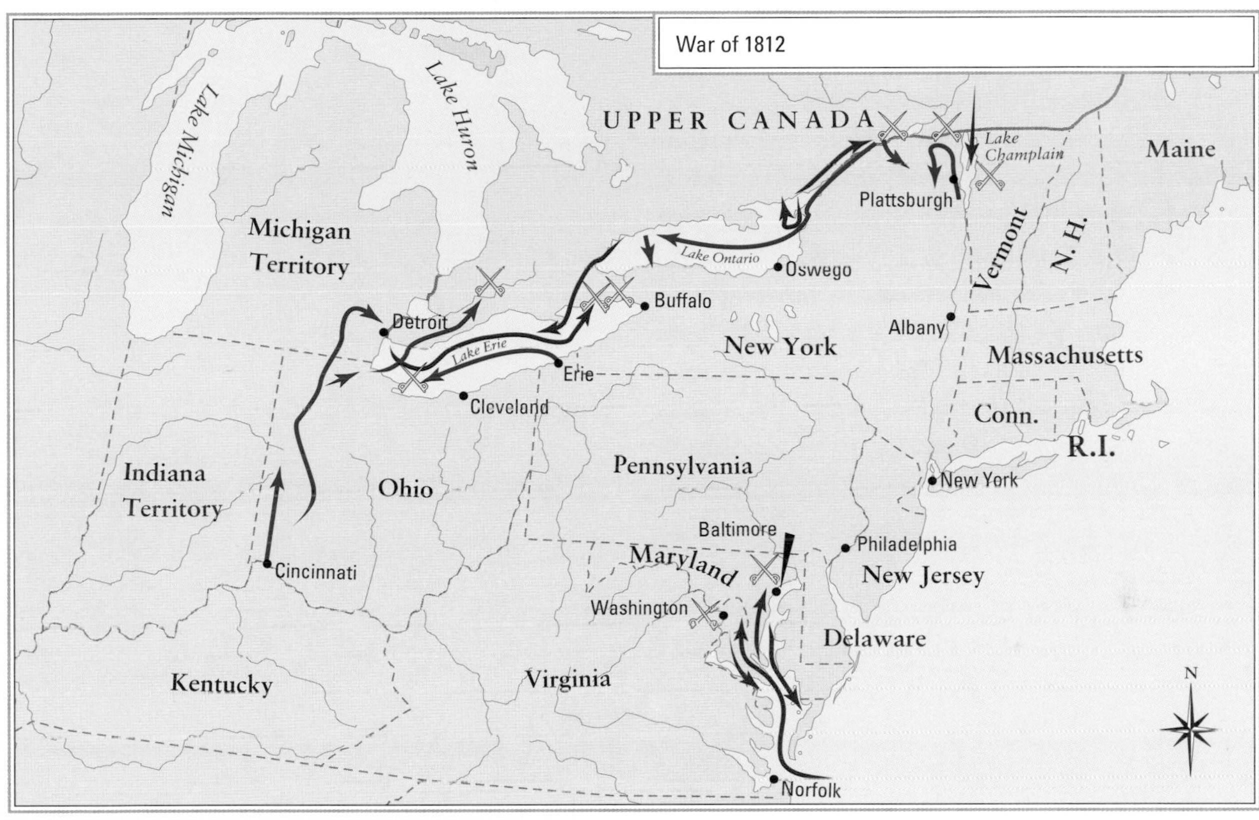

and 400 British and Indians attacked Miller and each other in confusion, Miller retreated to Detroit.

■ **Fort Dearborn, 15 August 1812**

Gen William Hull ordered this post, essentially a trading station, evacuated soon after the outbreak of hostilities with Britain and the fall of neighbouring Fort Mackinac. Capt Nathan Heald led out 67 garrison with 27 women and children after destroying Dearborn's stores. Four hundred Potawatomi and Winnebago Indians attacked the column of evacuees, killing 38 garrison, two women and 12 children, selling the survivors to the British for ransom.

■ **Detroit, 15–16 August 1812**

Gen William Hull received a commuted death sentence for cowardice after surrendering this bastion to British Gen Isaac Brock, after Brock warned that his Indians might massacre the garrison. Hull forbade his artillery to fire.

■ ***Constitution* vs. *Guerriere*, 19 Aug 1812**

This frigate duel between *Constitution* (44 guns), under Capt William Hull, and *Guerriere* (38), under Capt Richard Dacres, featured British shot bouncing off 'Old Ironsides's' hull and the *Guerriere*'s dismasting, surrender and sinking in a stinging British defeat.

■ ***Constitution* vs. *Java*, 19 August 1812**

'Old Ironsides' scored again when *Constitution* (44 guns), under Cdre William Bainbridge, engaged and took HMS *Java* (38), under Capt Henry Lambert. Java's greater speed allowed her to pummel *Constitution* severely before *Constitution*'s strength and battery prevailed.

■ **Fort Wayne, 5–12 September 1812**

As hostilities erupted, Potawatomi and Miami Indians attacked this post in Miami territory, firing homes nearby and seizing two wooden cannon, almost prompting Capt James Rhea to surrender. His two lieutenants declared him unfit to command and took over the defence of the fort, before a relief column 2200 strong under Gen (later President) William Henry Harrison arrived.

The resulting battle drove off the Miami, many of whom joined Tecumseh.

■ **Fort Harrison, 4–15 September 1812**

Gen (later President) William Henry Harrison had built this powerful wooden bastion, but left it weakly garrisoned under the command of Captain (later President) Zachary Taylor. Emboldened by a series of American defeats, 600 Indians attacked the fort, which Taylor defended with 10 soldiers and a handful of sheltering civilians. The Indians continued to invest the fort until a relief column arrived. The desperately needed stand stemmed further Indian uprisings south into American territory.

■ **Queenston Heights, 13 October 1812**

American plans for an invasion of Canada along the Niagara River frontier died along with British Gen Isaac Brock in this disastrous battle. With Gen William Hull's effort to launch an invasion in the Detroit area collapsing disastrously, Gen Stephen van Rensselaer led 6660 regulars and militia towards the Canadian town of Queenston, his officers quarrelling and his men exhausted by long marches and a previous crossing's failure in a rain storm. Brock was aware of the impending invasion with 2340 (mostly) regulars posted throughout the threatened area. Van Rensselaer planned to ferry his remaining 4600 men over the river in 13 bateaux, with a battery covering the crossing. The boats became damaged or swept away during the many trips the landing required. Van Rensselaer himself had to be evacuated wounded when British Cap James Dennis launched a fierce attack on the US bridgehead. What American success there was came from Capt John Wool who led 100 regulars up Queenston Heights and captured a battery and the British camp there. Brock fell leading a charge up the heights, the British then falling back as American LCol Winfield Scott attempted to organize the 1350 Americans on the Canadian side of the river, while the British brought up additional units from Chippewa and sent allied Indians to harass Wool's position. There

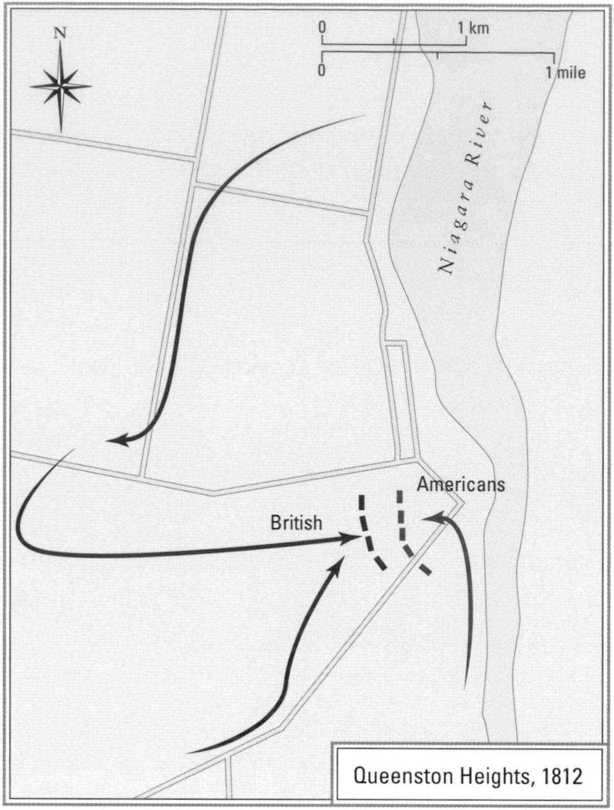

Queenston Heights, 1812

were no bateaux left to reinforce or rescue Scott's command, as Brock's replacement Gen Roger Sheaffe launched an attack that afternoon, which drove the exhausted Americans into flight. Scott surrendered some 925 prisoners. As many as 200 Americans were killed in the fighting and 20 British fell, mostly attacking Wool on the heights. Van Rensselaer resigned his commission. Winfield Scott was eventually exchanged.

■ ***United States* vs. *Macedonian*, 25 October 1812**

Weight of shot overcame rate of fire when frigate *United States* (44 guns), under Capt Stephen Decatur, pummelled frigate HMS *Macedonian* (38), under Capt John Carden, into surrender at long range. *Macedonian* became a gratifying US prize.

■ **Wildcat Creek, 22 November 1812**

Gen Samuel Hopkins with 1200 mounted militia and regulars moved south from Fort Harrison against Teumseh's Prophetstown and the Creeks. Destroying an abandoned Winnebago village here, Hopkins burned Prophetstown's homes and winter stores before withdrawing.

■ Mississinewa, 17–18 December 1812

The Miamis' failure to capture Fort Wayne and Fort Harrison prompted LCol John Campbell's expedition down this river with 600 mounted troops, which enjoyed some success before bad weather and Miami counter-attacks prompted Campbell's withdrawal.

■ Frenchtown/River Raisin Massacre, 18–23 January 1813

Gen James Winchester led 934 green militia north from Ohio. Col Henry Procter raised 1100 troops and Indians and overwhelmed the Americans here. Procter withdrew with his captives, the remaining Indians butchering 68 American prisoners.

■ Ogdensburg, 22 February 1813

American raids across the St Lawrence River prompted this powerful British retaliatory raid in which LCol George Macdonell scattered Maj Benjamin Forsythe's defenders and captured and plundered mostly military stores from this New York town.

■ York, 27 April 1813

An US force of 1800 under Gen Zebulon Pike landed at the Canadian capital and scattered 1100 British defenders under Gen Roger Sheaffe. During the occupation and plunder of the town, the parliament buildings burned.

■ Fort Meigs, 28 April–9 May 1813

British Gen Henry Procter with Tecumseh led an army of 2000 to reduce this strong American bastion in Ohio. The fort's powerful earthworks held, with the worst of the American casualties occurring when 1200 militia attacked the British camp.

■ Fort George, 25–27 May 1813

This wooden fort at the north end of the Niagara River and its ruins changed hands twice during the war. Given its location along an invasion route, the British enlarged the bastion at the start of hostilities; however, the Americans succeeded in capturing it in mid-1813. Later, US Gen George McClure blew up the fort. By year's end, the returning British used the ruins as a base to capture US Fort Niagara.

■ Sacket's Harbour, 28–29 May 1813

British Gen George Prevost and Cdre Chauncey Yeo launched an amphibious assault against this American naval yard on Lake Ontario. US Gen Jacob Brown grimly held the base's defences, the British successfully burning the naval stores.

■ Stony Creek, 6 June 1813

Advancing up from captured Fort George, 3400 US infantry under Gens John Chandler and William Winder retreated after British Gen John Vincent with 700 men surprised them in their encampment here, the British likewise withdrawing.

■ Craney Island, 22 June 1813

A British effort to 'cut out' the blockaded vessel USS *Constellation* in Norfolk failed after a British squadron in the Chesapeake landed as many as 3000 men in boats and barges to take Hampton and this island, upon which *Constellation*'s own gunners manned a battery of cannon. Congreve rockets and the fall of Hampton could not overcome the fire of the battery and American gunboats, forcing a British retreat up the Chesapeake.

■ Beaver Dams, 24 June 1813

After the fall of Fort George, LCol Charles Boerstler set out, armed with two cannon and 570 men, to strike a British outpost up the Niagara River country. Passing through Queenston, the column alerted an expatriate loyalist, Laura Ingersoll Secord, who walked 32km in the darkness while Boerstler halted, to a camp of Indians allied to the British, one of whom led her to Lt James FitzGibbon, commanding troops skilled in forest warfare. FitzGibbon joined with François Dominique Ducharme, an Indian agent, to post 400 allied warriors in especially thick brush in front of Boerstler's column here. The American cannon had no target and Boerstler's men could not get through the brush before the Indians arrived and fired upon them. Boerstler, under heavy attack, finally accepted FitzGibbon's proffer of surrender over the possible extinction of all his men by the Indians after 80 of his command had died.

■ Fort Stephenson, 1 August 1813

Withdrawing from Fort Meigs, Gen Henry Procter's siege train vainly attacked this Sandusky River bastion with cannon, Indians and gunboats. US Maj George Croghan and 160 garrison killed a quarter of Procter's regulars at close range.

■ St Michaels, 10 August 1813

As the British fleet in the Chesapeake attempted to burn the shipyards in this Maryland town, a landing party overran the harbour cannon. The battery protecting the town repelled the attackers and saved the shipyard.

■ Lake Erie, 10 September 1813

Fighting on the Great Lakes was a matter of each side's confidence as a function of warships constructed. Royal Navy Cdr Robert Barclay repeatedly sought to lure his counterpart, Master Commandant Oliver Hazard Perry, into a battle when the British fleet was the stronger. Perry could not be rushed behind his defences at Preque Isle as he built up his own force into a powerful squadron. Barclay decided to force the issue when the completion of HMS *Detroit* (11 guns), added her to *Queen Charlotte* (17), *Lady Prevost* (13), *General Hunter* (10) and two smaller ships. Barclay had stripped his own defending fort to secure cannon, with the result that his ships did not have a uniform weight of battery and were at times difficult to fire. Barclay was also short on supplies, and both sides faced a lack of skilled seamen.

Perry's two brigs, the *Lawrence* and *Niagara*, each mounted 20 short-range, but lethal 32-pound shot carronades, which could be reloaded rapidly. Seven smaller ships and gunboats made up the balance of Perry's fleet. When Barclay withdrew to make his own preparations for decisive battle, Perry moved his own fleet into deep water over a sandbar and sailed forth to engage Barclay. Shifting wind

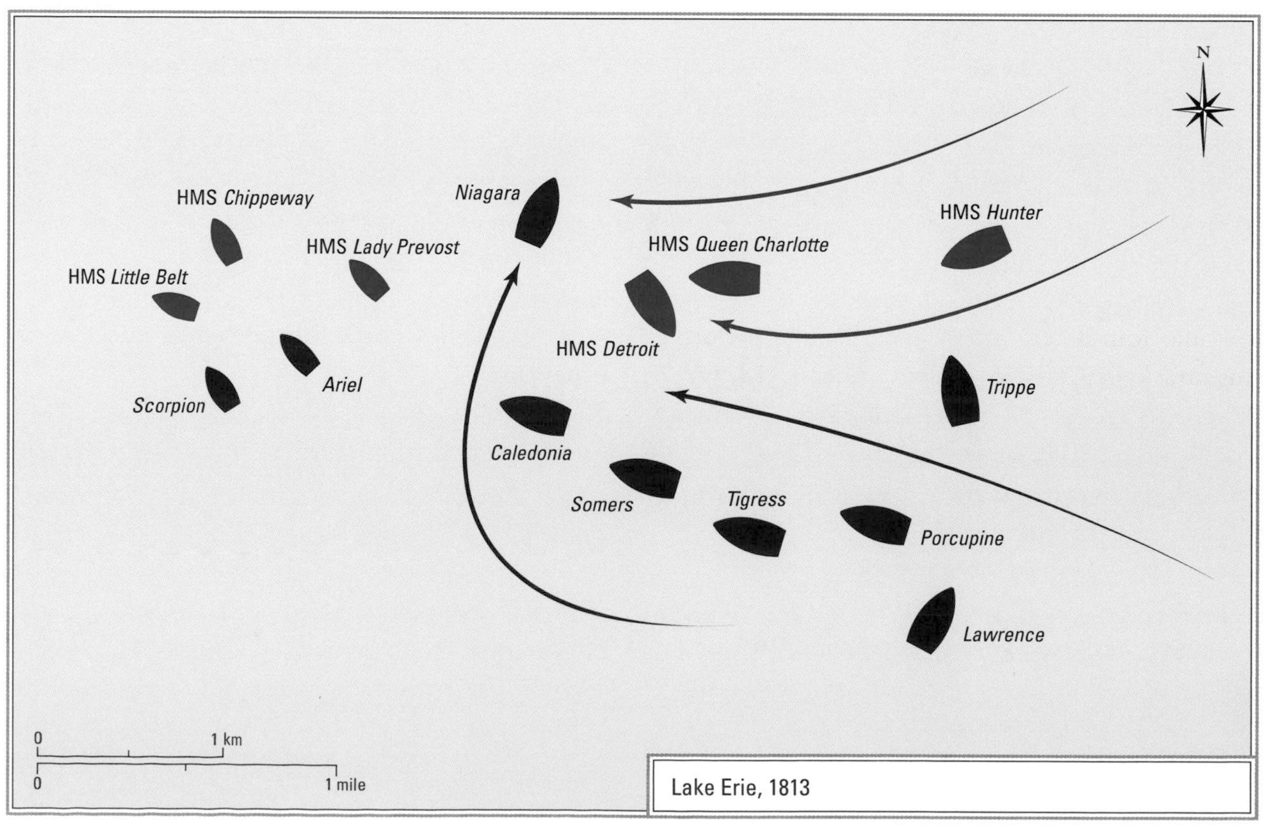

Lake Erie, 1813

allowed Perry's nimble brigs to close range rapidly upon the British, *Lawrence* in the lead engaging the British line before the balance of the US fleet arrived. Perry had to abandon *Lawrence* two hours later in a near-sinking condition, rowing past the mauled British to *Niagara*, hanging back under the command of his disgruntled predecessor, Cdr Jesse Elliot. The undamaged *Niagara* plunged into the fight, the remaining American ships arriving and capturing the British squadron.

■ Thames River, 5 October 1813

Having (despite Tecumseh's pleading) abandoned and partially burned Amherstburg after the defeat on Lake Erie, British Gen Henry Procter retreated along this river, burning ships and gunboats to forestall their capture. Procter finally made a stand with 430 soldiers and 600 Indians against US Gen William Henry Harrison's pursuing 3000 Kentucky militia, many of them mounted and vengeful. The British and surviving Indians retreated after suffering heavy casualties, including Tecumseh.

■ Chateauguay, 26 October 1813

US Gen Wade Hampton, leading 4000 green infantry, moved down this river en route to Montreal. LCol Charles-Michel de Salaberry with 400 local troops in a series of defensive lines defeated Hampton in detail.

■ Chrysler's Farm, 11 November 1813

Gen James Wilkinson's abortive advance into Canada foundered at Chrysler's Farm, during this attack in Ontario in November 1813, when 800 British regulars under LCol Joseph Morrison supported by gunboats repulsed the uncoordinated advance of his 7000 men. Wilkinson's command errors prompted a court martial into his actions.

■ Longwoods, 4 March 1814

US dismounted dragoons numbering 164 under Capt Andrew Holmes, with the aid of an abatis and a height, defeated an effort by British Capt James Basden and 240 regulars and militia to evict them from Canada.

■ Port Dover, 14–16 May 1814

Lt John Campbell and 800 regulars and militia sailed to loot and burn the Canadian town in retaliation for British raids in Maryland and New York. The British used this attack to justify burning Washington D.C.

■ Chippewa River, 5 July 1814

British Gen Phineas Riall and 2000 regular soldiers blocked the advance from Fort Erie of Gen Jacob Brown with 4800 men. Gen Winfield Scott's regulars drew the British into a punishing crossfire, both sides afterwards retreating.

■ Prairie du Chien, 17–20 July 1814

British LCol William McKay led 650 regulars and allied Indians against US Fort Shelby, recently built with 100 garrison. Under bombardment, a supporting American gunboat retreated, and Lt Joseph Perkins surrendered the fort.

■ Lundy's Lane, 25 July 1814

The British responding with 3000 men to Winfield Scott's presence near the Niagara River, US Gen Jacob Brown and British Gen Gordon Drummond fought a bloody and indecisive battle here in July 1814. A total of 81 British and 171 Americans perished.

■ Mackinac Island, 26 July–4 August

A US effort to retake this island in Lake Huron collapsed, when British LCol Robert McDouall with 200 soldiers at his disposal attacked the beachhead, capturing two American schooners, with US Col George Croghan retreating in the other three.

■ Fort Erie, 4 August–21 September 1814

Having seized this British post at the upper end of the Niagara, the US prepared to defend it in the aftermath of Lundy's Lane in what became the longest siege of the war. Gen Edmund Gaines enlarged the fort with batteries and entrenchments sheltering 2600 defenders. British Gen Gordon Drummond with siege artillery and 3000 regulars, militia and allied Indians surrounded the fort with batteries, but found the defenders, walls and trenches resistant to his bombardment. Several British efforts to storm the fort's bastions met with determined American resistance, while the besiegers were supplied by the river with less difficulty than the defenders via Lake Erie. Drummond finally withdrew when the Americans launched an attack with 2000 men against the British batteries, spiking cannon while inflicting and suffering heavy casualties. The Americans later abandoned and blew up the fort.

■ Lake Huron, 13 August–6 September 1814

A final series of American efforts to reassert control in the region of this lake generally did poorly in 1814. Five American schooners with 700 men landed and plundered an abandoned British base on St Joseph Island. The Americans next landed upon Mackinac Island, where a sudden British assault captured two of the schooners and prompted US Col George Croghan to abandon the effort to recapture the strategic island, which remained in British hands until the end of the war. The Americans next bombarded and destroyed a British fort protecting the supply base on Nottawasaga Bay. American foraging parties located schooner *Nancy*, which had been towed for safekeeping up the Nottawasaga River. The British had to destroy *Nancy*, the only British supply vessel on the lake, laden with winter supplies for the defenders, some of which they successfully concealed ashore. US Navy Capt Arthur Sinclair left schooners *Tigress* and *Scorpion* to patrol the northern part of the lake and intercept British traffic. Royal Navy Lt Miller Worsley, *Nancy*'s former commander, joined with army Lt Andrew Bolger and his Newfoundlanders in fitting out four bateaux with two cannon and sailing within 91m of *Tigress*, whose surprised gunners missed their first defensive salvo. The British then rushed in and captured the American ship in a sudden boarding combat.

Setting her crew ashore, the British used the undamaged vessel, still flying the American colours, to seize *Scorpion* at 24km distance. The British then employed the two ships to ferry winter supplies and the prisoners to the British garrison on Mackinac Island. British plans to further secure their control of the lake with additional ship construction ended with the cessation of hostilities at the end of the year.

■ Bladensburg, 24 August 1814

After Napoleon's exile, Britain directed considerable resources into the ongoing war in North America. Around 2500 of Wellington's regulars joined a force of 20 warships in an attack up the Chesapeake Bay directly into the central United States. The American defences included a flotilla of gunboats and a few forts, the one at Mount Vernon being blown up by its own garrison when the British approached. Adms Alexander Cochrane and George Cockburn sought profitable looting of Virginia tobacco, the crushing of Maryland privateering and the destruction of the US capital at Washington. American resistance varied from the heroic to the wildly incompetent, perfectly exemplified at this battle, when 4000 regulars marched through Maryland towards Washington. US Gen William Winder had 6000 green militia deployed at this town before the British advance, his positions changed at the last minute by Secretary (later President) of State James Monroe while President James Madison and most of his cabinet looked on.

Only 400 of US Cdre Joshua Barney's sailors and marines manning five navy cannon stood firm as the British approached up the pike, British Gen Robert Ross's Congreve rocket batteries scattering some militia, Winder ordering the remainder to retreat before they had engaged, while Madison and his cabinet escaped into the Maryland countryside. The British engulfed the sailors and marines, capturing the wounded Barney. About the only success in what later was known as the 'Bladensburg Races' was a day's time gained by the battle. The delay allowed First Lady Dolly Madison to evacuate some of the more important art and artefacts from the capital, which the British entered the following day and burned in a notorious action, ostensibly in retaliation for the burning of York and its parliamentary buildings in 1813.

■ **Burning of Washington, 24 August 1814**
British Adm George Cockburn planned and led this destructive and infamous raid on the US capital. The British regular soldiers under the command of Gen Richard Ross were methodical in their destruction, firing, among other structures, the Library of Congress, the executive mansion, the US Capitol, a ropewalk and the docks; the Washington Navy Yard was burned by the Americans. A providential rainstorm extinguished the fires the day the British withdrew.

■ **Alexandria, 29 August–2 September 1814**
The Virginia city of Alexandria drew ridicule for allowing British Adm Richard Cockburn to plunder their tobacco warehouses on the condition of sparing their homes. The citizens refused entry to Virginia militia attempting to repel the invaders.

■ **Caulk's Field, 31 August 1814**
British Adm Alexander Cochrane sought to disperse American resistance during his fleet's raid up the Chesapeake estuary with diversions to draw the defenders away from his primary objective of Baltimore. Capt Peter Parker succeeded at the cost of his life when, on this farm, his force of 200 encountered Col Philip Reed and 174 militia, who had anticipated Parker's plan to attack their camp. At Parker's death, his men fled.

■ **Hampden, 3 September 1814**
A British amphibious expedition into undefended Maine and up the Penobscot River resulted in their long-term occupation of this and other coastal towns, plus the scuttling of the USS *Adams* (28 guns), to prevent capture.

■ **Lake Champlain, 6–11 September 1814**
Guided by Perry's example at Lake Erie and his own considerable abilities as a leader and a sailor, US Cdre Thomas MacDonough – beginning in 1812 – constructed a powerful squadron upon this vital lake from green timber and imported fittings. British Cdre George Downie did likewise

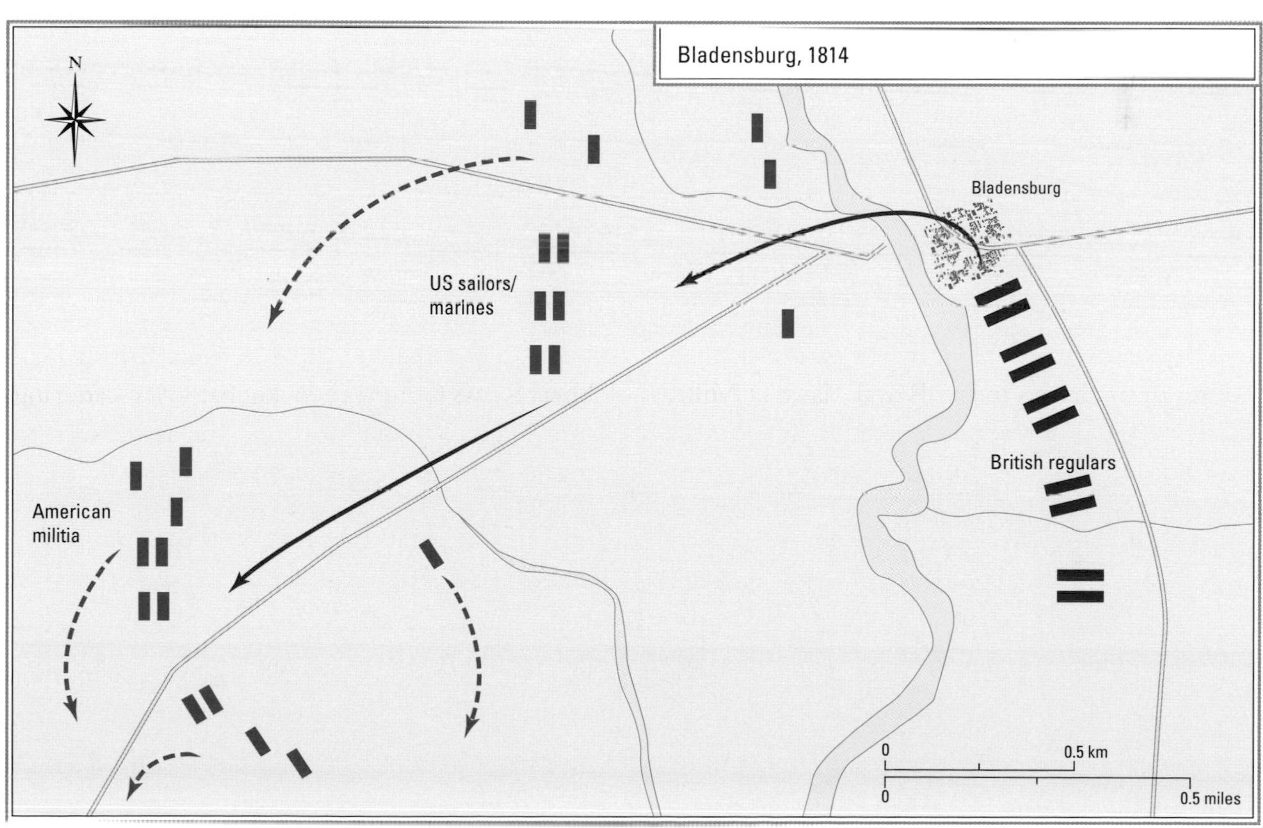

Marines in the rigging of USS *Wasp* fire at the crew of HMS *Reindeer* on 28 June 1814. HMS *Reindeer* was eventually captured and burned after a hard-fought battle in the English Channel.

upon the lake's northern shore, with both sides mindful of the lake's potential role as a British invasion route from Canada. The British squadron numbered four large ships and 12 gunboats, the frigate *Confiance* (37 guns), the most powerful on the lake. MacDonough anchored his four large vessels and a total of 10 gunboats across the mouth of Plattsburg Bay. British firepower devastated the American ships, but when the British were within effective shot of MacDonough's carronades, they suddenly found themselves facing undamaged broadsides as MacDonough rotated his vessels by their anchor lines. Downie fell, his large ships captured.

■ **Plattsburg, 6–11 September 1814**

British Gen George Prevost marched along the shore of Lake Champlain with 10,000 men, accompanied by a powerful fleet, as part of a plan to divide New England from the rest of the US. Prevost had reached this city in New York, where US Gen Alexander Macomb with 3400 resisted his attack until the news of the British fleet's destruction in the battle of Lake Champlain forced Prevost's retreat.

■ **North Point, 12 September 1814**

The British sought to punish and plunder Baltimore, source of tobacco and privateers. British Gen Robert Ross and 4600 men landed here, the land assault ceasing after Ross fell to Gen John Stricker's militia riflemen.

■ **Baltimore, 12–15 September 1814**

US Gen Samuel Smith poured 17,000 defenders into the city, the objective of the British fleet being to raid the Chesapeake. Entrenched militia blunted a British landing force at North Point, while harbour batteries withstood British bombardment.

■ **Fort McHenry, 13–14 September 1814**

This star-shaped brick fort's baptism of fire under the mortars, cannon and rockets of the British fleet was made legendary in song. The fort's defenders grimly stuck to their cannon, blocking the harbour and managing to save Baltimore. The defenders suffered four killed and 24 wounded.

■ **Fort Bowyer, First Battle, 14 Sep 1814**

A British naval squadron bombarded the Mobile Bay fort, while a detachment of Royal Marines attacked overland. The US garrison repulsed the attack and forced the British squadron to withdraw two days later.

■ **Malcolm's Mills, 6 November 1814**

British efforts to forestall US Gen Duncan McArthur's cavalry raid into the Niagara river country prompted a force of 400 Canadians to fight here. McArthur's 700 troopers launched a holding attack that scattered the militia.

■ **Farnham Church, 6 December 1814**

A small detachment of British soldiers landing under the bombardment of a portion of the Chesapeake fleet failed to capture this coastal Virginia church, protected by rallying Virginia militia. Arriving defenders discouraged further British raiding.

■ **Lake Borgne, 14 December 1814**

British forces in armed longboats and barges attacked an American gunboat flotilla. Despite the loss of the flotilla, the American gunboats delayed the British attack on New Orleans, allowing time to strengthen the city's defences.

■ **New Orleans, 23 December 1814**

A 1800-man British vanguard landed 15km south of New Orleans. That night, the American defenders attacked the British. The stalled attack halted the British advance, enabling the Americans to strengthen their defensive works.

■ **New Orleans, 8 January 1815**

After a week-long artillery bombardment, the British attacked the American defences on 8 January 1815. Well-placed American artillery disrupted the initial attack. Subsequent attacks failed with most of the senior British officers, including the commanding general, among the casualties. Consequently, the British failed to capitalize on the few battlefield successes they enjoyed. By the day's end, the British had suffered over 2000 casualties, whereas the Americans had fewer than 100.

■ Fort St Philip, 9 January 1815

British ships bombarding the fort were devastated by American artillery fire. Unable to silence the American batteries, the British withdrew after nine days, leaving the Americans in control of the Mississippi River.

■ Fort Peter, 13 January 1815

After seizing Cumberland Island, a British naval force sailed up the St Mary's River and captured the fort on 13 January 1815. A second British force advanced overland to St Mary's and occupied the town for 10 days.

■ Fort Bowyer, Second Battle, 7 Feb 1815

A 1400-strong British expedition attacked the fort, which surrendered after a five-day siege. Two days later, when news of the Treaty of Ghent arrived, the British postponed their attack on Mobile.

Second Barbary War 1815–16

■ Action of 17 June, 1815

With the War of 1812 ended, the United States' powerful and proven navy took the opportunity to deal with resurgent Muslim piracy in the Mediterranean, Congress declaring war against the Bey of Algiers in 1815. Commodore Stephen Decatur's squadron of nine ships arrived before the news and USS *Guerriere* combined with *Constellation* to maul and capture frigate *Meshuda*, killing the pasha of the Algerian navy.

Texas Revolution/ Texas-Mexican Wars, 1835–43

■ Velasco, 26 June 1832

American settlers attempted to ship a cannon to Anhuac, where they objected to the local commander's conduct. When this fort fired upon the ship, the Texans stormed the post, but settled down after Mexican concessions.

■ Gonzales, 2 October 1835

The Mexican government welcomed American settlers into the empty but fertile plains of Texas, but did not welcome slavery, which the Americans brought with them. Mexican instability joined with anti-Catholic sentiment to spark an uprising. Justified Mexican concern over the Texans' loyalty prompted Mexican soldiers to here demand the surrender of a cannon loaned to the settlers against Indian attack. Minor violence after the Texans refused began their revolt.

■ Goliad, 10 October 1835

The port of San Antonio fell after Mexican Gen Martín Perfecto de Cos transferred most of the main garrison to San Antonio. A Texas party under Capt George M. Collinsworth surprised the remainder, killing three.

■ Béxar, 12 October–11 December 1835

The garrison of Mexican Gen Martín Perfecto de Cos dwindled to 570 before 700 Texans finally stormed the town of Béxar (San Antonio). The Texans advanced house to house, while the desertion of his cavalry eventually prompted Cos to surrender.

■ Concepción, 28 October 1835

Stephen Austin had led some 1700 families into Texas in the 1820s, but his – and his followers' – frustration with the Mexican government (particularly after the Mexicans forbade further immigration from the United States) led to open warfare. The first shots were fired at Gonzales. Austin, when 400 Texan troops advanced upon the presidio in San Antonio, then called at Béxar, and the nearest large concentration of Mexican troops. The town was then under the command of Mexican Gen Martín Perfecto de Cos, who with 750 men fortified the town's plaza and the adjacent Alamo mission across the San Antonio River. From here, the Texans were gathering their forces and scouting the town's outlaying ring of missions for defenders and their possible use in the revolt. Cos sent out 200 cavalry to dislodge a party of 90 men that Austin had sent out to establish a position near the town at this location, the mission of Nuestra Señora de la Purísima Concepción de Acuña. Around 275 Mexican infantry with two

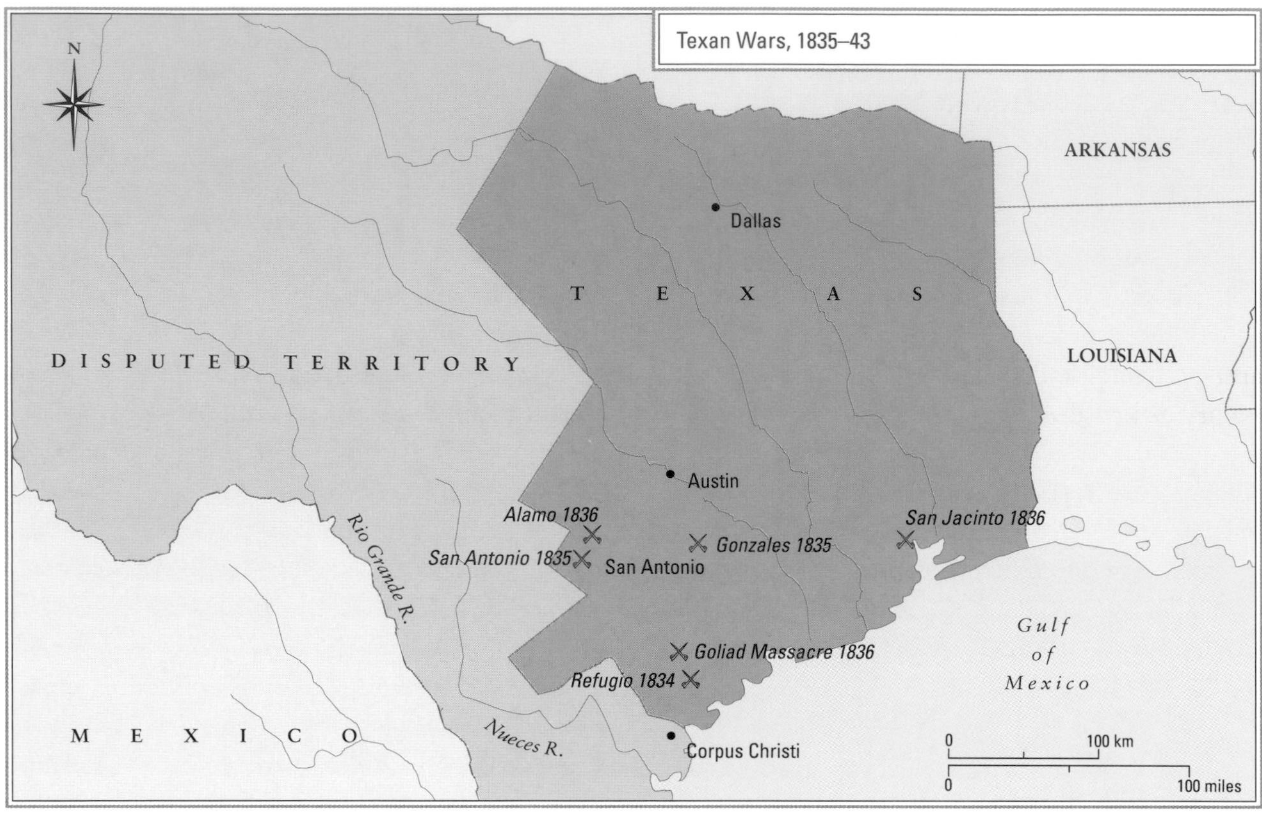

cannon moved out to support the cavalry against the Texans.

Capt James Bowie's party suffered the first casualty of the war as they advanced against the Mexican infantry. In response, Bowie's command opened rifle fire upon the Mexicans, inflicting casualties and capturing one of the cannon after repelling three charges by the Mexicans. The Mexican cavalry covered the retreat of the survivors back into San Antonio. A total of 200 East Texas reinforcements under Thomas Rusk prompted Austin to urge a full-scale attack upon the town, but the reluctance of his followers prompted Austin to settle into a siege over the winter, with his troops intercepting Cos's supplies and looking for weaknesses in the Mexicans' defences.

■ Lipantitlan, 4 November 1835

Approximately 90 Mexicans attempted to prevent the crossing of the Nueces River by 70 Texans under Ira Westover from this captured fort. The Texans established themselves in the riverside trees and killed 28 Mexicans as they approached.

■ Grass Fight, 26 November 1835

As the siege of Béxar continued, Col Edward Burleson, commanding in Austin's absence, maintained pressure upon Mexican Gen Martín Perfecto de Cos in San Antonio. The Texans kept scouting parties out in anticipation of Col Domingo de Ugartechea's return with Mexican reinforcements. One of these returned with the news of Mexican cavalry escorting a pack train towards the city, which the Texans suspected might be carrying the garrison's pay. Around 40 Texan cavalrymen under James Bowie fought to delay the train, with another 100 engaging about 150 Mexican cavalry soon afterwards, supported by 50 infantry with cannon from the garrison. A sharp battle ensued, the Texans caught in a crossfire by the Mexican forces, but rallying to capture the pack train's 40 animals, killing three Mexicans. The train's burden proved to be cut-grass fodder for the garrison's animals within the town.

■ Alamo, 23 February–6 March 1836

The deceptive strength of the old mission's walls convinced James Neill, commander of captured Béxar, to repair and fortify the bastion with 21 cannon of various calibre, despite Texan general Sam Houston's misgivings that the mission would be both easy for the Mexicans to attack and difficult for the Texans to supply. Governor Henry Smith decided to hold the post as it and Goliad blocked the roads to the Texas interior, sending Maj Green Jameson to bolster the Alamo's defences. Green's promise to Houston that the repaired bastion could hold off ten times the number of the garrison would prove to fail. James Bowie arrived and also supported maintaining the post as an outer barrier to the army of Mexican general, then-President, Antonio López de Santa Anna (by coup), seizing power and proclaiming his intention of executing the rebel settlers of Mexico as pirates. LCol William Travis arrived with 30 cavalry to give the Alamo warning of a Mexican attack, while former US Congressman David Crockett with 30 Tennessee volunteers answered a call to defend the bastion. Neill's departure for family reasons left Travis in command and Bowie and his supporters disgruntled.

Santa Anna's assembled force numbered some 1800 hand-picked soldiers, the Alamo's defenders totalling some 189 combatants after 32 scouts under George Kimbell slipped through Santa Anna's lines. Mexican artillery bombarded the mission over the 12 days of the siege, knocking holes in the walls and steadily lowering the morale of the doomed garrison. Santa Anna then ordered an assault, which soon crumbled under withering artillery and heavy rifle fire from the Texans. Approximately 600 Mexicans perished by the end of the second successful attack, with Santa Anna duly executing every surviving defender.

■ San Patricio, 27 February 1836

The Texans employed this town to corral horses for an expedition toward Matamoros. Gen José de Urrea attacked the post and an outlaying ranch at night, killing eight Texans and capturing 13, later executed at Goliad.

■ Agua Dulce, 2 March 1836

Some 60 Mexican cavalry under Gen José de Urrea overtook Dr James Grant and a foraging party of 27 volunteers here on their way to San Patricio with horses. Several Texans escaped, while de Urrea captured six prisoners.

■ Refugio, 12–15 March, 1836

Around 150 Texas troops from Goliad rode to this village under attack by the advance of Gen José de Urrea's army. After driving off the attackers, the Texans were overwhelmed, captured and executed by the Mexicans.

■ Coleto, 19–20 March 1836

James Fannin with 300 men evacuated Goliad before the Mexican advance, but slowed his march with wagons. Gen José de Urrea overtook the Texans with 80 cavalrymen and 360 infantry, capturing and executing them all.

■ Brazos Santiago, 3 April 1836

Off this port on the gulf, the Texas schooner *Invincible* engaged the Mexican brig *Montezuma*, with *Invincible* slowly manoeuvring *Montezuma* into the shallows until it grounded on Brazos Island. *Invincible* then set the Mexican ship afire.

■ San Jacinto (San Jacinto river), 21 April 1836

As commander-in-chief of the Texas settlers' revolution against Mexico, Sam Houston kept his force in readiness and awaited his opportunity to strike against Mexico's final great effort to crush the rebellion. The ranks of the Texas Army were gradually increasing in reaction to Mexican slaughters of the rebels at the Alamo and Goliad. Houston's forces shadowed the Mexicans as Mexican President Antonio López de Santa Anna moved up the Texas coast in a campaign directed at strongholds and centres of the rebellion. On 21 April, Houston's scouts located an unwary Santa Anna and his army bivouacked on the

Alamo, 6 March 1836

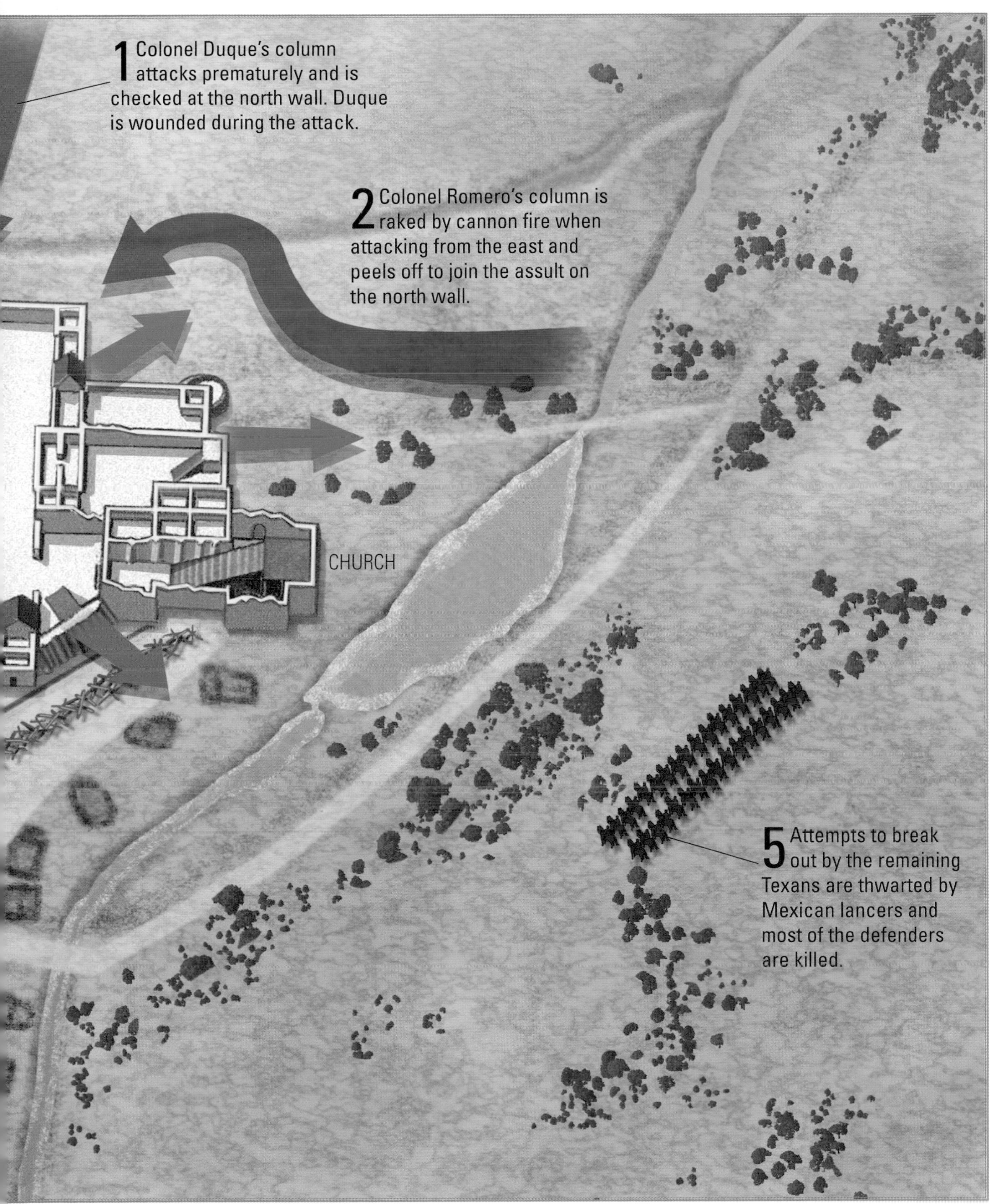
1 Colonel Duque's column attacks prematurely and is checked at the north wall. Duque is wounded during the attack.
2 Colonel Romero's column is raked by cannon fire when attacking from the east and peels off to join the assult on the north wall.
CHURCH
5 Attempts to break out by the remaining Texans are thwarted by Mexican lancers and most of the defenders are killed.

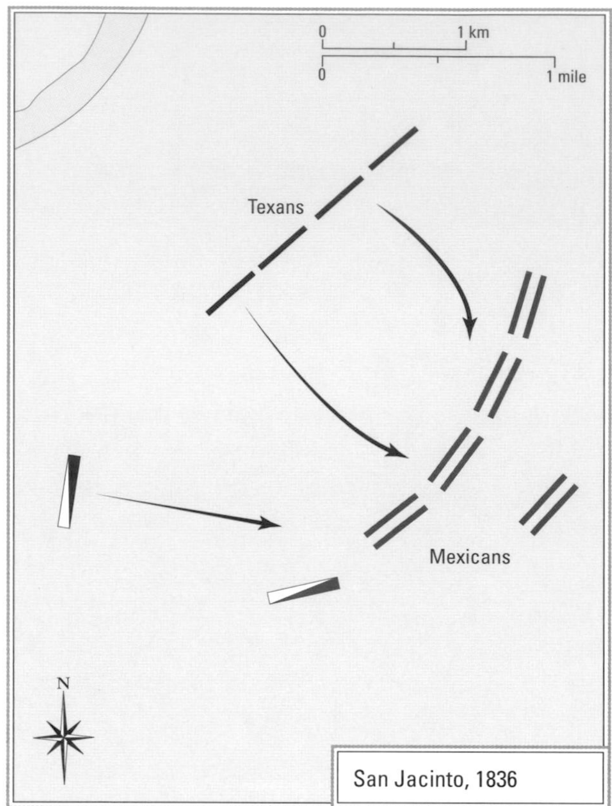

San Jacinto, 1836

Texans' side of the namesake river, near modern Houston. Houston with some 900 men moved stealthily against Santa Anna's fortified camp; 1360 Mexicans were caught taking their noonday meal while Santa Anna and his officers were engaged in making plans to attack and annihilate the Texans.

With two light cannon sent from Ohio, Houston's army initiated a headlong assault, with the Texans' cavalry on the flanks as they moved swiftly towards the Mexican encampment, the Texans' numbers and movements screened by riverside trees. 'Remember the Alamo! Remember Goliad!' was the first warning the Mexicans had of the onslaught, Santa Anna driven into flight without time to don his artificial leg. In a mere 16 minutes, 630 Mexicans had perished in disordered rout, with 200 more wounded, compared with only nine Texans falling. The pursuing Texans captured an additional 700 of the broken army over the next day, among them Santa Anna. The Texans forced the captured Santa Anna to sign a treaty recognizing Texas's independence, which Mexico later repudiated, but took no further military action to reconquer the rebel territory.

■ **Campeche, 30 April–16 May 1843**
Texas sloop *Austin* and brig *Wharton* joined with a small Yucatan squadron to engage Mexican steam warships *Moctezuma* and *Guadaloupe* and their consorts off this Yucatan port. The Mexicans withdrew, managing to escape the pursuing Texas ships.

US-Mexican War 1846–48

■ **Fort Texas (Fort Brown), 3–9 May 1846**
Mexico had announced that US annexation of Texas would mean war, Texas entering the Union in 1845. Gen Zachary Taylor cemented the US claim to the Rio Grande boundary with Mexico by constructing this earthwork at the tip of the disputed area. The garrison returned fire from Mexican batteries at Matamoros across the river with their own four cannon, Maj Jacob Brown being killed by injuries from the Mexicans' fire.

■ **Palo Alto, 8 May 1846**
Fighting began when Mexican cavalry crossed the Rio Grande, attacking a US patrol. Gen Mariano Arista crossed with 4000 infantry against US Gen Zachary Taylor's supply base at Port Isabel. Taylor moved 2200 troops towards Aras' line in this grassy plain. Taylor sent his 'flying artillery' batteries before his infantry's advance, the cannons' fire devastating the Mexicans. The Mexicans held their line until nightfall, suffering 400 casualties to Taylor's 55.

■ **Resaca de la Palma, 9 May 1846**
US Gen Zachary Taylor followed up Gen Mariano Arista's retreat, the Mexicans establishing a defensive position in this ravine in the midst of heavy brush. US troops eventually captured Arista's artillery, the Mexicans then fleeing.

■ **Monterrey, 21–24 September 1846**
Zachary Taylor seized Matamoros, moving towards this city where Gen Pedro de Ampudia waited with

7000 men and 32 cannon. Taylor divided his 6000 regulars and volunteers for a simultaneous attack upon the city's fortified approaches. Mexican artillery from the fortifications could not prevent the US capture of artillery and barricaded houses, which they turned against the Mexicans. Ampudia surrendered the city with 370 casualties to Taylor's 500.

San Pasqual, 6 December 1846

Unaware of local conditions, Col Stephen Kearny collected 136 US troops after his journey from Santa Fé to California and engaged 76 Mexicans under Maj Andrés Pico here. Pico's troops vanquished the Americans, killing 21.

Tucson, 16 December 1846

The 500-man Mormon Battalion under LCol Philip Cooke occupied this Mexican outpost without a battle as Capt Antonio Comaduran and Cooke averted bloodshed. Comaduran's 100-strong garrison camped outside of town while the Mormons resupplied.

Buena Vista, 22–23 February 1847

Antonio López de Santa Anna, dictator of Mexico, personally took the field with 15,000 soldiers against US general Zachary Taylor's 4700 troops as they took position on the far side of this pass having counter-marched before Santa Anna's army. Taylor made his preparations by ordering Gen John Wool to establish a defensive position on the heights overlooking the pass. Santa Anna left 5000 troops behind due to his forced march north in the hope of destroying Taylor's army, after President James Polk had transferred most of it to Gen Winfield Scott's amphibious invasion of central Mexico. First demanding Taylor's surrender, Santa Anna expended his light infantry under Gen Pedro de Ampudia in a daylong assault upon the heights under the fire of US artillery and the breech-loading rifles of the regulars.

On the second day, Santa Anna launched a full-scale assault, his greater numbers having some success on the US flanks as Wool gradually refused

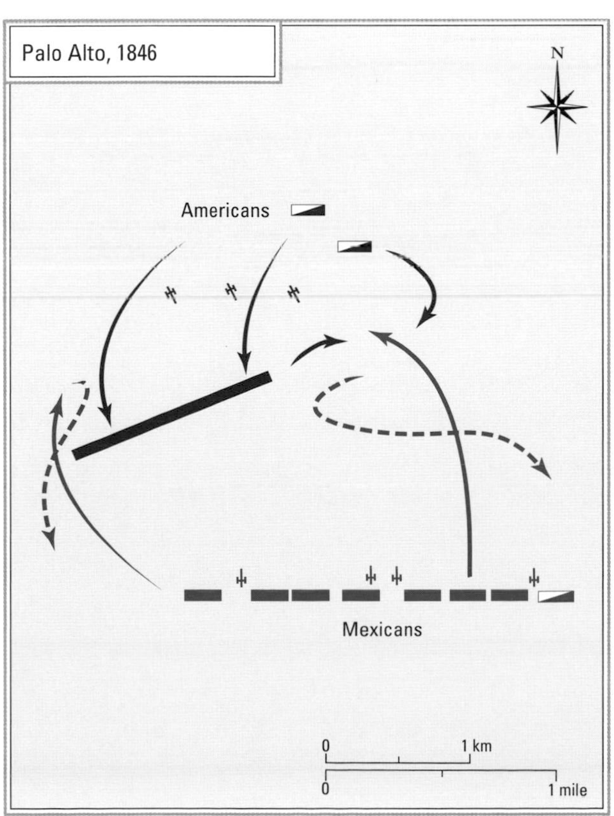

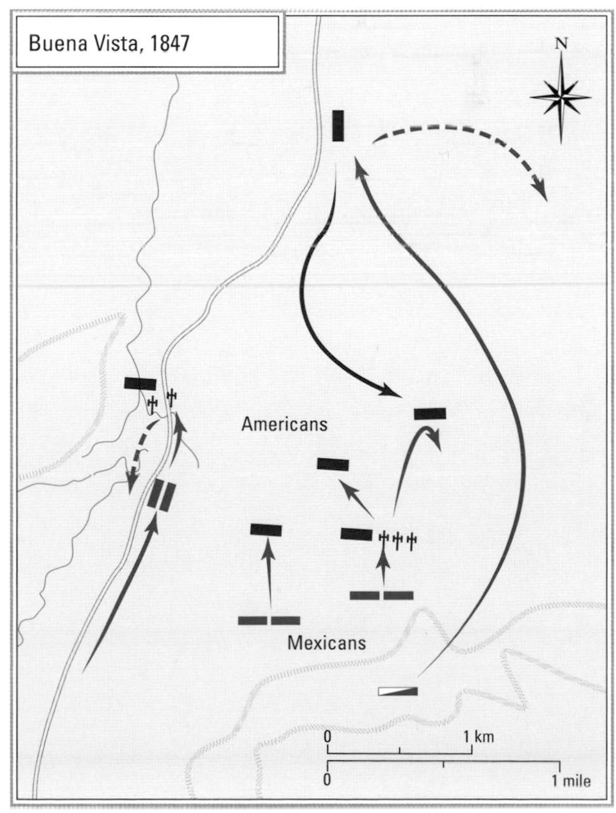

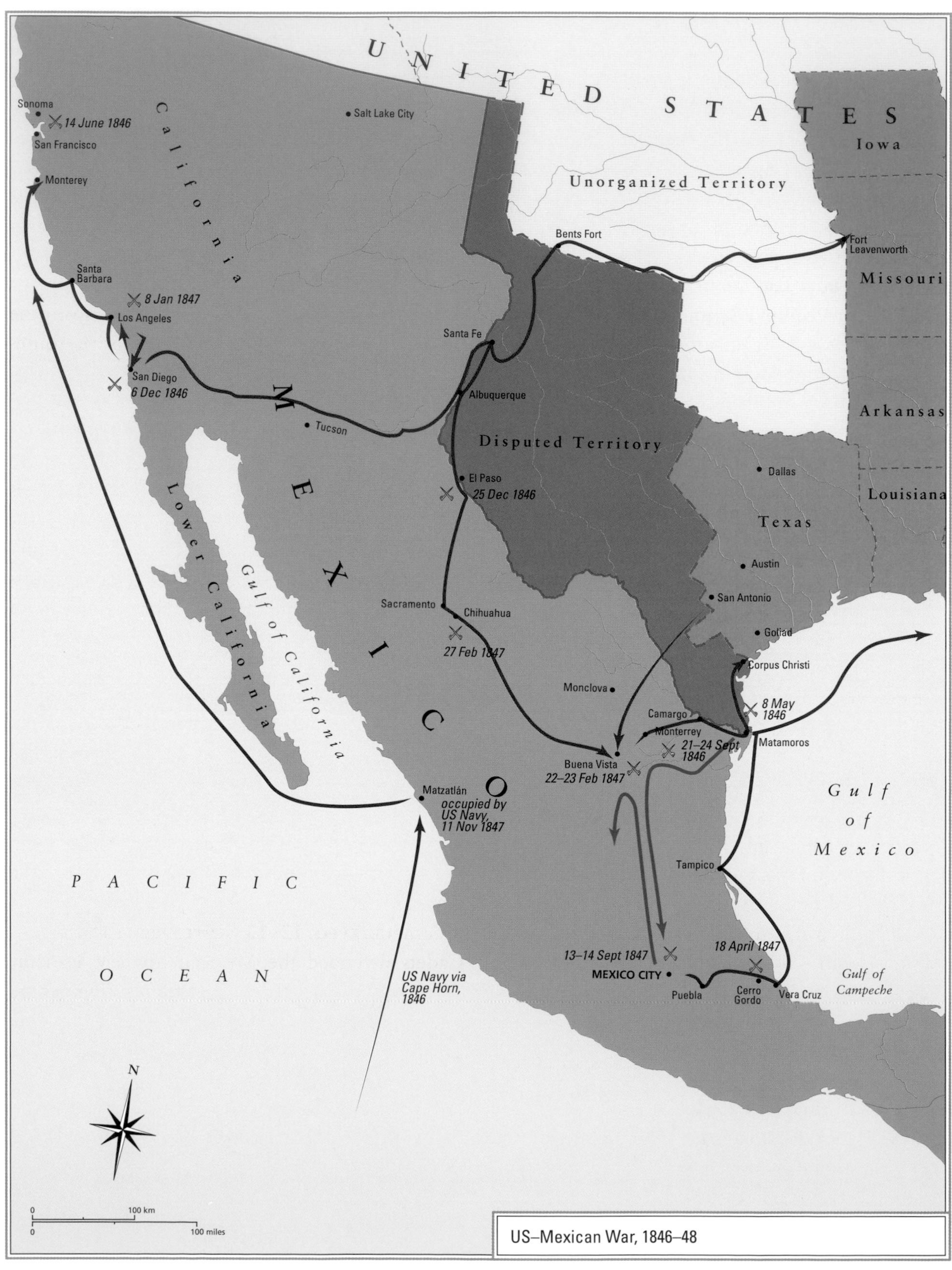

US–Mexican War, 1846–48

his centre to reinforce them. Guards and reserve troops repulsed a Mexican cavalry attack upon the Americans' wagons in the rear. US artillery at the front of the lines suffered significant losses, but inflicted more as the Mexicans repeatedly struggled up the heights, capturing two cannon. Taylor's reserve line moved forward and halted a Mexican breakthrough late in the day, the Americans surprised the next morning to find that Santa Anna had withdrawn southwards to move against Winfield Scott. The Americans had suffered 267 dead, 456 wounded and 23 missing, while Santa Anna had lost 1800 missing, 1000 wounded and 600 dead. Santa Anna's retreat allowed Taylor and his volunteers to stand unmolested on the defensive in the north for the remainder of the war.

■ Sacramento River (Rio Sacramento), 28 February 1847

Col Alexander Doniphan led 924 mounted volunteers and their supply train south towards Chihuahua, defended here by Gen García Conde with 3400 infantry, militia and artillery on a plateau across Doniphan's advance. Doniphan ascended that from the rear, fending off Conde's cavalry behind his wagons. Doniphan then rapidly attacked the Mexicans' flanks and rear, dismounting his men behind his mobile artillery, killing 300 Mexicans, scattering the rest and capturing Chihuahua.

■ Vera Cruz (Veracruz), 9–29 March 1847

A brilliantly planned and executed amphibious invasion with 10,000 soldiers reduced this Mexican fortified port, US Gen Winfield Scott landing unopposed and eventually forcing the city's surrender with a long bombardment from landed naval artillery.

■ Cerro Gordo, 18 April 1847

Antonio López de Santa Anna with 12,000 troops blocked a defile on the National Road towards Mexico City. Gen Winfield Scott wanted to get his 8500 troops into the interior before the Yellow Fever season, and had scouts investigate the Mexican position. Capt Robert E. Lee discovered a trail leading to this village behind the Mexican left flank, Scott's columns attacking and flanking the Mexicans, killing 1000 and capturing 1000.

■ Contreras-Churubusco (Churubusco), 20 August 1847

Antonio López de Santa Anna counted on a vast lava field before Mexico City to channel US Gen Winfield Scott's advance into one of two roads running across it, and parcelled out his defending forces to guard both. Scott approached from the south, his engineers finding alternative routes though the lava that allowed the Americans to rout Gen Gabriel Valencia's 6000 men at Padierna, whom Santa Anna did not reinforce. Scott's army next attacked the bridge over the Churubusco River, defended by the 200 deserters of the San Patricio Battalion and 1800 Mexicans at a fortified convent. Very hard fighting there lasted until the doomed deserters and Mexicans collapsed under numbers and a flank attack from US forces that crossed another bridge. Scott's soldiers had opened the way to Mexico City at the cost of 1053 killed, 4000 Mexicans falling.

■ Molino del Rey, 8 September 1847

Gen Winfield Scott ordered these fortified buildings near Chapultepec castle captured, 4000 Mexicans with artillery fighting first before, then within, the buildings. Hard fighting cost the 3400 victorious Americans 800 casualties, the Mexicans 2000.

■ Chapultepec, 12–13 September 1847

Cadets defended the Mexican military academy here, 1000 defenders in the castle resisting behind 14,000 around the base. Gen Winfield's Scott's bombardment preceded an attack by select storming parties, who took the castle.

■ Puebla, 14 September–12 October, 1847

This post, under Col Thomas Childs with 400 men, protected the US supply line from the Mexican coast. Gen Joaquin Rea with 4000 men besieged Childs for four weeks before a relief column from Veracruz arrived.

Native American Wars, 1791–1890

The westwards expansion of the United States soon brought the settlers and US Government into conflict with the Native Americans who had lived on the land for thousands of years. Peoples such as the Shawnee, Sioux, Comanche and Apache fought ferociously to defend their territories, but were systematically overwhelmed by greater numbers and superior weaponry. The destruction of George Custer's 7th Cavalry at Little Bighorn in 1876 was a rare reversal for the US Army, highlighting the fighting qualities of the Native Americans.

Left: George Custer and the men of the 7th Cavalry fight for their lives as numerically superior Sioux and Cheyenne warriors overwhelm his fragmented command, 25 June 1876.

Native American Wars 1791–1811

■ Harmar's Defeat, 18 October 1791

Near here, Miami chief Little Turtle and his warriors attacked and defeated part of US BGen Josiah Harmar's 1300 regulars and militia riflemen while they marched in three columns, inflicting 300 casualties before withdrawing.

■ Wabash, 4 November 1791

BGen Harmar's defeat had prompted the American Gen Arthur St Clair's march into Ohio with all 600 US regulars and 1500 militia. Miami Chief Little Turtle collected many warriors, who attacked St Clair's camp at this river. Neither St Clair nor his officers could establish any sort of order as the warriors inflicted 800 casualties in the worst defeat suffered by the Americans or British at the hands of Native Americans.

■ Fort Recovery, 1794

US Gen 'Mad Anthony' Wayne invaded Ohio, building this post at the end of his march into Little Turtle's territory near the Wabash battlefield and repelling a Miami attack upon his ready and better-trained troops.

■ Nickajack Expedition, 1794

The Chickamauga Cherokee faction had settled near Nickajack Cave in Tennessee after rejecting peace overtures before and after the revolution, launching sporadic attacks. With 15,000 militia mustered against them, the surrounded tribe surrendered and evacuated.

■ Fallen Timbers, 20 August 1794

Into this tornado-struck clearing, US Gen 'Mad Anthony' Wayne with a mixed force of 3000 drove out Little Turtle and his warriors, often employing the bayonet. Anthony's mounted force collapsed Indian resistance and created a rout.

■ Tippecanoe Creek, 7 November 1811

Shawnee Chief Tecumseh and his brother, known as 'The Prophet', with some British military support, rallied the neighbouring tribes for a stand against white encroachments. US Gen William Henry Harrison (later President), marched into Ohio against the Shawnee capital of Prophetstown, emulating Anthony Wayne's earlier tactics on the march and likewise building defences along his line of supply. With his army attacked in camp here, Harrison burned Prophetstown after his dragoons eventually scattered the Indians.

Peoria War 1812–13

The impending War of 1812 between the British and the US created difficulties and pressures for the Peoria and Potawatomi tribes in Illinois. There were successes such as the burning of Fort Dearborn and the repulse of the first Hopkins punitive expedition in 1812, but even British support could not prevent the subsequent destruction of the tribes' homes and winter stores, leading to their submission and evacuation across the Mississippi.

Creek War 1813–14

■ Burnt Corn Creek, 27 July 1813

The warring 'Red Stick' Creeks, having obtained weapons from the British and Spanish in Pensacola, at first fled and then routed an ambush by Alabama militia. The 'Red Sticks' then attacked Americans and assimilated Creeks.

■ Fort Mims, 30 August 1813

The warring 'Red Sticks' drove assimilated 'Lower Creek' tribesmen and settlers to shelter at this weak and undermanned post in Alabama. A massacre of the garrison and sheltering civilians followed a costly 'Red Stick' surprise attack.

■ Tallushatchee, 3 November 1813

A detachment of US Gen Andrew Jackson's 5000 Tennessee militia and some hundreds of allied Cherokee and assimilated 'White Stick' Creeks ambushed a 'Red Stick' domestic band here, killing 186 in retaliation for the earlier events at Fort Mims.

■ Talladega, 9 November 1813

The Creek War partook something of the War of 1812 and a civil war between the assimilated 'White Stick' Creeks and the 'Red Stick' faction, pursuing

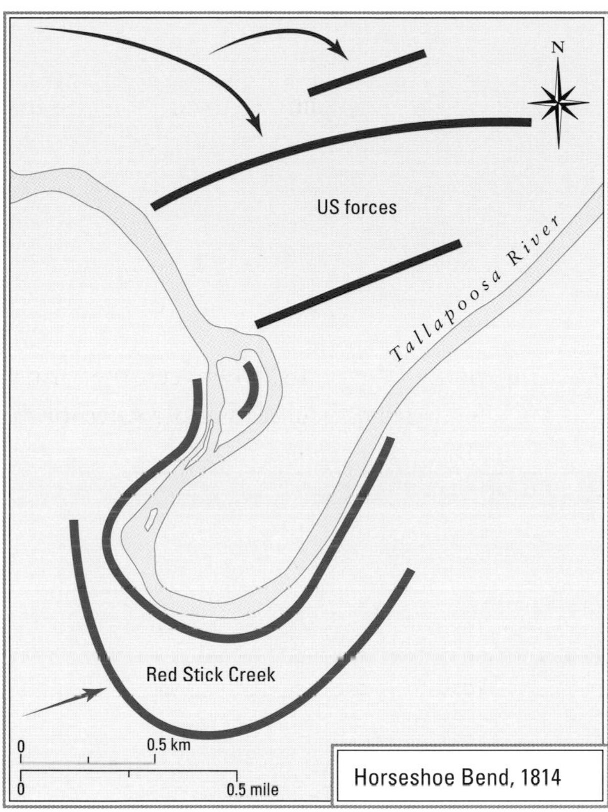

their original culture and waging war against white settlers and their former fellow tribesmen. Perhaps 1000 'Red Sticks' besieging this 'White Stick' Creek village suffered heavy losses, when US Gen Andrew Jackson marched quickly and raised their siege, killing some 290, suffering 15 losses.

■ **Emukfaw/Enotachopo Creek, Jan 1814**
US Gen Andrew Jackson's advance into 'Red Stick' Creek territory with 1000 green militia met a check at Emukfaw Creek and began retreating, the Creeks overtaking them at Enotachopo Creek, where the militia effectively resisted.

■ **Horseshoe Bend, 22–24 January 1814**
Hostile 'Red Stick' Creeks numbering 1200 had constructed a large and heavily fortified encampment, protected on three sides by the Tallapoosa River and on the fourth by an earthwork barricade 2.4m high with firing steps, with canoes left along the beach in case of evacuation. US Gen Andrew Jackson's force included 600 regulars, 1400 militia and 700 mounted troops, as well as 100 'White Stick' assimilated Creeks and 500 allied Cherokees. Jackson had to overcome the expiring enlistments of his militia and difficulties of supply. The attack on Horseshoe Bend began with a bombardment by Jackson's two cannon while the Cherokees swam the river to steal the canoes of the 'Red Sticks'. Allied Indian archers fired on the encampment with incendiary arrows.

Jackson then sent his regulars with fixed bayonets directly against the earthwork across the peninsula's neck, there meeting, but overcoming, stout resistance by the Red Sticks. Meanwhile, the balance of Jackson's force surrounded the peninsula across the river to prevent escapes, joining in the fight by crossing the Tallapoosa to the burning village, in which groups of 'Red Sticks' maintained a 'hut to hut' fight, some employing captured settlers and slaves as human shields during the battle.

When the fighting stopped, some 800 warriors were dead, and some 350 surviving women and children captured and dispersed among 'White Stick' villages. Jackson's force lost 26 killed, the allied Indians 23. The latter had a shock five months later when Jackson, in negotiating the Treaty of Fort Jackson, held them as responsible for the war as the 'Red Sticks' and forced all factions and the Cherokee to cede some 22 million acres of tribal land to the United States.

Claremore Mound Massacre, 1817

■ **Claremore Mound, October 1817**
The Osage tribe lost this struggle with the Cherokee nation when the Cherokee overran and burned Chief Claremore's village in northern Oklahoma while the men were out hunting, killing some 80 old men, women, and children.

Arikara War 1823

This plains tribe sought to preserve their role in the fur trade by attacking traders in their territory. Col Henry Leavenworth joined with Lakota Sioux

The Battle of Tippecanoe on 7 November 1811 was a victory for a seasoned US expeditionary force under Major General William Henry Harrison over Shawnee Indians led by Tecumseh's brother Laulewasikau, known as 'the Prophet'.

to bombard and attack Arikara villages along the Missouri River.

Winnebago War 1827

The Winnebago War was a limited war of a few skirmishes in June 1827 around Prairie du Chien, Wisconsin, by a large war party of Ho-Chunk warriors assisted by other tribes and a few civilians that eventually led to confrontation with a large contingent of US militia several hundred strong at Portage. Tribal leaders gave up six of their number – including the warrior Red Bird – who were imprisoned to prevent further violence.

Black Hawk War 1832

■ Stillman's Run, 14 May 1832
A detachment of 275 Illinois militia commanded by Maj Isaiah Stillman fled from a superior force of mainly Sauk warriors under Chief Black Hawk, leaving 12 dead behind on 14 May 1832, near a stream in Ogle County, Illinois.

■ Spafford Farm, 14 June 1832
On 14 June 1832, in Lafayette County, Wisconsin, a Kickapoo war party attacked and killed several farmers, including Spafford, while crossing the Pecatonica River in a prelude to the later battle of Horseshoe Bend.

■ Horseshoe Bend, 16 June 1832
On 16 June 1832, Col Henry Dodge and his militia attacked and killed an entire Kickapoo war party of 17 warriors at the battle of Horseshoe Bend, also called Pecatonica or Bloody Lake.

Kellogg's Grove, 16 June 1832
The battle of Kellogg's Grove, Illinois, involved two skirmishes over several days on 16 June 1832, when a large band of warriors under Chief Black Hawk fought US militia with small losses on both sides.

■ Wisconsin Heights, 21 July 1832
US militia commanded by Col Henry Dodge attacked and defeated a band of Sauk warriors under Chief Black Hawk on 21 July 1832, at Wisconsin Heights, in a static battle after a three-day chase.

■ Bad Axe, 1–2 August 1832
Chief Black Hawk led the Sauks and Fox back across the Mississippi into Illinois, counting on support from the British in Canada to regain lost territories as they attacked US settlements there and in Wisconsin. State militia, supported by Gen Henry Atkinson's Regulars, drove Black Hawk's 1500 back to the river. Black Hawk attempted surrender here, but some 200 men, women and children perished before the militia and soldiers relented.

Creek War 1836

The remnant of the Creek tribe in Alabama launched retaliatory raids when the state itself opened their treaty lands for settlement. After fierce fighting, troops eventually moved the rest of the Creeks to Oklahoma.

Comanche War 1836-75

■ **Fort Parker, May 1836**

Members of a Baptist sect built this fort in north Texas, having concluded treaties with the neighbouring tribes and farmers. A considerable force of Comanche, Kiowa, Kichai, Caddo and Wichita warriors converged upon the unprepared bastion, which at the time had but five adult male defenders and wide open gates. Some of the women escaped, with Cynthia and John Parker being captured and spending most of their lives with the Comanches.

■ **Stone Houses, 10 November 1837**

Eighteen Texas Rangers chased around 150 Kichai across the Colorado River after the Indians raided Fort Smith. The Indians turned and overwhelmed the Rangers with numbers and a prairie fire, only eight walking to safety.

■ **Neches, 15–16 July 1838**

The Republic of Texas moved against Cherokee Chief Bowl's settlement and the Indian presence in Easter, Texas, with 500 Texans overcoming around 600 Cherokee at this river crossing. The Cherokee retreated into Oklahoma.

■ **Council House, 19 March 1840**

The Comanche tribe resisted Texas President Mirabeau Lamar's efforts to evict them, taking many captives in their raids. A smallpox epidemic prompted Chief Muguara to lead a band of 65 chiefs and families into San Antonio to negotiate. The Texans had planned to hold the Comanche hostages against the captives' return. Half the Comanche died, the Indians reacting with fury to the treachery, launching more raids and executing their prisoners.

■ **Great Raid, 7 August 1840**

Comanche chief Buffalo Hump led this large-scale retaliatory raid upon San Antonio with careful planning and execution, avenging the Council House fight of three months ago. With the Texans' guard relaxed, 600 to 700 Comanche

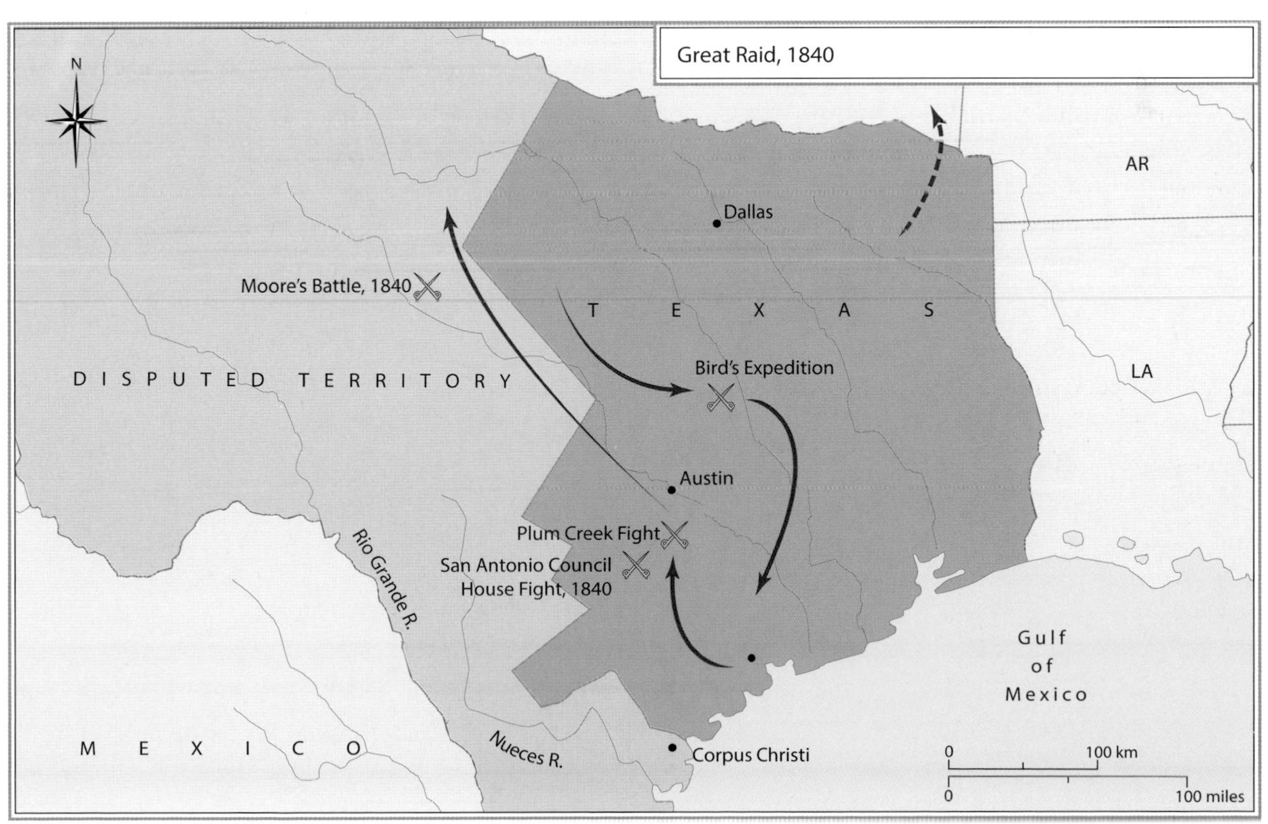

swept into the outlaying town of Victoria, killing the inhabitants found on the streets before the war party moved and slaughtered down the Guadalupe River into San Antonio's port of Linville. Once again, the Texans were caught unprepared, the survivors fleeing into boats or ships off shore as the Comanche plundered and burned their town. With a train of some 3000 pack animals, the Comanche set off with their loot, sufficiently slowly for Texas militia to collect and launch a running attack upon the band at Plum Creek. The Comanche escaped with most of their loot, the Texans suffering some 40 killed in the raid.

■ **Bandera Pass, 1841**

A party of 50 Texas Rangers under John Hays fell into a Comanche ambush in this pass, the traditional boundary. With men unhorsed, Hays dismounted his troop, repelling the Comanche with rapid fire from revolvers.

■ **Cayuse War, 1847–55**

Missionaries Marcus and Narcissa Whitman established their mission at Waiilaptu along what became the Oregon Trail, among the Cayuse tribe. The Whitmans taught the Cayuse farming techniques, but, as a trickle of white settlers along the trail became a stream, the Cayuse anticipated a takeover of their lands. When a measles epidemic broke out, in which Cayuse died while the whites recovered, the Cayuse leaders suspected Whitman of poisoning their people. The response was the butchering of the Whitmans and 11 others in 1847. The Cayuse also took 60 hostages for ransom. Subsequently, American militia warred with hostile and non-hostile area tribes, the US Army eventually arriving and prompting the Cayuse to hand over five men involved in the Whitman massacre for execution. Sporadic fighting continued until, in 1855, the army removed the surviving Cayuse to the Umatilla Reservation in eastern Oregon.

■ **Clark Massacre, 30 August 1851**

A Shoshone raiding party stealing horses attacked Thomas Clark and his wagon train in Idaho, killing two men and Clark's mother, leaving his sister for dead. The fleeing Indians resisted the train's efforts at pursuit.

Wakara War 1851–53

About 12 on each side died as Utah Mormons fought a series of skirmishes with Utes under Walker as the Mormons interfered with Ute horse raiding and trade with New Mexico. Negotiations ended the fighting.

The Jicarilla War 1849–55

■ **Cieneguilla, 30 March 1854**

Hundreds of Jicarilla Apaches and Utes combined to ambush 60 US Cavalry under Lieutenant John Davidson. Nearly all of Davidson's command were killed or wounded before the survivors managed to escape the onrushing warriors.

■ **Ojo Caliente, 8 April 1854**

A punitive expedition of 300 US troops set out against the Utes and Apaches who had ambushed 60 cavalry in New Mexico. At this river, the soldiers and troopers scattered the Indians, many of whom froze to death afterwards.

■ **Grattan Massacre, 19 August 1854**

A dispute with the Brulé Sioux over a stray cow in Wyoming resulted in a botched parley in which a Sioux chief, 2nd Lt John Grattan and his entire command of 30 men perished.

■ **Diablo Mountains, 3 October 1854**

Some 200 Lipan Apaches drove a stolen cattle herd over this Texas range, pursued by Capt John Walker and 40 Texas Rangers. Walker surprised the Apaches en route, scattering them.

Puget Sound War 1855–56

■ **Port Gamble, 1855**

A landing party from USS *Massachusetts* sought to remove Indian raiders from Victoria who occupied the port while attacking tribes in Washington.

When the Indians resisted, the *Massachusetts* party killed 27 and destroyed their canoes.

■ Klamath and Salmon War, Jan–Mar 1855

As more whites poured into the Pacific Northwest, the initially friendly Karok and Yurok Indian tribes began fighting using weapons and ammunition purchased from coastal traders. When the miners began arming to evict the Indians from this area in northern California, reprisals from both sides aggravated the situation. Army intervention finally pacified the violent Red Cap faction with the aid of non-hostile tribes; all were moved to a reservation.

■ Rogue River Wars, 1855

Resentment over a treaty removing the Rogue tribes to a reservation resulted in raiding and punitive attacks by militia against villages in this region. Army effort, to restore order failed, resulting in massacres and final pacification.

■ Klickitat War, 1855

Angered by treaties ignoring their own territorial claim, this tribe bought guns from the whites and launched raids against onrushing gold miners, prompting retaliation. Army probes met strong responses before the Indians relented.

■ Ash Hollow, 3 September 1855

Vengeance for the Grattan Massacre came in an attack by Gen William Harney and 700 soldiers from Fort Leavenworth upon this Sioux village in Nebraska. Over 100 Sioux, including women and children, perished in the assault.

Yakima War 1855–58

■ Seattle, 26 January 1856

USS *Decatur* bolstered the defences of the Washington settlement as a coalition of hostile tribes collected for an attack upon the Americans there. Raids from the surrounding tribes had prompted the whites to construct a network of blockhouses in which they could shelter at need, two of these providentially in the settlement. With friendly tribes and their agents warning of attack, the whites organized a volunteer company while *Decatur* anchored where her shell-firing cannon could protect the blockhouses. Some 500 warriors worked their way into the forest close to the town, some within the town mixing with non-hostiles. *Decatur* landed marines and a boat howitzer as the Indians began a sporadic fire, answered by the settlers' guns and the warship's shells. An unknown number of Indians were killed before the attackers withdrew with booty from the outlaying houses.

■ Tintic War, February 1856

Beliefs and practicality kept relations between the Mormons and the Utah Indian tribes fairly peaceful, but a drought and the disappearances of Mormon cattle led to some skirmishes in the area of this river valley.

■ Antelope Hills Expedition, 21 January–12 May 1858

Texas Rangers renewed their offensive operations against Comanche and Kiowa villages, making an extended foray into this area of Oklahoma. Their surprise attacks killed some 76 warriors and captured 16 prisoners and 300 horses.

■ Little Robe Creek, 12 May 1858

Texas Rangers from the Antelope Hills Expedition attacked three Comanche villages with the help of friendly Tonkawas. Chief Iron Jacket fell to the Rangers' powerful revolvers, the Comanche fleeing.

■ Fraser River War, 1858

Settlers in search of gold in British Columbia clashed with the Thompson River Salish tribe as they moved up from the diggings in California. Upon the Salish killing three French miners in retaliation for a rape, the miners formed themselves into three armed companies at Yale and marched into the interior, where both villages and mining camps were anticipating mutual slaughter as the Indians mustered their own warriors. The more aggressive of the armed miners having wiped each other out by friendly fire, the captain of the 'Austrian Company', John Centras, and Capt Snyder of the New York Pike Guards travelled into the Salish camp at Camchin, at which the tribes had agreed to end the conflict before matters got out of hand. Governor James Douglas in Victoria later dispatched British soldiers, who managed to keep the peace in the area.

Spokane-Coeur d'Alene-Paloos War 1858

■ Pine Creek, 17 May 1858

LCol Edward Steptoe attempted a show of force that impressed the hostile tribes with only his vulnerability. Surrounded by warriors, Steptoe's command held out on a rocky knoll, abandoning supplies and escaping after darkness.

■ Four Lakes, 1 September 1858

Steptoe's defeat prompted a harsher response when Col George Wright and 570 cavalry and an artillery train of six howitzers moved against the hostile tribes at this point near Spokane. Artillery and rifle fire decimated the Indians' charge upon the column, Wright's dragoons pursuing the Indians, capturing 800 horses, which Wright slaughtered as punishment. Wright executed 24 chiefs and imposed a peace treaty.

Mendocino War 1859

Slaughter of settlers' free-range cattle by Indians in need of sustenance resulted in open warfare, the whites making reprisals, attacking the nearest Indian community to the animals killed. Isolated California militia units would attack local Indians without any central command or authorization, several hundred Indians dying before the fighting ended. Captured young Indians were sold as labourers on white homesteads.

Other Wars 1859–1861

■ Bear River Expedition, 12 June and 18 October, 1859

An army detachment under Maj Porter investigated reports of an attack upon a California-bound wagon train by warriors of the Shoshone tribe. 2nd Lt Gay's company attacked a Shoshone camp, killing 20 Indians.

■ Mimbres River, 4 December 1860

Thirty heavily armed miners surprised the slumbering camp of Chiricahua Apache chief Mangas Coloradas at this New Mexican river, killing four Apaches before withdrawing as more Indians rushed to the scene. The miners attacked to recover what they said were cattle stolen by the Apaches. Sporadic fighting throughout the region led to the arrest and death of Mangas Coloradas in 1863 when he came to negotiate terms of a peace treaty.

■ Paiute War, 1860

Rape and fatal retaliation upon Williams Station on the Carson River led to the combined Paiute tribe of Nevada to prepare for war as 105 ill-prepared Nevada militia rushed headlong into a running Paiute ambush at Big Bend, with half perishing. The debacle prompted California to dispatch 750 militia into Nevada, where they met and overcame the Paiute at the battle of Pinnacle Mountain, another 40 whites falling. Sporadic fighting continued until a ceasefire was negotiated.

■ Pyramid Lake I and II, 12 May 1860, 2–4 June 1860

The Paiute chiefs met to debate war with onrushing miners. A subsequent militia attack upon the site having been ambushed and destroyed, a second attack forced the Paiutes' retreat and the end of the Paiute War.

■ Fort Defiance, 30 August 1860

Pressured by American encroachments, some 1000 Navajo under Chief Manuelito gathered to attack this unwalled post in Arizona. Capt Oliver Shepherd and 150 regulars held out in the compound's central buildings until relieved.

■ Pease River, 18 December 1860

The Texas Rangers under Capt Sullivan Ross continued stalking and attacking outlaying Comanche villages, finding this one unprepared and rescuing some white captives in the midst of the resulting slaughter, including the unwilling Cynthia Parker.

■ BASCOM AFFAIR, 27 JANUARY 1861

US-Apache warfare began with a boy's kidnapping, provoking 2nd Lt George Bascom to capture and later execute the family of Chiricahua chief Cochise. Resulting hostilities did not entirely die down until Geronimo's surrender in 1886.

■ TUBAC, AUGUST 1861

This Arizona town came under siege from Mexican banditos and Chiricahua Apaches, prompting Confederate militia to march to its rescue. The militia were able to evacuate the townsfolk before the raiders plundered and burned it.

■ COOKE'S CANYON, AUGUST 1861

After Confederate militia reached the besieged town of Tubac, the inhabitants chose evacuation rather than face annihilation by Apaches, who were vengeful after the murder of Chief Cochise's family. In the middle of this dangerous route, the Chiricahua Apaches attacked, moving up the canyon's slopes, firing upon the wagon train. The whites resisted the siege by means of mounted charges and fire from the wagons. The Apaches withdrew with the townsfolk's herds.

■ FLORIDA MOUNTAINS, AUGUST 1861

Confederate militia pursued the Apaches, who were retreating with animals taken from Tubac and Cooke's Canyon. Capt Thomas Mastin anticipated the Indians' route and dispersed the Apaches in a charge from ambush, recovering much of the livestock.

■ GALLINAS MASSACRE, 2 SEPTEMBER 1861

Four Confederate scouts watching for approaching Union troops fell foul of a Chiricahua Apache band of more than 30, who killed three of the scouts after a running fight over several miles, the fourth scout escaping.

■ PLACITO, 8 SEPTEMBER 1861

A Confederate patrol under Lt John Pulliam moved to succor this New Mexico town under attack by Chiricahua Apaches. After reaching the town, the Confederates and townsfolk pursued the raiders into the desert, killing five.

■ PINOS ALTOS, 27 SEPTEMBER 1861

Chiefs Mangas Coloradas and Cochise continued their vengeance war with the Confederacy, 300 Chiricahua Apaches attacking this mining town in the New Mexico mountains in late September 1861. Capt Thomas Mastin with 15 Confederates reached the town in time, where the Confederates turned an ancient cannon filled with nails and buckshot upon the Indians, killing 10. Mastin led a charge as the Apaches retreated, with Mastin later dying and most of the town's inhabitants evacuating.

■ PRYOR CREEK, 1861

A large Crow band made their stand here after the Sioux, Cheyenne and Arapahoe combined against these hereditary enemies. The attack began in Wyoming, the Crow fighting at a river crossing, with both sides suffering losses.

Dakota War/Minnesota Sioux Uprising 1862

■ FORT RIDGELY, 20–22 AUGUST 1862

Dakota chief Little Crow led 400 warriors against this post after the United States failed to provide support payments. The fort resisted two days' attacks by a total of 800 Sioux, who killed 21 soldiers.

■ NEW ULM, 19–23 AUGUST 1862

Wounded Dakota Sioux chief Little Crow with 400 warriors avenged undelivered promised annuities with a sudden attack on this hamlet. Part of the town burned and 100 settlers fell behind barricades repelling the vengeful Indians.

■ BIRCH COULEE, 2 SEPTEMBER 1862

After undelivered support drove the Minnesota Sioux into hostilities, Col Hastings Sibley sent part of his 1500 volunteers to bury the slain. Around 20 soldiers died with 60 wounded before the rest of Sibley's force arrived.

■ WOOD LAKE, 23 SEPTEMBER 1862

Col Hastings Sibley and a force of 1400 volunteers

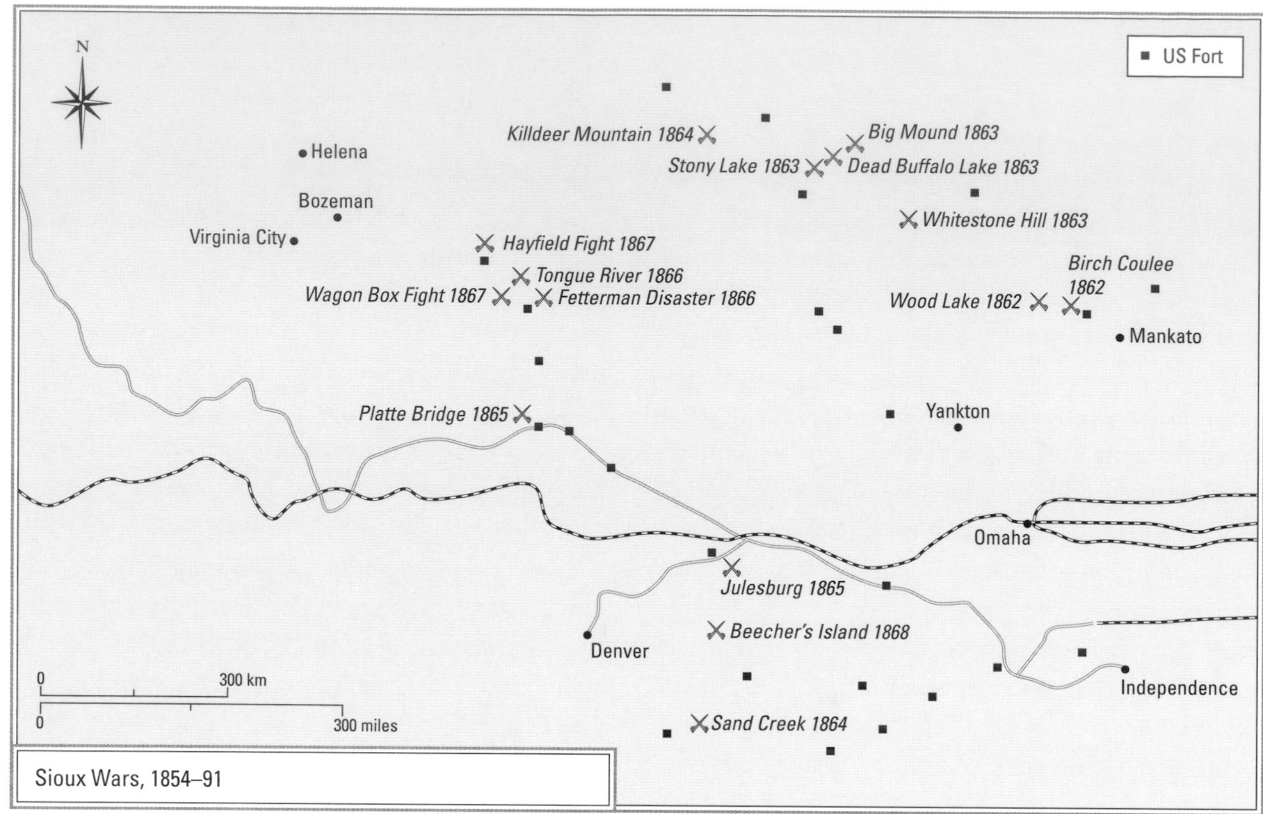

Sioux Wars, 1854–91

moved up the Minnesota River valley, pursuing some 2000 hostile Dakota Sioux who had attacked settlers after non-delivery of annuity payments. The drawn battle led to the Dakotas' surrender.

Arizona/New Mexico Apache War 1862–65

Dragoon Springs, 5 May 1862

Chiefs Mangas Coloradas and Cochise continued to fight the Confederacy, the Chiricahuas ambushing and killing four of a foraging party not far from Tucson, the Apaches capturing horses and cattle from the fleeing Confederates.

Apache Pass, 15–16 July 1862

In response to the Confederate presence in Arizona and New Mexico and the ongoing fighting with the Chiricahua Apaches, US colonel Edward Canby asked for reinforcements. Around 700 infantry from the California militia under Gen James Carleton moved south through this pass, where Mangas Coloradas and Cochise had collected 500 Chiricahua and Mimbres Apaches in the hope of ambushing the soldiers while they were encamped in the defile. Instead, warriors attacked the vanguard as it entered the pass, Capt Thomas Roberts continuing the march and finding some shelter in an abandoned stone station house while the Apaches fired upon his men from the slopes. Roberts's two mountain howitzers bombarded the Indians, causing enough casualties for the desperate soldiers to reach a vital spring. By the time the approaching column arrived and relieved Roberts's command, the Apaches had withdrawn into the Dragoon Mountains.

Bear River Massacre, 29 January 1863

Friction between Mormon settlers moving into Idaho and the Shoshone tribe worsened with the departure of Federal troops eastwards. Despite friction with the Mormons, California militia under Col Patrick Conner moved up the Bear River with 300 volunteers at the request of the Utah government. Conner's command surrounded and overran a fortified village here when the defending warriors' ammunition ran out, butchering some half of the village's 450 total population.

■ Big Mound, 24 July 1863

Attacks in retaliation for a murder resulted in this battle, in which Gen Henry Sibley's 3000 soldiers drove the Sioux from an entrenched position here after the Sioux fired upon him.

■ Dead Buffalo Lake, 26 July 1863

Gen Henry Sibley's 3000 soldiers followed up their battle against Red Cap's band at Big Mound with an engagement at Dead Buffalo Lake two days later, inflicting more casualties upon the retreating Teton and Santee Sioux.

■ Stony Lake, 28 July 1863

Chief Red Cap's band of Santee and Teton Sioux continued its retreat, here linking up with a much larger body of Sioux warriors just as Gen Henry Sibley's 3000 soldiers reached this battlefield having rested for a day on their march. Sibley at once ordered his men to defend their column, the Sioux at first probing for weaknesses, then scattering in all directions, ending Sibley's pursuit of Red Cap.

■ Whitestone Hill, 3–5 September 1863

Gen Alfred Sully's scouting party encountered and attacked Sioux chief Red Cap's large village here with 300 men. The Sioux, caught unprepared, scattered soon after the initial attack, with Sully destroying their tipis and provisions.

■ Canyon de Chelly, 12–14 January 1864

Col 'Kit' Carson with allied Utes and Union troops devastated the stores of this New Mexico Navajo stronghold, with starvation forcing some 8000 of the tribe into a difficult march to Fort Sumner and harsh confinement.

■ Killdeer Mountain, 28 July 1864

Gen Alfred Sully's 2200 regulars with artillery cleared away Sioux chief Red Cap's village on the slope of this North Dakota height. The Sioux attacked Sully's advance, scattering after 150 casualties from the artillery fire.

■ Adobe Walls I, 25 November 1864

Around 300 New Mexico militia under Col 'Kit' Carson fought a combined force of Kiowa and Comanche among these ruins of an abandoned trading post in north Texas. Carson's force retreated inside the remaining walls when a larger Indian force engaged after Carson's attack upon a Kiowa village. Indian numbers and ferocity could not overcome the fire of Carson's mountain howitzers, which broke up the Indian attacks and saved his command.

■ Sand Creek, 29 November 1864

Col John Chivington led 700 Colorado militia against Cheyenne chief Black Kettle's unprepared village and butchered some 148 men, women and children. The Indians were encamped in an agreed-upon safe area and were not prepared for war.

■ Julesburg, 7 January 1865

In the winter following the Sand Creek Massacre, some 1000 infuriated Cheyenne, Arapahos and Sioux twice laid waste to this Colorado transportation hub near Fort Rankin. Around 30 soldiers and civilians perished and the town itself burned.

■ Platte Bridge, 26 July 1865

Thousands of Sioux under Red Cloud and Cheyenne under Roman Nose moved to attack this isolated US post in Wyoming, annihilating cavalry under Lt Caspar Collins, but driven back from the post by artillery fire.

■ Powder River Expedition, 1 August–24 September 1865

The Bozeman Trail to the Montana goldfields bisected territory reserved to the Sioux, Cheyenne and Arapahoe tribes. Gen Patrick Conner, with Jim Bridger as a guide, led three converging columns of US volunteers along the trail to chastise the war parties raiding the trail in consequence. For the most part, the troops only fought skirmishes, the expedition ending when the volunteers' terms of enlistments lapsed with the conclusion of the Civil War.

■ Tongue River, 29 August 1865

The Powder River Expedition fought its one

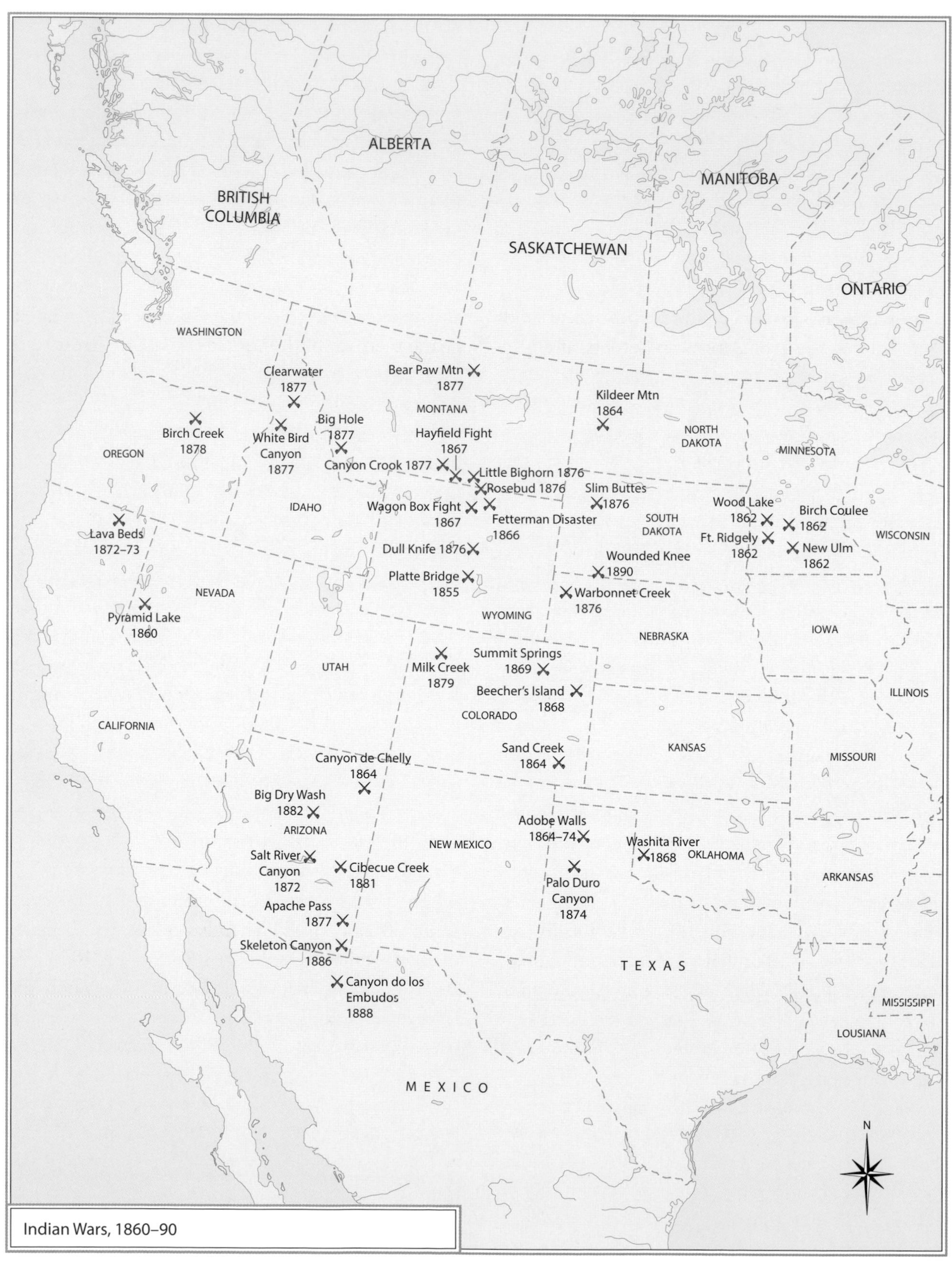

Indian Wars, 1860–90

major battle here against Arapahoe chief Black Bear's village. Gen Patrick Conner's 400 volunteers with two cannon attacked 500 Indians while more volunteers worked elsewhere, killing many Indian ponies.

Snake River War 1864–68

The Shoshone, Paiute and Bannock tribes of the Pacific Northwest, Nevada and Idaho united in sporadic raids to evict whites from their lands against the onrush of American settlers after the Civil War. Casualties on both sides were severe, with Indian raids resulting in white reprisals against uninvolved other natives, broadening the conflict. Army regulars freed after the Confederate surrender eventually replaced state militia units and pacified the region.

Powder River War 1866–68

Despite a treaty recognizing Sioux possession of the lands, the US Army built a string of posts along the Bozeman Trail directly through the heart of this region to speed the passage of miners to the Montana goldfields out of a need for income in the aftermath of the Civil War. The construction of Forts Reno, C.F. Smith and Philip Kearney supported the trail and violated earlier agreements with the Sioux, who considered the region a prime hunting area. Negotiations with the Indians failed because of that fait accompli and Lakota Sioux chief Red Cloud began one of the most carefully waged wars ever fought by the Indians. Red Cloud's Sioux, later joined by Cheyenne and Arapahoe with grievances of their own, ambushed supply trains and attacked farms, ranches and army work parties as they left the forts or moved along the trail, the raids forcing constant vigilance and inflicting noticeable physical and financial casualties. Red Cloud's tactics initially involved luring the whites into ambushes with small parties of warriors, then overwhelming small parties with much greater numbers of pre-positioned warriors before the whites could reload their weapons. Army logistics and the use of breechloading and repeating firearms made such ambushes more costly or futile, but the simple attrition of Red Cloud's tactics provoked the army into negotiations in 1867 on Red Cloud's terms. Red Cloud secured his conditions, including the abandonment of Forts Reno, C.F. Smith and Philip Kearney and the closing of the Bozeman Trail, all guaranteed and honoured by the Treaty of Fort Laramie.

■ **Fetterman Massacre, 21 Dec 1866**
Capt William Fetterman and 81 soldiers perished when Fetterman fell into Lakota Sioux chief Red Cloud's carefully planned ambush outside Fort Philip Kearney. Fetterman chased a small party into 2000 Sioux who prevented retreat.

■ **Kidder Massacre, 29 June 1867**
US 2nd Lt Lyman Kidder, an Indian scout and 10 soldiers perished at the hands of a Northern Cheyenne and Sioux war party while bearing dispatches to Gen Custer along the Republic River in Nebraska.

■ **Wagon Box Fight, 2 August 1867**
Lakota Sioux chief Red Cloud's ambush of Capt James Powell's 37 woodcutters fell afoul of the new breechloading M1866 rifle, with which Powell's command fought by their wagons until relieved from nearby Fort Philip Kearney, inflicting some 60 casualties. The Indian tactic had been to rush in while the soldiers reloaded. In 1868, the Army evacuated the fort under treaty, which the victorious Red Cloud then burned to the ground.

■ **Beecher Island, 17–19 September 1868**
Northern Cheyenne chief Roman Nose had successfully led repeated raids in Colorado in retaliation for Sand Creek. Maj George Forsyth's 50 scouts took refuge here when Roman Nose and 500 Cheyenne, Arapahoe and Sioux trapped them near the Arikaree River in Colorado. Around 30 warriors, including Roman Nose,

fell under the fire from the Scouts' repeating Spencer rifles before two messengers succeeded in bringing a relief column, which dispersed the Indians.

■ Washita River, 27 November 1868

LCol George Custer and 800 7th Cavalry attacked Cheyenne chief Black Kettle's village here in Oklahoma, the Indians considered hostile by their presence outside of a reservation and tracked by their traces in the snow. Black Kettle and 100 of his people perished in the winter dawn attack, 20 of Custer's men dying when outraged warriors boiled up from surrounding encampments that Custer had failed to scout before he withdrew.

■ Summit Springs, 11 July 1869

Pawnee scouts led Maj Eugene Carr and 500 men to a large camp of Cheyenne dog soldiers at the Platte river in Colorado. Caught unawares, the Cheyenne scattered as Carr took their camp.

■ Marias Massacre, 23 January 1870

After a period of quiescence, the Blackfoot tribe in Montana began resisting white incursions into their territory. Maj Eugene Baker attacked Mountain Chief's winter village on the banks of the Marias with subsequent indiscriminate slaughter. 173 died (mostly women and children) and 140 women and children were captured.

■ Camp Grant Massacre, 30 April 1871

1st Lt Royal Whitman's kindly treatment of surrendering Apaches at this post in Arizona resulted in more Apaches coming in to draw federal rations. As Apache raids upon Arizonan civilians continued, the Papago tribe joined with a local militia in making preparations for an attack upon the Camp Grant Apaches, now 500 in number. The Papago and Arizona locals attacked the camp while the men were out hunting, butchering 144.

■ Warren Raid, 18 May 1871

General of the Army William Tecumseh Sherman was touring the southwest when he encountered Henry Warren's wagon train delivering supplies to forts in western Texas. Warren ran into a large

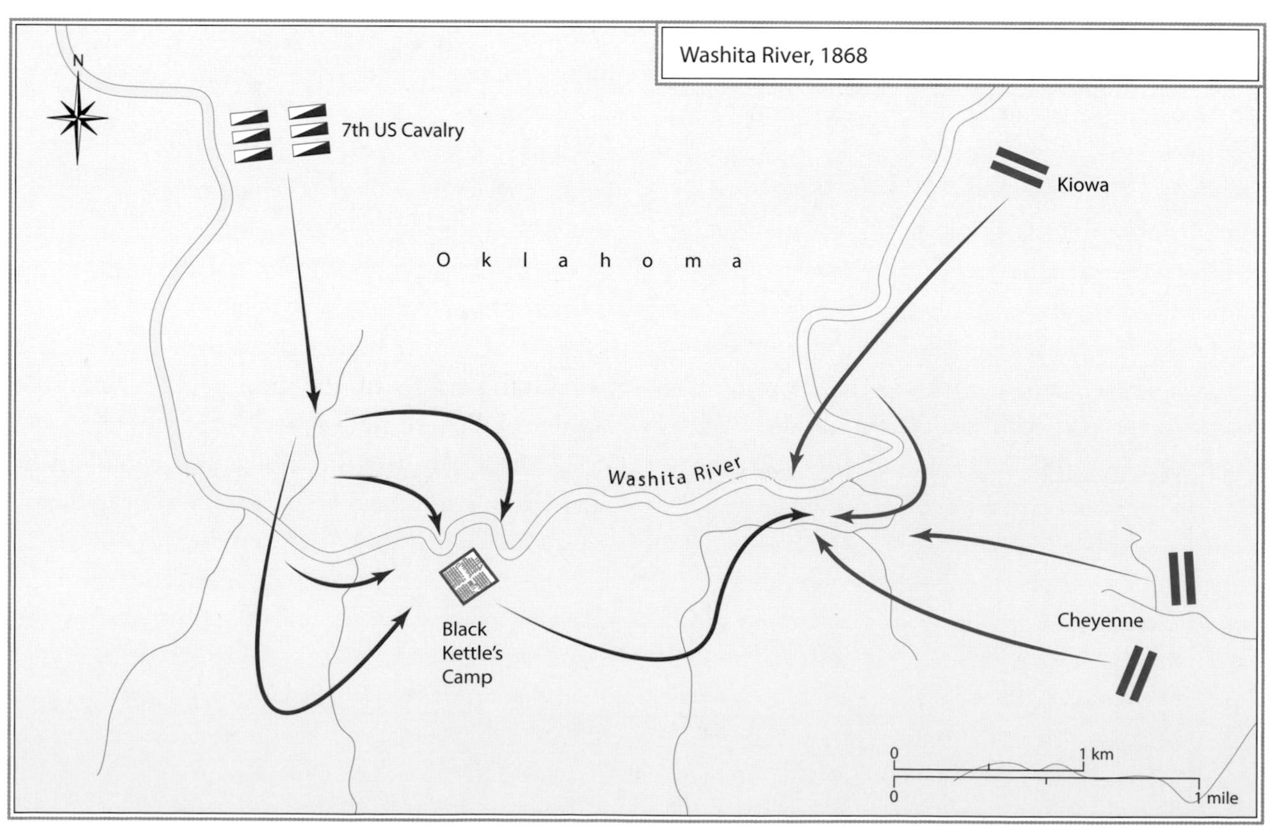

Indian raiding party, the Kiowas or Comanches torturing and killing seven teamsters and stealing the supplies, with five survivors able to describe the incident. Sherman sent out Col Ranald Mackenzie's command, which captured three of the chiefs considered responsible. Two were parolled and the other was killed while trying to escape.

■ Blanco Canyon, 10 October 1871

Col Ranald Mackenzie with 1000 regulars entered Comanche territory, encountering and defeating a large band, the army abandoning the pursuit as their animals wore out deep within areas previously considered a sanctuary for Comanche raiders.

■ Going Snake Massacre, 15 April 1872

Eight US marshals fell while attempting to remove an accused Cherokee murderer from tribal jurisdiction in Oklahoma for killing a white man. Four Cherokee perished defending the courthouse, with all charges in the affair later dropped.

■ North Fork, 28 September 1872

Col Ranald Mackenzie with 300 soldiers led by Tonkawa scouts carefully probed Comanche territory in North Texas, here on the Red River encountering a large village. Mackenzie's force attacked, killing some 23 Comanches and taking many horses.

■ Salt River Canyon, 28 December 1872

Gen George Crook's reliance on allied Indian scouts and trains of pack mules in the place of cumbersome wagon trains paid off handsomely for the US Army in this successful campaign against the Yavapai in Arizona. Crook's ability to find and pursue bands of hostiles resulted in the Yavapai retreating into the fastnesses of this canyon, in which Skeleton Cave served as a fort for the hostiles. Crook approached the site with 130 cavalry led by 30 Apaches, surprising some 110 Yavapai at the cave mouth. When the hostiles refused surrender and retreated into the cave, Crooks' men fired at the cavern roof, killing many with ricocheted bullets and stone shards, while Crook and others of his command rolled stones down upon Indians attempting to escape. With 76 dead, including Chief Nanni-chaddi, the Yavapai surrendered, their tribe henceforth greatly weakened.

■ Turret Peak, 27 March 1873

The Yavapai in Arizona considered this camp near the eponymous summit impregnable. Gen George Crook's Apache scouts and mule train convinced them otherwise when the US troopers attacked it, killing 57 of the hostile Yavapai.

■ Cypress Hills Massacre, 1 June 1873

Hostile Sioux fled to Canada after raids into the United States. Indians had stolen several horses from a party of Montana 'Wolfer' fur and buffalo hunters, who crossed the border, attacking an Assiniboine village, killing 23.

■ Honsinger Bluff, 4 August 1873

LCol George Custer's 7th Cavalry prepared to bivouac here when a party of Lakota Sioux under Chief Rain-in-the-Face tried to lure it into an ambush, then killed veterinarian Honsinger and retreated.

■ Modoc War (Lava Beds), 1872–73

The Modoc Indians lasted as long as they had in California by mostly scratching out a living in areas unwanted either by neighbouring tribes or encroaching white settlers. Finally expelled to the Klamath Reservation in Oregon, 300 Modocs under Kintpuash (Captain Jack), returned to their old lands along Tule Lake and began raiding nearby whites. Efforts to negotiate and disarm the Modocs failing bloodily, in the resulting 'Modoc War', the tribe withdrew across the lake into 'the Stronghold', a natural fastness of the nearby lava beds. The Modocs killed 18 settlers and repelled subsequent army efforts to evict them, also capturing Federal ammunition and supplies. Another 35 soldiers died attacking the Modocs in a heavy fog.

At President Grant's request, Gen Edward Canby headed a final effort at negotiations assisted by the Reverend E. Thomas, during which Kintpuash and other Modocs drew previously concealed firearms and murdered both men. Subsequently, overwhelming numbers of soldiers drove the Modocs out of the stronghold having cut off

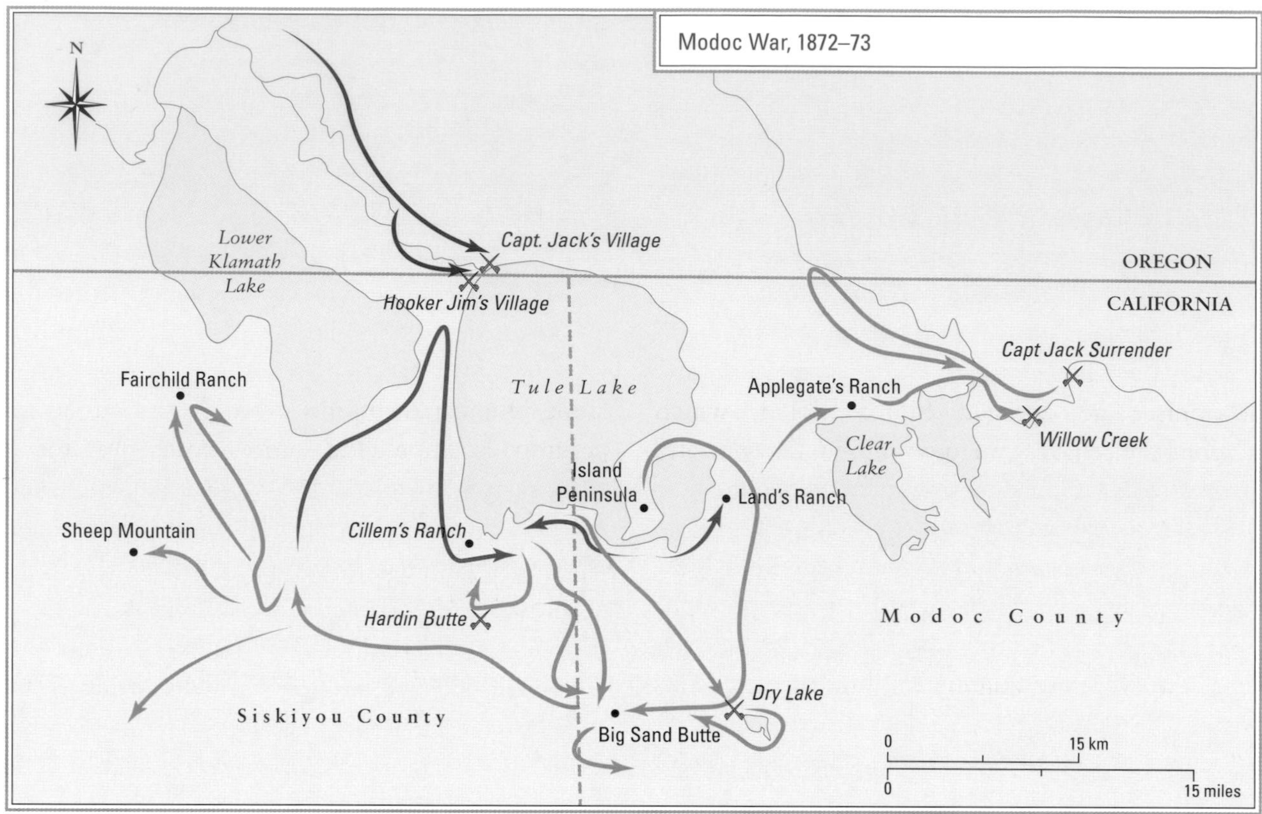

the Modocs' water supply. Kintpuash with 160 survivors fled into neighbouring lava caves, inflicting 17 dead upon an ambushed pursuing unit soon afterwards. Gen Jefferson Davis took over the war and encamped his forces at Dry Lake. There, the Modocs attacked them in the open, the army's charge defeating the Modocs and driving them into retreat, the tribe fragmenting under the stress of the defeat and their worsening situation. A band under 'Hooker Jim', who had been active in the fighting, negotiated a separate peace with the army, agreeing to capture and hand Kintpuash and the six others present at Canby's murder over to the US authorities. Kintpuash and four others were hanged, the survivors ended up in Oklahoma.

■ Adobe Walls II, 27 June 1874

A new trading complex near the old battlefield provoked 700 Cheyenne, Comanche, Arapahoe and Kiowa warriors into an effort to extirpate some 28 professional buffalo hunters operating out of the post's stores, corral and smithy. Just after a supply train reached the post, the warriors under Comanche chief Quanah Parker and medicine man Isa-Tai ran off the post's cattle herd and settled down to a four-day siege, Isa-Tai having previously prophesied the hunters' destruction. However, the Indians had failed to reckon with the extended accuracy and lethality of the hunters' long-range rifles, devastatingly employed against the buffalo and now against the warriors. The Indians abandoned their efforts on the fourth day in the face of 100 reinforcements, after hunter William Dixon with his Sharps rifle killed a warrior at a range later measured at 1406m.

■ Bates Battlefield, 1 July 1874

Capt Alfred Bates led 83 cavalry and Shoshone against a Cheyenne, Arapahoe and Sioux raiding party stealing horses from the Shoshone. An inconclusive fight cost both sides casualties and the Arapahoe a large horse herd.

■ Palo Duro Canyon, 28 September 1874

Col Ranald Mackenzie concluded his destruction

of the Comanche tribe. His scouts locating a large encampment, Mackenzie's regiment moved down the steep slopes of this canyon, scattering the Indians and capturing 1100 horses.

Black Hills War 1876–77

Rumours of gold in the Black Hills of South Dakota became a gold rush when LCol George Custer returned from the area confirming the accounts. The enraged Sioux nation, which claimed the region, joined with the Cheyenne and Arapahoe tribes in raids against the miners and settlements. In operations in Wyoming, Montana and the Dakotas, the army pursued the hostile bands under the general leadership of Sioux chiefs Crazy Horse and Sitting Bull. Indian successes at the Powder River augmented the hostiles' ranks to where they could blunt an army advance at the Rosebud and annihilate a third of the 7th Cavalry at Little Bighorn in 1876. That disaster prompted nearly half of the US Army's entry into the campaign, which continued until the winter of 1877 when the Indians' camps were much easier to locate and destroy.

■ Rosebud River, 17 June 1876

Gen George Crook's powerful column, consisting of 1050 regulars and 250 allied Crow and Shoshone Indians, encountered heavy resistance from the Sioux and Cheyenne under Chief Crazy Horse. The result was a brutal six-hour standing battle along the banks of this river, as the American column attempted to move north towards a planned rendezvous with Gen Terry's column and Custer's cavalry near the Bighorn River. Each side losing about 20 men, Crook withdrew.

■ Little Bighorn, 25–26 June 1876

More than a third of LCol George Custer's 7th Cavalry perished along with their commander when Custer ignored the warnings of his Indian scouts and precipitately engaged 3000 Sioux and Cheyenne warriors along this river in Montana.

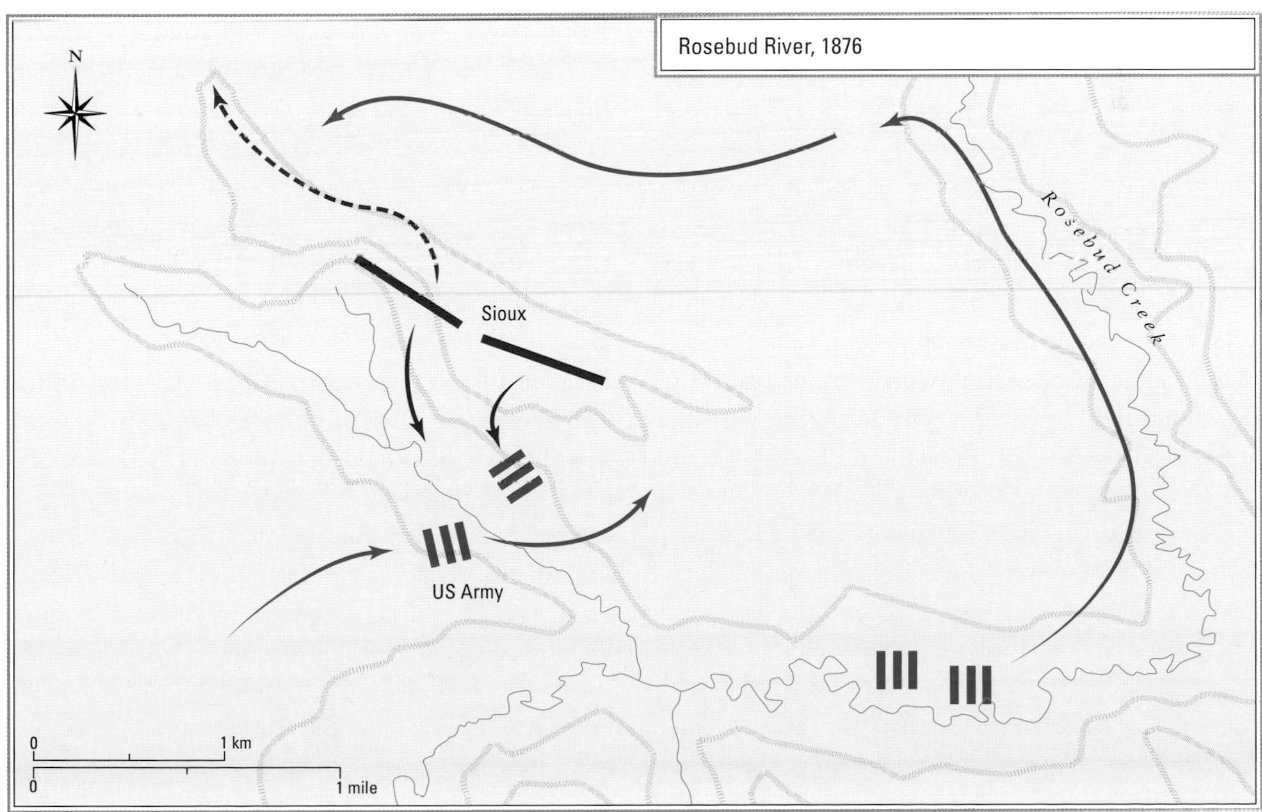

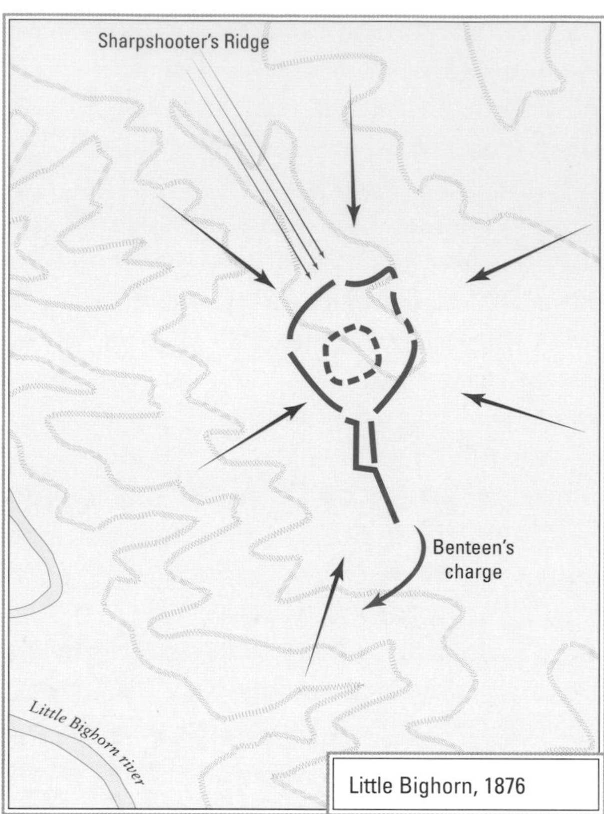

The numerous and powerful Sioux tribes and the organized and militarily skilled northern Cheyenne left their reservations in the late spring of 1876, with the intention of resisting the US Government's authority in response to past massacres and white incursions into the Black Hills of South Dakota, land which the Sioux considered theirs.

The US Army's response took the form of a powerful force of nearly 3000 infantry and cavalry in three converging columns pursuing the departed Indians. Gen Terry (in overall command) and his subordinates were initially unaware that the total agglomeration of Indian warriors was of approximately equal numbers and more concentrated than the army's columns. Custer's orders and his desire for another successful engagement on the plains allowed him to rush into attack with less than a third of the army's total force, the result being the most resounding defeat the US Army ever suffered in the wars against the plains Indians.

Generals Terry and Crook sent Custer's 7th Cavalry ahead of their two columns to locate the village and vital pony herd of the missing tribes. Custer's Crow scouts returned and told him that they had located the largest single village and pony herd that they had ever seen, claims Custer dismissed as exaggerated, despite reports of Indians shadowing his regiment and looting a fallen pack mule. Drawing closer to the village along the banks of the Little Bighorn, Custer divided his regiment of 647 men into four separate battalions, sending Maj Marcus Reno directly into the village, and Capt Frederick Benteen around the rear with the reserve ammunition, while moving his own two battalions toward the north, planning on containing and flanking the village against the river. Custer's final communication was an order to Benteen to bring up the ammunition quickly.

Reno's battalion moved directly into the village, where it encountered ferocious resistance, Reno taking casualties as he regrouped in a clump of trees before making a disorganized retreat toward a nearby hill. There, his men dug in and resisted sporadic attacks for the next two days, joined by Benteen's column with the vital ammunition. Unaware of Reno's repulse to the south and with Custer forgetting his own promise to support Reno's thrust, Custer's individual companies attacked the village or encountered groups of Indians under their own war chiefs boiling out of the village in a fierce response that began to overwhelm Custer's 241 men. Custer's command began to disintegrate as his movement north became a rout and then a headlong retreat away from Reno Hill. Individual units made their own 'last stands' while trying to escape destruction, their bodies found in situ by subsequent burial parties. Either because of Custer's death or due to his last order, his final remnant of the 7th stopped its flight on 'Custer Hill', where the warriors and their wives finished off the survivors, killing and mutilating the wounded in traditional fashion. Terry's column arrived and found Custer's body stripped, but otherwise untouched. The

One of Custer's Native American scouts, Bloody Knife, poses in profile in this photograph from 1873. The US Army used local scouts widely in their push for control of the West.

reinforcements informed Reno's and Benteen's dazed survivors of the fate of their comrades, with 268 perishing in total.

■ **Warbonnet Creek, 17 July 1876**

Col Wesley Merritt with the 5th US Cavalry soon after Little Bighorn here intercepted several hundred Cheyenne as they attempted to leave the Red Cloud Agency to join the hostiles in the Black River War.

■ **Slim Buttes, 9–10 September 1876**

Gen George Crook's column stumbled into a large village of the Miniconjou Sioux under Chief American Horse in South Dakota. Attacking immediately, the soldiers scattered the village and deprived the Indians of vital winter stores.

■ **Cedar Creek, 21 October 1876**

Gen Nelson Miles' force moving up the Yellowstone River located Sitting Bull's village when the Sioux attacked its wagons near Spring Creek. Although the Sioux initially drove away the supply train, the wagons' escorts rallied and made the rendezvous with Miles. As the resupplied column approached Sitting Bull's village, Sitting Bull began negotiations, but attempted to slip away the following morning. Miles pursued, capturing much of the Indians' winter supplies.

■ **Dull Knife Fight, 25 November 1876**

Col Ranald Mackenzie led 1100 cavalry against a large northern Cheyenne village here celebrating in the aftermath of Little Bighorn. Mackenzie drove the Indians from their camp and captured ponies and vital winter stores.

■ **Wolf Mountain, 8 January 1877**

Crazy Horse led his band of Sioux and Cheyenne against the pursuing column of Gen Nelson Miles, some 500 warriors finding Miles's 436 soldiers entrenched and ready for the assault. Weather and howitzers eventually drove Crazy Horse off.

■ **Yellow Horse Canyon, 18 March 1877**

Black Horse's Comanche concluded their efforts against the buffalo hunters having set forth on a permitted hunting expedition, plundering camps, then torturing and killing one hunter who fell into their hands. A militia of 46 men set out in pursuit and tracked the Comanches to a camp in this canyon. Despite being outnumbered 12:1, the hunters attacked the Comanche from three sides before being forced to retreat under the fire of women and the infuriated warriors, 12 of the hunters perishing. The Comanche set a prairie fire to camouflage their own movements and the hunters used a decoy bonfire that night to elude pursuit by the Indians. Black Horse and his band returned to the reservation after news that regular army units were en route, a brief skirmish serving to confirm that news violently.

Nez Perce War 1877

■ **White Bird Canyon, 17 June 1877**

Nez Perce, when rejecting cessions in an 1855 treaty, began attacking white settlers. Capt David Perry's column of 150 men retreated after losing 32, the Indians capturing weapons and ammunition.

■ **Clearwater, 11–12 July 1877**

Nez Perce chiefs Joseph and Looking Glass combined their 300 warriors and moved northwards, here in Idaho overtaken by Gen Oliver Howard's 350 soldiers. Mauled by Howard's artillery, the Nez Perce inflicted casualties and retreated.

■ **Big Hole, 9–10 August 1877**

The Nez Perce rested here, where US Col John Gibbon surprised them with 206 men, the 200 warriors then rallying to protect their families and forcing Gibbon on the defensive, killing 32 soldiers; 52 Indians died.

■ **Camas Creek, 20 August 1877**

Gen Oliver Howard's 250 men, shadowing the Nez Perce here in southeastern Idaho, suffered and inflicted some six casualties when the Nez Perce attempted to dismount the soldiers by stealing their horses, the Indians retreating.

■ **Canyon Creek, 13 September 1877**

The Nez Perce abducted and killed tourists in Yellowstone Park, pursued to this point by Gen Samuel Sturgis, who retreated from the fire of the Nez Perce holding a ridge. The Nez Perce eluded pursuit, however, and disappeared into the wilderness.

■ **Bear Paw Mountain, 30 September–5 October 1877**

The Nez Perce War ended when Gen Nelson Miles with 400 soldiers trapped 800 exhausted Nez Perce and blocked the escape route to Canada, with 200 Indians eluding the snare and escaping. The warriors dug in to defend their families, aiming in particular at Miles' officers, killing two officers as well as 21 enlisted men. Gen Oliver Howard arrived four days later with 120 reinforcements and two cannon with exploding shells. The Nez Perce endured for six days until a sniper killed Chief Looking Glass. Surviving chief Joseph ended his tribe's 2414km effort to escape the war when he left the beleaguered camp and made an impassioned speech of surrender to Howard, only 87 warriors and 331 women and children remaining with him. The army first shipped the captives to Kansas and then to Oklahoma, although some later returned to central Washington.

Other Indian Wars 1878–90

■ **Buffalo Hunters' War, 1877**

Commanche chief Black Horse led a final large raiding band out into the Staked Plains where they and allied Apaches plundered the camps of buffalo hunters. The hunters tracked and attacked the band, killing 35.

■ **Staked Plains Horror, 1877**

Black 'Buffalo Soldiers' and buffalo hunters under Capt Nicholas Nolan wandered for days while tracking Comanche in the Staked Plains region. Reported massacred by the Indians, most of the party actually managed to reach rescue.

■ **Bannock War, 1878**

The Bannock Shoshone vented their rage at settlers' destruction of their food supplies in an ongoing series of raids and murders, prompting Gen Oliver

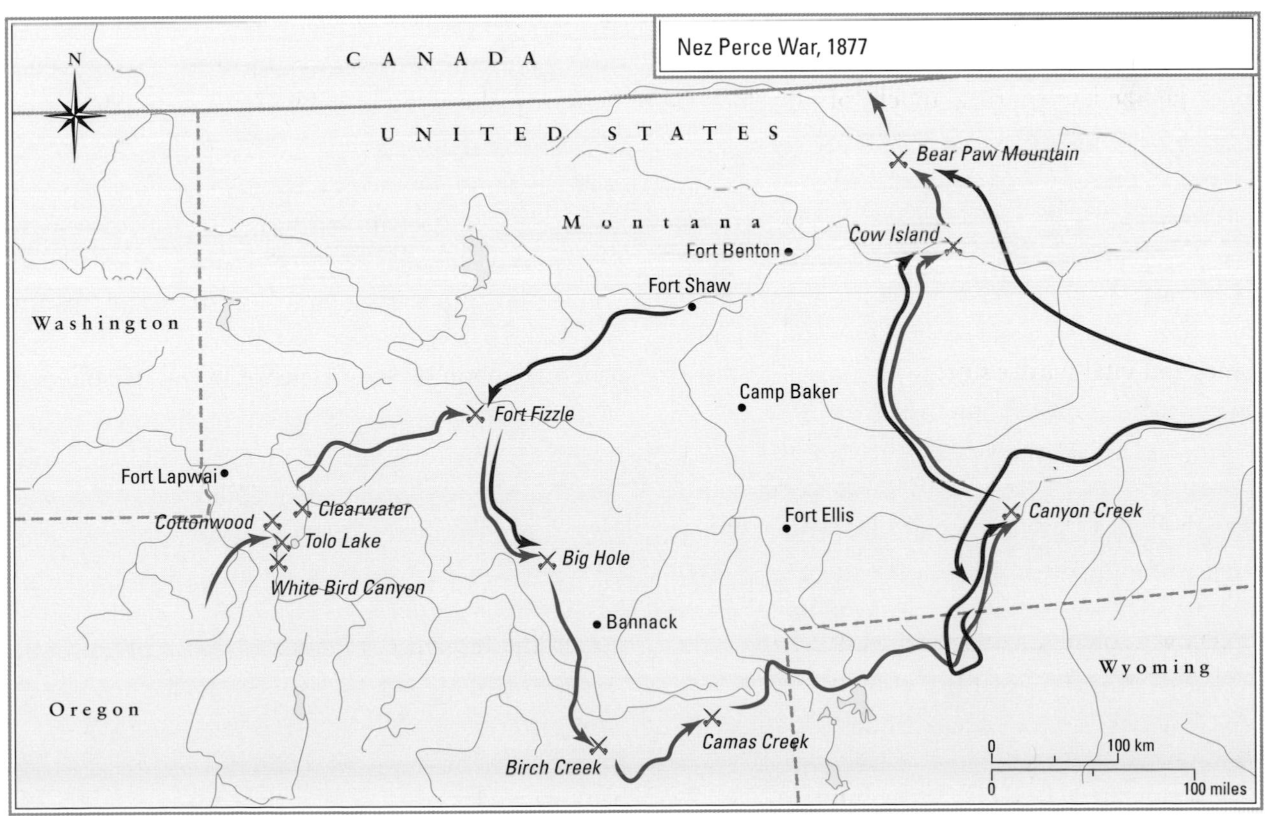

Howard and the army to move in pursuit of the hostile factions. Capt Reuben Bernard ambushed the group, killing 50, and 500 hostiles were beaten while attacking Capt Evan Miles' camp. The Bannocks next attacked the Umatilla Reservation; those Indians joined the army in tracking and capturing the survivors.

■ Cheyenne War, 1878–79

Reservation conditions were poor enough to prompt Cheyenne chief Dull Knife and some 100 followers to leave Oklahoma for Montana. Captured and held at Fort Robinson, Nebraska, over half the Cheyenne died while attempting to escape.

■ Sheepeater Indian War, 1879

The army pursued northwestern Indian holdouts called 'Sheepeaters' for the murder of seven people near the Salmon. The Indians defeated a badly led cavalry column in heavy winter snows before relentless army pursuit forced their surrender.

■ White River War, 1879

The Utes continued to resist the army and acclimatization to white culture along this river in Utah and Colorado. After setbacks such as Milk Creek, increasing army numbers and pressure drove the Utes onto reservations.

■ Milk Creek, 29 September–5 October 1879

Tensions with the Utes in Colorado resulted in this battle and the Meeker Massacre as Maj Thomas Thornburgh's 150 troopers were trapped for a week. Twice reinforced, the cavalry eventually drove the Utes into flight.

■ Alma Massacre, 28 April 1880

Chiricahua Apache chief Victorio led a raiding party against a silver mine and this town in New Mexico, killing three in town and three more while fleeing, then slaughtering 35 sheepherders before eluding army pursuit.

■ Fort Tularosa, 14 May 1880

The 9th US Cavalry's black 'Buffalo Soldiers' here moved quickly to the relief of this New Mexican post when Chiricahua Apache chief Victorio and his 100 warriors attacked it and the civilians nearby. Arriving as the Apaches withdrew having killed several settlers, the 9th's troopers worked to increase the town's defences, killing Apaches attempting to capture the settlers' cattle. The full regiment unsuccessfully gave chase to the Apaches when assembled.

■ Cibecue Creek, 30 August 1881

An Apache shaman's prayer to raise the dead and drive out the whites led to his arrest and death, plus the mutiny of army Apache scouts, as Apaches throughout Arizona and New Mexico turned hostile.

■ Fort Apache, 1 September 1881

Apaches, infuriated by the death of the shaman at Cibecue Creek, attacked this post in Arizona, firing on the fort at long range, the army returning fire and suffering three dead before the Apaches disappeared.

■ Big Dry Wash, 17 July 1882

Capt Adna Chaffee with 350 troopers overtook 54 Chiricahua Apache who planned an ambush. Informed, Chaffee launched a decisive holding attack, pinning the warriors while a part of his command attacked from the sides of this declivity to ambush the Apaches.

■ Geronimo Campaign 1886

The last and perhaps grimmest of Indian leaders, Chiricahua Apache chief Geronimo resisted three campaigns and two generals' efforts to contain and catch him before his final surrender. Geronimo never forgave the Mexicans' slaughter of his wife and children. Having fought and learned in the campaigns of Mangas Coloradas and Cochise, Geronimo achieved fame after he led out several hundred Apaches from the barren San Carlos Reservation in 1882, undoing Gen George Crook's peace treaties with previous chiefs.

Surrendering to Crook in 1884, Geronimo again rebelled and escaped in 1886, prompting the appointment of Gen Nelson Miles to command the campaign against him. Repeated failures on the part of Miles and slaughters on the part of Geronimo forced Miles to adapt Crook's measures of employing mule trains and Apache scouts from rival bands to track the elusive Geronimo and his core band of highly seasoned followers. One of Geronimo's favourite tactics was to elude US or Mexican forces by crossing a border his pursuers could not cross without risking a diplomatic incident. For several years, he kept southeastern Arizona and northern Mexico in turmoil. Around 5000 army troops with 500 native scouts participated in Miles' final campaign against Geronimo's camp in the Sonora Mountains.

The pursuers took five months and 2647km of travel before Miles was able to convince Geronimo to surrender for a final time, the Apaches down to 16 warriors, 12 women and six children. Crook bitterly criticized Miles' broken promise that Geronimo and his followers would be allowed time to return to Arizona. Instead, Geronimo, his followers and Miles' own Apache scouts spent years in Fort Pickens, Florida, Geronimo eventually dying in Fort Sill, Oklahoma, in 1909.

■ Wounded Knee Creek (Wounded Knee Massacre), 29 December 1890

The spreading net of railroads completed the ability of white settlers and buffalo hunters to obliterate the plains tribes' way of life when the army returned to the plains after the civil war. Treaties, dependency upon government supplies and systematic military action forced the beaten Indians onto reservations, where some of the tribes turned to religion as their final hope to bring back better days still vivid in their memories.

Wovoka, a Paiute shaman, preached his vision of a Ghost Dance that would return the dead and the buffalo to the plains without additional outbreaks of fruitless violence. More aggressive Oglala Sioux in the band of Chief Big Foot claimed that a Ghost Dance shirt would protect against bullets, word of which quickly reached the nervous and scanty forces stationed to control and pacify the Indians.

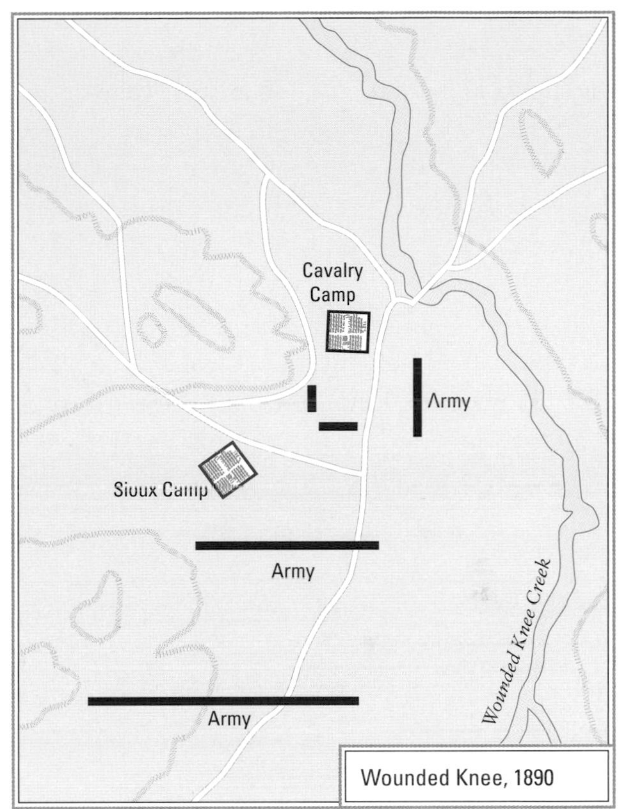

Wounded Knee, 1890

Government unease and his stated support for the Ghost Dance led to the death of Chief Sitting Bull, when native police sought to arrest him despite the chief's long record of peaceful conduct since his role at Little Bighorn in 1876.

In another echo of that celebrated battle, Big Foot's band left their reservation and moved towards other militant bands in an unauthorized departure that prompted an army pursuit. With the Indians surrounded by soldiers on all sides at Wounded Knee Creek, members of the reconstituted 7th Cavalry moved into the crowd of Oglala Sioux on 29 December 1890 with orders to disarm the Indians.

A resulting scuffle rapidly escalated into an outright and bloody slaughter, when jittery troopers outside the crowd turned Hotchkiss repeating cannon upon the surrounded Indians and other troopers still intermingled with the Sioux. Big Foot and 149 other Indians perished, along with 25 cavalry.

American Civil War, 1861–65

The Civil War was one of the bloodiest periods in American history, resulting in the death of at least 600,000 Americans, with many more maimed and wounded. The United States was only 84 years old when it began to break apart. The conflict was caused by differences in the economies and cultures of the North and South, especially over the issue of slavery. In January 1861, seven Southern slave states declared their secession from the United States and formed the Confederate States of America, setting them in direct opposition to the Federal government.

Left: Union General Ambrose Burnside's corps captures a bridge at the Battle of Antietam as Confederate forces press forwards. Fought on 17 September 1862, Antietam saw the bloodiest single day's fighting of the Civil War, with combined losses of more than 22,000.

American Civil War 1861–65

■ Pea Ridge, 7–8 March 1861
MGen Earl Van Dorn launched an ill-planned attack against BGen Samuel Curtis's overextended lines at Elkhorn Tavern, Arkansas. The defeat forced the Confederates to retreat from Arkansas, surrendering the initiative there to the Federals.

■ Fort Sumter, 12–14 April 1861
Fort Sumter was a brick fort built on an artificial island in the middle of the main ship channel at Charleston, South Carolina. Even though South Carolina seceded on 20 December 1861, Federal commander Maj Robert Anderson refused to surrender his 84-man force. A weak Federal attempt to resupply and reinforce the beleaguered garrison by the unarmed *Star of the West* was turned back on 9 January 1861. In early March, BGen Pierre Gustave Toutant Beauregard arrived to assume command of the Confederate forces, and on 10 April he issued a demand that Anderson surrender or face bombardment. On 12 April, Beauregard commenced his attack. After a 34-hour bombardment of some 4000 shells, Anderson surrendered on 13 April and the Federals were evacuated to New York. The action compelled President Abraham Lincoln to call for volunteers to suppress the rebellion.

■ Philippi, 3 June 1861
As Confederate and Federal forces battled for control of western Virginia early in the war, a minor action was fought at Philippi. Federals commanded by Col Thomas Morris surprised Confederates under Col George Porterfield in a two-pronged attack before dawn. The Confederates suffered 26 casualties and retreated towards Huttonsville in what critics called the 'Philippi Races'. The Federals suffered four casualties. Philippi is sometimes credited as being the first battle of the war.

■ Big Bethel, 10 June 1861
This Federal attack on a Confederate outpost northwest of Newport News, Virginia, was easily

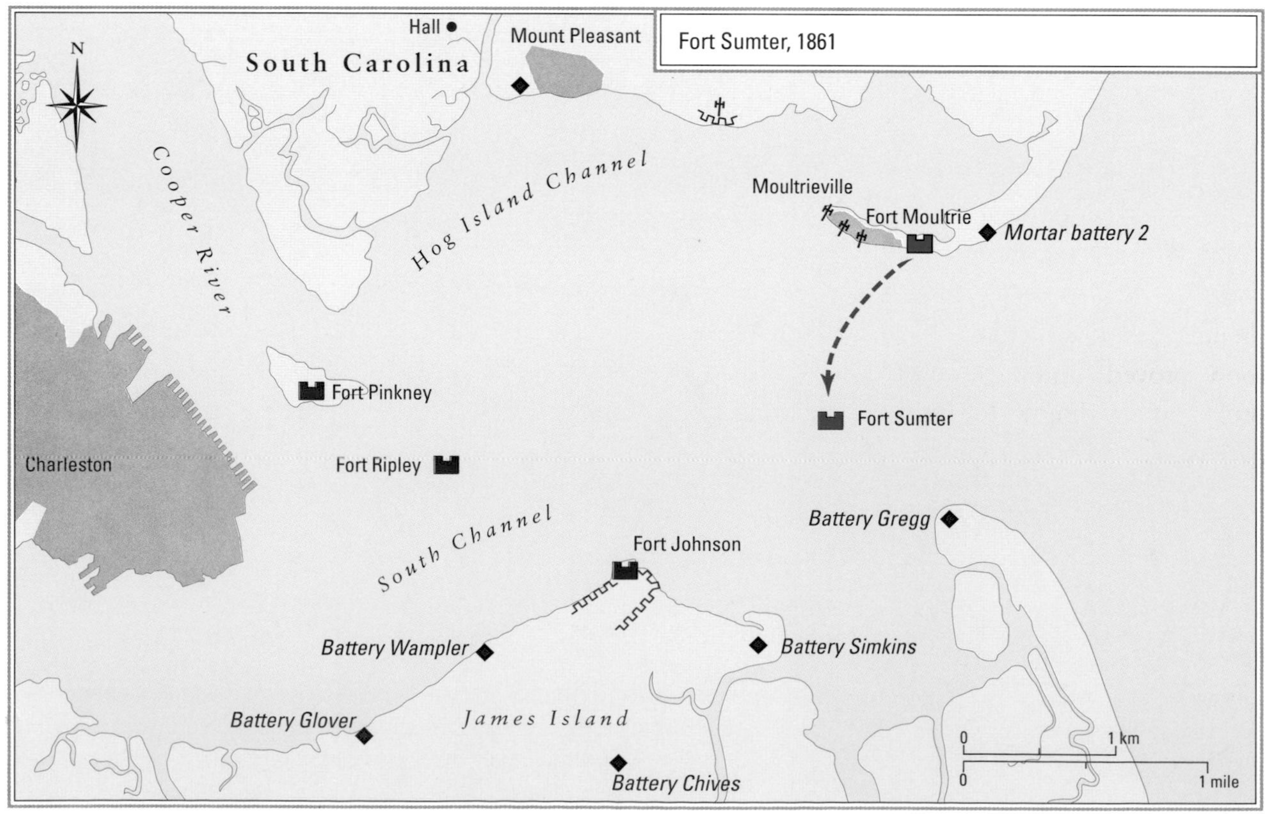

repulsed by Col John Magruder. Although a small action, at the time the battle was widely reported and elevated Magruder to the status of a minor celebrity.

■ **Rich Mountain, 11 July 1861**

MGen George McClellan attacked Confederate troops who had retreated from Philippi. The victory helped remove the Confederate presence from the northwestern counties of Virginia. West Virginia was admitted to the Union as a new state in 1863.

■ **First Bull Run, 21 July 1861**

Under pressure from President Abraham Lincoln to act, BGen Irvin McDowell began moving his army toward Manassas Junction. Confederates commanded by BGen Pierre Gustave Toutant Beauregard soon ascertained the threat and requested reinforcements from Gen Joseph Johnston in the Shenandoah Valley. Johnston slipped away from MGen Robert Patterson, who had been ordered to hold him in place, and Johnston moved by railroad to join Beauregard. On 21 July, McDowell launched a diversionary attack on the Confederate line at the Stone Bridge. A Confederate signal station noticed the flanking movement the attack had been designed to cover, and Col Nathan Evans moved to the southern slope of Mathews' Hill to counter this threat. Evans was joined by Confederate brigades commanded by BGen Barnard Bee and Col Francis Barlow, but the Matthews' Hill position soon proved untenable, and the Confederates broke into a disorderly retreat back towards the Henry House. It seemed as if a Federal victory was at hand until BGen Thomas Jackson arrived with reinforcements from the Shenandoah Valley and took up a position on Henry Hill. The remnants of the other Confederate commands rallied around Jackson's line, prompting Bee to point to Jackson and declare he was standing there 'like a stone wall', giving Jackson the nickname he carried ever after. As the Confederates rallied, McDowell was slow to renew his attack and he forfeited his numerical advantage by piecemeal attacks. After stopping the attack on Henry Hill, the Confederates focused their attention on Chinn Ridge and turned back another Federal attack there. Panic soon swept the Federal ranks, and McDowell chaotically retreated to Washington. By now, however, the victorious Confederates had also become disorganized and exhausted and were unable to pursue.

■ **Wilson's Creek, 12 August 1861**

Federals commanded by BGen Nathaniel Lyon and Col Franz Sigel attacked Confederates under BGen Ben McCulloch at Wilson's Creek, Missouri. The victory gave the Confederates temporary control of south-western Missouri and encouraged secessionist sympathizers.

■ **Cheat Mountain, 12–15 September 1861**

Gen Robert E. Lee ordered Col Albert Rust to attack BGen Joseph Reynolds's Federals defending Cheat Mountain in western Virginia. A mere 300 determined Federals held off Rust, and Lee withdrew to Valley Head.

■ **Cockle Creek, 5 October 1861**

In spite of Virginia's secession, residents of Chincoteague Island were decidedly pro-Union. At Cockle Creek, the USS *Louisiana* sank the CSS *Venus*, helping secure the area from Confederate blockade runners and privateers.

■ **New Orleans, 12 October 1861**

Cdre George Hollins attacked the remarkably unprepared Federal naval detachment commanded by Capt John Pope. Hollins's force included the ironclad *Manassas*. The Federals fled in what critics labelled 'Pope's Run.'

■ **Ball's Bluff, 21 October 1861**

Col Nathan Evans defeated a bungled Federal attempt to cross the Potomac River. Col Edwin Baker was killed in the fighting and the overall Federal commander, BGen Charles Stone, became the scapegoat for the debacle.

■ **Belmont, 7 November 1861**

Confederates commanded by MGen Leonidas Polk manned an observation post called Camp

Colonel J.E.B. Stuart's Confederate cavalry charge Union artillery and Zouave infantry during the First Battle of Bull Run, July 1861.

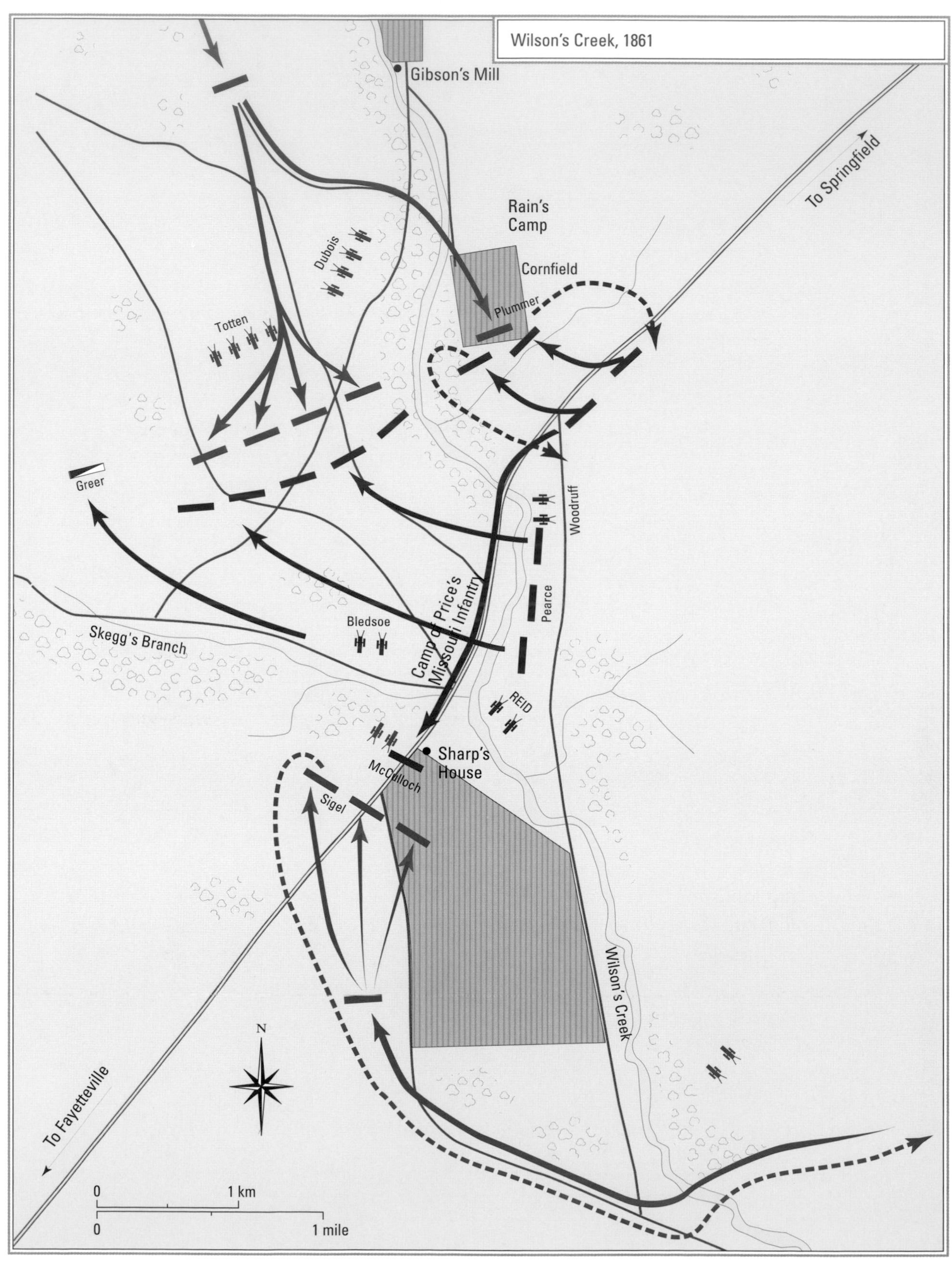
Wilson's Creek, 1861
Gibson's Mill
Rain's Camp
Cornfield
Plummer
To Springfield
Dubois
Totten
Greer
Woodruff
Camp of Price's Missouri Infantry
Pearce
Bledsoe
Skegg's Branch
REID
Sharp's House
McCulloch
Sigel
Wilson's Creek
N
To Fayetteville
0
1 km
0
1 mile

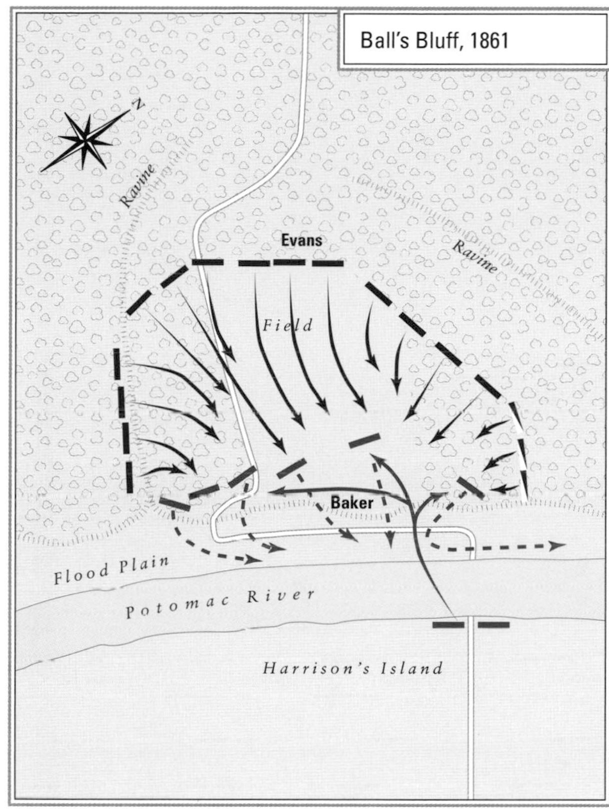

Johnston at Belmont, Missouri. BGen Ulysses Grant believed that Polk was planning to reinforce pro-Confederate forces under BGen Sterling Price in southwest Missouri. To prevent this move, Grant embarked from Cairo, Illinois, and landed a force of over 3000 men 3.2km above Belmont. As Grant advanced, he scattered Confederates commanded by BGen Gideon Pillow and then descended on Camp Johnson from two directions. While the Confederates withdrew, Grant lost control of his men as they celebrated and looted the camp. Polk then sent two steamers with reinforcements across the Mississippi River from Columbus, Kentucky, and threatened to surround Grant. Grant rallied his men and fought back to their transports and returned to Cairo, Illinois. Although a largely unnecessary battle, Belmont proved to be a formative experience for Grant.

■ Mill Springs, 19 January 1862

Confederate MGen George Crittenden advanced from Mill Springs, Kentucky, and struck BGen George Thomas in a pre-emptive attack at Logan's Crossroads. Crittenden was forced to retreat to Murfreesboro, Tennessee. Confederate BGen Felix Zollicoffer was killed in the battle.

■ Fort Henry, 6 February 1862

Fort Henry was a relatively weak Confederate position intended to guard the Tennessee River approach into the heart of Tennessee and north Alabama. In early February 1862, it was manned by a force of about 100 artillerymen under the command of BGen Lloyd Tilghman, who had sent the bulk of his force to Fort Donelson, a stronger position on the Cumberland River. BGen Ulysses Grant loaded 15,000 troops on to Flag Officer Andrew Foote's transports and headed up the Tennessee River. MGen Henry Halleck had previously rejected the plan, but when Foote lent his support, Halleck acquiesced. Grant landed a few miles below Fort Henry, while Foote steamed ahead to shell the position. After a brief bombardment, Tilghman surrendered. The capture of Fort Henry opened the Tennessee river to Federal vessels as far as Muscle Shoals, Alabama, and was a precursor to the capture of Fort Donelson.

■ Roanoke Island, 7–8 February 1862

BGen Ambrose Burnside and Flag Officer Louis Goldsborough brushed aside a weak Confederate force on this island off the North Carolina coast in what was the Federals' first major land victory east of the Alleghenies.

■ Fort Donelson, 13–16 February 1862

A joint force commanded by BGen Ulysses Grant and Flag Officer Andrew Foote besieged this Confederate position on the Cumberland River. On 16 February, the Confederates surrendered, giving the Federals their first major victory of the war.

■ Hampton Roads, 9 March 1862

Confederate engineers raised the scuttled USS *Merrimack* and converted it into an ironclad rechristened as the CSS *Virginia*. On 8 March, the *Virginia* sailed into Hampton Roads off Norfolk, Virginia, and began destroying Federal ships

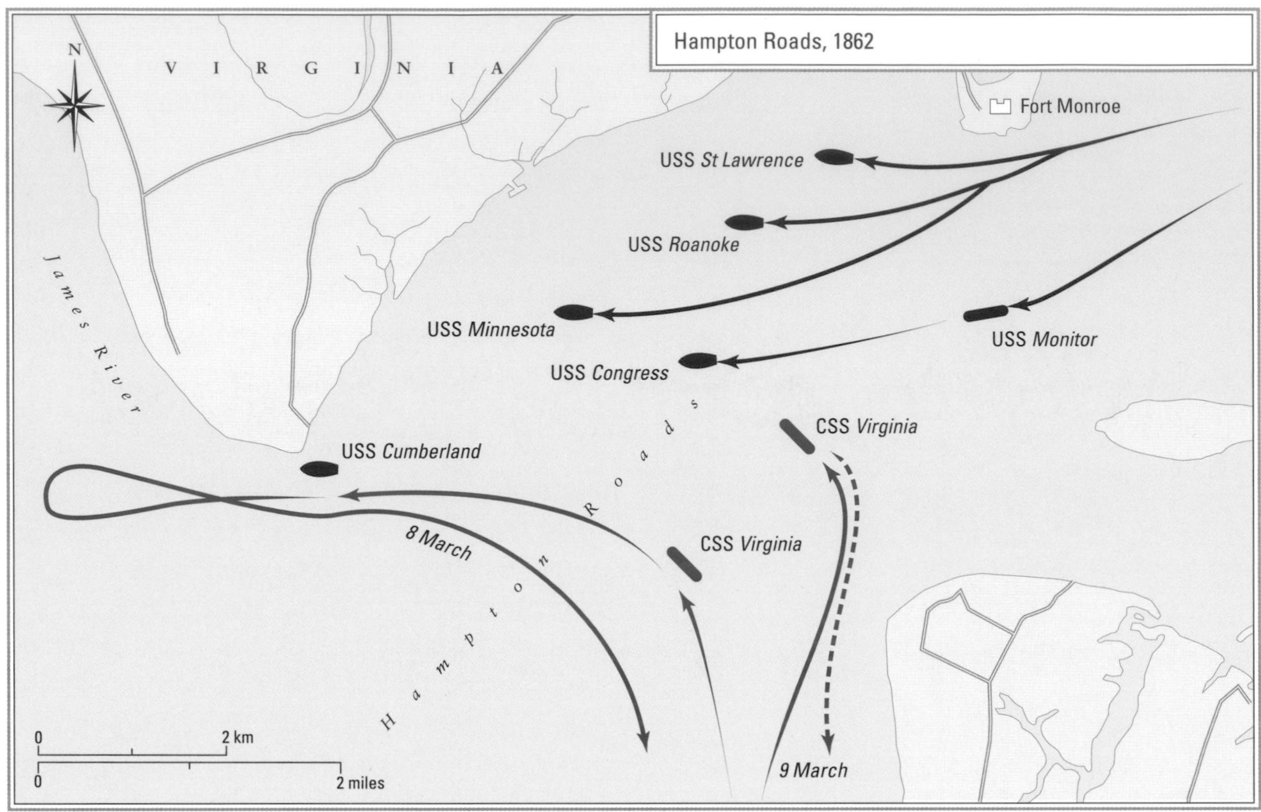

anchored there. On 9 March, the *Virginia*'s rampage was challenged when the Federal ironclad, the USS *Monitor*, arrived on the scene. Taking advantage of its superior manoeuvrability, the *Monitor* scored several hits on the *Virginia*, cracking its railroad iron armour, but failing to penetrate its 60cm pitch pine and oak backing. The two combatants continued to duel indecisively for two hours, and then both ships withdrew for a half-hour respite.

In the second two-hour engagement, the *Virginia* made an attempt to ram the *Monitor*, but, having lost her ram-beak in the previous day's fighting, was unsuccessful. Then Lt Catesby ap Roger Jones, who had assumed command of the *Virginia* after Cdre Franklin Buchanan was wounded, tried to take advantage of his larger crew size and made several attempts to board the *Monitor*. The *Monitor* repulsed all efforts. Finally, Jones brought the *Virginia* to within 10m of the *Monitor* and struck her pilot house at point blank range with a 9in (28cm) shell. Stationed immediately behind the point of impact, the *Monitor*'s commander, Lt John Worden, personally felt the full effect of this concussion and commanded his helmsman to sheer off. The *Virginia* had also taken a beating, and with the ebb tide running, she withdrew across Hampton Roads to Norfolk. After the battle, the *Virginia* was still a threat, but thanks to the presence of the *Monitor*, it no longer was able to thwart MGen George McClellan's developing Peninsula Campaign.

■ New Madrid, 13 March 1862

Island No. 10 and New Madrid, Missouri, blocked Federal navigation of the Mississippi River. As BGen John Pope prepared to begin siege operations against New Madrid, the Confederate force there withdrew.

■ Kernstown, 23 March 1862

MGen George McClellan was eager to shift forces from the Shenandoah Valley to help him with his Peninsula Campaign. Confederate MGen Stonewall Jackson's mission was to prevent that from happening. Col Turner Ashby reported Federal

Campaigns of 1861–62

troops were preparing to join McClellan, and Ashby skirmished with Federals commanded by BGen James Shields on 22 March. At about 14:00 on 23 March, Jackson met Ashby at Kernstown, 6.5km south of Winchester. Jackson's men were tired from marching and the pious Jackson was reluctant to fight on the Sabbath, but he could not afford to let reinforcements slip away to McClellan. Jackson launched a disjointed attack and suffered a tactical defeat with 718 casualties compared to 568 for the Federals. Strategically, however, Kernstown was a huge Confederate victory. Jackson's presence and aggressive action caused Federal authorities to halt plans to shift forces to McClellan.

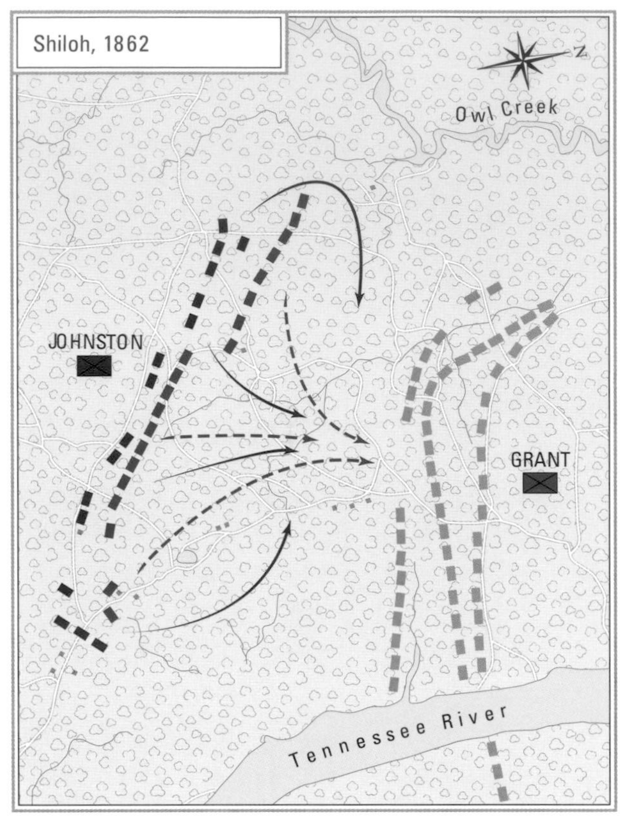

■ Shiloh, 6–7 April 1862

Stinging from MGen Ulysses Grant's victories at Forts Henry and Donelson in February 1862, Gen Albert Sidney Johnston withdrew from Tennessee and concentrated his Confederate forces at Corinth, Mississippi. At the same time, Grant assembled some 45,000 men at Pittsburg Landing, Tennessee, about 32km northeast of Corinth, where he waited for the arrival of MGen Don Carlos Buell's Army of the Ohio from Nashville. Perhaps 2km south-west of Pittsburg Landing was Shiloh Church, the feature that would give the upcoming battle its common name. Grant arranged his command in a largely administrative camp configuration while he waited for Buell to join him to conduct a combined attack on Corinth. Grant never considered Johnston might launch his own offensive, and was caught by surprise when Johnston marched from Corinth and attacked before dawn on 6 April. The Confederates attacked with MGen William Hardee's Third Army Corps and MGen Braxton Bragg's Second Army Corps deployed in line, followed by MGen Leonidas Polk's First Army Corps and then BGen John Breckinridge's Reserve Corps advancing in column formation.

The Confederate attack hit the part of the Federal line occupied by BGen Benjamin Prentiss's 6th Division, whose stubborn defence of the 'Hornet's Nest' bought time for Grant to reorganize his force. When Johnston was killed leading an attack through a peach orchard just to the right of the Hornet's Nest, Gen Pierre Gustave Toutant Beauregard assumed command and launched a series of frontal assaults that eventually forced the Federals to withdraw back to Pittsburg Landing. Although initially caught off guard, Grant used Prentiss' stubborn defence to organize the stragglers into units and form a new defensive line that ran inland at a right angle from the Tennessee River above Pittsburg Landing northwestwards towards Owl Creek. There he held on until reinforcements from Buell's 35,000-man army began arriving at 19:00. In spite of the early Confederate success, the tide of the battle was beginning to turn in favour of the Federals.

Still, Beauregard believed the Confederate attack had carried the day and stopped the pursuit, declaring 'the victory is complete'. Beauregard was later subjected to much historical scrutiny for missing what became known as the 'Lost

Opportunity' to destroy Grant's army. For his part, Grant continued to receive reinforcements and resolved to counter-attack the next day. Striking before dawn and taking advantage of the numerical advantage gained by the arrival of Buell, the Federals enjoyed quick success. Grant easily recaptured most of the ground he had earlier lost, and by 14:30 Beauregard decided to withdraw back towards Corinth. Grant's men were too exhausted to effectively pursue.

The battle of Shiloh was the biggest battle fought in North America to that date. Of the 62,000 Federals engaged, 13,047 were killed, wounded or missing. The Confederates suffered 11,694 casualties from their 44,000-man army. The Confederate forces in the west were now committed to an unwinnable war of attrition.

ISLAND NO. 10, 7 APRIL 1862

BGen John Pope dug a canal to allow his boats to bypass the Confederate defences and ferried four regiments across the Mississippi River, cutting off the Confederate line of retreat. BGen William Mackall surrendered 3500 Confederates while another 500 escaped through the swamps. The victory opened the Mississippi River to Fort Pillow, Tennessee, and enhanced Pope's reputation enough that he became commander of the Army of Virginia two months later.

NEW ORLEANS, 25 APRIL 1862

Adm David Farragut attacked New Orleans, the South's largest city and a key port and shipbuilding centre, shortly after midnight on 24 April 1862. After the Federals forced their way past the ram *Manassas* and Forts St Philip and Jackson, Confederate commander MGen Mansfield Lovell retreated. The city was in panic, and as Farragut pulled alongside, he hammered it with broadsides. He then dispatched his marines to take possession of the Federal mint, post office and customs house, and replace the Confederate flag with the Stars and Stripes on all public buildings. Capt

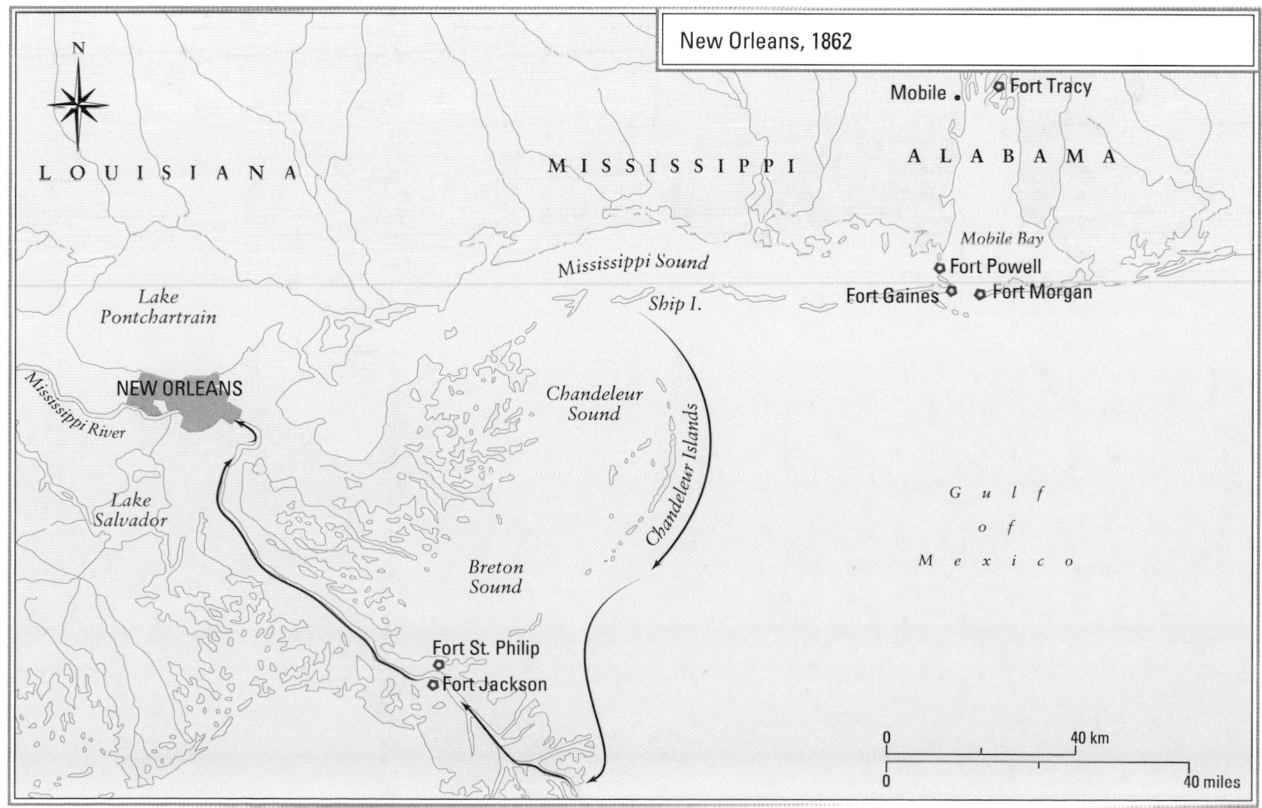

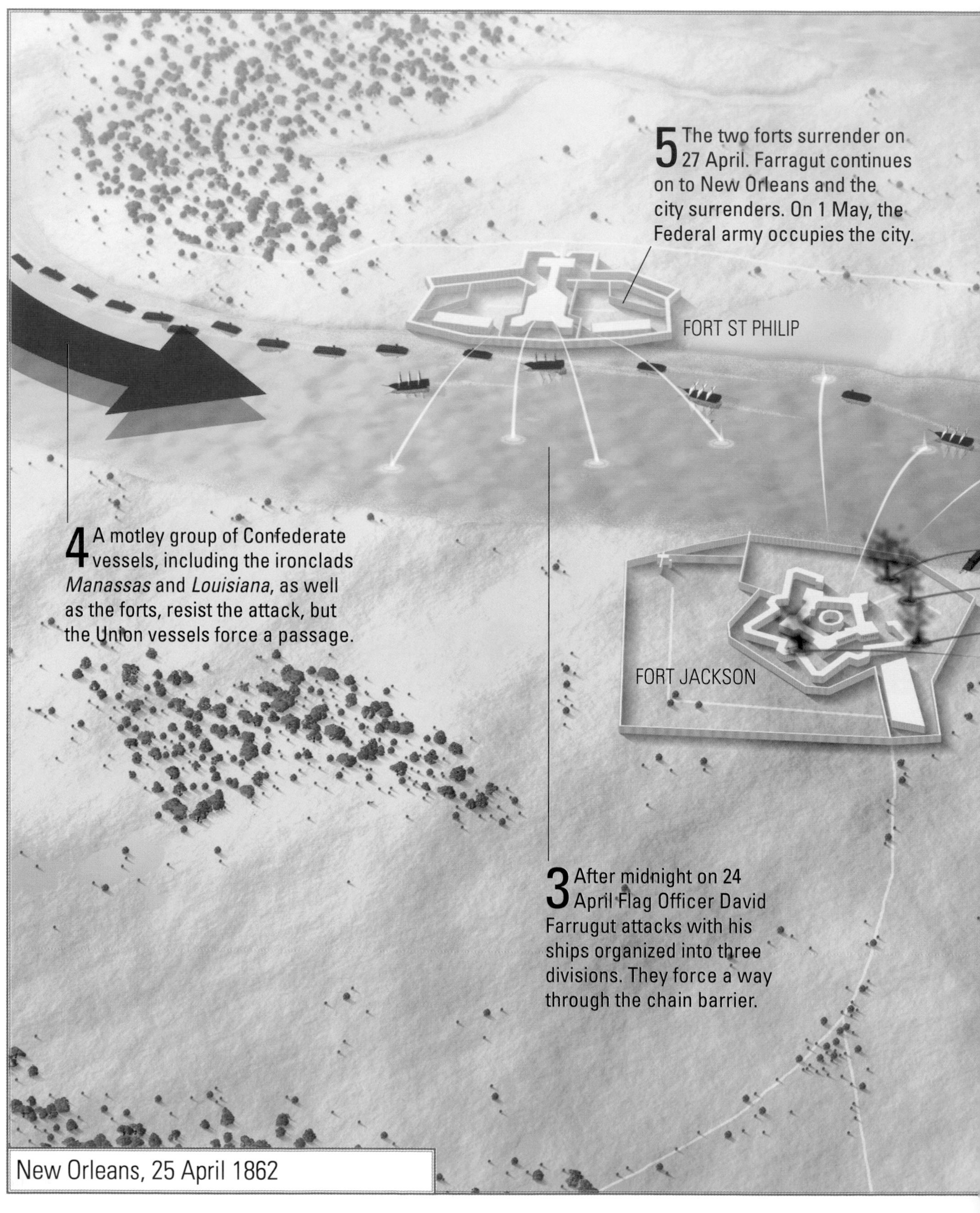

New Orleans, 25 April 1862

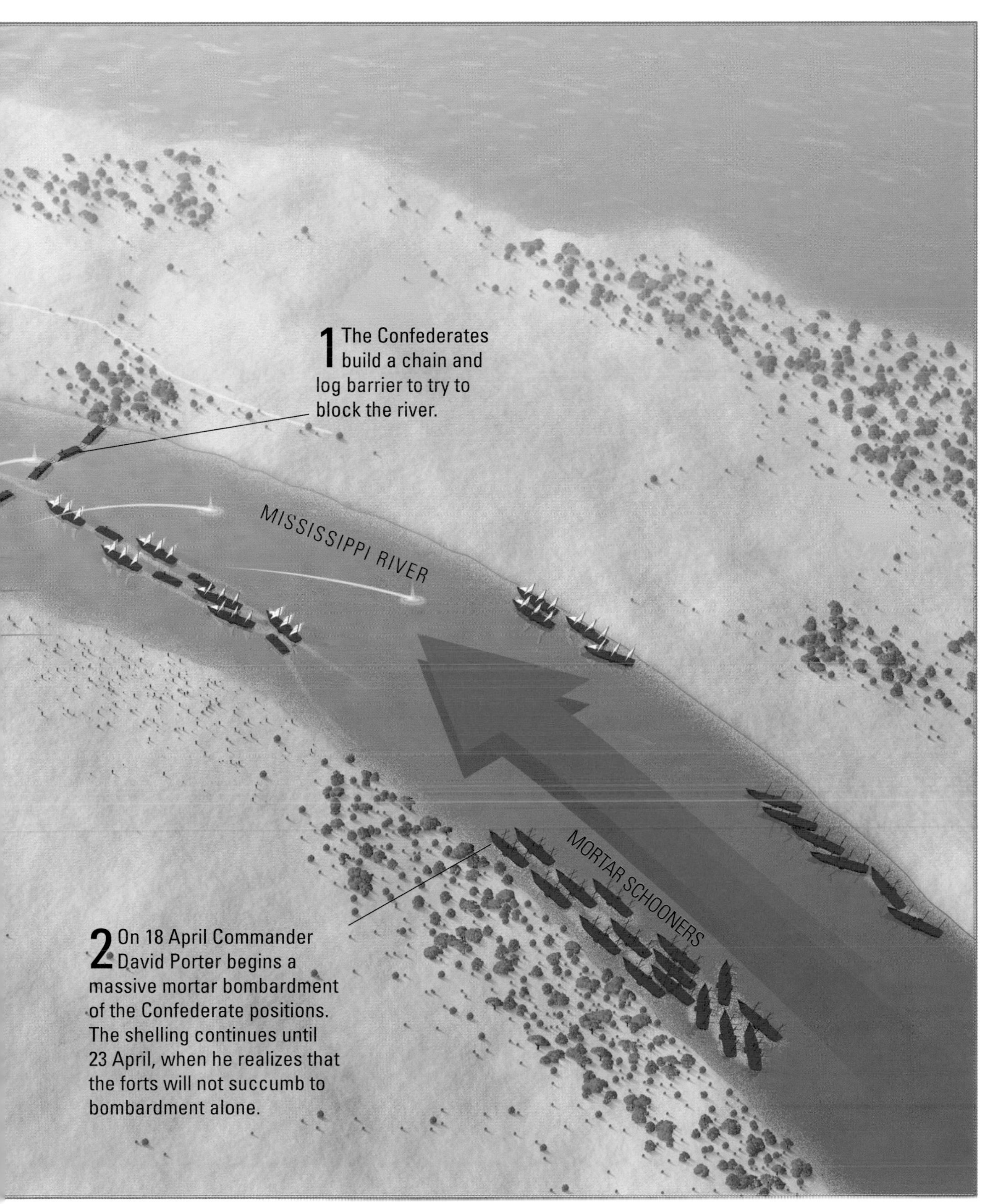
1 The Confederates build a chain and log barrier to try to block the river.
MISSISSIPPI RIVER
MORTAR SCHOONERS
2 On 18 April Commander David Porter begins a massive mortar bombardment of the Confederate positions. The shelling continues until 23 April, when he realizes that the forts will not succumb to bombardment alone.

Theodorus Bailey worked his way through an angry mob and demanded the city's surrender, but the mayor claimed to be under martial law and without authority. When Farragut threatened a bombardment, the mayor and Common Council declared New Orleans an open city. On 1 May, MGen Benjamin Butler and the army began a controversial occupation of New Orleans.

■ **Fort Jackson and Fort St Philip, 25–28 April 1862**

Forts Jackson and St Philip guarded the Mississippi River approaches 120km south of New Orleans. On 18 April, Adm David Porter began a two-day mortar bombardment of the forts that failed to cause them to surrender. After Adm David Farragut captured New Orleans, Porter subjected the forts to additional shelling. Confederate morale waned, and at midnight on 27 April, the troops refused to continue resistance. BGen Johnson Duncan was left with no choice but to surrender his forces to the enemy.

■ **Yorktown, 3 May 1862**

On 5 April, a Federal force commanded by BGen Erasmus Keyes came under fire at Lee's Mill as it marched up the Virginia Peninsula. Based on this small contact, Keyes reported that the Confederate position was too strong to be carried by assault. MGen George McClellan decided to reduce Yorktown by a siege that lasted until 3 May when the Confederates abandoned Yorktown and withdrew up the peninsula.

■ **Williamsburg, 4–5 May 1862**

After abandoning Yorktown, Gen Joseph Johnston withdrew up the Virginia Peninsula, hoping to retreat rapidly to the immediate vicinity of Richmond before MGen George McClellan could get there first. Johnston withdrew along two roads which came together 18km past Yorktown and 3km short of Williamsburg.

BGen Jeb Stuart's cavalry provided the rearguard, and on 4 May, Federal troops caught up with Stuart. Johnston then ordered MGen James Longstreet to fight a delaying action to allow the remainder of the Confederate force to continue withdrawing along the single road from Williamsburg to Richmond. In a sharp battle on 5 May, the Federals committed their forces piecemeal, allowing Longstreet to halt their advance, and then break contact and rejoin the Confederate retreat. Longstreet's successful delay was essential in allowing the Confederates to reorganize to defend Richmond.

■ **McDowell, 8 May 1862**

Leaving MGen Richard Ewell to hold MGen Nathaniel Banks in place, MGen Stonewall Jackson clandestinely moved to McDowell where he defeated MGen John Frémont, preventing him from uniting with Banks.

■ **Plum Rum Bend, 10 May 1862**

The Confederate River Defense Fleet guarded Mississippi River approaches to Memphis, Tennessee. An eight-ship flotilla attacked Federal ships at Plum Rum Bend. During the action the CSS *General Sterling Price* rammed the USS *Cincinnati* and sank it.

■ **Front Royal, 23 May 1862**

Aided by hard marching, deception and intelligence from the legendary spy Belle Boyd, MGen Stonewall Jackson concentrated 16,000 men against about 1000 Federals at Front Royal, Virginia. Jackson inflicted 904 Federal casualties while losing fewer than 50 of his own men. The Confederates also captured some $300,000 worth of supplies. However, when the Federals counter-attacked on 30 May, the commander whom Jackson left to guard the supplies panicked and withdrew towards Winchester.

■ **Winchester, 25 May 1862**

After the Confederate victory at Front Royal, MGen Nathaniel Banks withdrew to Winchester. MGen Stonewall Jackson attacked and routed the Federals there, but was unable to conduct an effective pursuit.

■ **Fair Oaks, 31 May 1862**

On 30 May, Gen Joseph Johnston learned that two Federal corps were south of the Chickahominy River, making MGen George McClellan's army vulnerable to an attack. Johnston developed a plan to use a series of three roads emanating from Richmond to conduct a double envelopment against the isolated corps. The plan quickly began to unravel when MGen James Longstreet marched down the wrong road and became entangled with troops belonging to BGen Charles Whiting and MGen Benjamin Huger. The ensuing confusion delayed Johnston's attack by some five hours, and resulted in MGen D. H. Hill attacking alone. Longstreet attacked later, but of the 29,500 men in the three divisions under his command, he managed to get only 12,500 into the battle. Confederate efficiency was further hamstrung by the fact that an unusual combination of atmospheric conditions precluded Johnston from hearing the sounds of the firing from his headquarters, and he was late in learning the battle was under way.

Towards nightfall, Johnston was severely wounded in the chest and thigh from fragments from an artillery shell and was succeeded by MGen Gustavus Smith who was quickly overwhelmed by his responsibilities. The Confederates launched a weak attack on 1 June that was stopped by Federal reinforcements that had moved from north of the river during the night. At about 14:00, Gen Robert E. Lee, who previously was serving as President Jefferson Davis' military advisor, assumed command of the Confederate forces. After midnight on 2 June, the Confederates retreated to the west. The Confederates lost 6134 killed, wounded or missing and the Federals 5031 during the battle. Its most significant outcome was Lee's rise to command of what became the Army of Northern Virginia.

■ Memphis, 6 June 1862

After the Federals occupied Corinth, Mississippi, Gen Pierre Gustave Toutant Beauregard ordered the Confederate troops to withdraw from Fort Pillow and Memphis, Tennessee. Federal troops occupied Fort Pillow on 4 June, and Flag Officer Charles Davis left one gunboat there in support. Davis and Col Charles Ellet then launched a naval attack on Memphis early on 6 June. Although Ellet and his Ram Fleet were authorized to operate independently of the navy, he and Davis achieved a working arrangement that involved surprisingly little friction. During the hour-and-a-half battle, the Federals sank or captured all vessels of the Confederate River Defense Fleet except for the *General Van Dorn*, the fastest of the Confederate gunboats. Memphis surrendered and was occupied by Federal forces. Ellet was severely wounded in the fighting and he subsequently died a few days later.

■ Cross Keys/Port Republic, 8–9 June 1862

After avoiding a Federal attempt to trap him at Strasburg, MGen Stonewall Jackson positioned MGen Richard Ewell at Cross Keys and stationed his own men at Port Republic. On 8 June, Ewell easily repulsed MGen John Frémont's attack and then withdrew to assist Jackson at Port Republic. Jackson and Ewell defeated BGen James Shields while Frémont watched helplessly from the far side of a bridge that Ewell's men had burned.

■ Seven Days' Battles, 25 June–1 July 1862

MGen Stonewall Jackson reinforced Gen Robert E. Lee after Jackson's Shenandoah Valley Campaign. Lee then went on the offensive, and, in a series of battles collectively known as The Seven Days, forced MGen George McClellan to abandon his Peninsula Campaign.

■ Mechanicsville, 26 June 1862

Gen Robert E. Lee's planned envelopment was thwarted by MGen Stonewall Jackson's uncharacteristic slowness. Instead, MGen A.P. Hill launched four separate unsuccessful frontal attacks against MGen Fitz John Porter's formidable Beaver Dam Creek positions.

■ Gaines' Mill, 27 June 1862

After Mechanicsville, MGen George McClellan ordered MGen Fitz John Porter to fall back to a defendable position covering the Chickahominy River bridges. Porter occupied an excellent defensive position at Turkey Hill about a 1.5km from Gaines' Mill. Porter's line was finally broken by an assault spearheaded by BGen John Bell

Hood. The loss caused McClellan to announce his plans to abandon the Peninsula Campaign and shift his base to Harrison's Landing.

■ **Savage's Station, 29 June 1862**

After Gaines' Mill, Gen Robert E. Lee realized MGen George McClellan was in full retreat. Lee hoped to intercept McClellan using a network of four roads that fanned out to the east and south from Richmond. Leading the immediate pursuit was MGen John Magruder, whom Lee hoped could overtake the Federal rearguard and force it to turn and fight. Magruder caught up with BGen Edwin Sumner at 09:00 on 29 June at Allen's Farm, 3.2km short of Savage's Station. Both Magruder and Sumner fought cautiously, with Sumner delaying back to Savage's Station. Neither general engaged the majority of his force. Darkness and a thunderstorm brought an end to the stalemated fighting, and the Federals withdrew across White Oak Swamp, having lost 1038 men compared to 473 for the Confederates.

■ **Frayser's Farm, 30 June 1862**

Gen Robert E. Lee missed an excellent opportunity to cut off MGen George McClellan from the James River, in part due to MGen Stonewall Jackson's continued slowness. Instead McClellan continued his retreat.

■ **Tampa, 30 June–1 July 1862**

Capt J.W. Pearson's Osceola Rangers turned back a weak attack by the Federal gunboats *Sagamore* and *Ethan Allen* and refused a small landing party's demand to surrender. Neither side suffered any casualties, and the Federals withdrew.

■ **Malvern Hill, 1 July 1862**

After Frayser's Farm, MGen George McClellan retreated to Malvern Hill, another formidable defensive position. There the Federal artillery defeated a Confederate attack, enabling McClellan to complete his withdrawal to Harrison's Landing and entrench.

■ **Baton Rouge, 5 August 1862**

MGen John Breckinridge led Confederate forces

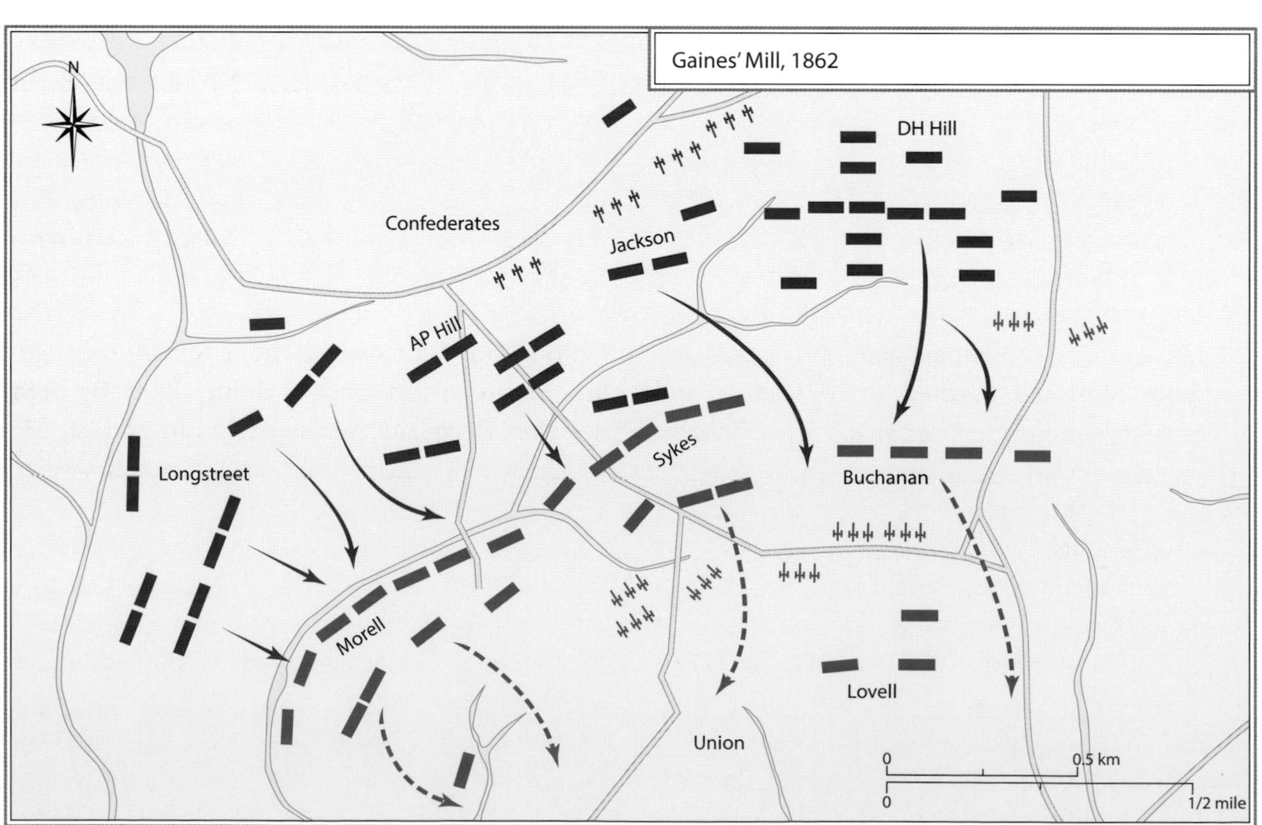

from Camp Moore in an attempt to regain the Louisiana capital city. Breckinridge anticipated assistance from the ironclad CSS *Arkansas*, but the vessel had repeated engine problems, could not participate in the attack, and ultimately was destroyed to prevent capture. Without the support of the *Arkansas*, Breckenridge's force was subjected to shelling by Federal gunboats, and his attack failed to carry the Federal works.

■ **Cedar Mountain, 9 August 1862**

Hoping to attack Federal forces moving towards Culpepper, MGen Stonewall Jackson was instead attacked by MGen Nathaniel Banks. MGen A.P. Hill rescued Jackson, who suffered 1338 casualties compared to 2353 for Banks.

■ **Second Bull Run, 29–30 August 1862**

Once Gen Robert E. Lee determined MGen George McClellan was withdrawing from the Virginia Peninsula, Lee ordered MGen Stonewall Jackson to cut MGen John Pope's line of communication along the Orange and Alexandria Railroad, threatening Washington in the process. Pope was commander of the newly formed Army of Virginia and in his address to his officers and men upon assuming command he crowed, "Let us understand each other. I have come to you from the West, where we have always seen the backs of our enemies; from an army whose business it has been to seek the adversary, and to beat him when he was found; whose policy has been attack and not defense." Pope's boast alienated his men, many of whom remained devoted to McClellan, and also reflected an overconfidence that did not serve Pope well in the upcoming battle.

While Pope was making his grand pronouncements, Jackson marched 92km in two days, descended upon the railroad, destroyed the Federal supply depot at Manassas Junction and occupied a strong defensive position a few kilometres west of Manassas. Still, Pope had 62,000 men compared to Jackson's 20,000, and on 29 August at about 07:00 the Federals attacked. Fighting continued throughout the day, but Jackson was able to absorb the series of piecemeal and uncoordinated frontal assaults from behind the protection of a railroad cut. MGen James Longstreet arrived on Jackson's right flank at about 11:00, but did not attack. Instead he brought his corps next to Jackson's, giving the Confederate line the shape of an open V along a 6.5km front facing the enemy to the east. Throughout the day, Pope had at least four opportunities to follow up a tactical success with a concerted attack. Each time he failed to send reinforcements, and Jackson held on.

Pope, who did not fully realize Longstreet was on the scene, thought Jackson had been weakened in the first day's fighting and attacked again on 30 August. Pope was unknowingly entering a trap and as Pope attacked the Confederate left, Longstreet would be able to envelop the weakened Federal left with five divisions. Pope would be caught between Jackson's anvil and Longstreet's hammer. Adding to the Confederate firepower was the well-placed artillery of Col Stephen Lee that was able to engage the Federals throughout the attack.

By 15:00, the Federals were directly to Jackson's front, and Jackson requested General Lee to send reinforcements. Lee ordered Longstreet forward in a massive counter-attack against the exposed Federal left. Desperately, Pope threw together a makeshift defence that bought the Federals enough time to save his army. The fighting raged along Chinn Ridge for over an hour until the Federal line began to give way at about 18:00. By then, however, Pope had been able to create another line on Henry House Hill. The retention of this position allowed the Federals to escape across Bull Run via the Stone Bridge and nearby fords. By now it was getting dark, and Longstreet ended his attack. Pope withdrew his demoralized force northeast towards Washington, having suffered 14,500 casualties compared to 9500 for Lee. The battle of Bull Run cleared northern Virginia of any major Federal presence and shifted the momentum in the eastern theatre to the Confederates. With Pope defeated

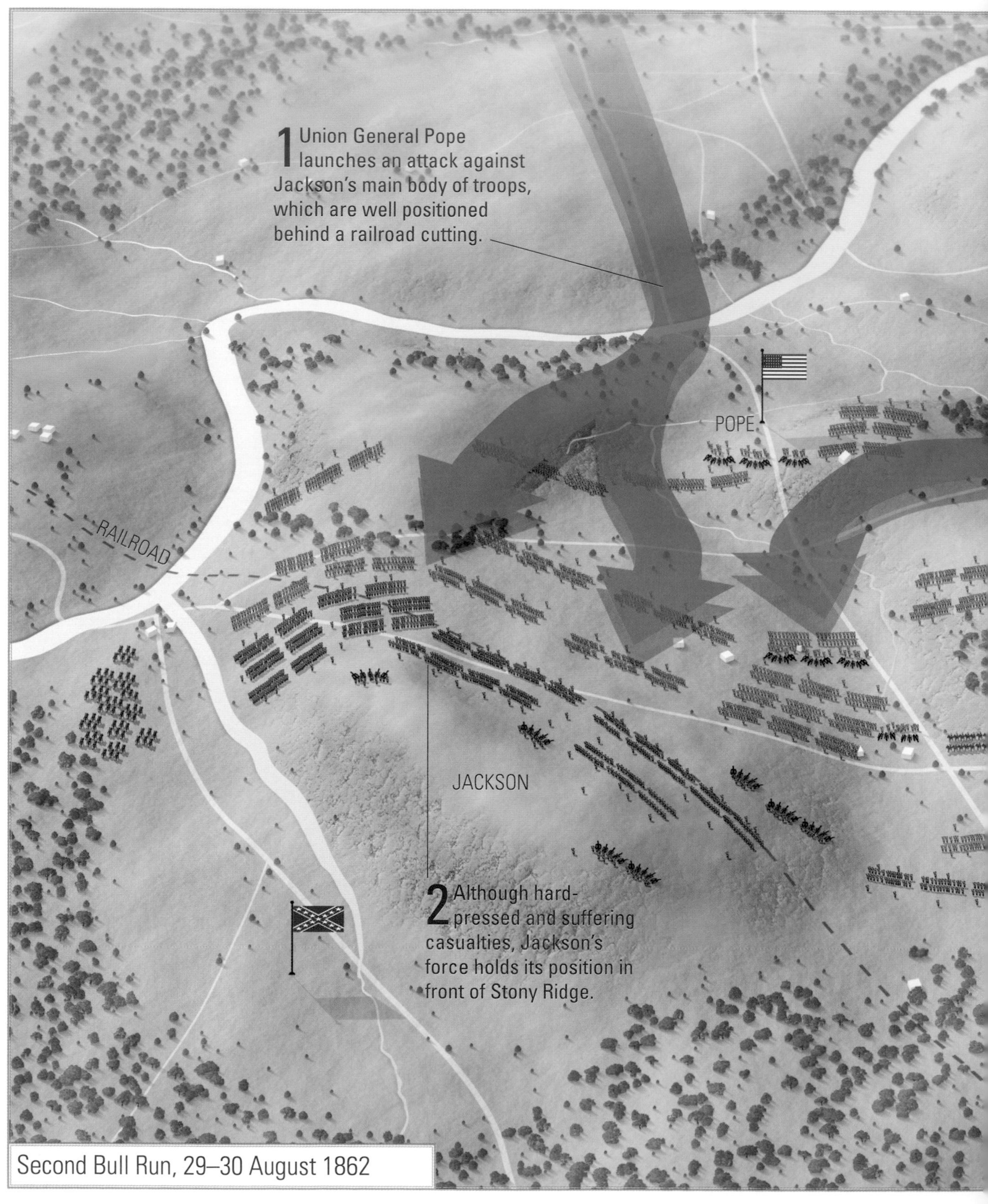

Second Bull Run, 29–30 August 1862

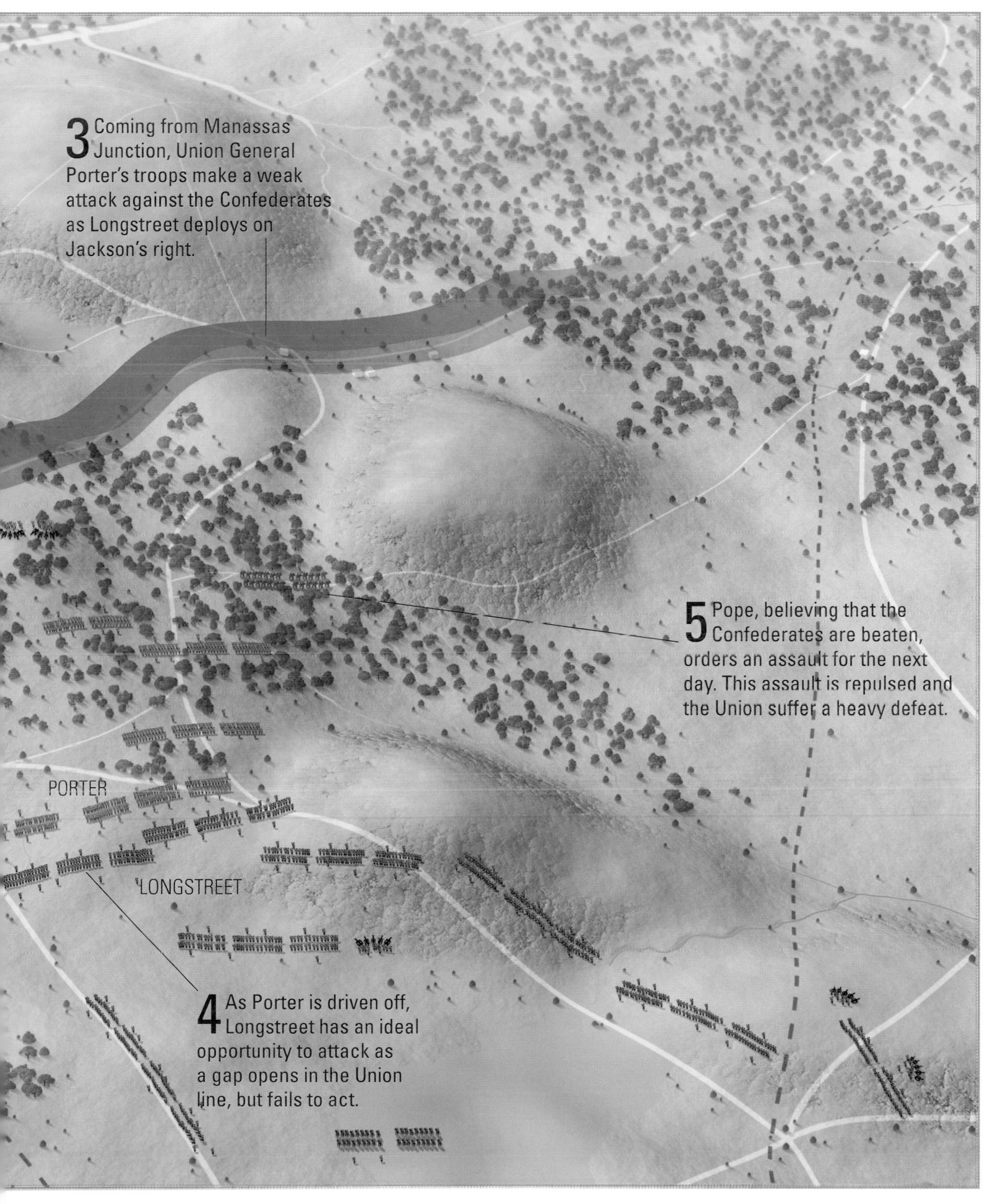
3 Coming from Manassas Junction, Union General Porter's troops make a weak attack against the Confederates as Longstreet deploys on Jackson's right.
5 Pope, believing that the Confederates are beaten, orders an assault for the next day. This assault is repulsed and the Union suffer a heavy defeat.
PORTER
LONGSTREET
4 As Porter is driven off, Longstreet has an ideal opportunity to attack as a gap opens in the Union line, but fails to act.

and McClellan's army withdrawn behind the defences of Washington, Lee saw an opportunity to carry the war into Northern territory and began planning his Antietam campaign.

■ **Groveton, 28 August 1862**

As MGen Stonewall Jackson moved against MGen John Pope's line of communications outside Washington, Jackson fought a sharp skirmish with BGen Rufus King's division. As a result, Pope mistakenly thought Jackson was withdrawing towards the Shenandoah Valley.

■ **Richmond, 29–30 August 1862**

On 29 August, the day after Gen Braxton Bragg began moving towards Kentucky, MGen Edmund Kirby Smith ran into Federal skirmishers, who withdrew to Richmond, Kentucky, after a brief engagement. The next day, Smith attacked the town and sent the Federals in full retreat. The Federals suffered 206 killed, 844 wounded and 4000 captured. Smith lost only 78 killed and 372 wounded. This important victory left Smith virtually unopposed in the territories of eastern Kentucky.

■ **Chantilly, 1 September 1862**

After Second Bull Run, Gen Robert E. Lee kept the pressure on the Federals, causing MGen John Pope to withdraw to the defences of Washington. MGen Philip Kearny was the most notable Federal casualty.

■ **Harper's Ferry, 12–15 September 1862**

As Gen Robert E. Lee began his Antietam campaign, he expected the Federals to abandon their 13,000-man garrison at Harper's Ferry. Instead, they remained in place, forcing Lee to send MGen Stonewall Jackson to deal with this threat. Jackson reached Harper's Ferry on 13 September and encircled the position, but Col Dixon Miles, the Federal commander, did not surrender until 15 September. Jackson then marched to join Lee at Sharpsburg.

■ **Crampton's Gap, 14 September 1862**

Although the Federal forces under BGen William Franklin forced the Confederate defenders from this South Mountain pass, MGen Lafayette McLaws succeeded in preventing Franklin from relieving the besieged Federals at Harper's Ferry.

■ **South Mountain, 14 September 1862**

MGen George McClellan attacked defences at South Mountain and suffered 1813 casualties compared to 2685 for the Confederates. The slowness of McClellan's attack allowed Gen Robert E. Lee to concentrate at Sharpsburg.

■ **Antietam, 17 September 1862**

After his victory at Second Bull Run, Gen Robert E. Lee hoped to offer some relief to the Virginia countryside, influence European intervention and capitalize on Confederate sympathies by invading Maryland. On 4 September he led his 45,000 men across the Potomac River. Opposing him were some 85,000 Federals commanded by MGen George McClellan.

In the preliminary actions, Lee escaped close calls after having to divide his force to reduce Harper's Ferry and having his campaign plan accidentally fall into Federal hands. McClellan's slow responses to these opportunities allowed Lee to concentrate his force at Sharpsburg and establish a defensive line that stretched across the angle formed by the junction of the Potomac River and the Antietam Creek. The terrain favoured the defence and would allow Lee to use interior lines to move forces from one threatened location to another. McClellan's plan was to attack both Confederate flanks in a risky double envelopment and then use his reserve to attack the centre.

The Federal attack began around daybreak with MGen Joseph Hooker's striking the Confederate left. MGen Stonewall Jackson parried each of Hooker's uncoordinated assaults and Lee used the delays between attacks to reposition his forces. By the time MGen Joseph Mansfield launched his echeloned attack next to Hooker's attack, Hooker's men were spent, having withdrawn to the cover of the Federal batteries in front of East Woods. BGen George Greene's division pierced the Confederate line, only to be stopped in front of

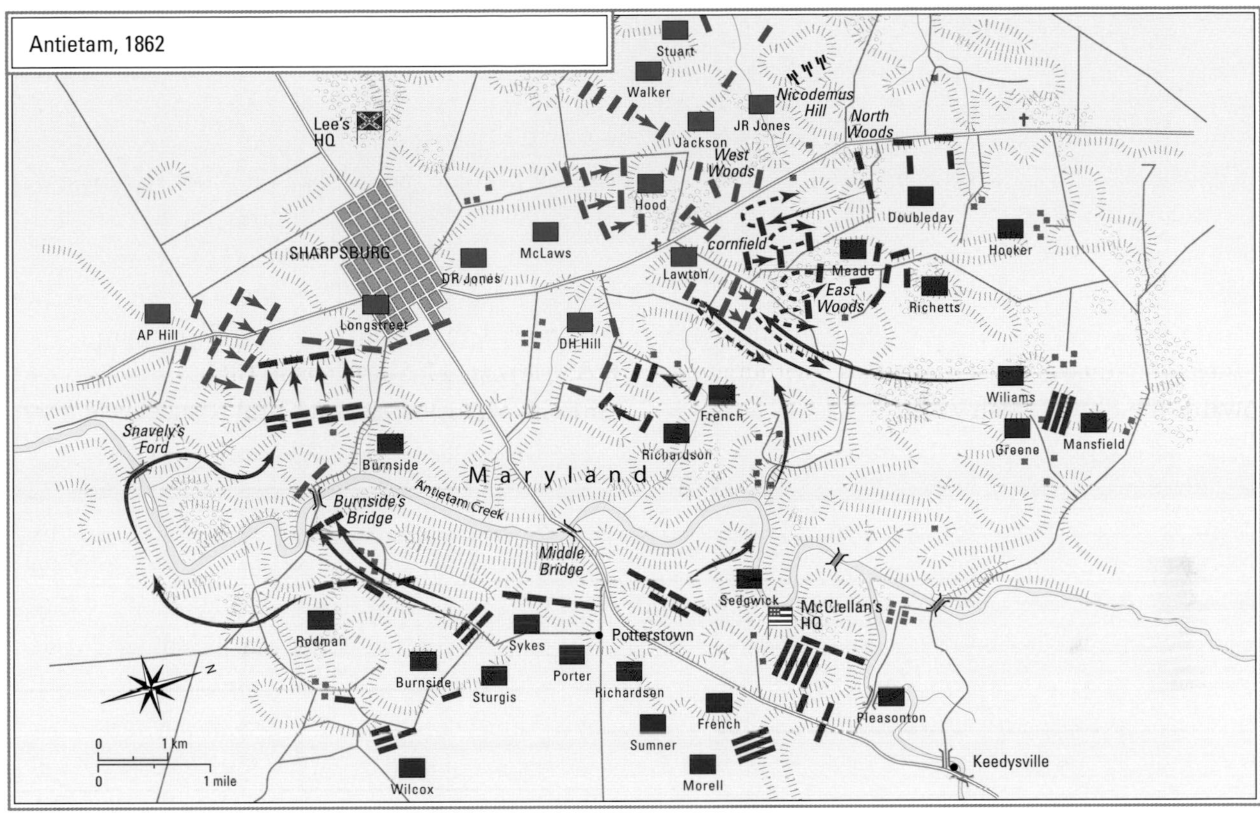

Antietam, 1862

the Dunker Church. In the centre, MGen Edwin Sumner's attack also ground to a halt as MGen John Sedgwick's division was caught in an ambush by Jackson in West Woods and BGen William French's brigade ran into strong Confederate defences in the Sunken Road, the first thousand yards of which became known as the 'Bloody Lane'. The defenders were eventually forced to withdraw from the Sunken Road, exposing a huge gap in the Confederate line. However, rather than pressing the attack, McClellan foolishly kept MGen William Franklin's and MGen Fitz John Porter's corps idle. The Federal attack had broken down into a series of piecemeal and uncoordinated assaults. Still further to the left was perhaps the most notable example of Federal mismanagement of the battle. There, at the Rohrbach Bridge, just 550 Confederates commanded by BGen Robert Toombs delayed 11,000 Federals under MGen Ambrose Burnside. In the nick of time, MGen A.P. Hill's hard-marching 3000-man division arrived from Harper's Ferry, having covered the 27km in seven hours. Hill attacked through a cornfield owned by John Otto, breaking the far left of Burnside's force and causing the Federals to retreat. Hill lacked the numbers to pursue, and by 17:30 the battle was over. Over the course of 12 hours of fighting, 12,400 Federals and 10,300 Confederates were casualties. It was the bloodiest single day in American military history. On the night of 18 September, Lee was forced to abandon his invasion of Maryland and retire across the Potomac.

While the battle of Antietam itself was a tactical draw, the fact that Lee was forced to withdraw back to Virginia made it effectively a strategic victory for the Federals, and that was enough to give President Abraham Lincoln the opportunity he had been waiting for to issue the Emancipation Proclamation, a document that changed the fundamental nature of the war and made the European intervention the Confederacy hoped for highly improbable.

■ Iuka, 19 September 1862

LGen Ulysses Grant attacked MGen Sterling Price at Iuka, hoping to trap him in a pincer between MGens William Rosecrans and E.O.C. Ord. Price escaped, suffering 1516 losses compared to 782 for the Federals.

■ Corinth, 3–4 October 1862

In early October 1862, Confederate commander MGen Earl Van Dorn attacked Federals under MGen William Rosecrans, hoping to seize Corinth's railroad junction. Van Dorn was forced to withdraw after suffering 4467 casualties, compared to 3090 for the Federals.

■ Perryville, 7–8 October 1862

Climaxing Gen Braxton Bragg's invasion of Kentucky, Perryville cost the Federals 4211 casualties compared to 3396 for the Confederates. Although Bragg won a tactical victory, he was forced to withdraw from Kentucky, ending the campaign.

■ Prairie Grove, 7 December 1862

MGen Thomas Hindman launched an offensive that was defeated by the combined Federal forces of BGens James Blunt and Francis Herron. The loss ended any Confederate hopes of regaining northern Arkansas. Both sides lost slightly over 1000 men.

■ Fredericksburg, 13 December 1862

On 7 November 1862, President Abraham Lincoln replaced MGen George McClellan with MGen Ambrose Burnside as commander of the Army of the Potomac. Within a week of assuming command, Burnside launched a new 'On to Richmond' campaign. The plan was to slide past Gen Robert E. Lee's right flank and cross the Rappahannock River at Fredericksburg, about 80km north of Richmond. Burnside would have to cross the Rappahannock quickly before the Confederates could oppose him in force. In order to cross the river, Burnside needed to build a pontoon bridge, but the necessary materials did not arrive until December. By then, Lee had plenty of time to concentrate in and around the town. This development made Burnside's plan obsolete, but he continued with it anyway.

On 11 December, the Federals began crossing the river. Lee did not contest the town, leaving just BGen William Barksdale and 1600 Mississippians there to slow the Federal advance while the main Confederate defence was based on the nearly impregnable positions on Marye's Heights just west of Fredericksburg. There Lee had some 20,000 men under MGen James Longstreet behind a stone wall at the crest of the ridge.

On 13 December, Burnside made six major assaults against Marye's Heights. All failed, but the constricted battlefield prevented Lee from counter-attacking the weakened Federal army. The Federals lost more than 12,500 men while the Confederates fewer than 5500. After the defeat, Burnside attempted to move upstream and cross at Banks' Ford on 23 January 1863, but heavy rains produced a two-day 'Mud March' that stymied the offensive. Amid mounting complaints from his subordinates, Burnside returned to camp near Fredericksburg.

■ Chickasaw Bluffs, 27–29 December 1862

While Confederate cavalry raids forced MGen Ulysses Grant to turn back his supporting attack, MGen William Sherman was repulsed in a frontal assault in this effort to reach Vicksburg. Sherman lost 1776 casualties, compared to 187 for the Confederates.

■ Stones River, 31 December 1862–2 January 1863

After withdrawing from Kentucky, Gen Braxton Bragg established a position alongside the Nashville to Chattanooga railroad line at Murfreesboro, Tennessee. MGen William Rosecrans replaced MGen Don Carlos Buell as the Federal commander and slowly built up his readiness. After amassing a huge logistical base at Nashville, Rosecrans finally began advancing on 26 December. On the night of 29 December, the two armies of 44,000 Federals and 37,000 Confederates were camped within earshot of each other. Rosecrans had ordered an

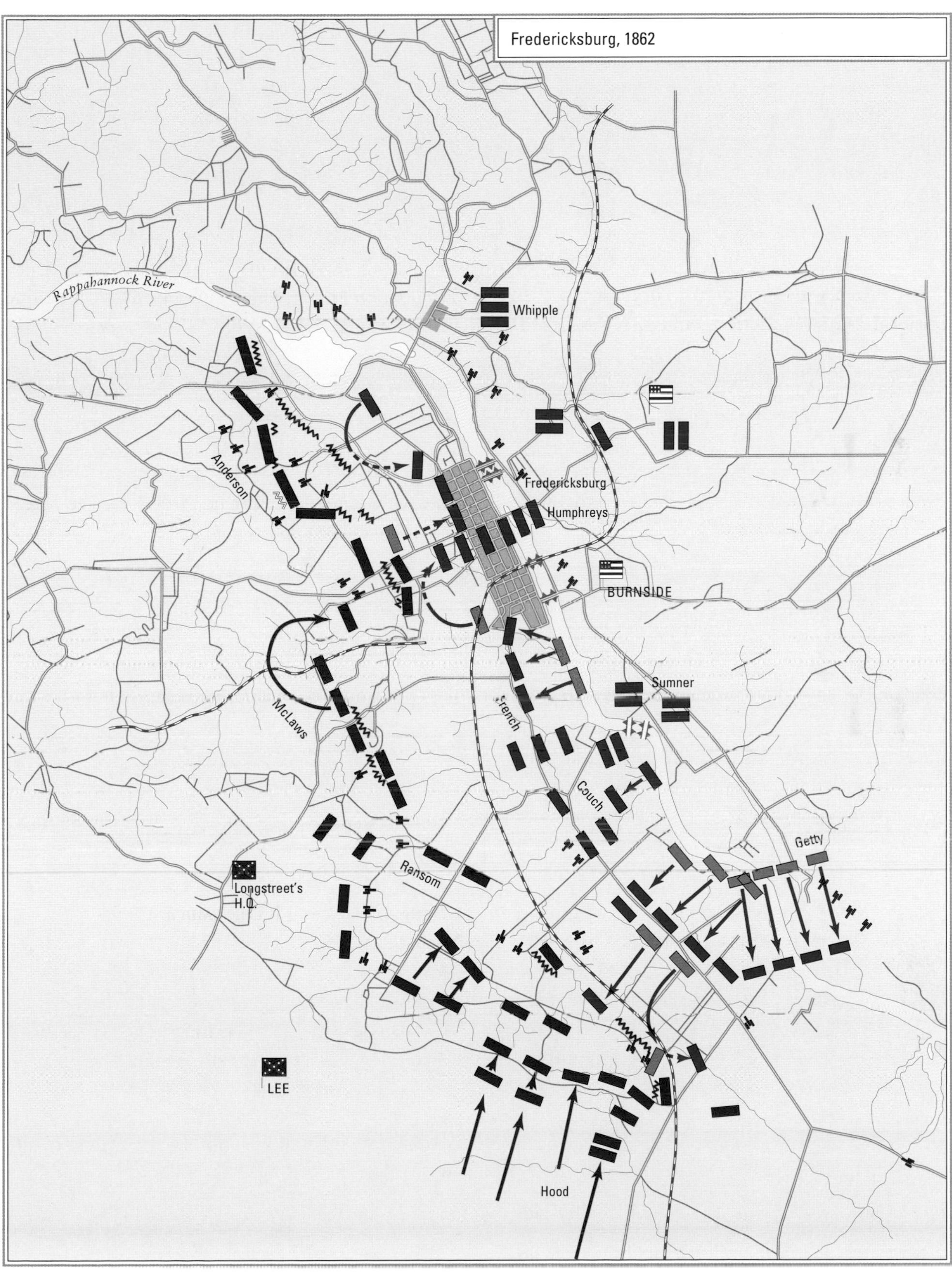
Fredericksburg, 1862
Rappahannock River
Whipple
Anderson
Fredericksburg
Humphreys
BURNSIDE
McLaws
French
Sumner
Couch
Getty
Ransom
Longstreet's H.Q.
LEE
Hood

attack at 07:00, after his men finished breakfast, on 31 December, but before he could put the plan in motion, Bragg struck the Federal right flank in a surprise attack. The Federals repulsed two Confederate attacks, but a third attack succeeded in enveloping the Federal flank. BGen Philip Sheridan counter-attacked and re-established a new Federal line, but a fourth attack all along the Federal front eventually forced Sheridan to withdraw. However, subsequent Confederate attacks were all turned back. Fighting was especially fierce in the Round Forest, where MGen John Breckinridge's Confederates battled Col William Hazen's Federals in an area that became known as 'Hell's Half Acre'.

Both armies were silent on 1 January, and then Bragg renewed the attack, hitting the Federal left on 2 January. The Confederate attack was slow in developing and was defeated by the massed fire of 58 Federal artillery pieces, which had been posted by Maj John Mendenhall. Confederate losses were 11,739 out of a total of 34,739 engaged, while the Federals suffered 12,906 casualties out of 41,400 soldiers. Although Bragg had scored a tactical victory, his army was physically exhausted, and he fell back 50km to Tullahoma. Rosecrans also was spent and did not resume operations until June.

■ **Arkansas Post, 10–11 January 1863**

A land and naval attack by MGen John McClernand and Adm David Porter forced the surrender of this Confederate strongpoint 80km up the Arkansas River from Vicksburg. Most of the 5000 Confederate defenders were captured.

■ **Charleston, 27 April 1863**

Adm Samuel Du Pont's plan to run past the in-depth defences of Charleston Harbor was foiled by Confederate obstacles and fire. The failure led Du Pont to conclude Charleston could not be taken by naval action alone.

■ **Port Gibson, 1 May 1863**

MGen Ulysses Grant began an unopposed crossing of the Mississippi River at Bruinsburg on 30 April. BGen John Bowen attempted to halt Grant's advance inland, but Grant brushed this small force aside and established a foothold at Port Gibson.

■ **Chancellorsville, 1–4 May 1863**

After receiving a report from MGen Jeb Stuart that MGen Joseph Hooker's 'flank was in the air', Gen Robert E. Lee sent LGen Stonewall Jackson on a 17km route to the Federal flank. When Jackson attacked, the Federal line collapsed, causing Hooker to panic and withdraw north of Chancellorsville. Lee inflicted 17,000 casualties while suffering 13,000 himself, but among the Confederate losses was the invaluable commander Stonewall Jackson.

■ **Salem Church, 3–4 May 1863**

In the midst of LGen Stonewall Jackson's success at Chancellorsville, MGen John Sedgwick defeated MGen Jubal Early at Fredericksburg and began moving west. BGen General Cadmus Wilcox and an ad hoc Confederate force stopped Sedgwick at Salem Church.

■ **Vicksburg, 19 May–4 July 1863**

After a series of five failed attempts to break through to Vicksburg between December 1862 and March 1863, MGen Ulysses Grant marched south down the Louisiana side of the Mississippi River and made an unopposed crossing at Bruinsburg on 30 April. Grant's forces closed on Vicksburg on 19 May after a brilliant campaign of manoeuvre that included victories at Port Gibson, Raymond, Jackson and Champion Hill. After two failed assaults on 19 and 22 May, Grant began a siege of Vicksburg. Grant and Confederate commander LGen John Pemberton had similarly sized armies, but the presence of the Federal navy gave Grant a decided advantage. On 25 June and 1 July, Federal troops exploded mines under the Confederate positions, but made no more general assaults. Instead, the city was subjected to incessant shelling throughout the 47-day siege. The Confederate surrender on 4 July gave the Federals control of the Mississippi River and served to split the Confederacy into eastern and western halves.

■ **Jackson, 14 May 1863**

On May 13, MGen Ulysses Grant sent commanders William Sherman and James McPherson on two separate axes toward Jackson. The Federals attacked the next day, capturing the city with little resistance and destroying anything of military value.

■ **Champion Hill, 16 May 1863**

During this decisive battle of the Vicksburg campaign, MGen Ulysses Grant forced LGen John Pemberton to retreat to the defences of Vicksburg and surrender the initiative to Grant. Grant suffered 2441 casualties compared to 3851 for Pemberton.

■ **Big Black River, 17 May 1863**

After his defeat at Champion Hill, LGen John Pemberton retreated to the east side of the Big Black River. MG John McClernand attacked Pemberton, but the Confederates escaped to the defences of Vicksburg.

■ **Port Hudson, 27 May–9 July 1863**

This Confederate stronghold withstood repeated land and naval attacks and finally surrendered after a siege. The capture of Port Hudson, along with the earlier victory at Vicksburg, left the Federals in complete control of the Mississippi.

■ **Franklin's Crossing, 5 June 1863**

MGen Joseph Hooker ordered reconnaissance to determine Gen Robert E. Lee's location as Lee began his Gettysburg campaign. The Federals suffered 41 casualties and captured 35 prisoners in forcing the Confederates from this site.

■ **Brandy Station, 9 June 1863**

After his victory at Chancellorsville, Gen Robert E. Lee pushed north for his Gettysburg campaign behind MGen Jeb Stuart's cavalry screen. In order to determine Lee's dispositions, MGen Joseph Hooker dispatched a cavalry reconnaissance led by MGen Alfred Pleasonton. Pleasonton attacked across the Rappahannock River at 04:00 in two columns. MGen John Buford struck Confederates under BGen W.E. 'Grumble' Jones from across Beverly Ford. Some 10km downstream at Kelly's Ford, BGen David Gregg also attacked. Although Stuart was initially surprised, a counter-attack by MG Wade Hampton helped the Confederates maintain control of the battlefield. The Confederates were also helped by the fact that Col Alfred Duffie, a Frenchman who was supposed to attack with Gregg, was delayed in a fight with Confederates at Stevensburg, 9km to the south. Duffie did not reach Brandy Station in time to participate in the battle. Although Federal infantry was on the field and Confederate infantry was moving to it, Brandy Station was predominantly a cavalry battle. In fact, it was the biggest cavalry battle of the war. Overall, the battle of Brandy Station was tactically inconclusive, with the Confederates suffering 523 losses compared to 936 for the Federals. However, Pleasanton had succeeded in learning the Confederates whereabouts, and Stuart had failed in his screening mission. It was a humiliation for Stuart, and many consider his ill-advised extended reconnaissance at Gettysburg to have been an attempt to repair his reputation after this setback. The battle is also considered a turning point after which Confederate cavalry no longer dominated their Federal counterparts in the Eastern Theatre.

■ **Winchester, 13–15 June 1863**

As the Army of Northern Virginia moved north on the Gettysburg campaign, MG Richard Ewell soundly defeated MGen Robert Milroy. The Federals lost 4443 in the disaster, compared to just 269 for Ewell.

■ **Gettysburg, 1–3 July 1863**

Building on the momentum of his victory at Chancellorsville, Gen Robert E. Lee launched a second invasion of Northern territory. In the meantime, President Abraham Lincoln replaced MGen Joseph Hooker with MGen George Meade on 28 June. Lee advanced north into Pennsylvania virtually unopposed, but because MGen Jeb Stuart, Lee's eyes and ears, had gone on an ill-advised raid around the Federal army, Lee was ignorant of the Federal dispositions. By 30 June, Lee had gathered most of his army in the area of Chambersburg, Cashtown and Heidlersburg. Meade had been pushing his army north, staying to the east of Lee's army in order to protect Washington and Baltimore.

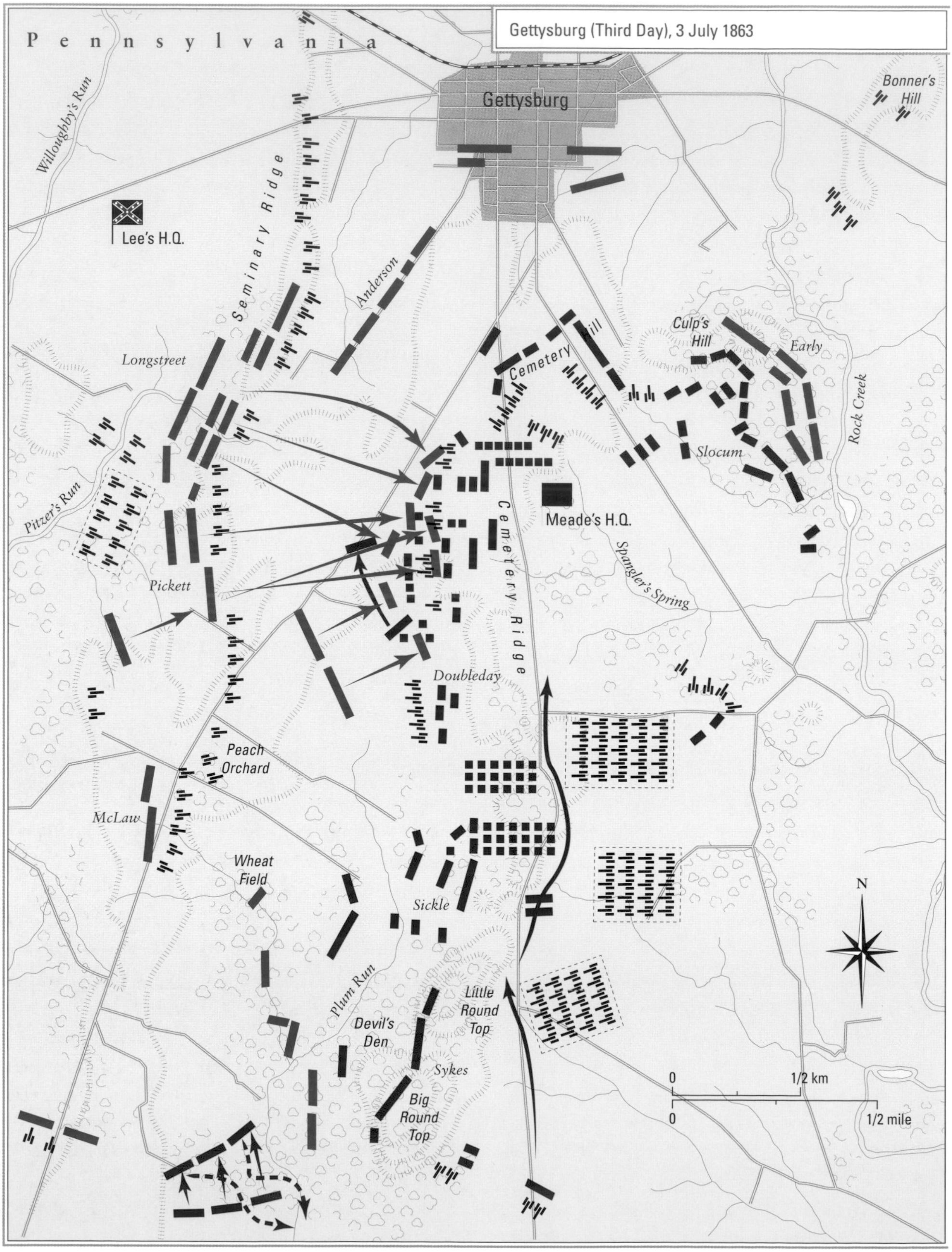

Gettysburg (Third Day), 3 July 1863

Pennsylvania
Gettysburg
Bonner's Hill
Willoughby's Run
Seminary Ridge
Lee's H.Q.
Anderson
Culp's Hill
Early
Cemetery Hill
Longstreet
Rock Creek
Slocum
Pitzer's Run
Meade's H.Q.
Cemetery Ridge
Spangler's Spring
Pickett
Doubleday
Peach Orchard
McLaw
Wheat Field
Sickle
Plum Run
Little Round Top
Devil's Den
Sykes
Big Round Top
N
0 1/2 km
0 1/2 mile

On 30 June, Meade advised MGen John Reynolds that it seemed Lee would concentrate his forces near the small town of Gettysburg. Reynolds thus sent BGen John Buford and two cavalry brigades towards Gettysburg to find Lee.

On 1 July, Buford encountered a Confederate brigade that had marched to Gettysburg in search of some shoes reported to be there. A meeting engagement ensued in which both Lee and Meade competed to rush forces to the location. Because the Confederates were closer, Lee was able to gain the upper hand. However, MGen Oliver Howard wisely occupied Cemetery Hill for the Federals. This hill on the north end of Cemetery Ridge dominated the approaches to Gettysburg and would be key to any defensive effort. Receiving only a discretionary order from Lee, LGen Richard Ewell did not attack the position, giving the Federals a critical piece of terrain.

Lee wanted to press the advantage he had gained in the first day's fighting, and, over the objections of LGen James Longstreet, who favoured assuming a strong defensive position, Lee ordered an attack against the left of the Federal line in the vicinity of Little and Big Round Tops on 2 July. Longstreet did not attack until 16:30 and by then Meade had rushed defenders to Little Round Top. After hard fighting, the Federals retained the key hill and the second day of the battle ended in a stalemate.

Having struck the Federal right the first day and the left the second, Lee now resolved to attack the Federal centre on 3 July. At 13:00, the Confederates initiated a 172-gun pre-assault bombardment, but most of the rounds sailed over the heads of the Federal defenders on Cemetery Ridge. With the Federal line still largely intact, MGen George Pickett began his charge at about 13:45. His men met a devastating fire from the Federal artillery, and gaps soon appeared in the Confederate line. BGen Lewis Armistead led his men to the 'High Water Mark of the Confederacy', but MGen Winfield Scott Hancock repulsed the attack, and the scattered remnants of 'Pickett's Charge' staggered back across the field. The attack had caused 54 per cent losses to the Confederates. As Pickett's beaten men fell back, Lee said, "It's all my fault." Although Meade had defeated Lee, it had been a close call, and Meade was in no mood to press his victory. Both sides had been badly hurt, with Lee suffering 28,063 losses and Meade 23,049. In spite of urgings by President Lincoln, Meade allowed Lee to withdraw back into Virginia, ending his second invasion of the North. The defeat cost Lee manpower he could ill-afford to lose and ended his ability to launch further offensives.

■ **Fort Wagner, 10 and 18 July 1863**
The Federals launched multiple attacks on this position guarding the land approach to Charleston from Morris Island. In the famous 18 July attack, the Federals suffered 1515 casualties compared to 174 for the Confederates.

■ **Chickamauga, 19–20 September 1863**
Enjoying the rare advantage of numerical superiority, Gen Braxton Bragg inflicted 16,170 casualties on MGen William Rosecrans while suffering 18,454 of his own. Then, instead of aggressively pursuing, Bragg laid siege to Rosecrans in Chattanooga.

■ **Bulltown, 13 October 1863**
Confederates led by Col William Jackson attempted to capture the small fort overlooking the Little Kanawha River in West Virginia. Jackson was repulsed after suffering light casualties. The Federals were commanded by Capt William Mattingly.

■ **Bristoe Station, 14 October 1863**
Misinterpreting the size of the Federal force, LGen A.P. Hill was soundly defeated by Federal forces defending behind the Orange and Alexandria Railroad embankment. The Confederates lost 1428 men compared to 446 for the Federals.

■ **Knoxville, 17 November–5 December 1863**
After a rearguard action at Campbell's Station, MGen Ambrose Burnside withdrew to the fortifications around Knoxville, Tennessee. LGen James Longstreet began a siege which he abandoned after the Federal victory at Chattanooga.

Union and Confederate troops exchange close-range volleys at Chickamauga, September 1863. The Federals experienced their biggest defeat in the Western Theatre, suffering 16,000 casualties.

■ Chattanooga, 23–25 November 1863

In a pivotal campaign in which the Federals lost 5800 and the Confederates 6700, MGen Ulysses Grant forced Gen Braxton Bragg to retreat to Dalton, Georgia, opening the gateway to the heartland of the Confederacy.

■ Orchard Knob/Indian Hill, 23 November 1863

BGen Thomas Wood and MGen Philip Sheridan drove in Confederate outposts on Orchard Knob, a low ridge between Chattanooga and Missionary Ridge. Gen Braxton Bragg then reinforced the extreme right of his line.

■ Lookout Mountain, 24 November 1863

MGen Joseph Hooker attacked the Confederate left at Lookout Mountain to the south of Chattanooga. MGen Carter Stevenson commanded the defence. Hooker won this 'Battle above the Clouds', suffering 710 casualties and inflicting 521 on the Confederates.

■ Missionary Ridge, 25 November 1863

MGen Ulysses Grant ordered MGen George Thomas to create a diversion in the centre of the Confederate defence outside Chattanooga to allow MGen William Sherman to continue making progress to the left. Thomas's attack was supposed to be just a limited one, but individual soldiers seized the initiative and turned the operation into a full-scale attack. Gen Braxton Bragg was forced to withdraw, ending the siege of Chattanooga.

■ Olustee, 20 February 1864

After an unopposed landing at Jacksonsville, Florida, BGen Truman Seymour advanced inland to Baldwin where he was joined by MGen Quincy Gillmore. Seymour met little resistance until approaching BGen Joseph Finnegan's 5000 Confederates entrenched near Olustee. After driving in Finnegan's outposts, Seymour incurred heavy losses as Finnegan launched several attacks. Seymour retreated back to Jacksonville, having suffered 1860 casualties. Finnegan, who had lost 946 of his own men, did not pursue.

■ Sabine Crossroads/Pleasant Hill, 9 April 1864

MGen Nathaniel Banks advanced some 240km up the Red River, forcing LGen Richard Taylor to withdraw to defensive positions 5km southeast of Mansfield, Louisiana, at Sabine Crossroads. Taylor was an independent-minded subordinate, and, without coordinating with his commander Gen Edmund Kirby Smith, he attacked Banks' advancing force at Mansfield on 8 April. Although Taylor was unsuccessful in his effort to turn the Federal right, he did force Banks to withdraw to Pleasant Hill, where Taylor attacked him the next day. Although Taylor was outnumbered, he expected the Federals to be demoralized and cautious after the fighting at Mansfield. He attacked at 17:00, hoping to fix the Federals with a frontal attack while another attack led by BGen Thomas Churchill enveloped the left flank and Taylor's cavalry blocked the escape route on the right. Churchill succeeded in breaking the Federal left, but as he pressed on to attack the Federal centre from the rear, his right flank came under attack. Taylor ordered BGen C.J. Polignac's reserve brigade forward to stop the Federal counter-attack, but Polignac did not arrive in time. Instead, Polignac acted as a covering force while Churchill retreated. In spite of this victory, Banks began withdrawing from west Louisiana, abandoning his objective of capturing Shreveport for fear of suffering further damage to his army. Although he had repulsed Banks, Taylor complained that Smith's unwillingness to concentrate his forces prevented the annihilation of the Federal army. The Federals suffered 2000 losses compared to 1100 for the Confederates. After the battle, the Confederates left a cavalry force to screen Banks's men entrenched at Grand Ecore and began moving against MGen Frederick Steele in Arkansas.

■ Fort Pillow, 12 April 1864

MGen Nathan Bedford Forrest surrounded this position in Lauderdale County, Tennessee, and,

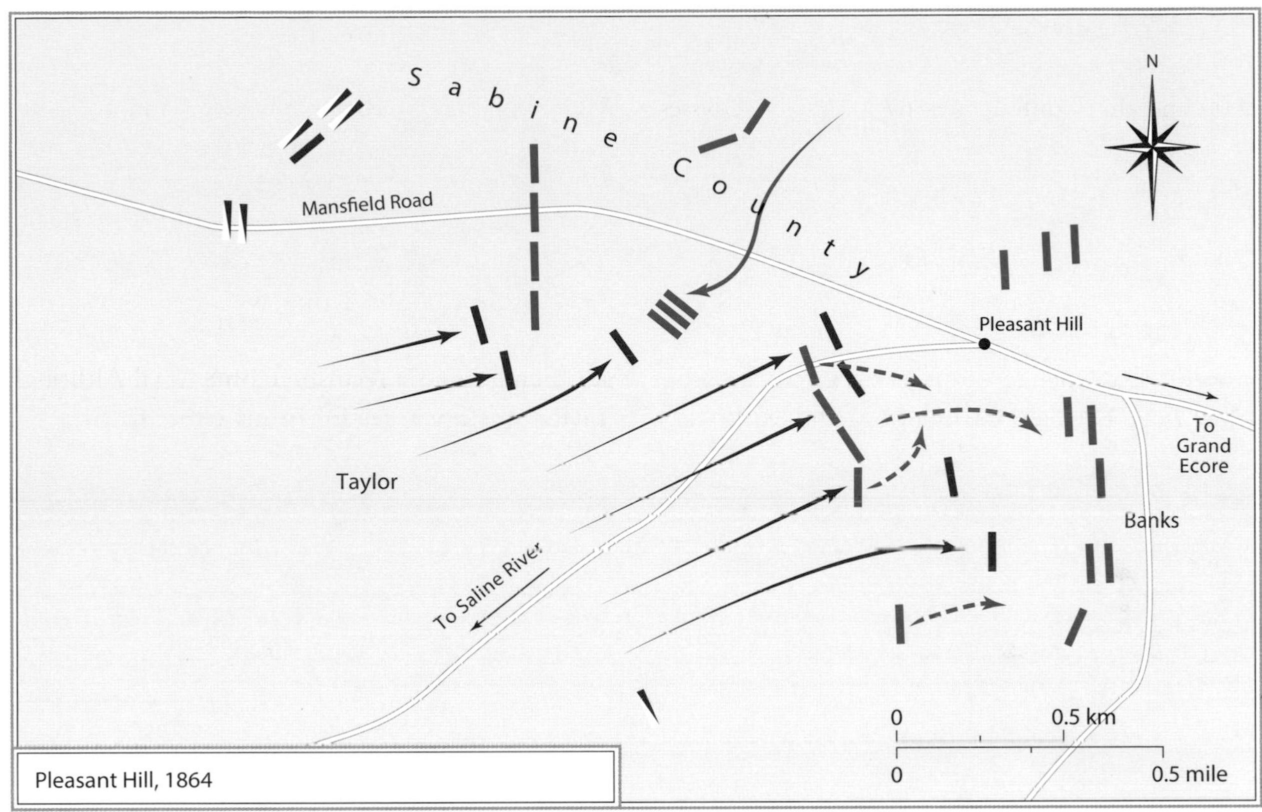

Pleasant Hill, 1864

when the Federals refused to surrender, Forrest attacked. During the overwhelming Confederate victory, Forrest's men were accused of massacring black soldiers after they had surrendered.

■ **Alexandria, 1–8 May 1864**

In a series of actions, Confederate forces, including BGen J.P. Major's cavalry, harassed MGen Nathaniel Banks during his Red River campaign, destroying five Federal boats and blocking the Red River between 4 and 13 May.

■ **Wilderness, 5–7 May 1864**

As part of his comprehensive strategy to press the Confederacy on all fronts, LGen Ulysses Grant crossed the Rapidan River on 4 May 1864, into an area of Virginia appropriately called the Wilderness. Neither side knew the other's exact location until 5 May, when the Federals made contact with LGen Richard Ewell's corps and launched a hasty attack, which the Confederates halted. When the fighting resumed the next day at 05:00, Gen Robert E. Lee used the restrictive terrain to offset Grant's numerical advantage. The thick vegetation made the battle a small-unit fight. At one point, Lee vowed personally to lead BGen John Gregg's Texas Brigade into the fray, only to be dissuaded by the men's passionate pleas of 'Lee to the rear'. Although Lee scored a tactical victory, inflicting 17,000 Federal casualties compared to 10,000 of his own, the Confederacy could ill afford the lost manpower.

■ **Spotsylvania, 7–12 May 1864**

In spite of his defeat at the Wilderness, LGen Ulysses Grant continued to keep pressure on the Confederates. Grant began a march to flank Gen Robert E. Lee and cut him off at Spotsylvania Courthouse. Lee ascertained Grant's intentions and narrowly beat Grant to the strategic location. Once there, Lee established a defence, the flanks of which Grant probed on 9 and 10 May without success. During the attack on 10 May, Grant took notice of a technique used by Col Emory Upton to attack in column formation against

Spotsylvania, 1864

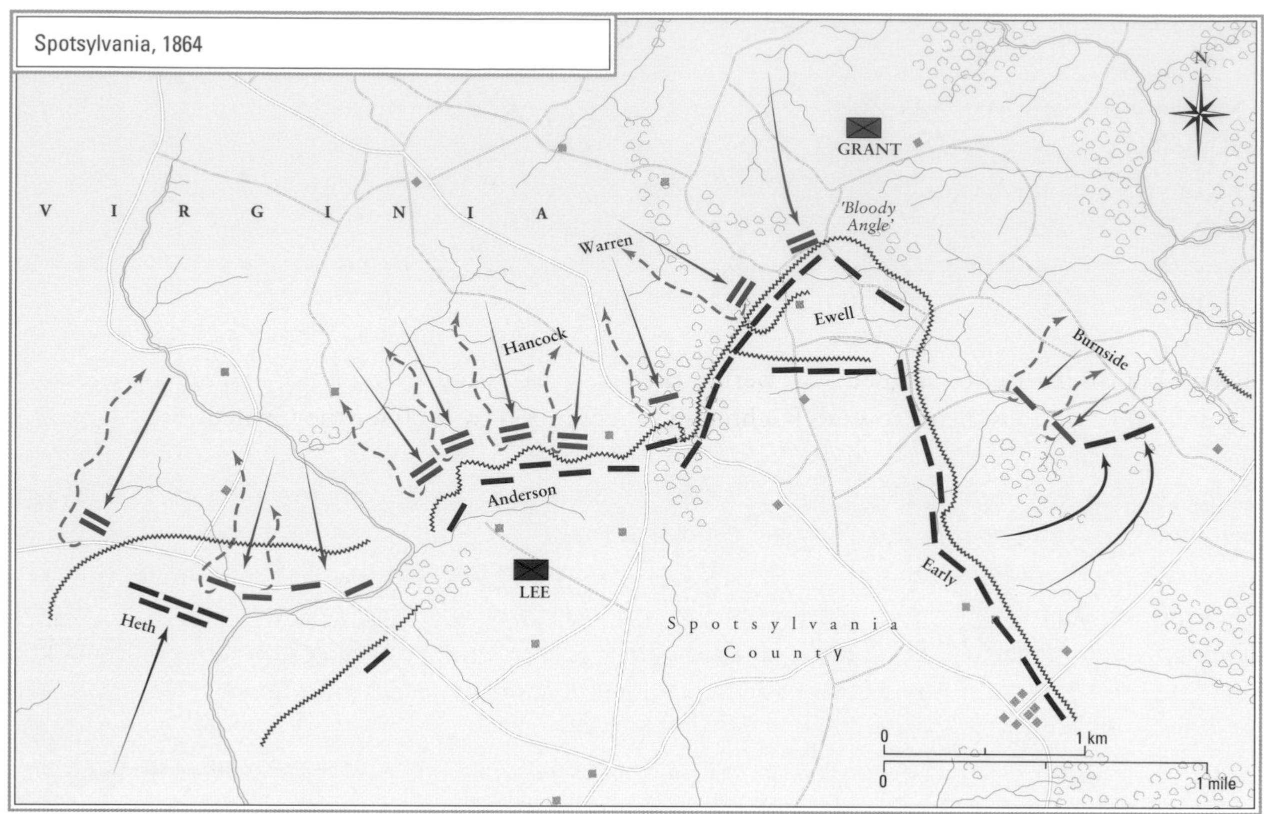

a salient in the Confederate line known as the 'Mule Shoe'. Upton had not been able to hold his original gains because of a lack of troops, but Grant saw promise in the new tactic. He decided to send MGen Winfield Scott Hancock's entire corps against the Mule Shoe. On 12 May at 04:30, a massed attack of 20,000 Federals advanced, and in just 15 minutes they were pouring through gaps in the Confederate lines. Hancock captured 4000 Confederate prisoners. In a desperate attempt to restore the breach, Lee counter-attacked and succeeded in completing a new line of entrenchments across the base of the salient. For nearly 20 hours the ferocious fighting continued almost without pause. The contested area became known as "the Bloody Angle". There was more inconclusive fighting on 18 and 19 May, but the Confederate line held. Fighting mostly behind the protection of entrenchments, Lee suffered just 12,000 casualties compared to Grant's 18,000. Among the Federal losses was MGen John Sedgwick. Lee withdrew on 20 May to a new position at Hanover Junction, thwarting another attempted turning movement by Grant.

■ Yellow Tavern, 11 May 1864

MGen Jeb Stuart attempted to block MGen Philip Sheridan's raid towards Richmond. Sheridan overran the Confederates, but decided to move to the James River rather than continuing to Richmond. Stuart was mortally wounded in the fighting.

■ Resaca, 13–16 May 1864

As MGen William Sherman began his Atlanta campaign, Gen Joseph Johnston withdrew from Rocky Face Ridge to the hills to the north and west of Resaca before becoming decisively engaged. Sherman attacked Johnston's new position, and the fighting was inconclusive until Sherman sent a force across the Oostanula River at Lay's Ferry that threatened Johnston's railroad communications with Calhoun. Johnston then withdrew, having suffered 2800 casualties compared to 2747 for Sherman.

■ New Market, 15 May 1864

MGen Franz Sigel's advance up the Shenandoah Valley was challenged by MGen John Breckinridge, whose force included a battalion of cadets from the Virginia Military Institute. Sigel was forced to retreat to Strasburg.

■ Drewry's Bluff, 16 May 1864

MGen Benjamin Butler landed at Bermuda Hundred and began advancing towards Richmond. Gen Pierre Gustave Toutant Beauregard attacked, forcing Butler to withdraw and leaving him 'bottled up' on the peninsula between the Appomattox and James rivers.

■ North Anna River, 23–27 May 1864

Although Gen Robert E. Lee's novel defensive configuration forced LGen Ulysses Grant to split his army in three places, Lee was unable to capitalize on this advantage and Grant withdrew across the North Anna River.

■ New Hope Church, 25–27 May 1864

MGen William Sherman marched around Gen Joseph Johnston's left flank, heading towards Dallas. Johnston intercepted Sherman at New Hope Church. Thinking Johnston had only a token force, Sherman attacked and was easily repulsed.

■ Cold Harbor, 3 June 1864

LGen Ulysess Grant outnumbered Gen Robert E. Lee 108,000 to 59,000, but the Confederates delivered enfilading fire from carefully prepared trenches. Grant lost 7000 men in a disastrous frontal attack while Lee lost only 1500.

■ Piedmont, 5 June 1864

MGen David Hunter replaced MGen Franz Sigel after Sigel's defeat at New Market and renewed the Federal offensive in the Shenandoah Valley. As Hunter advanced, he divided his force to avoid BGen W.E. 'Grumble' Jones's defensive position en route to Staunton. In order to prevent the two Federal columns from reuniting, Jones attacked Hunter, only to be driven back to defensive positions at Piedmont, about 11km southwest of Port Republic. Amid attacks and counter-attacks, the Confederates were routed and Jones was killed. Hunter entered Staunton unopposed the next day. After he was joined by BGen George Crook, Hunter marched to Lynchburg, destroying much military and public property as he went. Among the targets of Hunter's rampage was the Virginia Military Institute, which he ordered burned on 12 June. Federal losses at Piedmont were 875 compared to 1500 for the Confederates.

■ Brice's Crossroads, 10 June 1864

LGen Nathan Bedford Forrest soundly defeated BGen Samuel Sturgis, inflicting 2610 casualties compared to just 495 of his own. In spite of the defeat, Sturgis succeeded in distracting Forrest from MGen William Sherman's lines of communication.

■ Trevilian Station, 11–12 June 1864

LGen Ulysses Grant hoped to create a diversion and draw off the Confederate cavalry while he crossed the James River to attack Petersburg. He ordered MGen Philip Sheridan to cut the Virginia Central Railroad. Gen Robert E. Lee sent MGen Wade Hampton to meet this serious threat. Fighting on 11 June was inconclusive, but when Sheridan attacked the next day, he was repulsed with heavy losses and forced to abandon his campaign.

■ Lynchburg, 17–18 June 1864

After his victory at Piedmont, MGen David Hunter advanced to the important rail centre at Lynchburg. Gen Robert E. Lee dispatched LGen Jubal Early to the Shenandoah Valley to reinforce MGen John Breckinridge. The Confederate forces defeated Hunter's attack on Lynchburg, preventing him from joining MGen Philip Sheridan for Sheridan's Trevilian Raid. After the defeat, Hunter withdrew to West Virginia, opening the way for Early's advance into Maryland.

■ Petersburg, 19 June 1864–13 April 1865

Unable to turn Gen Robert E. Lee's flank and break through to Richmond, LGen Ulysses Grant decided to shift his line of advance south of the

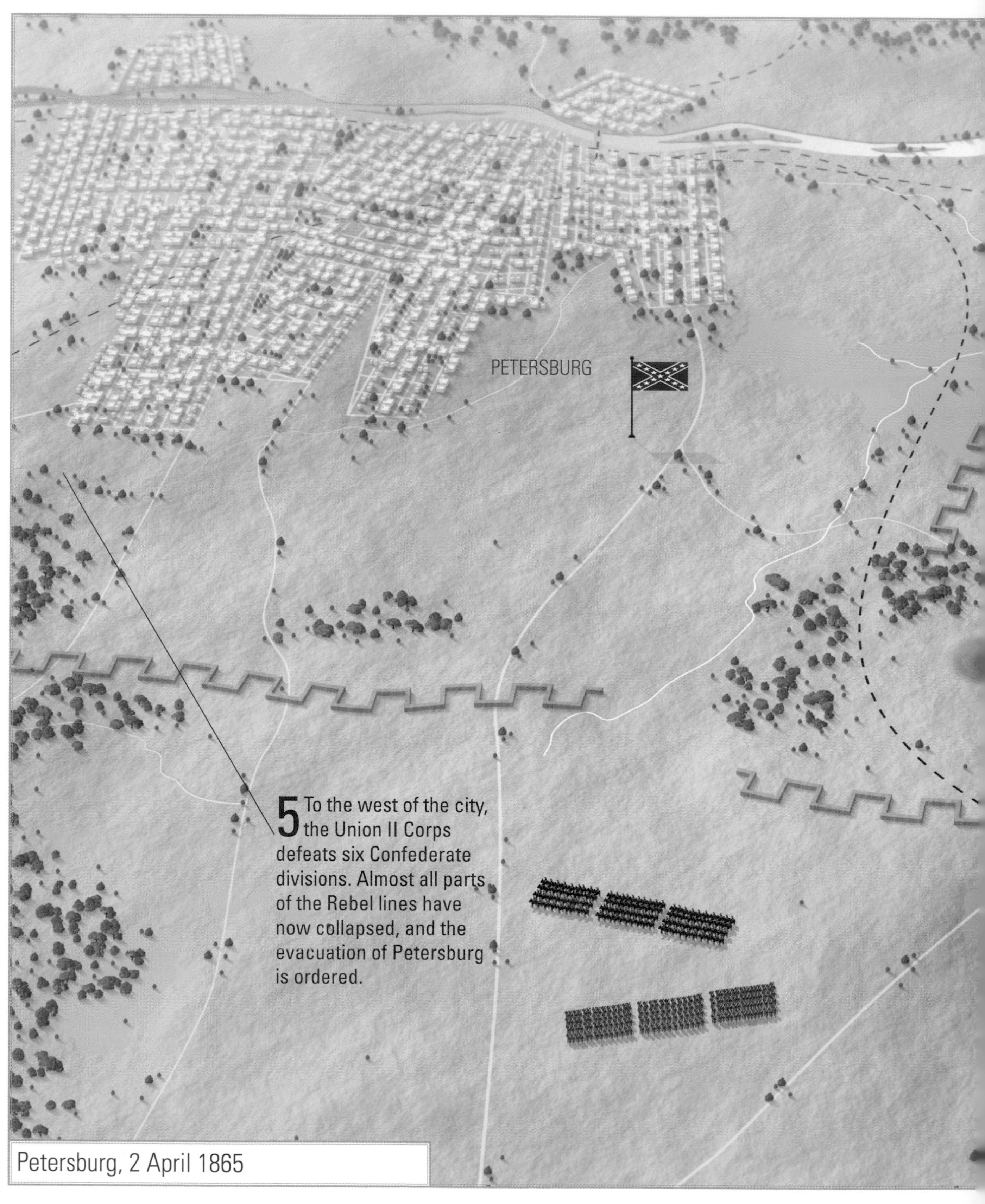
PETERSBURG
5 To the west of the city, the Union II Corps defeats six Confederate divisions. Almost all parts of the Rebel lines have now collapsed, and the evacuation of Petersburg is ordered.
Petersburg, 2 April 1865

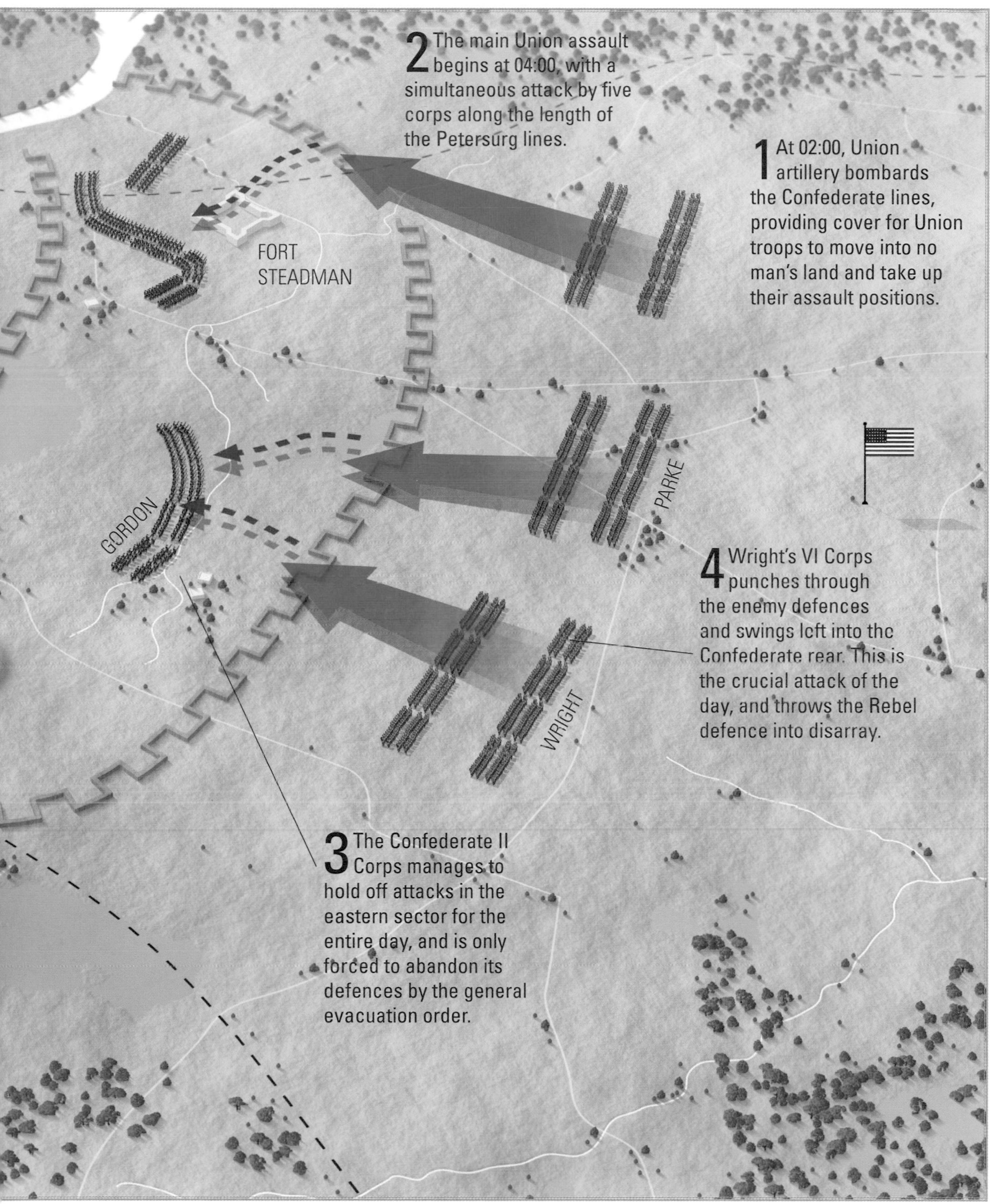
2 The main Union assault begins at 04:00, with a simultaneous attack by five corps along the length of the Petersurg lines.
1 At 02:00, Union artillery bombards the Confederate lines, providing cover for Union troops to move into no man's land and take up their assault positions.
FORT STEADMAN
GORDON
PARKE
4 Wright's VI Corps punches through the enemy defences and swings left into the Confederate rear. This is the crucial attack of the day, and throws the Rebel defence into disarray.
WRIGHT
3 The Confederate II Corps manages to hold off attacks in the eastern sector for the entire day, and is only forced to abandon its defences by the general evacuation order.

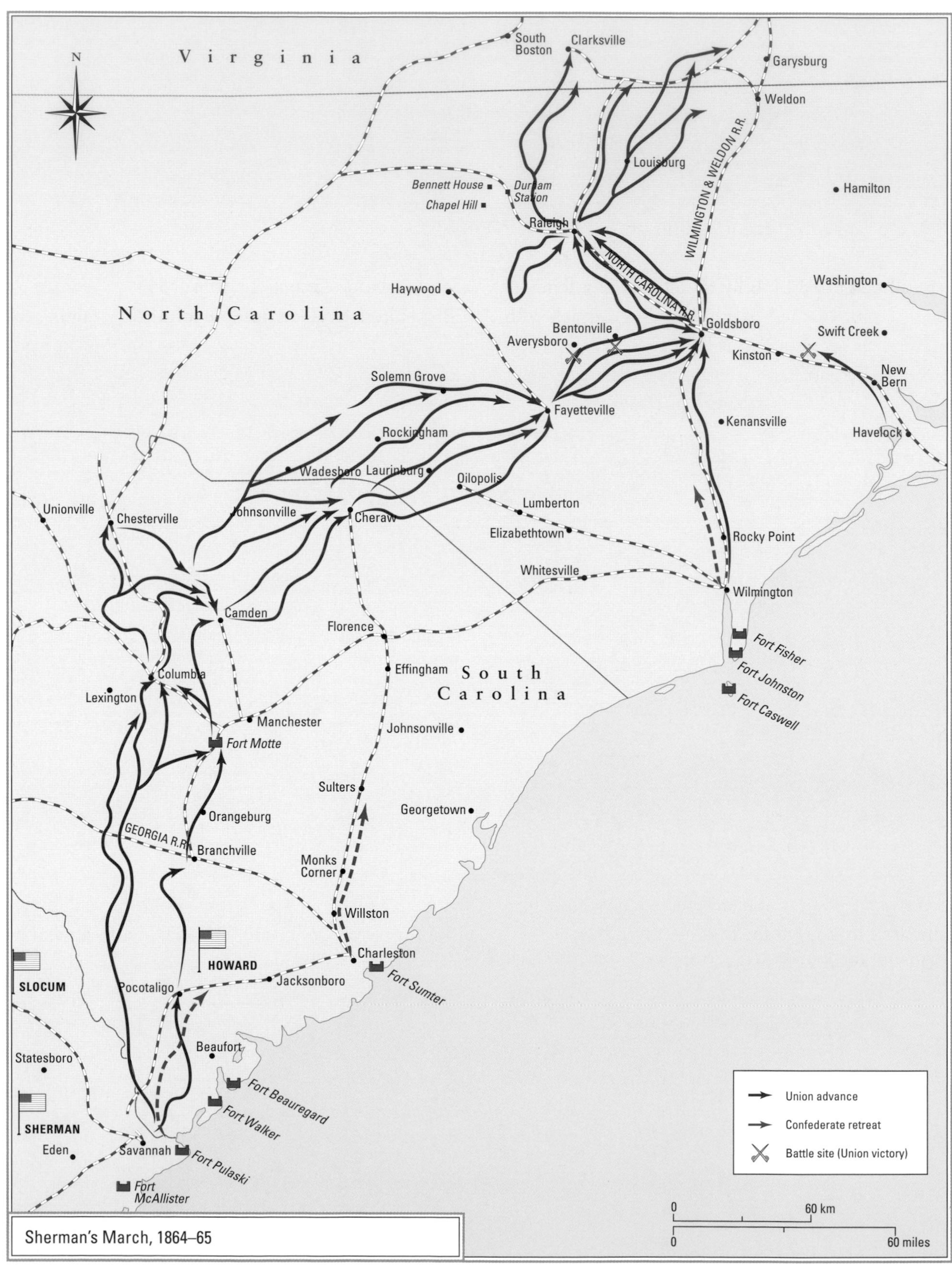

Sherman's March, 1864–65

James River and use the river as his line of supply for an advance on Petersburg, about 32km south of Richmond. Petersburg was a shipping port as well as a rail centre and many of the supplies headed for both Richmond and Lee's army passed through there, making it critical to the survival of the Army of Northern Virginia. Once Grant decided to shift his line of advance, he got a jump on Lee, crossing the James River and reaching Petersburg while it was still defended by only a skeleton Confederate force. Grant launched an uncoordinated attack with his entire army on 18 June 1864, but was repulsed. By then Lee had arrived with reinforcements. The next day Grant began what would become the longest siege of the war.

During the siege, Grant built up a huge logistical base at City Point that benefited from outstanding rail and water communications. Grant had access to excellent supply, repair and medical facilities to help sustain his force. The result was that as Lee weakened inside Petersburg, Grant grew stronger outside. Pressing this advantage, Grant kept extending his lines to the west. When MGen Philip Sheridan joined Grant from the Shenandoah Valley, Grant gave him an infantry corps and told him to break Lee's western flank. In the ensuing battle of Five Forks on 1 April 1865, Sheridan pressed Lee, and Grant then ordered a general attack all along the Petersburg front. Faced with this threat, Lee was forced to abandon Petersburg, and the city fell on 3 April. Grant's men suffered 42,000 casualties compared to 28,000 for Lee.

■ **Kennesaw Mountain, 27 June 1864**

MGen Sherman deviated from his series of turning movements en route to Atlanta and was soundly defeated by Gen Joseph Johnston in a disastrous frontal attack. Sherman lost about 3000 compared to 1000 for Johnston.

■ **Monocacy, 9 July 1864**

With LGen Jubal Early advancing on Washington, MGen Lew Wallace rushed a hastily organized defence to Monocacy Junction, Maryland. Although the Federals suffered 1880 casualties compared to just 700 for the Confederates, the threat to the capital subsided.

■ **Tupelo, 13–15 July 1864**

Attempting to prevent LGen Nathan Bedford Forrest from interfering with MGen William Sherman's Atlanta campaign, MGen Andrew Jackson Smith was engaged by the combined forces of Forrest and LGen Stephen Lee and forced to withdraw towards Memphis.

■ **Peachtree Creek, 20 July 1864**

Exasperated by Gen Joseph Johnston's failure to make a stand north of Atlanta, President Jefferson Davis replaced him with the combative LGen John Bell Hood. With Sherman closing in from the north and east, Hood ordered an attack as MGen George Thomas crossed Peachtree Creek. After a series of failed assaults, Hood was forced to withdraw to the defences of Atlanta, having suffered 4796 casualties compared to 1710 for the Federals.

■ **Atlanta, 22 July 1864**

As part of LGen Ulyssess Grant's coordinated strategy for the spring of 1864, MGen William Sherman was directed "to move against [Confederate Gen Joseph] Johnston's army, to break it up, and to get into the interior of the enemy's country as far as you can, inflicting all the damage you can against their war resources". Atlanta, with its vital supply, manufacturing and transportation assets, was such an objective. Johnston fought a retrograde battle from Dalton, Georgia, to the outskirts of Atlanta until he was relieved by President Jefferson Davis and replaced with the more aggressive and impulsive LGen John Bell Hood. In a desperate attempt to keep Sherman from taking Atlanta, Hood launched the battle of Peach Tree Creek on 20 July. Repulsed, Hood attacked again on 22 July. All told, Hood suffered 8499 casualties and failed to break the Federal line. MGen John McPherson was among the 3641 Federal casualties.

■ **Kernstown, 23–24 July 1864**

LGen Jubal Early attacked a weakened Federal force commanded by BGen George Crook after

Union troops wait in a shallow trench during the siege of Petersburg. The siege consisted mainly of trench warfare, with General Grant's stranglehold on the city finally causing Confederate commander Lee to withdraw in March 1865, after holding out for nine months.

Early withdrew from the outskirts of Washington on 12 July. Crook suffered 1200 casualties and was forced to retreat across the Potomac River.

■ **Crater, 30 July 1864**

In a bungled attempt to break the stalemate at Petersburg, LGen Ulysses Grant detonated an explosion under the Confederate position. The Confederates inflicted 5300 casualties on the Federals while suffering just 1032.

■ **Mobile Bay, 5 August 1864**

Adm David Farragut's attack on one of the few Confederate ports still open to blockade runners was challenged by a series of well-placed forts, the ironclad CSS *Tennessee* and a dangerous minefield. When Farragut's ironclad *Tecumseh* struck a torpedo and went down swiftly, Farragut famously declared, "Damn the torpedoes! Full speed ahead." As the Federal fleet pressed forward, its starboard batteries unloaded on Fort Morgan. The Confederates hit some of the ships, but Farragut was able to complete his run past the fort. His main threat now was the *Tennessee*, commanded by Adm Franklin Buchanan. The Tennessee withstood repeated Federal broadsides, but with only six hours of coal left, Buchanan was forced to attack. As Buchanan approached, Farragut ordered his fleet to descend on the *Tennessee*, and after a spirited fight, Buchanan was forced to surrender. The Federals suffered 319 casualties in the brief naval battle, including 93 who drowned when the *Tecumseh* sank. Confederate losses were much higher with 312 casualties of the 470 engaged.

The Confederate forts held out only slightly longer against Federals commanded by BGen Gordon Granger. The Confederates abandoned tiny Fort Powell, blowing it up as they departed. Fort Gaines mustered a faint-hearted show of resistance and then surrendered the next day on 8 August. Fort Morgan was a stronger defence, but BGen Richard Page had only 400 men to oppose Granger's 5500. After receiving a siege train from New Orleans, the Federals began a heavy land and naval bombardment. The Confederate defenders raised a white flag over Fort Morgan on 22 August. The Federals captured 1464 prisoners.

■ **Winchester, 19 September 1864**

MGen Philip Sheridan used some 40,000 men to attack LGen Jubal Early's 11,500 Confederates positioned to the north and east of Winchester. The Federals suffered 5020 casualties compared to 3610 for the Confederates. Early then withdrew past Strasburg.

■ **Fisher's Hill, 21–22 September 1864**

After Winchester, LGen Jubal Early took up a defensive position south of Strasburg, which he was forced to abandon when MGen Philip Sheridan attacked. The battle opened the unfortunate Shenandoah Valley to Sheridan's scorched-earth tactics.

■ **Centralia, 27 September 1864**

'Bloody Bill' Anderson, a notorious Confederate bushwacker, unleashed a massacre on this Missouri town 80km north of Jefferson City. Anderson captured a train and murdered 24 unarmed soldiers. He also defeated a Federal attack 5km from the town.

■ **Cedar Creek, 19 October 1864**

After his success in the Shenandoah Valley, MGen Philip Sheridan began preparing to join LGen Ulysses Grant against Gen Robert E. Lee. While Sheridan was at a conference in Washington, LGen Jubal Early crossed the Shenandoah River at Fisher's Hill and attacked the surprised Federals along Cedar Creek. Sheridan rushed back from Washington and reversed Early's initial success. The Federals suffered 5665 casualties and the Confederates 2910.

■ **Spring Hill, 29 November 1864**

Gen John Bell Hood missed his best chance to damage MGen John Schofield's army as it moved from Columbia to Franklin. Instead, Hood made his disastrous attack on Franklin the next day.

■ **Franklin, 30 November 1864**

LGen John Bell Hood evacuated Atlanta on 1 September 1864, and the Federals moved in to

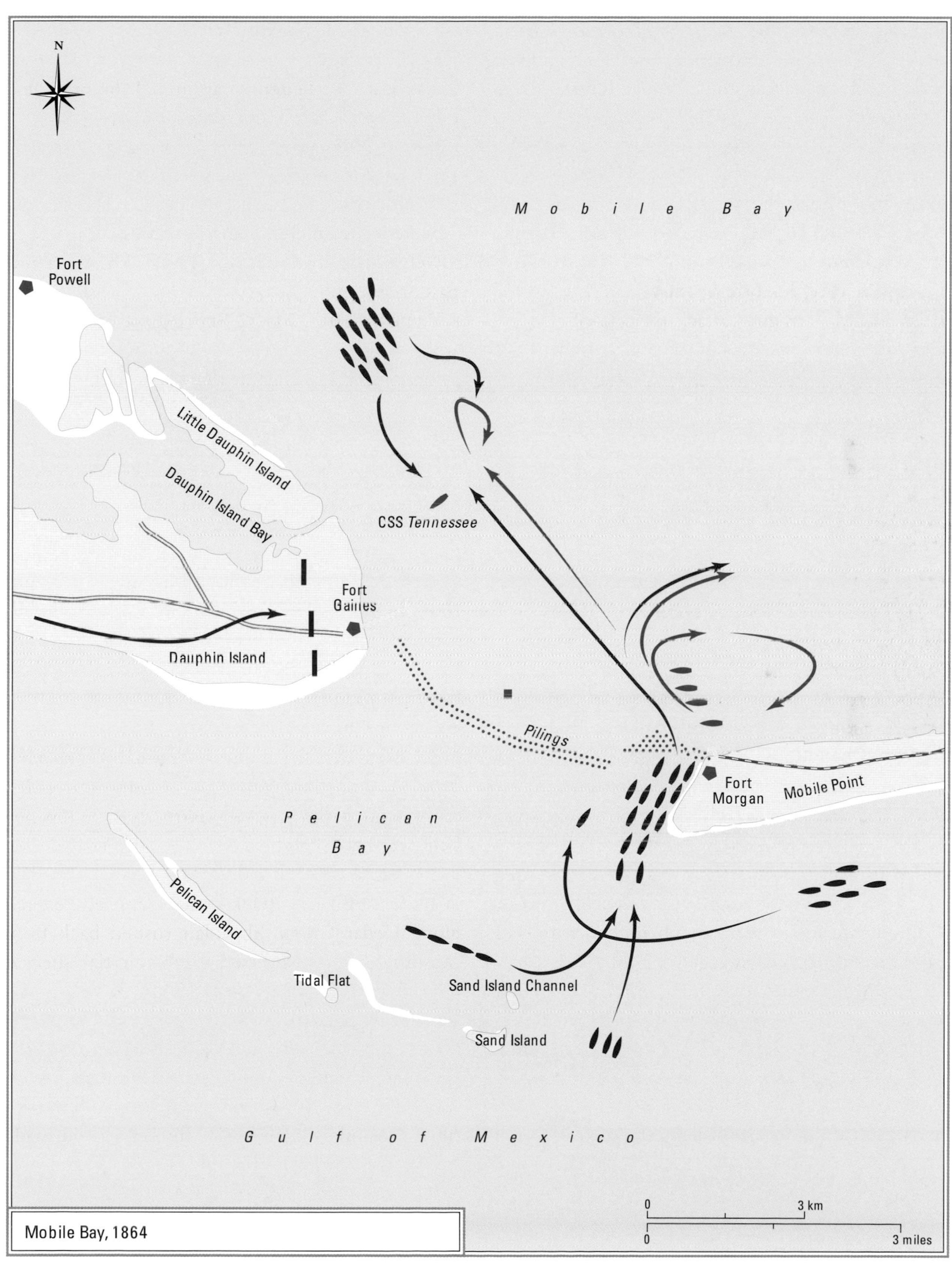

Mobile Bay, 1864

occupy the city the next morning. Hood then marched north into Tennessee, hoping to recover middle Tennessee and force MGen William Sherman to abandon Atlanta by threatening his communications. Rather than following Hood in force, Sherman dispatched only MGen George Thomas's corps. Contrary to LGen Grant's desire that he attack, the methodical Thomas opted to delay Hood, who succeeded in turning MGen John Schofield's position near Columbia, Tennessee.

By 30 November, Schofield had taken up a position at Franklin, about 50km south of Nashville. The wisest course would have been to execute another turning movement, but, instead, the impetuous Hood attacked in a disastrous frontal assault. Hood lost more than 6000 men, as well as whatever limited offensive capability he had once had. He withdrew his 30,000 men to the outskirts of Nashville, a place occupied by 70,000 entrenched Federals.

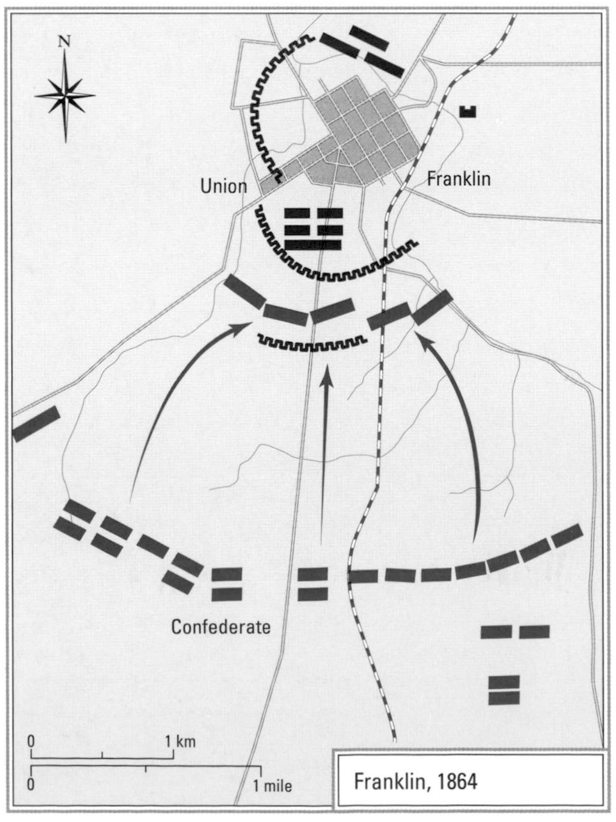

Franklin, 1864

■ **Nashville, 15 December 1864**
MGen George Thomas launched a massive flank attack from his entrenched position that overwhelmed the Confederates. After suffering 4500 casualties, Gen John Bell Hood retreated to Tupelo, Mississippi, and asked to be relieved of command.

■ **Savannah, 21 December 1864**
MGen William Sherman reached Savannah on 10 December on his famous 'March to the Sea' campaign. After LGen William Hardee evacuated it on 20 December, Sherman presented Savannah as a 'Christmas present' to President Abraham Lincoln.

■ **Fort Stedman, 25 March 1865**
MGen John Gordon attacked this strongpoint in the Petersburg siege line in hopes of threatening the Federal supply depot at City Point. It was not to be – a Federal counter-attack forced Gordon to retreat from his early gains after suffering 2900 losses.

■ **Fort Fisher, 12–15 January 1865**
MGen Alfred Terry replaced MGen Benjamin Butler after Butler's failed attack in December 1864. Supported by an accurate naval bombardment from the offshore guns of Adm David Porter, Terry attacked Fort Fisher with a force of 8000 men. Col William Lamb's force of just 1500 Confederate soldiers defended stubbornly, but the superior Federal numbers captured the fort. With the loss of Fort Fisher, Wilmington, the last remaining Southern port was closed, completing the Confederacy's isolation from overseas goods.

■ **Bentonville, 19 March 1865**
Bentonville was the last time Gen Joseph Johnston could muster the strength to fight MGen William Sherman as the Federals advanced through North Carolina. Johnston asked for an armistice on 14 April and surrendered on 26 April.

■ **Five Forks, 1 April 1865**
After his success in the Shenandoah Valley, MGen Philip Sheridan joined LGen Ulysses Grant in the siege of Petersburg, Virginia. Grant gave Sheridan

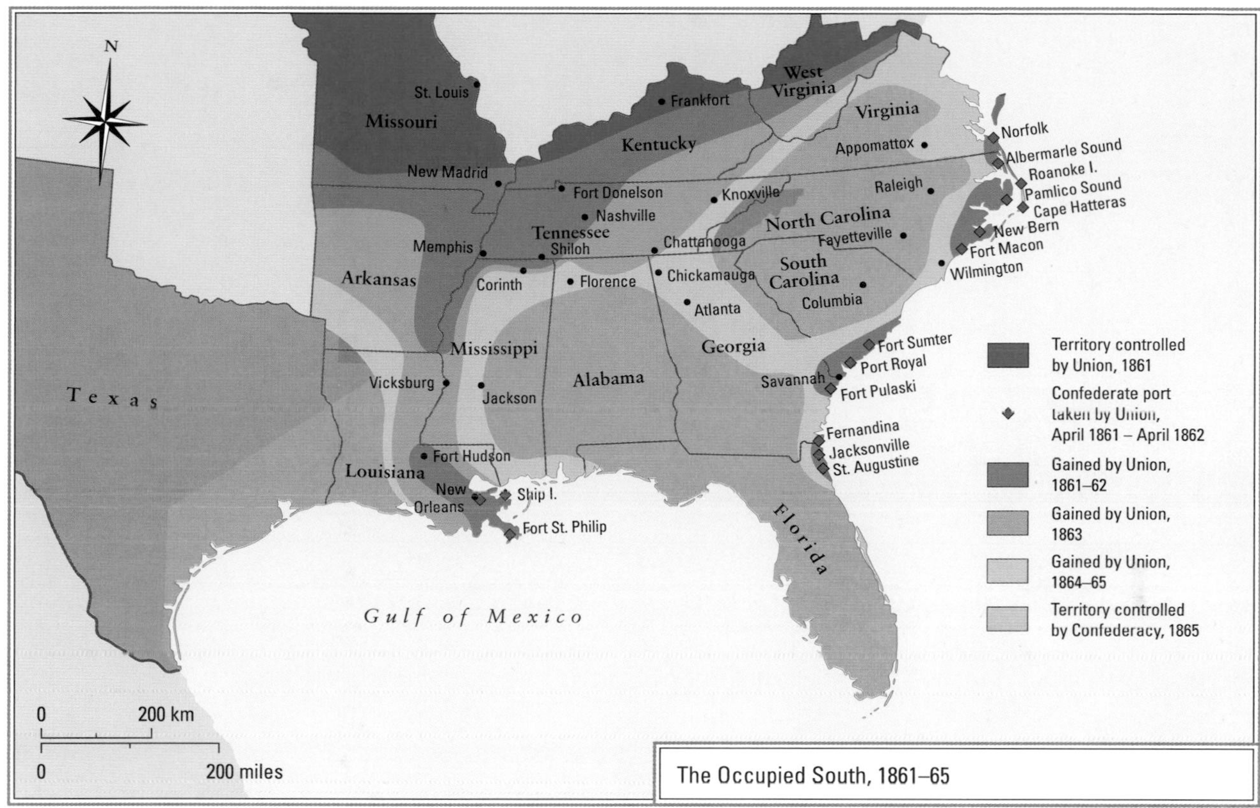

The Occupied South, 1861–65

an infantry corps and told him to break the Confederate western flank. Gen Robert E. Lee had anticipated this move and dispatched MGen George Pickett with 19,000 infantry and cavalry towards Five Forks. However, when Sheridan attacked, Pickett and MGen Fitzhugh Lee were away at a shad bake north of Hatcher's Run. Pickett raced back to Five Forks and joined the battle in progress, but there was little he could do. Once Grant learned of Sheridan's success, he ordered a general attack all along Lee's front. The loss of Five Forks made it impossible for Lee to maintain the Southside Railroad as a link to Gen Joseph Johnston in North Carolina, and Lee was forced to abandon Petersburg.

■ Sayler's Creek, 6 April 1865

Moving west from Aemlia Corthouse, nearly a quarter of Gen Robert E. Lee's retreating Confederate army was cut off by MGen Philip Sheridan's cavalry and two corps. Most of the Confederates surrendered, including LGen Richard Ewell.

■ Appomattox River, 6–7 April 1865

While other Federal forces fought at Sayler's Creek, MGen E.O.C. Ord advanced his Army of the James on a parallel route to the south towards Burke's Junction. LGen Ulysses Grant ordered Ord to burn the Appomattox River bridges at Farmville and High Bridge to block Gen Robert E. Lee's line of retreat. However, BGen Thomas Rosser attacked BGen Theodore Read as Read approached High Bridge, capturing about 780 Federals. The Confederates suffered about 100 casualties. After LGen James Longstreet crossed the Appomattox, MGen William Mahone failed to burn High Bridge promptly and the wagon bridge that ran under and alongside it. BGen Francis Barlow was able to capture the wagon bridge and push across while Col Thomas Livermore led a party of pioneers who extinguished the fire on High Bridge. By crossing these bridges, the Federals were able to continue pursuing Lee to Farmville.

Wars of the Industrial Age, 1870–1920

During the late 19th and early 20th centuries, the United States began to flex its political and military muscle, pursuing a policy of colonial expansion that brought it into conflict with the remnants of the Spanish empire in the Caribbean and the Philippines. US troops served on the Western Front during the final year of World War I, providing a much needed boost to Allied efforts and contributing to the victory in November 1918. The United States' entry into World War I saw a significant expansion of the US military that was to set the tone for the rest of the 20th century.

Left: American troops man a French '37' in firing position on a parapet in a second-line trench, Spring 1918. The gun was designed to destroy enemy machine-gun nests.

US Expedition to Korea, 1871

■ Ganghwa, 10–11 June 1871

Taewongun, Regent of Korea, resisted all external efforts to open the kingdom to trade. When two Korean forts fired upon two American ships of RAdm J. Rodgers' squadron, the Americans landed and destroyed both.

Westwards Expansion, 1874–94

■ Brooks-Baxter War, 15 April–15 May 1874

After a legal challenge over the result of the election of the Arkansas state governor failed, the losing candidate attempted to take over by force. The result was a series of skirmishes between militias until the Federal government was forced to intervene.

■ Reading Railroad Massacre, 1877

Depressed economic conditions resulted in a financial crisis for many US railroad companies, which had previously been enjoying a boom period. Wage cuts and job losses also resulted in resentment among the railroad workers, many of whom rioted or prevented rail traffic from moving. At Reading, Pennsylvania, state militia attempted to free a train blocked by rioters and were attacked. Shots fired by the militia resulted in several deaths among the rioters.

■ San Elizario Salt War, 1877

Several attempts were made to exert private control over the salt-extraction industry near San Elizario, Texas, gradually replacing the traditional system whereby the salt lakes were considered to be communal property. This led to an ongoing feud between factions in the town, which was mainly political, legal and economic in nature and was mostly fought using those means.

The situation changed when Charles Howard filed a legal claim of ownership to the salt lakes. This brought him into conflict with his former political ally Louis Cardis, who championed the idea of communal ownership. The local population were also concerned about the situation and made plans to disregard the pro-private ownership county government and set up their own local committees.

Howard used his legal position to have some local men arrested for planning to extract 'his' salt, which outraged the community sufficiently that he was taken captive and held for several days. During this time Howard agreed to relinquish his salt rights, but instead shot and killed his rival Cardis before fleeing to New Mexico.

The situation in San Elizario was apparently calmed by negotiation. The local population agreed to respect the county government. In return, Howard was to be brought back to San Elizario to face trial. A force of 20 new Texas Rangers was raised for the purpose of returning him.

The Rangers brought Howard back to San Elizario, but were immediately attacked by the townsfolk. The Rangers, and Howard with them, were besieged in the town church and, after two days, surrendered to the townsfolk. Most of the Rangers were disarmed and expelled from the town. Two, and Howard, were murdered by the mob. The situation was restored by deploying a force of cavalry to nearby Fort Bliss.

■ Lincoln County War, 18 February–19 July 1878

Rivalry over the dry goods trade in Lincoln County, New Mexico, grew into a range war between competing factions, in which both sides made use of legal measures as well as recruiting outlaws to fight the gunmen of the opposing side. The flashpoint was the murder of rancher John Tunstall, who was shot by a posse sent to seize his assets in what was ostensibly a legal move. In revenge, members of the original posse were murdered after surrendering. Their murderers were the Regulators, a group formed to arrest Tunstall's killers – again, supposedly in accordance with a legally issued warrant.

As the violence escalated, political and legal machinations resulted in the Regulators being outlawed when their faction's legal sponsor, Justice of the Peace John Wilson, was dismissed from his post. Pursued by an increasingly large force, some of the Regulators were killed and others exchanged fire with US troops, drawing Federal forces into what had thus far been a local dispute.

The Regulators were eventually forced to take up defensive positions in the town of Lincoln, where they held out for three days. Federal reinforcements, equipped with artillery, forced the Regulators to attempt an escape from one of their positions. Some of the Regulators were able to escape, but remained in the general area.

The final Regulator stronghold caught fire, forcing the last of the gang to flee. Some were shot as they came out of the building, and others were killed in a close-quarters fight with Federal troops who attempted to arrest them. Others were able to link up with those who had escaped earlier and fled the area. Notable among those who escaped was the outlaw Billy the Kid.

Lincoln County, 1878

■ Skeleton Canyon Massacre, 1879

A party of Mexican Guardia Rural (mounted police), pursuing cattle rustlers into Arizona despite this being a border violation, were ambushed in Skeleton Canyon. Skeleton Canyon is located in the Peloncillo Mountains (Hidalgo County), which straddle the modern Arizona and New Mexico state line border. Most of the Mexicans were killed in the attack or were murdered after surrendering.

■ Second Skeleton Canyon Massacre, 1881

Hearing that Skeleton Canyon was used as a route to smuggle silver from Mexico into the United States, a party comprising several men who had taken part in the original Skeleton Canyon massacre staged another ambush, killing all 19 smugglers.

■ Guadeloupe Canyon Massacre, 1881

US outlaws, who had been rustling cattle across the US–Mexican border, were ambushed as they camped in Guadeloupe Canyon. The majority were killed in the fierce attack, which was probably carried out by Mexican Guardia Rural personnel. It is known that Mexican personnel were in the area, commanded by an officer who had survived the 1879 Skeleton Canyon attack. Those killed in the ambush included perpetrators of the 1879 incident.

■ Johnson County War, 1892

Conflict over land and water rights in Wyoming began after the harsh winter of 1886, with many smaller ranchers driven off by their more powerful neighbours. Allegations of cattle rustling were often used as an excuse for violence against the ranchers. This led to the existence of two rival organizations, the well established Wyoming Stock Growers Association (WSGA) and the newly formed Northern Wyoming Farmers and Stock Growers Association (NWFSGA), which was created to protect the interests of newer and less powerful ranchers. Under the pretence of eliminating cattle

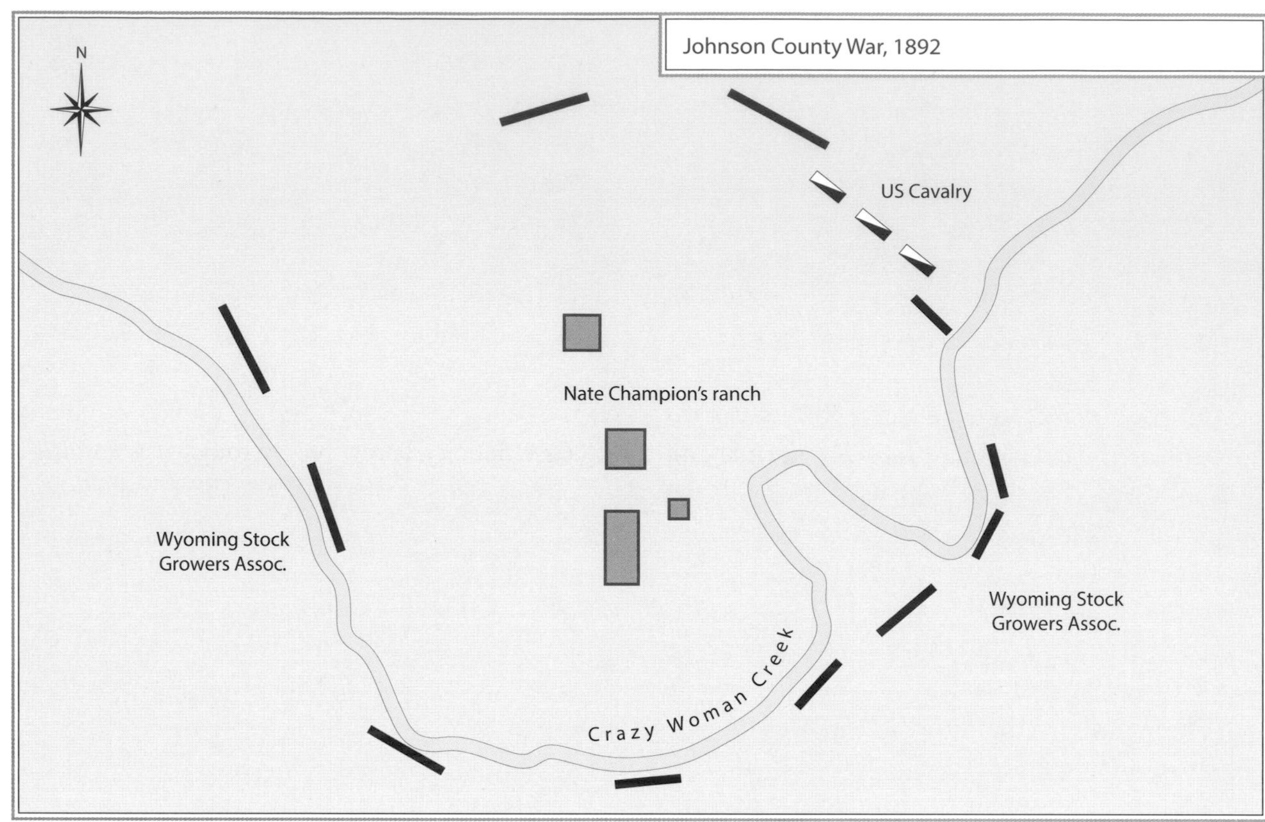

rustling, the WGSA sent an armed band known as the Invaders into Johnson County. The Invaders attacked the ranch of Nate Champion, leader of the NWFSGA, and killed him as he tried to flee his burning home. They were then intercepted by a posse from Johnson County and a protracted skirmish ensued before US cavalry arrived and arrested the Invaders.

■ **Enid-Pond Railroad War, 1893–94**

A dispute between railroad companies and the US Department of the Interior escalated into violence as citizens of towns where trains refused to stop began to attack the railroad infrastructure and even the trains themselves.

Spanish–American War, 1898

■ **Manila Bay, 1 May 1898**

The destruction of the Spanish fleet in Manila Bay and the reduction of the harbour forts allowed the US squadron to blockade the Spanish capital in the Philippines, despite the lingering presence of other foreign warships. Some 10,000 nationalist Filipino forces, led by Gen Emilio Aguinaldo, completed the landward investment of the city. US Gen Wesley Merritt arrived in June with the first land forces, eventually totalling 10,800 men by August. Adm Dewey maintained US control of Manila Bay over the intervening months with increasing difficulty, particularly as a reinforced German cruiser squadron under RAdm Otto von Diederich committed several violations of recognized procedures in the blockaded port. US policy was to avoid all formal terms of alliance with the Filipino rebels against Spain's rule. Notwithstanding, Merritt and Aguinaldo cooperated in trapping Fermin Jaudenes, Governor-General of the Philippines, and his 13,000 troops within Manila's walls while two monitors mounting large cannon suitable for shore bombardment joined Dewey's squadron. At the start of August, Merritt delivered an ultimatum to Jaudenes, offering a chance to evacuate noncombatants before the reduction of the city. The Spanish refused, citing the hostility of the Filipinos as justification.

On 13 August, the American forces attacked Manila, the Spanish resisting until the following day, when Jaudenes formally surrendered the city. Even as their own forces attacked and entered Manila, the Americans denied entry to the surrounding Filipino troops, setting the stage for additional months of fighting as the United States asserted control over a fierce native force set upon independence for the Philippines. The formal end of the Spanish-American War had come with the signature of the Treaty of Paris some two months before Manila's fall.

Cardenas, 11 May 1898

The US torpedo boat *Winslow* twice entered here trying to lure Spanish armed tugs away from the port's defences. On the second run, shore batteries killed five aboard, while seven Spanish died from US fire.

Cienfuegos, 11 May 1898

Three naval skirmishes took place outside this Cuban harbour as Spanish gunboats and shore batteries engaged American ships taking prizes or cutting cables near the harbour, American fire damaging the gunboats and destroying the lighthouse.

San Juan, 12 May 1898

With the Spanish blockaded in Santiago, Adm William Sampson took two battleships, four cruisers and two monitors to bombard Puerto Rico's chief city, hampered by rough seas and high winds. Two Americans and two Spanish died.

Guantanamo Bay, 6–10 June 1898

The American authorities decided that this location in Cuba would make a good base for operations against neighbouring Santiago. The US Navy cleared away Spanish ships, then 623 Marines were landed at Fisherman's Point, where there were 5000 defenders in blockhouses and a fort at Cayo del Toro.

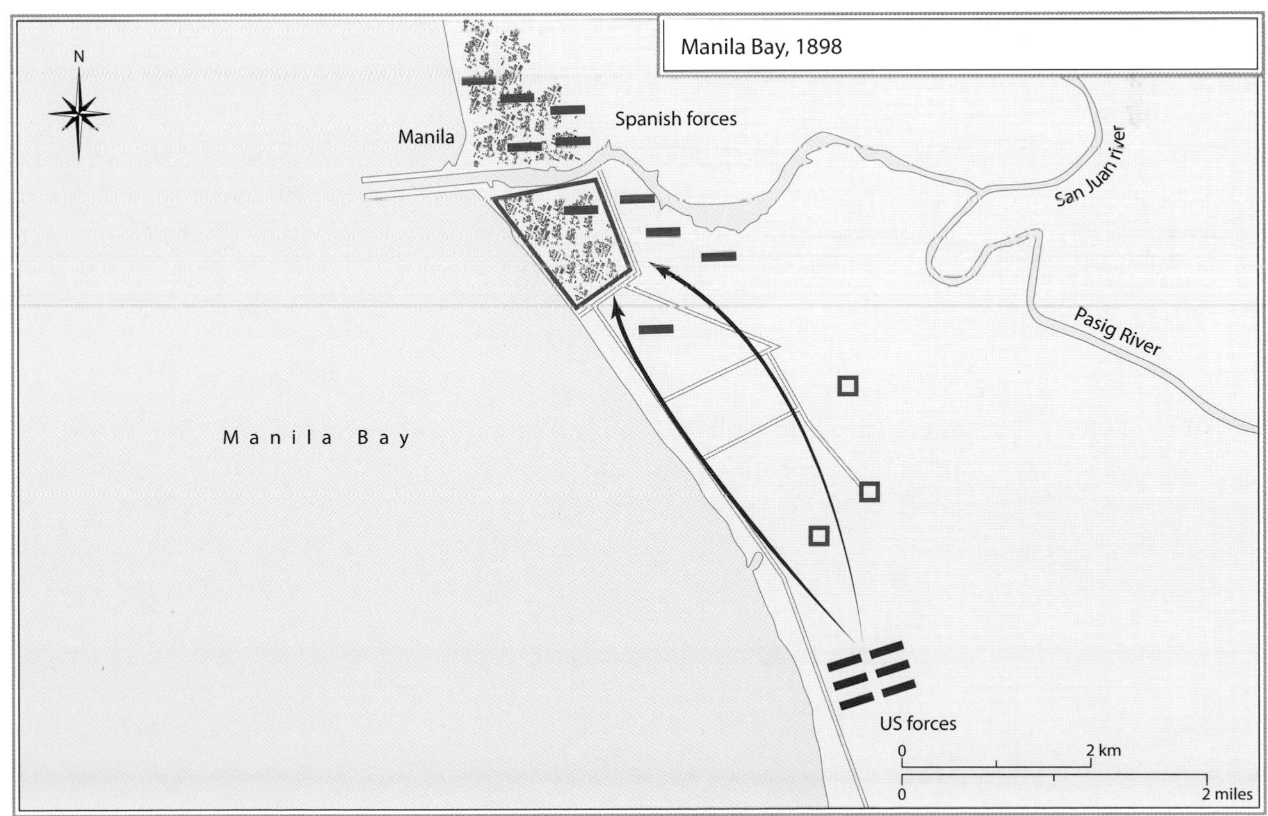

The surprised Spanish left the fortifications nearest the landing, but launched harassing attacks against the US Marines, who lacked artillery and machine guns. Cuban rebels cleared the brush and Spanish snipers away from the position, while naval gunfire supported the landing. With the assistance of Cuban rebels and naval fire coordinated by flag signals, the US Marines destroyed the well supplying the Spanish attackers, killing 68 soldiers while driving the Spanish back from the beachhead. The Spanish retreated back to the inland city of Guantanamo, which they fortified in expectation of an attack. The Americans instead employed the base on the bay.

■ Guam, 20–21 June 1898

In a rather benign engagement, the USS *Charleston*'s opening bombardment was taken for a salute, prompting negotiations and a bloodless surrender of 54 soldiers to the cruiser's captain by the island's governor, Juan Marina, previously unaware of the outbreak of war.

■ Second San Juan, 22 June 1898

The converted liner USS *Saint Paul* under Capt Charles Sigsbee prevented Spanish destroyer *Terror* and old cruiser *Isabel II* from escaping this blockaded harbour in Puerto Rico. *Terror*, having left Cervera's squadron for repairs in the port, attempted to torpedo *Saint Paul* while *Isabel II* disengaged, *Terror* abandoning its attack when *Saint Paul*'s shot disabled her rudder and left it unable to manoeuvre effectively. *Terror*, with two dead, beached herself on the Spanish shore, later being repaired.

■ Las Guásimas, 24 June 1898

Gen Joe Wheeler overtook Spanish retreating into Santiago at this ridge, sending Gen Leonard Wood's brigade to attack the Spanish flank. The Spanish resumed retreating after a two-hour holding action, the Americans suffering 16 killed.

■ Third San Juan, 28 June 1898

Spanish blockade runner *Antonio Lopez* slipped

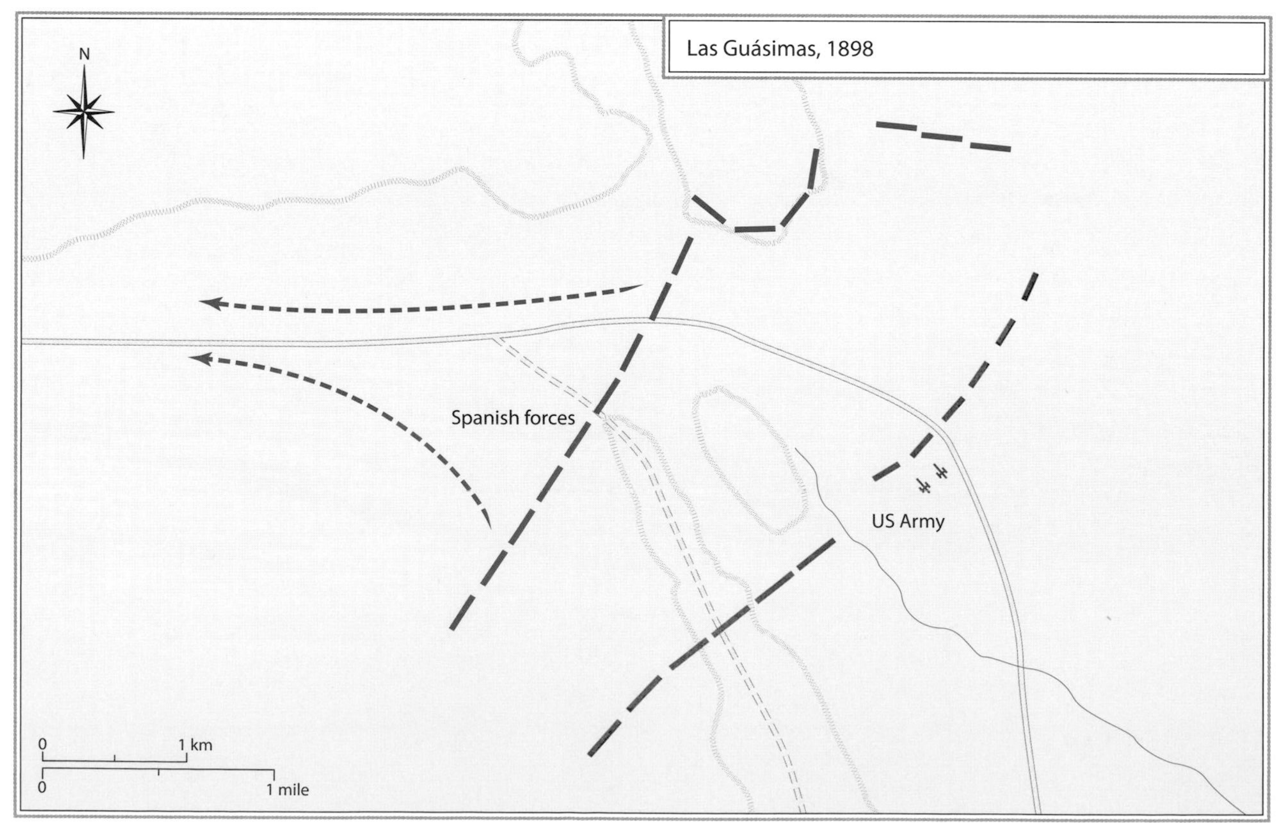

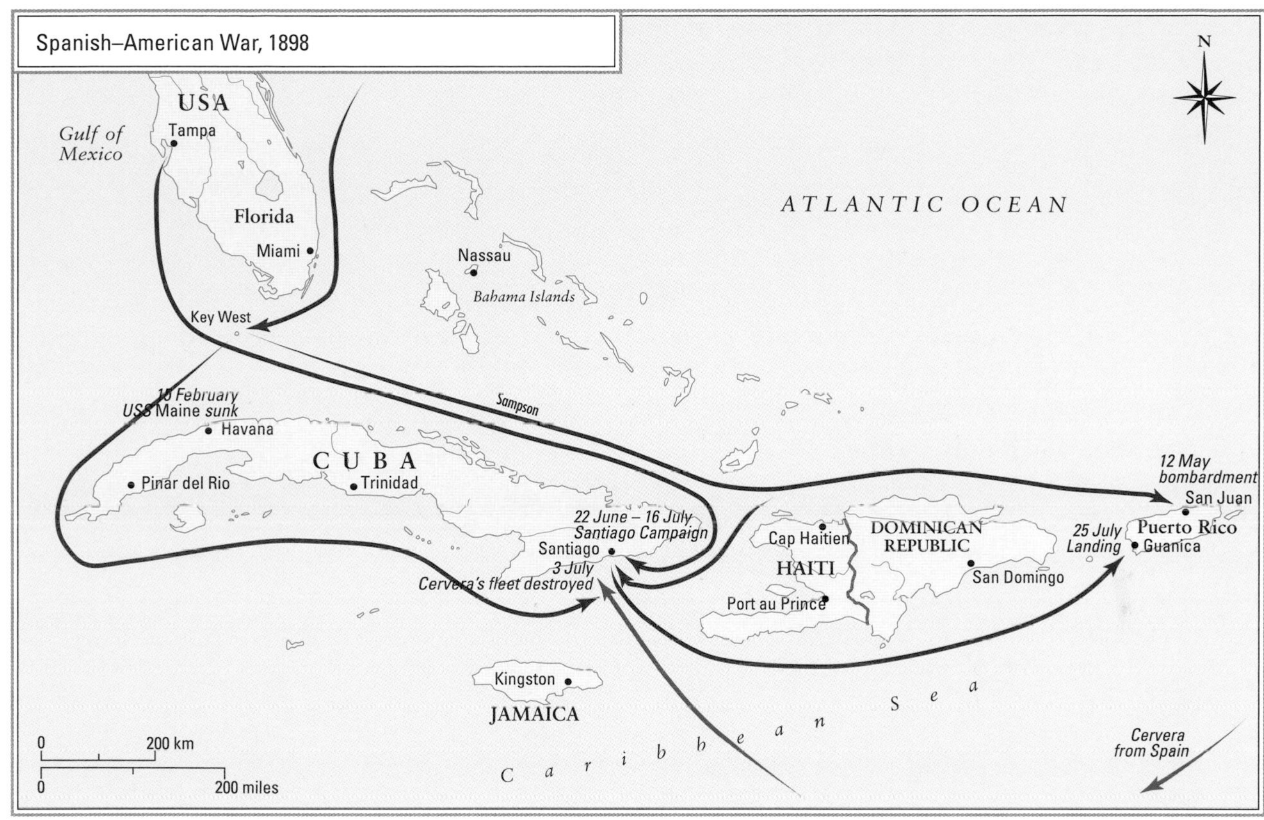

past USS *Yosemite* with a munitions cargo for the blockaded port. *Yosemite* drove *Lopez* aground despite fire from ships and forts in the harbour, the Spanish salvaging *Lopez*'s cargo.

■ I Manzanillo, 30 June 1898

Three US gunboats escorted a prize past this harbour, Spanish gunboats, pontoons and field artillery engaging and disabling USS *Hornet*.

■ Tayacoba, 30 June 1898

A small US landing party attempting to supply Cuban rebels fighting against the Spanish ran afoul of Spanish scouts, the landing party retreating under fire on the beach only to find themselves trapped on there with their boats destroyed by Spanish artillery. After the first four efforts to rescue the wounded Americans failed under heavy Spanish fire from the surrounding jungle, boats from USS *Florida* offshore finally rescued the party.

El Caney, 1 July 1898

Gen William Shafter's army moved inland after landing unopposed at Daiquiri. Gen Henry Lawton with 6653 men attacked blockhouses, his artillery at first ineffective before Lawton finally ordered his gunners to concentrate on individual targets, the most important being El Viso. Firing from their loopholes, the Spanish inflicted disproportionate losses before artillery cracked their strongpoints. The US lost 81 dead; the Spanish had 235 casualties, and 125 taken prisoner.

■ Aguadores, 1 July 1898

Some 274 Spanish in a fortified position on the western side of the San Juan River killed two Americans trying a diversionary attack supported by naval bombardment during the main assault on San Juan Ridge.

■ II Manzanillo, 1 July 1898

The Spanish continued to accumulate smaller armed vessels in this defended harbour, three American gunboats entering and inflicting some damage until repelled by the combined fire of the gunboats inshore, troops and clustered shore batteries.

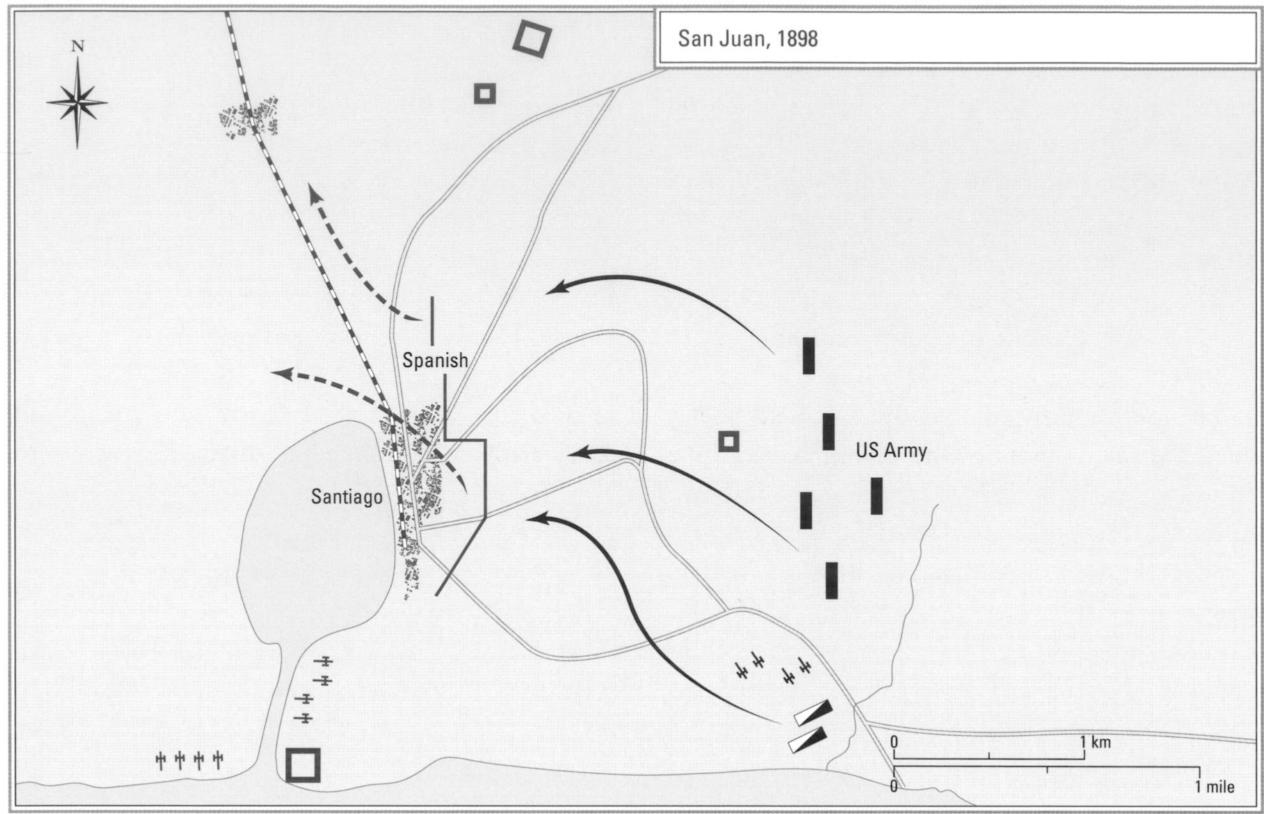

■ San Juan (Kettle) Hill, 1 July 1898

The San Juan Ridge was the last obstacle to the complete investment of Santiago, the principal port on the southern coast of Cuba. This hill was just off the southern end of the ridge, crowned by a strong blockhouse with 750 Spanish defenders. They were led by Gen Arsenio Linares and armed with Model 1893 Mausers, which reloaded from a stripper clip. After waiting under fire for the troops from El Caney, Gen Samuel Sumner ordered his Dismounted Cavalry Division up the hill, supported by the fire of Gatling guns, while the infantry moved up San Juan Ridge and its own blockhouse, taking casualties from accurate Spanish fire.

Leading the charge mostly on horseback was former Assistant Secretary of the Navy Theodore Roosevelt and his 'Rough Riders', a volunteer cavalry regiment equipped with Winchester repeating carbines. Alongside them were the African-American 'Buffalo Soldiers' of the 9th US Cavalry. The Spanish withdrew from the blockhouse, and the dismounted cavalry on Kettle Hill supported the attacks upon San Juan Ridge and the higher San Juan Hill behind the ridge, although the Spanish resisted stubbornly. The Americans' field guns and some rifles fired black powder, which obscured the battlefield, while the more modern Spanish artillery fired smokeless charges more rapidly.

The Spanish on San Juan Hill continued firing from the trenches as the US infantry moved forward. Linares kept most of his garrison within the walls of Santiago, taking the Americans under fire and launching one attack to retake San Juan Hill, which fire from the American Gatlings on Kettle Hill repulsed.

For the eventual American victory, casualties on Kettle Hill were 35 US dead, a total of 170 infantry perishing in the assault on San Juan Ridge and the Suan Juan Hill. Fifty-eight Spanish were also killed.

■ **Santiago de Cuba, 3 July 1898**
Spanish Adm Pascual Cervera slipped his fleet of four cruisers and two torpedo boats into harbour here despite US efforts at interdiction. Upon the location of Cervera's ships in the protected harbour, the US Navy moved to blockade the harbour while Cervera sought to coal his ships and make them ready for sea. Adm William Sampson arrived with the US North Atlantic Squadron and bombarded the harbour fort, an attempt to sink a blockship in the channel mouth failing. Cdre Winfield Schley added the fast cruisers of the Flying Squadron as US Army troops landed and surrounded Santiago. With *Massachusetts* coaling and Sampson taking *New York* for a meeting, Cervera sortied, Schley in *Brooklyn* interfering with the pursuit as the Spanish cruisers burst forth. All the Spanish ships were sunk in the resulting chase, *Oregon* overhauling the fastest, *Vizcaya*.

■ **III Manzanillo, 18 July 1898**
The battle of Santiago freed three cruisers and two gunboats of the US fleet to obliterate the shipping and defences at this port. The Spanish lost four gunboats, three merchant steamers and three floating batteries.

■ **Nipe Bay, 21 July 1898**
Three US gunboats and an armed yacht attacked the Spanish sloop *Juan Jorge*, clearing this Cuban harbour for use against Puerto Rico. A Spanish gunboat was scuttled upriver, *Juan Jorge* was sunk and the harbour forts were damaged.

■ **Rio Manimani, 23 July 1898**
An American force of 250 infantry supported by a gunboat came ashore near Havana to deliver supplies to Cuban rebels operating against remaining Spanish resistance. Spanish cavalry located and fired upon the party, which withdrew.

■ **Manila, 25 July–13 August 1898**
US Gen Wesley Merritt with 10,800 men and Filipino Gen Emilio Aguinaldo with 10,000 nationalist troops invested the landward defences of the Spanish provincial capital. The Spanish surrendered 13,000 troops after a token defence.

Philippine–American War, 1899–1902

■ **Zapote River, 13 June 1899**
Philippine nationalist leader Emilio Aguinaldo collected 5000 nationalist troops at the bridge over this river in Luzon and entrenched them in the path of American troops moving from Manila into the Philippine countryside, as Gen Henry Lawton advanced north with 3000 regulars. Fire from gunboat *Helena* allowed the Americans to turn the Filipino position while US field and naval artillery combined with machine guns to rout the nationalists. A total of 150 died.

■ **San Jacinto, 11 November 1899**
With war joined in earnest between US occupying forces and Philippine nationalist troops under the leadership of Emilio Aguinaldo, US Gen Elwell Otis made large-scale preparations to subdue the area of Luzon north of Manila around Malolos, proclaimed by the rebels as capital of their Philippine Republic. His first move was against the nationalists' supply line, dispatching Gen Lloyd Wheaton towards Laguna de Bay in a campaign that successfully rendered those territories in southeastern Luzon unable to support the rebel army. Gen Arthur MacArthur took 9000 men north along the rail line from Caloocan, two brigades in the main advance, a third 'flying brigade' intended to trap the Filipino Army of Liberation in between the two columns. Aguinaldo's army avoided that trap, but, despite the Americans' slow progress through the Luzon jungle, the nationalists had to burn and abandon their new capital before MacArthur's advance.

Summer rains forced a halt in the campaign. The pause allowed Aguinaldo to rally as many as 80,000 Filipinos to the nationalist cause. When the rains ceased in the autumn, Lawton's objective was to capture Aguinaldo and scatter the Army of Liberation, the US force moving north along the Rio Grande de Pampanga, driving the nationalists 160km through rough terrain. The battle of San Jacinto occurred when Wheaton, with his flying

Kansas Volunteer Infantry fire at enemy positions in Bigaa, the Philippines, during the Philippine–American War, 1899.

column, moved by sea to the Lingayen Gulf, where 2500 men with artillery landed at San Fabian after a preparatory bombardment by the US fleet. There they faced a Filipino force under the command of Manuel Tinio; the Americans scattered the force as they united the flying column to MacArthur's main body, capturing Aguinaldo's mother and infant son, but not the nationalist leader.

■ **Tirad Pass, 2 December 1899**
Emilio Aguinaldo's aide Gregorio del Pilar undertook to hold this narrow passage with 60 men against 500 US Marines pursuing Aguinaldo's retreating forces moving into the Concepcion highlands. Pilar's life bought them five vital hours.

■ **Paye, 19 December 1899**
Filipino resentment of the US occupation of the Philippines expressed itself in this ambush, in which 200 Filipino snipers killed Gen Henry Lawton and 13 of his command, the survivors retreating back into San Mateo.

■ **Cagayan de Misamis, 7 April 1900**
Mindanao Filipino Gen Nicolas Capistrano's surprise dawn attack upon this large town on Mindanao island failed with 52 dead, when a native warrior gave his battle cry while killing an American sentry, alerting the US troops. Three more Americans were killed.

■ **Siege of Catubig, 15–19 April 1900**
Hundreds of Filipino nationalists on Samar gathered to attack a US post at this port garrisoned by 31 volunteers. The barracks burned and the 12 entrenched survivors were rescued two days later. Some 150 Filipinos perished.

■ **Agusan Hill, 14 May 1900**
US Capt Walter Elliot and 80 men surprised Col Vincente Roa's 500 nationalists in this Mindanao village, killing Roa and 38 men and capturing stores of rifles and ammunition for the loss of two killed.

■ **Makahambus Hill, 4 June 1900**
Col Apolinar Velez had heavily fortified this position on a steep height in Mindanao, with rocks and logs ready to roll down upon attackers, as well as pits filled with punji sticks waiting as Capt Thomas Millar's company attacked. Nine Americans fell in the assault for the loss of only one Filipino. As the Americans retreated, Velez' troops captured a prisoner and a number of rifles.

■ **Pulang Lupa, 13 September 1900**
Filipino Col Maximo Abad on the island of Marinduque ambushed Capt Devereux Shields and 54 US troops with his 250 nationalists assisted by a hostile island population. Shields was wounded, and his force surrendered, having taken four casualties.

■ **Mabitac, 17 September 1900**
Filipino Gen Juan Cailles' troops dug in behind a mud flat and successfully resisted LCol Benjamin Cheatham's assault upon their position with 300 men and support from a gunboat offshore. The Americans lost 21 soldiers.

■ **Dolores River, 12 December 1900**
US Lt Stephen Hayt commanded 38 Philippine Constabulary in a patrol here through Cebu. Some 1000 Pulajan religious extremists suddenly attacked the contingent, killing all but Hayt after the constables killed large numbers of the attackers.

■ **Lonoy, March 1901**
Capt Gregorio Caseñas planned to ambush US troops en route to attack his camp at this location on the island of Bohol, imitating the success of earlier Filipino commanders by constructing a network of pits and trenches in the expected line of the Americans' advance. Instead, a local betrayed the ambush to the Americans, who on Easter Sunday circled around and attacked the entrenched Filipinos from behind, killing some 400.

Boxer Rebellion, 1899–1901

■ **Peking, 20 June–14 August 1901**
An mixed international force defended the American, British, German, Italian, Japanese, French, Austro-Hungarian and Russian legations in the Legation Quarter in Peking for 55 days.

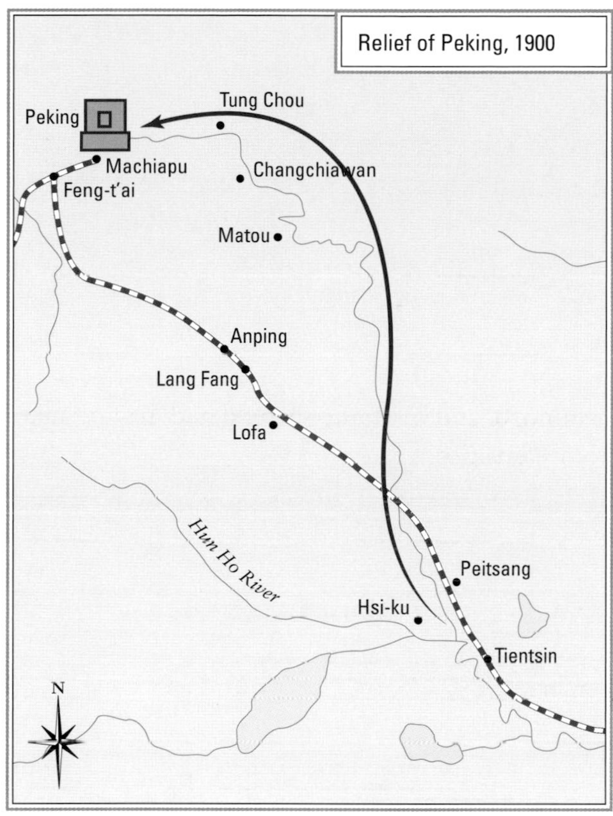

A Chinese nationalist movement calling itself 'The Fists of Righteous Harmony', known as the 'Boxers' internationally, formed a powerful force that began attacking Westerners, Japanese and Chinese Christians throughout China in an effort to reassert Chinese internal sovereignty, eroded for a half century following the Opium Wars. Drought conditions swelled the Boxers' ranks with recruits from the barren countryside. Sensing an opportunity to strike back against Western encroachments, on 20 June the Qing Empress's own army joined the Boxers in an attack on the diplomatic compound. Within the compound's walls were some 500 diplomats and 405 guards who had taken shelter as anti-foreign riots broke out throughout the city. Some 150 embassy personnel joined the armed defenders, among whom numbered future US President Herbert Hoover. Two cannon and three machine guns countered Chinese snipers and artillery, while 2800 Chinese Christians who had fled into the compound previously assisted with the defence. Lacking a unified command, the Boxers and Qing Army had difficulty coordinating a strong enough attack to overwhelm the defenders, who were fighting literally for their lives and making forays outside the compound to destroy hostile emplacements. The Boxers established roadblocks, burned railway stations and severed telegraph communication between the compound and the outside world as an international relief column of some 50,000 troops moved from Tientsin to rescue the diplomats. Fifty-five of the defenders and 13 civilians within the compound died before the relief column arrived on 14 August and scattered the armed Chinese, the foreign troops then plundering Peking for days.

Moro Rebellion, 1906

■ Bud Dajo, 5–7 March 1906

MGen Leonard Wood's US force of 790 men defeated 1000 Moro rebels at Bud Dajo on Jolo Island in the Philippines. Wood's force virtually wiped out the rebels for the loss of 96 men.

Mexican Revolution, 1912–18

■ Veracruz, 21 April–25 November 1914

As the United States became more and more involved in the fallout from the Mexican Revolution of 1911, tensions between the two countries grew. In April, the Mexican Government arrested nine American sailors for trespassing into off-limits areas. At the same time, the Wilson administration learned of an expected delivery to Veracruz of German weapons for Victoriano Huerta, the president Wilson sought to remove from power.

In fact, the weapons were American, and they had been transported through Germany so the manufacturer could skirt an American embargo. Nevertheless, the United States responded forcefully by sending sailors and US Marines to seize the customs house, the railroad station, the telegraph and telephone exchanges, the post office, and any weapons they found. They took up positions as bewildered residents watched, at first impassive.

Soon, however, cadets at the Veracruz Naval Academy and local residents began to form opposition to the Americans. The senior American official, Adm Frank F. Fletcher, sent in more sailors in the hopes of calming the situation, but it only led to more violence. Fletcher looked for a local authority with whom he could negotiate, but found no one. He then expanded the mission to the occupation of the entire town. He also called for reinforcements which included five battleships and a battalion of US Marines from Panama. Within three days, the Marines had restored order, but the incident had been violent. More than 150 Mexicans and 22 Americans died. Among the former was José Azueta, who became a hero for his defence of the Mexican Naval Academy against American Marines. President Huerta cut all diplomatic ties to the United States and Mexican–American relations worsened even further. American forces remained in the city until November.

■ **Columbus, 9 March 1916**

Following his defeat at Celaya, Francisco (Pancho) Villa's Mexican revolutionaries were increasingly short of supplies. Desperate after months of foraging with little success in northern Mexico, Villa raided the US border town of Columbus, New Mexico. The town was defended by a 330-strong detachment of the 13th Cavalry, which beat off the attack by 500 of Villa's men. US forces inflicted 90 casualties for the loss of 26 men.

■ **Carrizal, 21 June 1916**

Francisco (Pancho) Villa's attack on Columbus provoked the USA to organize a punitive expedition under MGen John J. Pershing to capture Villa. A 100-strong US detachment drawn from C and K troops of the 10th Cavalry attacked what was thought to be 150 of Villa's men at Carrizal. The Mexicans were, in fact, government infantry who drove off the cavalrymen, inflicting 35 casualties for the loss of 67 men.

■ **Bear Valley, 9 January 1918**

Yaqui tribes fighting to maintain their autonomy within Mexico raided US border ranches for food. A group of 30 Yaqui was defeated by a detachment of the US 10th Cavalry at Bear Valley, Arizona.

■ **Ambos Nogales, 27 August 1918**

A minor incident at Nogales on the US–Mexican border became a clash between an 800-strong US detachment and 600 Mexican troops. US forces inflicted 400 casualties for the loss of 35 men.

World War I

■ **Château-Thierry, 1–4 June 1918**

Having captured and held Cantigny in May, the American Expeditionary Force (AEF) helped the French to check the advance of German Gen Bruno von Mudra's First Army and Gen Max von Boehn's Seventh Army. The 3rd American Division, under Gen John Dickman, held the line at the Marne against Ludendorff's exhausted and overextended troops. The success of the 'Rock of the Marne' complemented the 2nd American Division's victory at Belleau Wood.

■ **Belleau Wood, 6–26 June 1918**

'Retreat – hell, we just got here.' So, supposedly, called out an American Marine when told by a French counterpart that the fight for the small forest was lost. The American 2nd Division fought for three weeks as part of an effort to stop the German momentum during their 1918 offensives. The Americans suffered almost 10,000 casualties to take back the wood against heavily defended German positions. The Americans fought hard, but at times recklessly, including an open charge across a wheat field swept by German machine guns. The Marine Corps lost more men on the first day of battle than on any other day in their history up to that point.

■ **Marne River II, 15 July–6 August 1918**
Ludendorff's gamble against Paris had failed (at the cost of over 800,000 German casualties during five offensives). FM Foch ordered a massive counter-attack, involving three French armies, two American divisions and British and Italian support. This marked the beginning of the drive north to reach the Armistice line by 11 November.

■ **Champagne-Marne River, 15–17 July 1918**
Three German armies attacked the French in the vicinity of Reims. After pushing a short distance across the Marne, Gen von Boehn's Seventh Army crashed into the French Ninth Army and the American 3rd Division. The attack cost 139,000 German and 133,000 Allied casualties.

■ **Aisne–Marne Rivers, 18 July–6 August 1918**
The French Tenth, Sixth and Fifth Armies, supported by American, British and Italian divisions, thrust into the German salient. Allied armoured cavalry, including 350 new tanks, helped roll the Kaiser's troops back across the Marne.

■ **Amiens, 8–12 August 1918**
On the opening day of the Hundred Days' Offensive Allied forces advanced over seven miles, one of the greatest advances of the war. Total German losses were estimated to be 30,000, leading Erich Ludendorff to describe the first day of the battle as 'the black day of the German Army'. The battle was a turning point in the war, with the American Expeditionary Force taking 44,000 prisoners.

■ **St Mihiel, 12–16 September 1918**
The first major operation by the independent US Army targeted the St Mihiel salient just south of Verdun. It involved the largest air armada ever assembled at that time: 1481 airplanes from all of the Allied nations under the unified command of American Col William 'Billy' Mitchell. Having held the ground largely unopposed since 1914, German defences in the region were formidable, but German leaders saw the precariousness of their position. They began to evacuate units as soon as they deduced that a major attack was imminent. Still, the campaign posed challenges. Terrain features, including lakes, forests and hills, channelled the movement of the infantry, creating a complex battlefield. The Americans assembled 550,000 troops, alongside 110,000 French troops, for the attack. St Mihiel was the largest US military operation since 1865. It targeted the southern and eastern parts of the salient with a supporting attack to the west. It achieved all of its first-day goals, disrupting German movements and pinching off the salient near the town of Hattonchâtel. The American capture of the heights near Montsec broke open crumbling German defences and cleared the way. By 16 September, the entire salient was in Allied hands and the threat to Allied communications in the Champagne area had been neutralized. The operation had been a big success. The Americans took 7000 casualties, but captured more than twice that number of enemy soldiers.

■ **Meuse River-Argonne Forest, 26 September–11 November 1918**
Gen Henri Gouraud's French Fourth Army and Gen 'Black Jack' Pershing's American First Army successfully attacked the German Fifth Army's lines east of Reims. This was the AEF's largest battle of the war, involving more than half a million Allied troops and approximately 200,000 Germans.

■ **Cambrai–St Quentin, 27 Sept–9 Oct 1918**
The attack on the Cambrai–St Quentin sector was intended as the British portion of a joint offensive all along the Western Front. French Marshal Ferdinand Foch, the architect of Allied strategy, wanted attacks on the entire length of the front to prevent the Germans from focusing their dwindling resources in one area only. The British attempt, in tandem with the American attack in the Meuse-Argonne sector and French attacks to the north, aimed to force the Germans out of the powerful set of fixed defences known as the Hindenburg Line. If the Allied armies could unhinge that line, they would face no insurmountable obstacles to the Rhine River. Breaking the line before winter afforded the Germans a chance to pause

A group of US Marines pose in this 1918 photograph entitled 'First to Fight'. From 1–26 June, Marines fought at Belleau Wood, at the time the largest battle in the history of the Corps.

U.S. MARINE CORP

and refit could produce victory before the end of the year. Although primarily a British operation, the forces dedicated to breaking the Hindenburg Line in the Cambrai sector included one French army, the Australian Corps, and the American II Corps. Preliminary assaults on German positions along the Canal du Nord succeeded in forcing the Germans back almost 6.4km, a huge achievement by World War I standards. The attack also produced 10,000 German prisoners of war, an indication that the enemy's morale might be breaking. Nevertheless, the American/Australian attack on the St Quentin Canal on 29 September at first fared poorly, in part due to American inexperience. The 'Yanks' tended to advance too far too fast, failing to neutralize German positions in their rear. Surviving German troops could then fire into the backs of advancing American troops. Staff coordination between British and American officers was also imperfect, leaving the Americans with inadequate artillery support.

Another reason for the setback emerged from the strength of well planned German positions. The Germans had emptied a key tunnel of the St Quentin Canal and turned it into a mini-fortress, complete with field kitchens, hospitals and barracks. Once inside the tunnel, troops were well protected from Allied artillery barrages. The Germans had also carefully defended the approaches to the canal with barbed wire, interlocking machine-gun positions and pre-registered artillery pieces. The canal tunnel thus represented part of one of the most formidable defensive systems to be found anywhere in 1918. Despite their initial setback, the Americans regrouped and assaulted the canal again. Two raw and inexperienced American National Guard divisions attacked with support from British heavy artillery and tanks. Driving forward, the Americans captured the critical part of the German trench system around the present-day American military cemetery of Bony. Then, alongside the Australians, they attacked both ends of the St Quentin tunnel simultaneously, trapping the Germans inside and

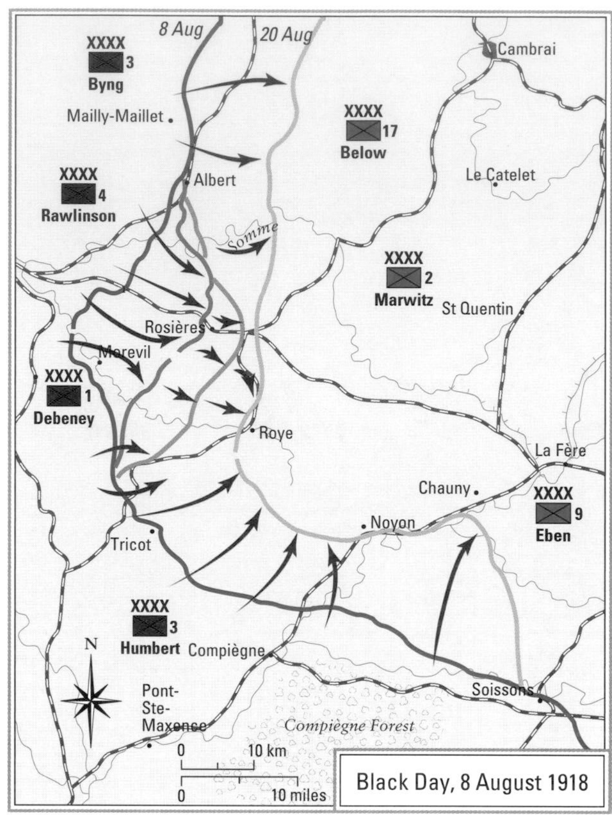

Black Day, 8 August 1918

winning an important victory. That success allowed the British to press on towards the strategic road juncture of Cambrai, which Canadian troops took on 9 October. The conditions of the pillaged town and the demoralized state of German prisoners of war convinced the Allies that the end of the war might indeed be in sight. Meanwhile, at the German resort town of Spa, the German High Command had come to the same conclusion. They therefore began preparations to sue for peace.

Russian Civil War 1917–20

■ Archangelsk, March 1918–July 1919

Under the so-called Northern Russia Expedition, more than 13,000 Allied soldiers occupied important Russian ports along the Barents and White Seas. Seizing Murmansk in March and Arkhangelsk in August 1918, the Allies attempted unsuccessfully to expel 14,000 Bolshevik troops from the area.

American troops cheer for the camera as they await evacuation from a northern Russian port, 1920.

World War II, 1941–45

Following the Japanese attack on the US Navy base at Pearl Harbor on 7 December 1941, the US entered the global conflict against the Axis powers of Japan, Germany and Italy. Over 16 million Americans served in the United States armed forces, with 290,000 killed in action and 670,000 wounded. US forces led the amphibious landings in North Africa, Sicily and Italy in 1942–43, the Normandy landings in 1944, as well as the island-hopping campaign across the Pacific from 1943 to 1945. American air power proved decisive, with the strategic bombing campaigns against Germany and Japan contributing to eventual victory.

Left: American infantry wade ashore during the assault on Omaha Beach, 6 June 1944. US forces suffered more than 2000 casualties while capturing the heavily defended beach.

Battle of the Atlantic, 1939-44

■ U-boat war, 1939–44

Despite the Treaty of Versailles prohibiting the German Navy from possessing U-boats, a covert programme kept the skills alive for rebuilding and, at the outbreak of war, the U-boat force was 57 strong, of which 39 were available for operations. The campaign began in 1939 with minelaying as well as direct attacks on merchant ships; initially 'prize rules' were followed, but these scruples lasted little more than a month. Overall, international law was not allowed to be the hindrance it was in World War I.

The campaign began slowly as U-boat production was not yet a priority. From mid-1940 – a period referred to by U-boat crews as the 'happy time' – the losses inflicted on shipping began to increase for several reasons. First, although the Allies introduced a convoy system from the outset, it was far from comprehensive and there were few escorts available, giving the gradually increasing force of U-boats plenty of targets. Second, the U-boats tended to attack on the surface (which negated the Asdic/sonar on which British anti-submarine planning had relied) and at night (which made visual detection very difficult). Third, the fall of France allowed U-boats to be based on the French Atlantic coast. This, with the occupation of Norway, made the passage of U-boats from their bases to their hunting grounds much easier and faster (and meant they could avoid the heavily mined Straits of Dover); it also let them spend longer on patrol and reduced the time needed for rearming and repair. The result was a huge increase in the number of boats operational at any one time, even before higher production took effect. The conquered territory also provided bases for long-range aircraft that spotted convoys for the U-boats. Fourth, the U-boats began to use 'wolfpack' tactics, which Adm Karl Dönitz, who commanded the campaign, had devised in the

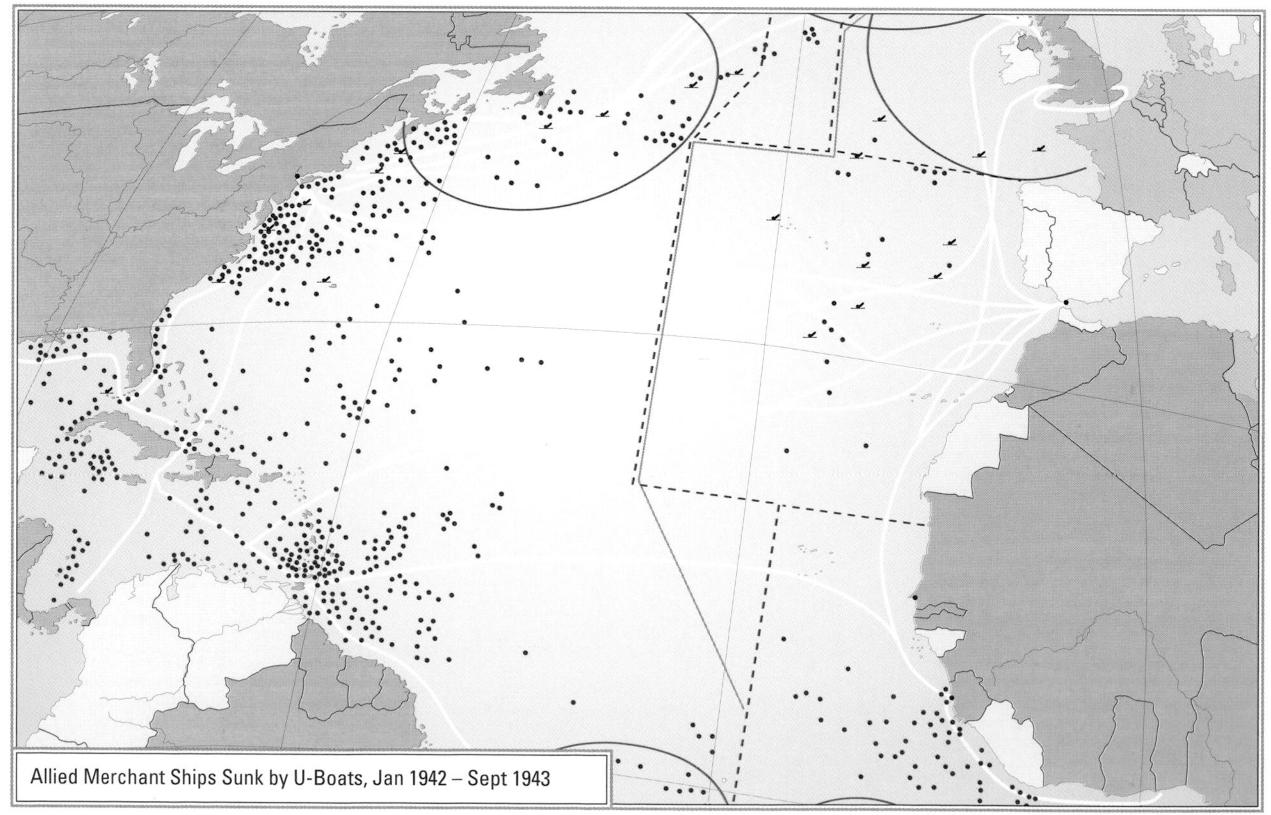

Allied Merchant Ships Sunk by U-Boats, Jan 1942 – Sept 1943

interwar years. These sought to defeat the convoy system by concentrating large numbers of U-boats to overwhelm its escorts and inflict devastating losses rather than simply sinking one or two ships. German codebreaking helped to locate convoys, although the ability to do this eventually lapsed.

Gradually, the campaign tipped against Germany. With the United States joining the war against Germany from December 1941, the number of escorts available to their enemies steadily increased, as did their effectiveness. The Allies also had the priceless advantage of Ultra signals intelligence, which – apart from a dark period through much of 1942 – allowed them to route convoys away from patrolling U-boats. Allied counter-measures improved, notably with radar fitted to warships and aircraft, which could detect surfaced U-boats.

The U-boats inflicted heavy losses during 1942, not least during Operation *Drumbeat* off the American coast, when they took full advantage of the unpreparedness of the US following its entry into the war. November 1942 saw the highest losses of shipping inflicted throughout the war, leading to shortages of fuel, food and raw material in Britain. During 1943, however, there were fewer successful attacks by each U-boat, while their own losses increased (see map opposite), as the escorts – particularly escort carriers – became more numerous and effective, and as the Atlantic 'air gap' was closed. In May 1943, Dönitz effectively admitted defeat by withdrawing his U-boats from the North Atlantic. The campaign continued, but the escorts were increasingly dominant. The U-boat war saw over 14.5 million tons of merchant shipping sunk, for the loss of 785 of the 1100 U-boats.

The Pacific 1941–42

Pearl Harbor, 7 December 1941

The surprise Japanese attack on the United States Pacific Fleet at Pearl Harbor on Oahu in the Hawaiian Islands, on 7 December 1941, initiated World War II in the Pacific. During 1930–41, Japanese military and economic expansionism into China and Southeast Asia led to significantly deteriorating relations with the US. Many Japanese leaders felt that America would prevent Japan from acquiring the colonies in British Malaya and the Dutch East Indies it required to assume Japan's rightful place near the top of the league of states. Strategic planning by the Japanese military concluded that Japan was unlikely to win a war with America, given the United States's immense economic and military potential. As this level of disparity in military and economic potential was only likely to increase in future years, some military commanders advocated the immediate initiation of hostilities against the United States. If a surprise and sudden Japanese strike could place the enemy on the back foot, Japanese forces might be able to exploit this by capturing Malaya and the East Indies, thus gaining additional economic resources and altering the course of the war in Japan's favour.

Japan thus decided to use carrier-based naval aircraft to mount a surprise strike on the Pacific Fleet as it sat in Pearl Harbor. The operation's main aims were to destroy the three American fleet carriers *Enterprise*, *Lexington* and *Saratoga*, as well as the rest of the American fleet. On 26 November 1941, Adm Isoroku Yamamoto's Combined Fleet set sail from Japan; this included an escort force of two battleships, three cruisers and nine destroyers, plus Adm Chuichi Nagumu's strike force of six carriers with 408 aircraft on board.

By early morning on 7 December, the fleet had reached a point north of Oahu. At 07:38, the first wave of 183 aircraft, mainly torpedo- and dive-bombers, left the carriers and attacked the American fleet. Subsequently, the 171 aircraft of the second wave attacked, concentrating on enemy airfields. Simultaneously, five Japanese submarines each launched a single midget submarine, but these operations achieved little. Just after the first attacks had commenced, the Japanese ambassador in Washington issued the Japanese declaration

Taken from a Japanese aircraft during the attack on Pearl Harbor in December 1941, this photograph shows 'Battleship Row' in the foreground, including USS *Nevada* and USS *Arizona*.

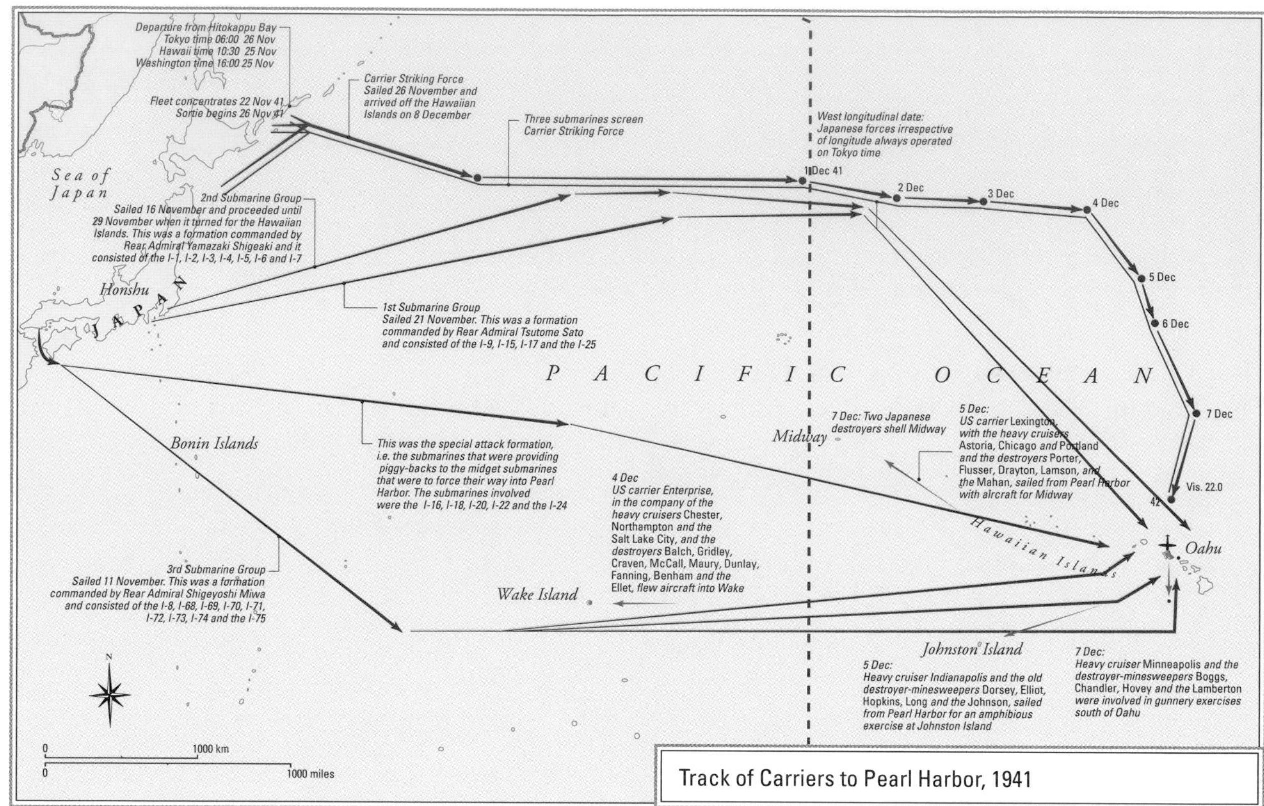

Track of Carriers to Pearl Harbor, 1941

of war. By the end of the day, the Japanese aerial strike on Pearl Harbor had been a stunning success, in what was probably the greatest feat of naval aviation witnessed in any war. The Japanese attacks sank four battleships and two destroyers, and severely damaged three battleships, three cruisers and four other vessels. The attacks also wrecked 188 aircraft and damaged a further 153, and caused significant personnel casualties, amounting to 2402 killed and 1282 wounded. The Japanese suffered only light casualties, including 29 aircraft and five midget submarines lost, together with 66 personnel casualties.

■ Wake Island, 8–23 December 1941

Within hours of the air attack on Pearl Harbor, the Japanese pounced on Wake Island, an outpost in the North Pacific and a strategic link in the chain connecting the mainland with American possessions in the Philippines. The US Marine garrison repelled the first landing. However, the Japanese returned with 2500 infantry (including 1500 marines). The landing force overwhelmed the defenders and captured the atoll, which the Japanese held until the end of the war.

■ Guam I, 8–10 December 1941

After air raids softened Guam's defences, nine Japanese transport ships brought ashore 5900 troops of the South Seas Detachment and Special Naval Landing Forces. Within hours, the invaders overwhelmed the garrison of US Marines, sailors and Guam Insular Force Guards.

■ Philippine Islands, 8 December 1941–6 January 1942

On 22 December, after several feints, the Japanese Fourteenth Army, under Gen Masaharu Homma, landed in force at Lingayen on Luzon. Building up approximately 130,000 troops, the Japanese confronted around 150,000 defenders, including more than 30,000 soldiers of US Army MGen Jonathan Wainwright's Philippine Division (the 23rd Infantry Brigade and supporting units). Blasting through five defensive lines en route south to Manila, the Japanese bottled up the defenders on the Bataan peninsula.

■ **Bataan-Corregidor, 7 Jan–6 May 1942**

The Japanese Eleventh Air Fleet had destroyed the US Far East Air Force on the Philippines. The Imperial Japanese Navy's 3rd Fleet and Gen Masaharu Homma's Fourteenth Army had successfully landed on Luzon, advancing south to the capital. Outmanoeuvred, Gen Douglas MacArthur, commander of US Army Forces Far East, gave up Manila and ordered his American and Filipino troops to fight a delaying action at the Bataan peninsula and on the island fortress of Corregidor. Supported by heavy artillery fire and aerial bombardment, the Japanese reduced Bataan's defences on 9 April. Corregidor held on for another month, until MGen Wainwright surrendered on 6 May. The Japanese took 15,000 American and 60,000 Filipino prisoners, many of whom would perish under harsh treatment (e.g. the 'Bataan Death March'). MacArthur withdrew to Australia to organize a counter-offensive. Adm Thomas Hart, commanding the US Asiatic Fleet, joined in the futile defence of the Dutch East Indies.

■ **Doolittle Raid, 18 April 1942**

The aircraft carrier USS *Hornet* launched 16 US Army B-25 medium bombers within 1200km of Japan in a raid on Tokyo. After the largely symbolic raid succeeded, American President Franklin D. Roosevelt facetiously told his people the mission had originated in the mythical Himalayan kingdom of 'Shangri La'.

■ **Coral Sea, 7–8 May 1942**

Notable as the first naval engagement in which the opposing surface fleets never saw one another, this battle was fought entirely by carrier-based planes. As such, it clearly signalled the shift in naval warfare from the importance of the 'big gun' battleships and cruisers to aircraft carriers. Both the American and Japanese fleets were attempting to gain control of the area around Port

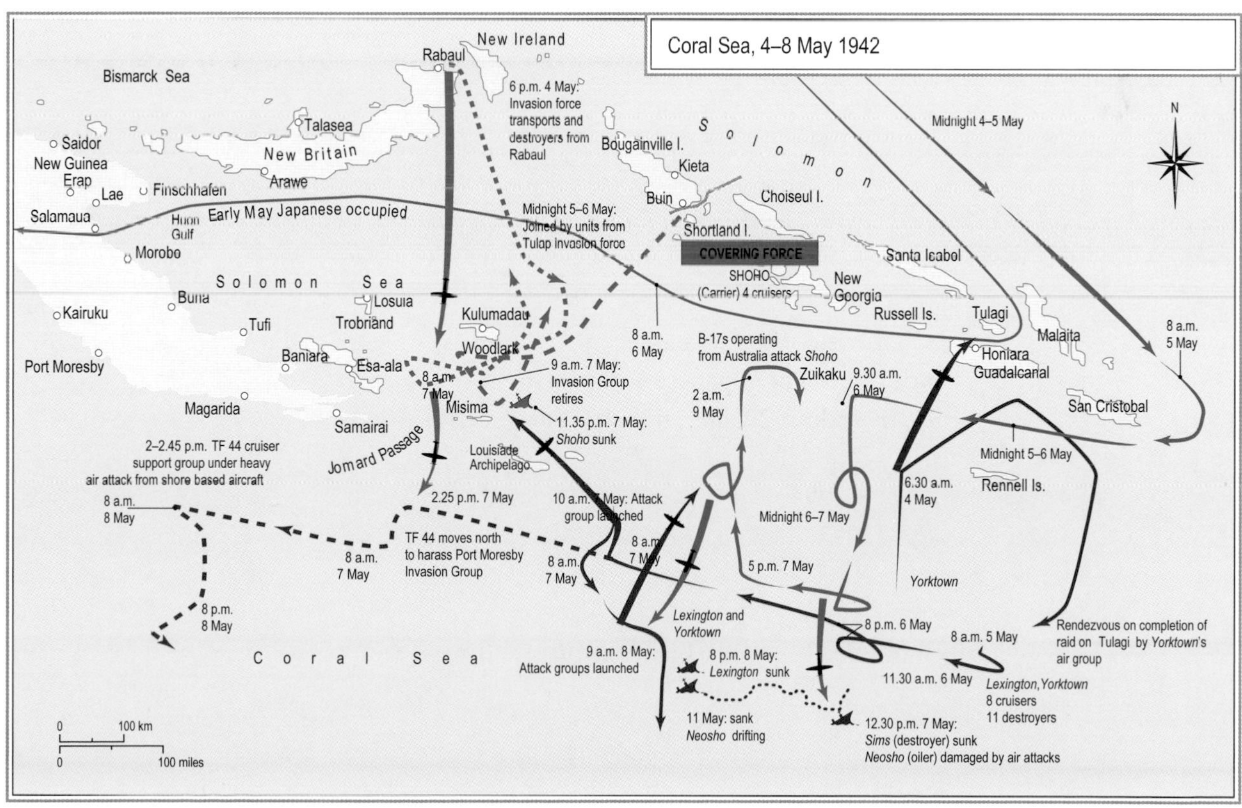

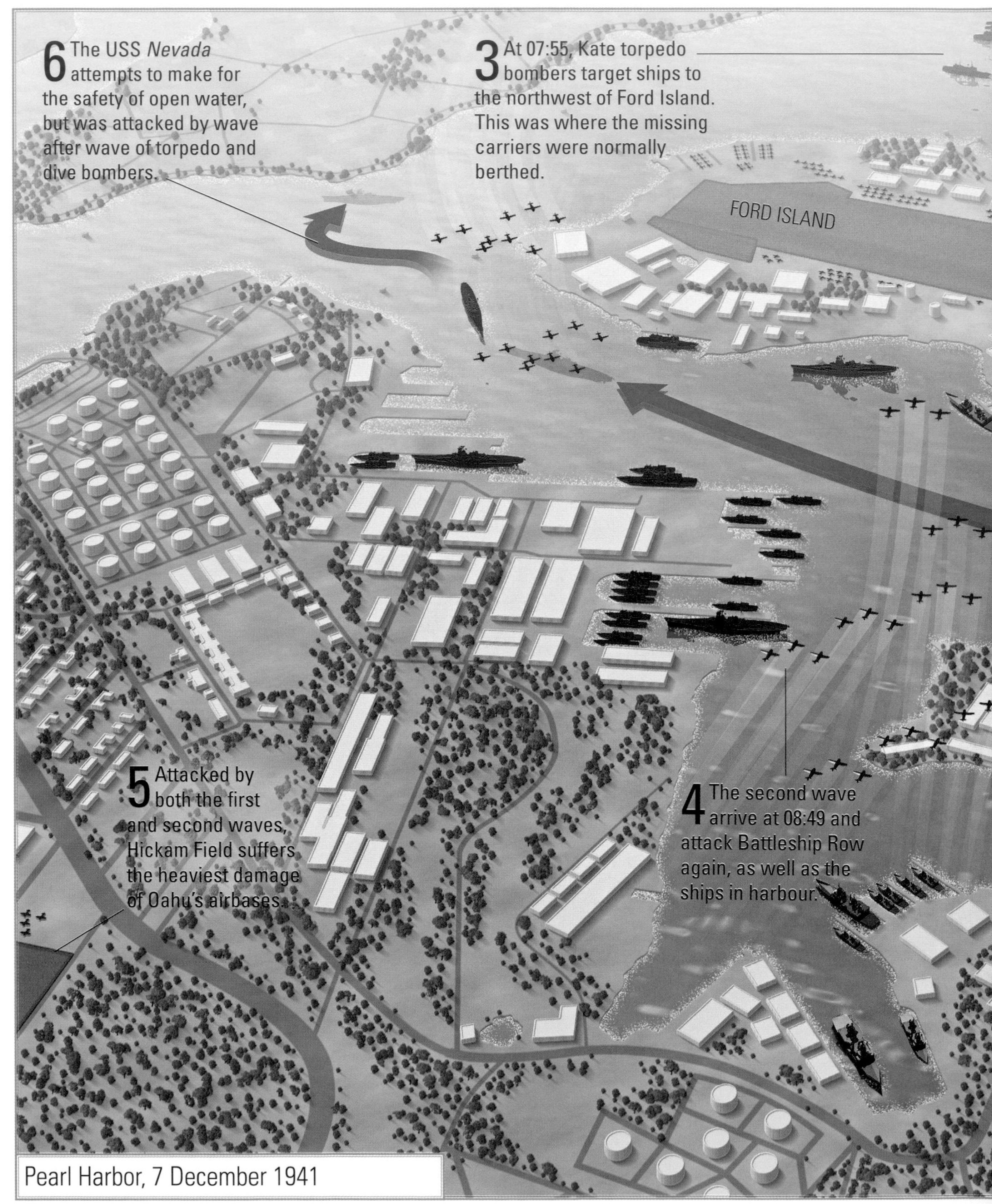

Pearl Harbor, 7 December 1941

2 At 07:53, Val dive bombers approach from the northwest. Their targets are the aircraft parked on Hickham Field and Pearl Harbor Naval Air Station on Ford Island.
BATTLESHIP ROW
1 The first wave of Kate torpedo bombers attack Battleship Row from the southeast at 07:50 AM. They are followed by waves of Kates bombing from high level.
OIL TANKS

Moresby, Papua, which was critical to the defence and resupply of Australia. The Japanese hoped to use three aircraft carriers to draw the Americans towards two of their heavy cruisers, showing that they still prioritized surface warfare. The US Pacific Fleet, taking advantage of radio decrypts, was able to avoid the trap. The Americans had two carriers, the *Yorktown* and the *Lexington*, which they planned to use to disrupt Japanese landings at Port Moresby, but poor weather and poor navigation placed them in an exposed position.

On 8 May, the two fleets' reconnaissance aircraft located one another in the vast ocean. Each side had approximately 120 aircraft, although the Japanese planes were qualitatively superior and had a better range of offensive options. The Americans nevertheless did well. They sank the Japanese carrier *Shoho* and damaged the *Shokaku* badly enough to force it to withdraw to the north, thus tilting the odds towards the Americans. That advantage soon dissipated, however, when the Japanese sank the *Lexington* and badly damaged the *Yorktown*. The Japanese, nevertheless, abandoned efforts to take Port Moresby, handing the Americans a strategic victory despite their severe losses. The *Yorktown* was so badly damaged that the Japanese counted it as sunk; although limping, it did take part in the battle of Midway later that summer. Coral Sea showed the wisdom of the American decision to base its naval power around aircraft carriers rather than battleships.

South Pacific 1942–45

New Guinea, 3 February 1942–22 January 1943

At the beginning of 1942, the Japanese had established at Rabaul, New Britain, a major base from which their air forces and navy could check the Allied advance through the Solomons, especially in the contest for Guadalcanal. From New Britain, Japanese land forces also deployed to New Guinea and sought to take Port Moresby, over the Owen Stanley Range in Papua. The naval battle of the Coral Sea prevented a direct Japanese landing at Port Moresby. As a result, MGen Tomitaro Horii's 144th Infantry secured a beachhead at Buna, on Australian New Guinea, in order to attempt an overland conquest of Papua. Although this was initially successful, the Australian 7th Division eventually checked the Japanese advance at Kokoda. By 22 January 1943, six months of bloody fighting had cost Australia almost 5700 casualties and the US almost 3000. The Japanese lost more than half of Horii's force of 20,000 before withdrawing survivors for deployment elsewhere.

Midway, 4–7 June 1942

The battle of Midway (4–7 June 1942) was a major turning point in the Pacific Theatre during World War II, inflicting a blow upon the Japanese from which they never fully recovered. The battle's origins lay in the decision of Adm Yamamoto to attempt to lure the US Navy's major units into a trap where they could be destroyed by the Japanese fleet. Yamamoto's plan was predicated on faulty intelligence about the status of the US Navy's aircraft carriers in the Pacific (erroneously believing that only two were likely to be available), and further undermined by American signals intelligence breaking the Japanese code and being able to work out the basis of the enemy plan.

Yamamoto intended to launch an attack on Midway Atoll as the means of bringing the Americans to battle; the Americans, cognizant of his intentions, duly obliged. Adm Chester Nimitz, Commander-in-Chief, Pacific Ocean Areas, was able to call upon not two, but three carriers after the badly damaged USS *Yorktown* was made fit for service. The major damage sustained at the battle of the Coral Sea was rectified in 72 hours, with further work being carried out while *Yorktown* was under way to join the carriers *Enterprise* and *Hornet*.

The day before the battle, on 3 June, USAAF B-17 bombers operating from Midway attacked

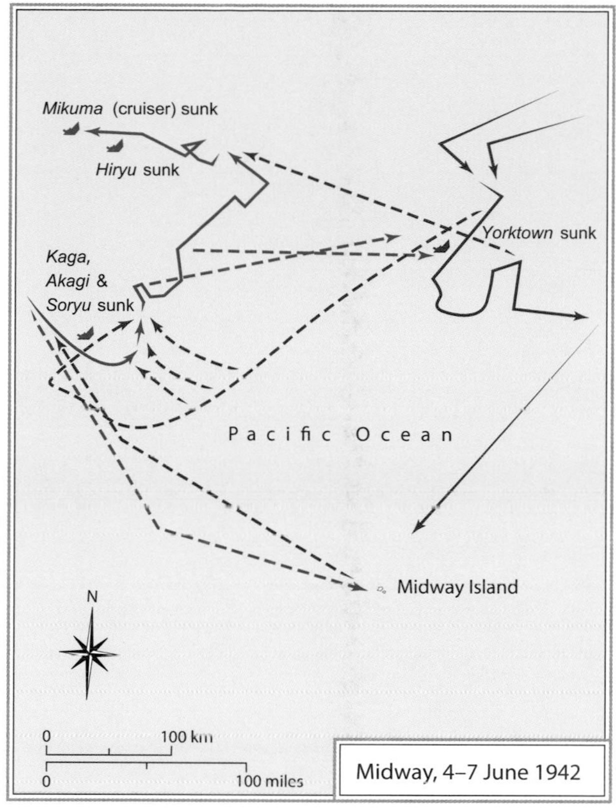

Midway, 4–7 June 1942

the Japanese fleet's transport group and bombed it without result. On 4 June, the Japanese launched their carrier aircraft to attack Midway, which was hard hit, but not put out of action. The Japanese then learned of the presence of an American carrier thanks to air reconnaissance, and Adm Nagumo, commanding the Japanese carriers, decided to launch an attack on the American fleet. By this point, the Americans were well aware of the location of the Japanese carriers, and launched aircraft from *Enterprise* and *Hornet* to attack. The first attacks were conducted by TBD Devastator torpedo-bombers from Torpedo Squadron 8; all of them were shot down as they attacked. Their sacrifice was not in vain, however, since they drew the Japanese defensive fighters out of position, leaving the carriers *Kaga*, *Akagi* and *Soryu* vulnerable to three squadrons of approaching American SDB Dauntless dive-bombers. The dive-bombers hit all three carriers, leaving *Kaga* and *Soryu* ablaze, while *Akagi* sustained serious damage to its rudder and flight deck. All three Japanese carriers were out of action, leaving just the fourth Japanese carrier, *Hiryu,* capable of operations.

Hiryu's air group then launched a major counter-attack, badly damaging the *Yorktown* and putting that ship out of action. The remaining two American carriers were untouched, however, and upon the discovery of the *Hiryu* by a scout-plane, they launched a further dive-bomber assault on the Japanese ship. The attack set the *Hiryu* ablaze from bow to stern, and it sank the following day, another crushing loss to the Japanese Navy. As darkness fell on 4 June, the Americans had knocked out four Japanese carriers in exchange for the *Yorktown* being badly damaged. There was little fighting on 5 June, but over the course of the next 48 hours, the Americans managed to sink the Japanese cruiser *Mikuma* in another air strike. Yamamoto finally decided that he must withdraw. A Japanese submarine found the *Yorktown* and hit it with two torpedoes, which caused the ship to sink on 7 June 1942.

■ Owen Stanley Range, 21 July–16 November 1942

MGen Horii's 144th Infantry had seized the strategically important airfield at Kokoda. To repel the Japanese advance, the Australian 7th Division and the US 126th Infantry fought a difficult campaign along rugged mountain tracks, north to Buna.

■ Solomon Islands, 7 August 1942–25 December 1943

By April 1942, the Japanese line extended from the Burma–India border, east to the Philippines, New Britain and the Solomon Islands. Air and naval bases at Bougainville and New Georgia supported their campaign on New Guinea. To check and isolate Japanese air and naval power, the Allies planned a counter-offensive, beginning with the amphibious conquests of Tulagi and Guadalcanal. By 9 February 1943, the Japanese had been expelled from both places at tremendous

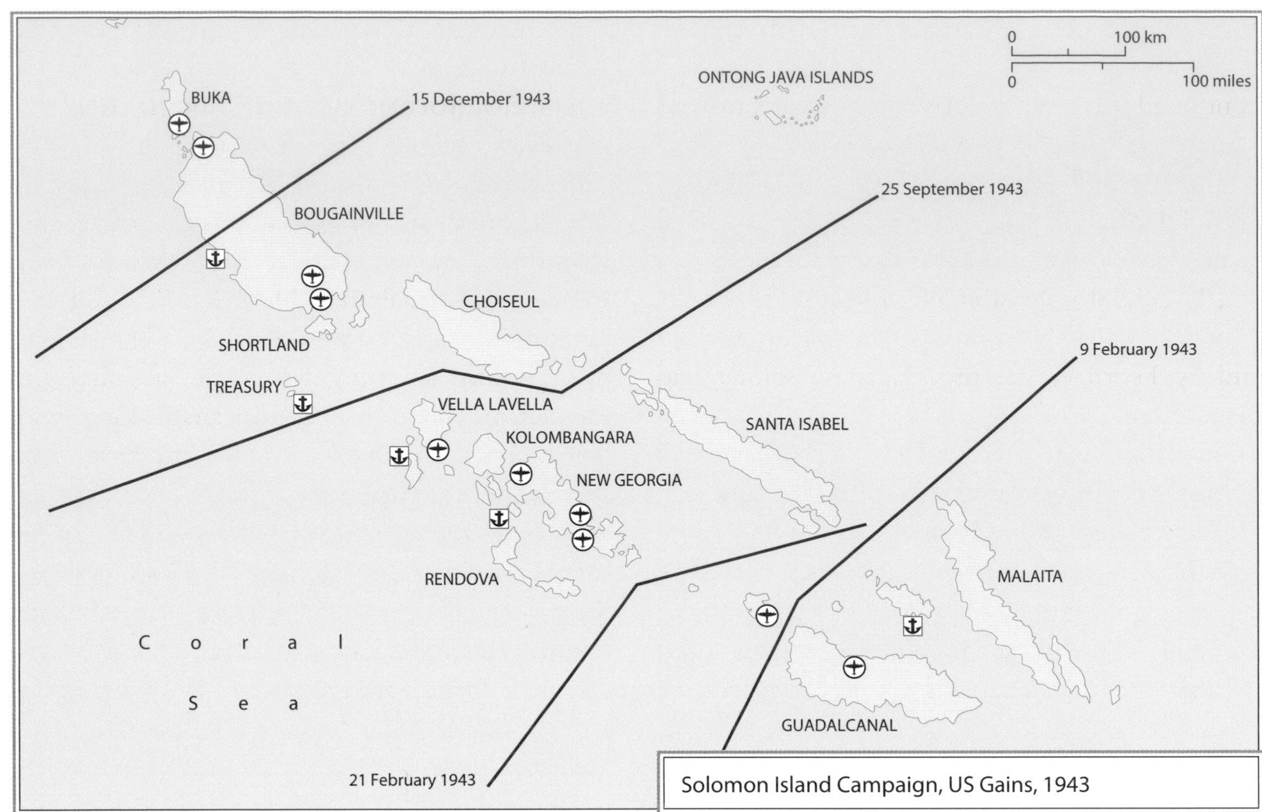

Solomon Island Campaign, US Gains, 1943

cost: more than 7000 Allied and 30,000 Japanese lives.

The naval battles nearby were equally costly, with so many ships sunk in the passage north of Guadalcanal that it earned the sobriquet 'Iron Bottom Sound'. Countering Japanese naval power in the region became a central challenge throughout the campaign. Adm Yamamoto's powerful fleet outnumbered that of Adm Halsey. While often tactically successful, however, the Japanese ultimately suffered from attrition, unable to replace lost ships, aircraft and experienced personnel. Both sides suffered setbacks, including the loss of the carriers *Ryujo* and USS *Hornet*. The American industrial base could absorb these losses; the Japanese, increasingly, could not.

The second phase of the campaign, Operation *Cartwheel*, included the conquest of Bougainville, the largest island in the archipelago. By Christmas 1943, US Destroyer Squadron 23 had sunk more than half the Japanese resupply effort, in the battle of Cape St George. Ashore, US Marines had wiped out the Japanese 23rd Infantry at the battle of Piva Forks. Soon the heart of Japanese power in the region, the base at Rabaul, New Britain, was to be surrounded and isolated, though fighting would continue in the area until 1945.

By the end of the war, the Solomon Islands campaign had cost the Allies more than 10,600 dead, along with 40 ships and 800 aircraft and the Japanese had lost more than 80,000 men, 50 ships and 1500 aircraft.

■ Guadalcanal, 7 August 1942–8 February 1943

With information that the Japanese had started airfield construction on Guadalcanal, the Americans landed 19,000 Marines there, driving the Japanese troops away from the airfield (known to the Americans as Henderson Field). The Japanese responded by sending a task force of cruisers to the area, the force defeating an Allied naval group in the battle of Savo Island on 9

August. This success did not create conditions with which to dislodge the Marines, and the Japanese continued attempts to drive the Americans out throughout August, September and October. A final attempt by the Japanese to land their 38th Division in early November 1942 ended with their transport ships being sunk by air attack and 38th Division left with just 2000 men. This marked the turning point in the battle, and by February the final Japanese soldier had been withdrawn.

■ **Savo Island, 9 August 1942**

Japanese VAdm Gunichi Mikawa's Eighth Fleet attacked Allied warships screening the Guadalcanal landings. Within an hour of night fighting, the Allies lost four heavy cruisers (three US and one Australian) and more than 1000 sailors, and had damaged three Japanese cruisers. Both sides had made mistakes. Prior to the battle, American VAdm Frank Fletcher moved his task force's carriers, depriving the Allies of air cover. Mikawa failed to exploit his victory, leaving the Allied landing force unmolested.

■ **Eastern Solomons, 24–25 August 1942**

American carrier task groups, including USS *Enterprise* and USS *Saratoga*, attacked the Japanese carriers *Shokaku*, *Zuikaku* and *Ryujo*, which were screening a supply column bound for Japanese troops on Guadalcanal. Neither side's warships sighted the other's in this battle, fought entirely by opposing air wings. American aircraft from Henderson Field on Guadalcanal, along with seven USAAF Boeing B-17 bombers from Espiritu Santo, also joined in the fracas. VAdm Nagumo's intention was to destroy the American carriers and deliver 1400 fresh troops to recapture the island's important airfield. *Saratoga*'s dive-bombers sank *Ryujo*. The Japanese strike force crippled *Enterprise,* but it survived the battle. While indecisive, the fight enabled the Americans to slow, though not to halt, Japanese resupply and reinforcement. More significant for Japan was the

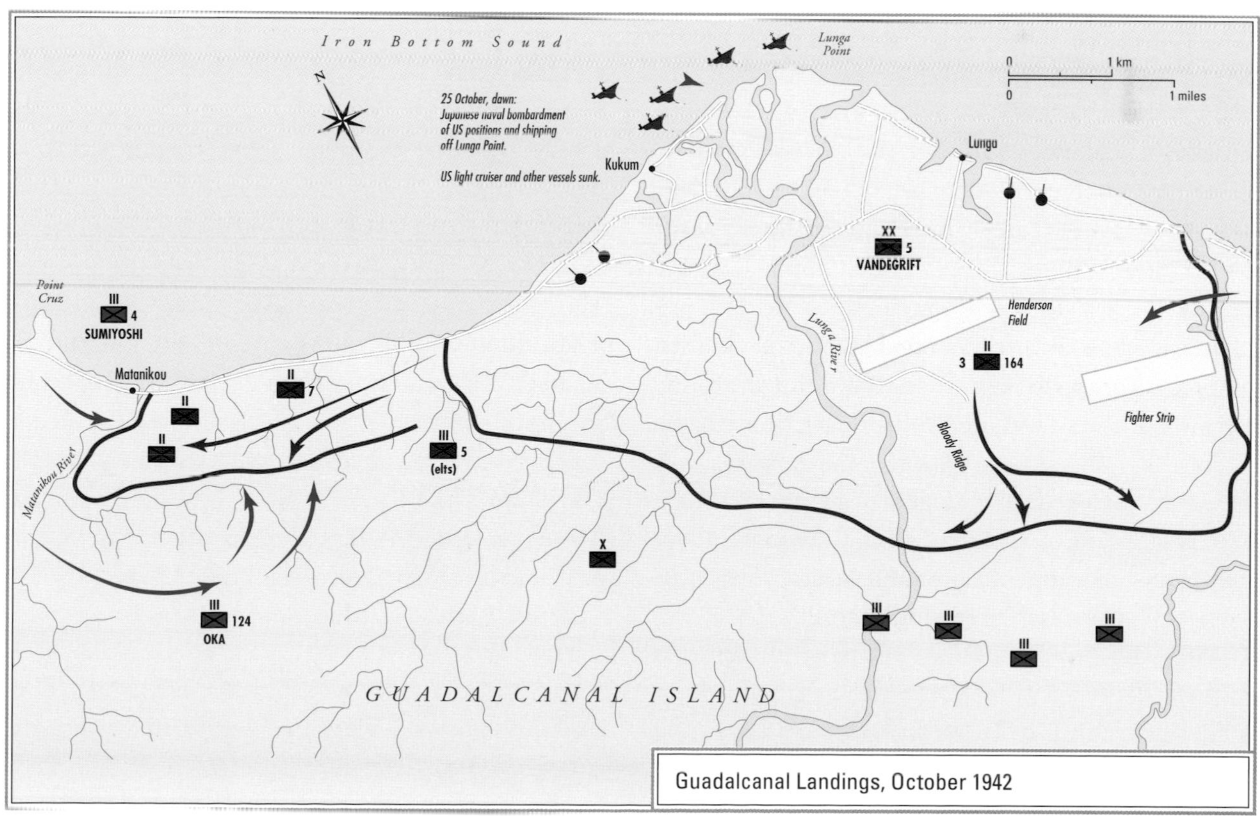

Guadalcanal Landings, October 1942

loss of some of its most experienced aviators, who were irreplaceable.

■ Cape Esperance, 11–12 October 1942

American RAdm Norman Scott's Task Force 64 surprised Japanese Cruiser Division 6, led by RAdm Arimoto Goto, on a night sortie to Guadalcanal. The heavy cruiser USS *San Francisco* and light cruisers USS *Salt Lake City*, USS *Boise* and USS *Helena*, together with five destroyers, 'crossed the T', bringing all guns to bear on the Japanese. Goto's flagship, *Aoba*, quickly lost communication and fire control and was forced to retire. US fire sank the cruiser *Furutaka* and three Japanese destroyers. Goto himself was mortally wounded when armour-piercing shells struck *Aoba*'s bridge.

■ Bismarck Sea, 1–3 March 1943

US Gen George Kenney's Allied Air Force, Southwest Pacific, carried out a devastating attack on Japanese merchant and naval shipping, sending eight transports and eight warships to the bottom and killing more than 3000 enemy troops in the process. The three-day battle, carried out by 335 American and Australian aircraft, with US Navy motor torpedo boats supporting, targeted a Japanese convoy bound for New Guinea. Allied bombers skilfully surprised the Japanese with low-level attack runs, evading the convoy's high-flying fighter escort. The attacking planes 'skipped' their bombs along the wave crests into their targets' hulls, puncturing the vessels close to or below the waterline. At the battle of Bismarck Sea, the Allies also destroyed 20–30 Japanese aircraft, in the air and at Lae. After the battle, the Japanese abandoned large supply missions to New Guinea, hastening its reconquest by the Allies.

■ New Georgia, 20 June–25 August 1943

During the summer of 1943, the US invaded the islands of New Georgia, the next important objective after Guadalcanal. Despite unopposed landings and overwhelming numerical superiority (30,000 US troops to 9000 Japanese), the American advance stalled. At Bairoko Harbor, the 1st and 4th US Marine Raider Battalions, with two US Army infantry battalions, attempted to seize Japanese naval facilities. The attack failed at the price of 50 US and 30 Japanese lives before the Americans withdrew. In July, the Americans attacked Munda Point, where the Japanese had built and fortified an airfield. Adding that facility to the Allies' growing network of bases was an important objective for LGen Millard Harmon, commander of US Army Forces Pacific. The Americans used flamethrowers and explosives to envelope and destroy the last Japanese positions. With the airfield captured, the remaining Japanese forces evacuated the island.

■ Kula Gulf, 6 July 1943

US RAdm Ainsworth's cruiser-destroyer Task Group 36 attacked Adm Akiyama's Third Destroyer Group at night in the 8km gulf between Kolobangara and New Georgia. The Americans sank the destroyer *Nizuki* and drove *Nagatsuki* aground. In return, the Japanese sank the light cruiser USS *Helena*.

■ Vella Lavella, 15 August–9 October 1943

The US 25th and New Zealand 3rd Divisions crushed a Japanese garrison on Vella Lavella, west of New Georgia. From mid-August 1943 to January 1944, the island's airbase hosted the Vought F4U Corsairs of US Marine Corps VMF-214 – Col 'Pappy' Boyington's 'Black Sheep' Squadron.

■ Markham Valley, 5–15 September 1943

The US 503rd Parachute Infantry Regiment made the first American airborne landing of the Pacific War, seizing an airfield at Nadzab in the Markham River valley, New Guinea. With the Australian 25th Infantry Brigade, the Allies forced the Japanese to abandon the city of Lae.

■ Huon Peninsula, 22 Sept 1943–1 Mar 1944

The Australian 9th Division's superb amphibious landing captured Finschhafen, bottling up the Japanese 20th Division in eastern Papua. In a series of battles on the peninsula, the Japanese lost approximately 3000 soldiers while the Australians lost 1028.

■ Bougainville, 1 Nov 1943–21 August 1945

Bougainville, largest and most westerly of the Solomons, was an important campaign objective. Adm Halsey's plan included an amphibious landing at Empress Augusta Bay on 1 November 1943. Within the first day, US Marines had established and fortified a 4000m beachhead. Later, the US Army's XIV Corps, including the Americal and 37th Divisions, landed. The beachhead put Japanese airfields on Bougainville and at Rabaul within reach of Allied attack planes. More than 62,000 American troops dug in to await a counter-attack by 19,000 Japanese troops of Gen Harukichi Hyakutake's Seventeenth Army. The two sides bitterly contested the island's central ridgeline. By November 1944, the Americans had the upper hand. However, the Japanese continued to fight Australian and Commonwealth replacement troops until 21 August 1945. Final victory cost more than 1200 Allied and more than 20,000 Japanese lives.

■ Rabaul, 1943–44

After a crippling US air raid on Rabaul on 2 November 1943, which inflicted severe damage on the port, the Allied forces surrounded and strangled Japanese-held bases on New Britain by seizing airfields and naval facilities at Cape Gloucester, the Green Islands and the Admiralty Islands.

■ Cape Gloucester, 26 December 1943–22 April 1944

During Operation *Cartwheel*, the US 1st Marine Division landed on New Britain to seize the airfields at Cape Gloucester. Opposed by the Japanese 17th Division, the US Marines used their new M4A1 Sherman tanks to overwhelm the defenders.

■ Admiralty Islands, 29 Feb–18 May 1944

In the final phase of the Allied effort to isolate the critical Japanese-held port of Rabaul, 35,000 troops of the US Cavalry Division attacked a Japanese garrison of 4000 men during Operation *Brewer*. The fighting cost 3280 Japanese and 326 American lives.

■ Aitape, 22 April 1944

After a two-hour naval barrage on 22 April, troops from the US 41st Infantry Division, together with Australian engineers, landed at Aitape, New Guinea. The Allies easily overwhelmed a Japanese garrison of 2000 men. Nearby Tadji airfield became a base for Allied fighters.

■ Hollandia, 22 April 1944

Covered by carrier air strikes, a landing force of 80,000 US troops (a total of two divisions) seized this Japanese air base on New Guinea's north coast. Gen MacArthur's success isolated the Japanese force at Wewak, although the victory cost 4000 American casualties.

■ Biak, 29 May–13 June 1944

Northwest of New Guinea, Biak was a battleground between the US 41st Division and the Japanese 222nd Infantry. After a grinding combat that annihilated more than 6000 Japanese and 400 Americans, US troops captured the Mokmer airfield.

■ Morotai, 15 September–4 October 1944

On the southern approach to the Philippines, this island in the Dutch East Indies was the scene of an unopposed landing by the US 31st Infantry Division. The island's topography made the landing and subsequent air and naval base development challenging.

■ Leyte, 17 October 1944–1 July 1945

The US Sixth Army, under LGen Walter Krueger, confronted Japanese LGen Shiro Makino's 16th Division. The Japanese took 70,000 casualties and lost irreplaceable aircraft and ships in this decisive battle of the American reconquest of the Philippines.

■ Leyte Gulf, 24 and 25 October 1944

In terms of tonnage of warships deployed, the battle of Leyte Gulf is the largest naval battle ever fought, engaging 282 vessels as well as 180,000 sailors and pilots. The Imperial Japanese Navy (IJN) hoped to use the battle to destroy the US

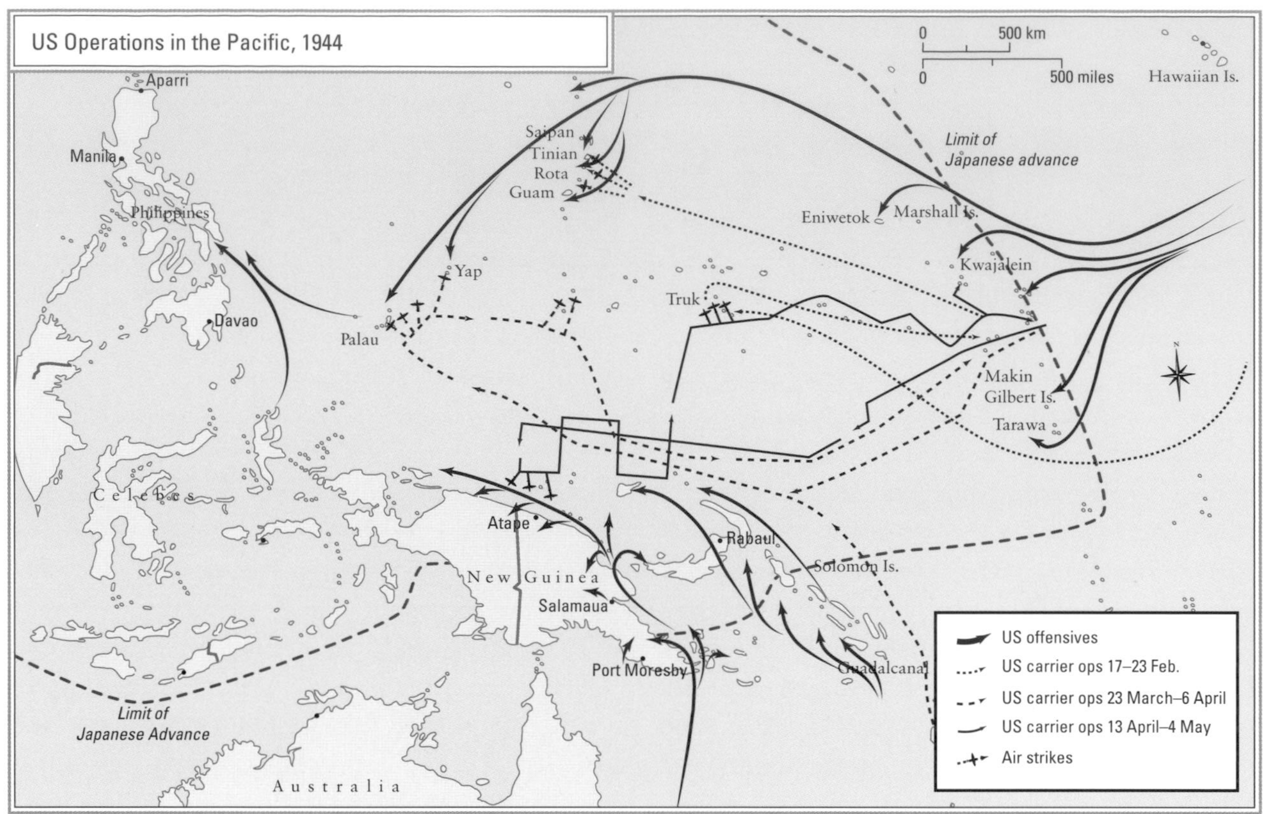

Third and Seventh Fleets outside the Philippine Islands, then isolate the US ground forces invading the Philippines themselves. The Japanese plan, developed by Adm Soemu Toyoda, envisioned amassing the Japanese fleet from disparate bases then dividing it into two in the waters off the Philippines. A decoy fleet of four carriers would steam to the northeast of the islands and attract the attention of the carriers of the US Third Fleet before running off to the northeast. Given that these carriers had few planes or pilots owing to Japan's earlier defeats, Toyoda did not believe that they could do much more. If, however, they could distract the US carriers, then the Japanese battleships coming from the west could even the odds against the US Seventh Fleet.

Aware that Leyte was possibly the last major engagement Japan was capable of fighting, the Japanese Navy committed almost everything it had, including its two enormous 72,000 ton battleships, the *Yamato* and the *Musashi*. Five other battleships and 16 cruisers joined them, supported by land-based planes on Japanese airfields in the Philippines. If they could lure the US Seventh Fleet away from the carriers and perform a pincer movement, the Japanese might deny the Americans access to the Philippines, giving them the major strategic victory they needed.

The battle of Leyte Gulf involved four related engagements in the gulfs and straits of the Philippines. Gen Douglas MacArthur's landing of the Sixth Army on the island of Leyte drew both navies towards Leyte Gulf like a magnet and made it the centre of gravity for the subsequent battle. Neither side had one admiral in overall command of the entire engagement and confusion therefore reigned from beginning to end. With the clash spread out over hundreds of miles, it was nearly impossible for the commanders to develop a sense of the entire battle as it unfolded. Superior intelligence and quick decision-making gave the

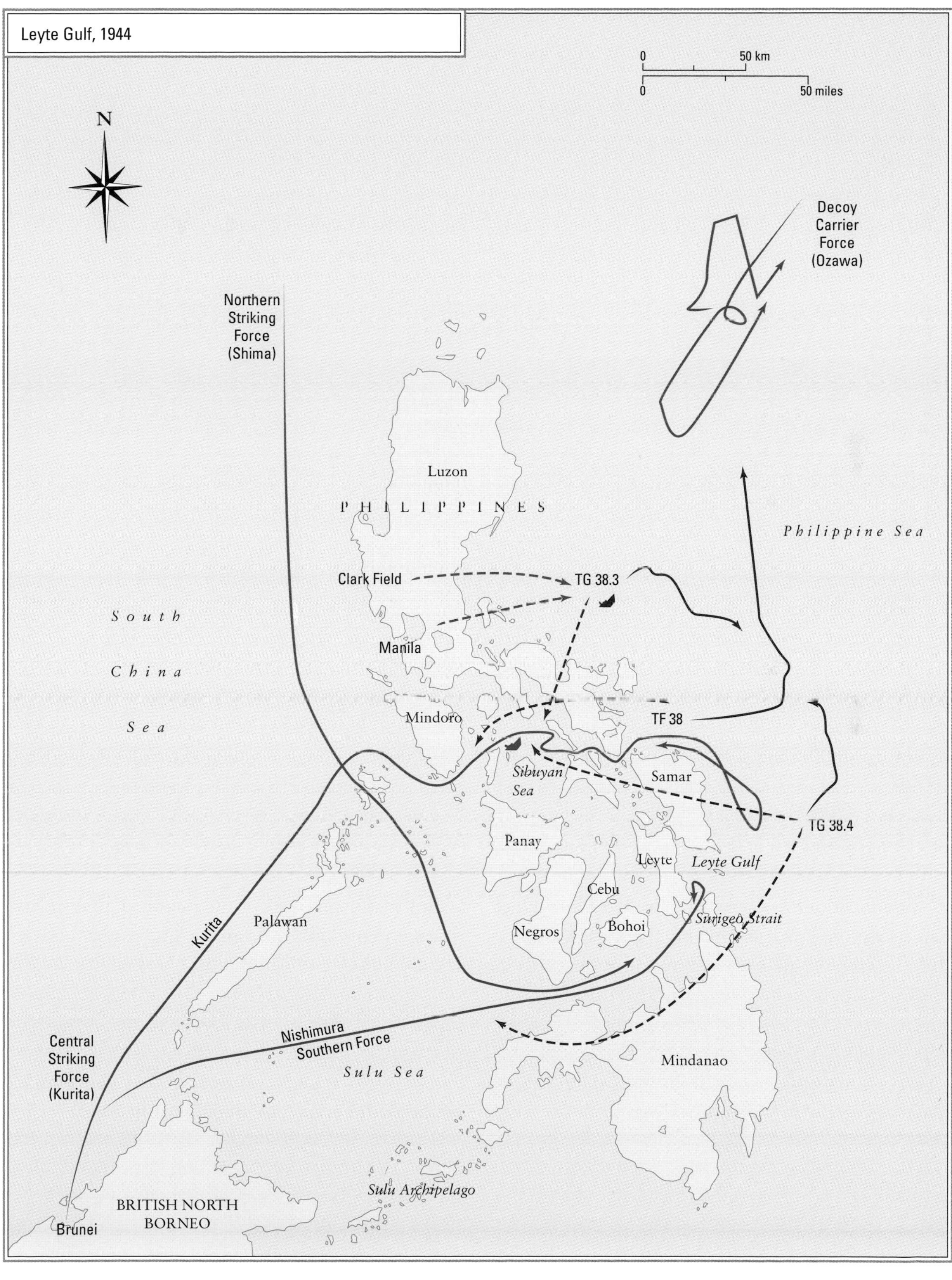
Leyte Gulf, 1944
0 50 km
0 50 miles
N
Decoy
Carrier
Force
(Ozawa)
Northern
Striking
Force
(Shima)
Luzon
PHILIPPINES
Philippine Sea
Clark Field
TG 38.3
South
China
Sea
Manila
Mindoro
TF 38
Sibuyan
Sea
Samar
TG 38.4
Panay
Leyte
Leyte Gulf
Cebu
Kurita
Palawan
Negros
Bohoi
Surigeo Strait
Central
Striking
Force
(Kurita)
Nishimura
Southern Force
Sulu Sea
Mindanao
Sulu Archipelago
BRITISH NORTH
BORNEO
Brunei

Americans a fundamental geographic advantage, although the Americans did initially fall for the carrier bait and divide their forces.

The decision to chase the decoys limited the power the Americans could bring to bear, although in fairness it must be noted that the Americans had no way of knowing how depleted of aircraft the Japanese decoy carriers really were. The Americans thus might have scored even greater triumphs at Leyte Gulf had they concentrated their ships, but they won a major victory nevertheless.

The Japanese Navy suffered devastating losses of all four decoy carriers, three battleships, 10 cruisers and nine destroyers. Most of the other capital ships the Japanese engaged were damaged and they also lost more than 500 planes. Perhaps most crucially, some 10,000 irreplaceable pilots and sailors died in the battle. Japan could not make good these losses, and was forced to rely increasingly on poorly trained replacements, who were virtual cannon fodder for the Americans. The American losses were three light carriers (out of 16 deployed), two destroyers, and 200 aircraft, but American industry could more than make good these losses. American personnel losses equalled 2800 men, about half of them from suicide attacks that previewed the deadly *kamikazes*. The battle of Leyte Gulf effectively destroyed Japanese naval power and opened the way for the American reconquest of the Philippines.

■ Surigao Strait, 25 October 1944

During the battles for Leyte Gulf, Japanese VAdm Shoji Nishimura's Southern Force clashed with US RAdm Jesse Oldendorf's Seventh Fleet. Despite having been observed in enemy-controlled waters, Nishimura's task force proceeded. The Americans ambushed and successfully 'crossed the T' of their adversaries, raking Nishimura's line mercilessly with torpedoes and heavy gunfire, which decimated the Japanese fleet. Nishimura went down with his flagship, the Fuso-class battleship *Yamashiro*. This was the last large-scale surface engagement between battleships in the Pacific War.

■ Cape Engano, 25–26 October 1944

VAdm Jisaburo Ozawa's Northern Force baited Adm Halsey's Third Fleet into a risky pursuit. Ozawa commanded four aircraft carriers, making him an attractive target, but the depleted Japanese force actually had fewer than 30 aircraft. Halsey's 64 warships and more than 300 planes caught them up, sinking all four carriers in a crushing defeat. Halsey was later criticized for leaving the San Bernardino Strait unguarded.

■ Samar, 25 October 1944

In the San Bernardino Strait, six US escort carriers of task unit 'Taffy 3' attacked the mighty Japanese Central Force. Badly outgunned, Taffy 3 sank three Japanese cruisers at the cost of more than 1000 American sailors, two destroyers and two escort carriers, including one sunk by *kamikaze* attacks.

■ Wewak, mid-December 1944–10 May 1945

Allied amphibious operations at Hollandia and Aitape had isolated the Japanese Eighteenth Army in northern New Guinea. After five months' hard campaigning, the Australian 6th Division took Wewak, at the cost of 451 killed. More than 7000 Japanese died.

■ Luzon, 9 January–15 August 1945

On the Philippine island of Luzon, the Japanese force included 152,000 soldiers of LGen Yamashita's Shobu Group, 30,000 soldiers of MGen Tsukada's Kembu Group (near Bataan) and 80,000 soldiers of LGen Yokoyama's Shimbu Group (along the Bicol peninsula). US Sixth Army commander, LGen Walter Krueger, landed 175,000 troops along a 40km beachhead between Lingayen and San Fabian. MacArthur ordered them to capture Manila, Bataan and Corregidor. In February, the US 37th and 1st Cavalry Divisions raced towards the capital. Although lightly garrisoned, by 4 March Manila was razed to the ground in the most intense urban combat of the Pacific War. US amphibious and airborne landings then seized Bataan and Corregidor, leaving the Allies firmly in control of Subic Bay. Fighting continued in the centre and north. By the end of the war, the Americans had killed or captured almost all of the approximately 230,000 Japanese on Luzon. US casualties were 47,000 (killed and captured).

■ **Southern Philippines–Borneo, 1 May–1 August 1945**

Between 1943 and 1944, Borneo had provided 40 per cent of Japan's fuel oil and as much as 30 per cent of her crude oil. Having landed, the Australian 9th Division (with US and Dutch support) defeated the Japanese Thirty-Seventh Army to seize these vital resources.

Central Pacific 1943–45

■ **Tarawa-Makin, 20–24 November 1943**

Operation *Galvanic* was the first joint US Army and US Marine Corps amphibious operation of the Central Pacific Campaign. This represented a shift in the Americans' regional strategy from defence to offence. US Adm Chester Nimitz, Commander-in-Chief, Pacific Ocean Areas, and Marine LGen Holland Smith, V Amphibious Corps, ordered the plan to seize Makin Atoll, a Japanese seaplane base, and Tarawa Atoll, a fortified airfield.

Naval Task Force 52 landed the army's 27th Infantry Division on Makin, where they faced fewer than 800 defenders. Nevertheless, MGen Ralph Smith met fierce resistance. His soldiers shot dead 395 Japanese while suffering 218 casualties. On 23 November, Smith radioed his superiors: "Makin taken". Tarawa was a different scene. There, Task Force 53 had put the Marines' amphibious tractors (amtracs) ashore amid withering enemy artillery and automatic weapons' fire. MGen Julian Smith's 2nd Marine Division faced 4800 well-entrenched Japanese. The battle for Tarawa was one of appalling ferocity, as the Japanese soldiers fought to the death. By the time the smoke cleared on 24 November, nearly all the defenders were killed

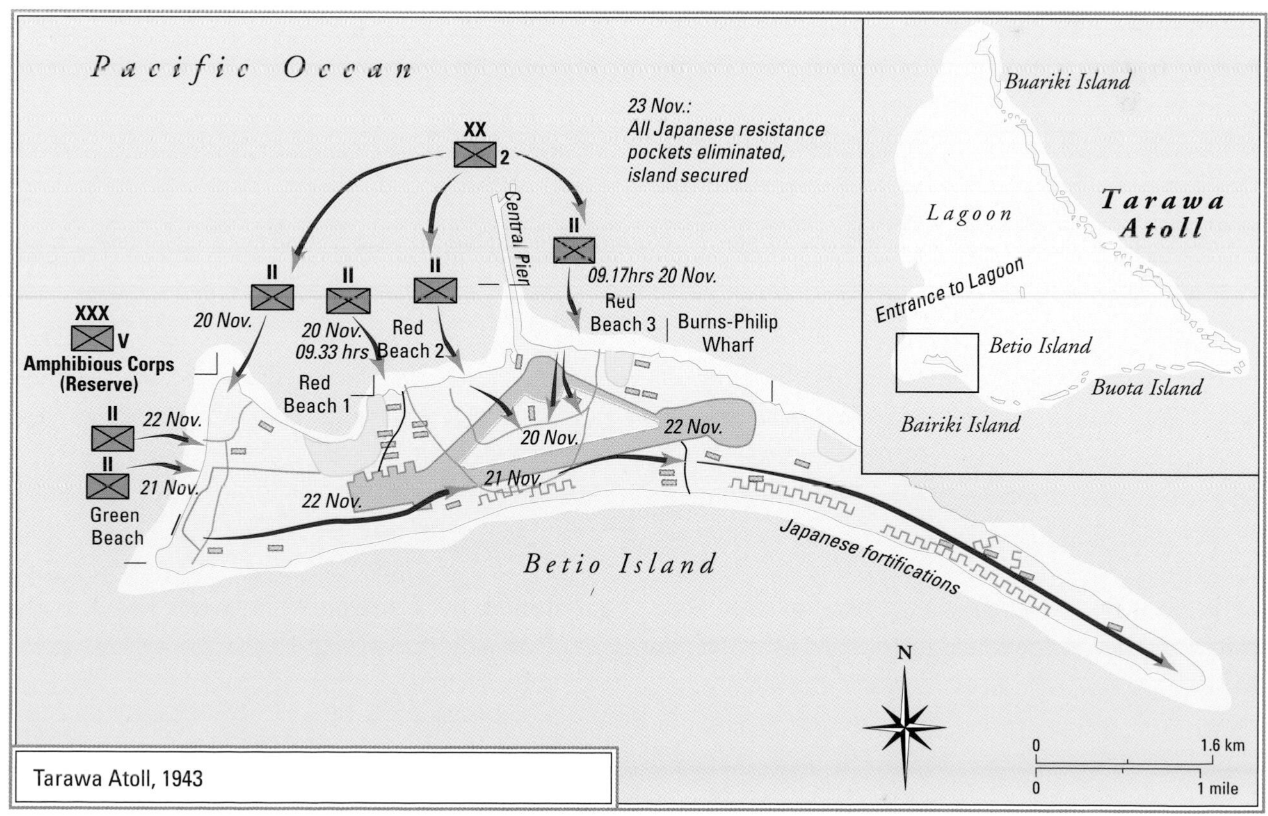

Tarawa Atoll, 1943

and the Americans had suffered more than 3000 casualties.

■ **Kwajalein-Eniwetok, 31 January–3 February/17 February–23 February 1944**

The American 4th Marine Division and 7th Infantry Division sought to break Japan's 'outer ring' defences. At Roi and Namur, northernmost islands of the Kwajaleien Atoll, they wiped out almost the entire Japanese garrison of 3500 men.

■ **Truk, 17–18 February 1944**

Almost 600 US aircraft, from 12 carriers, attacked Japan's large naval base at Truk. The Americans destroyed 15 Japanese warships, more than 30 freighters and almost 300 aircraft. The Japanese shot down 25 US planes.

■ **Mariana Islands 15 June–1 August 1944**

The Mariana Islands offered many benefits as a base for the Americans, particularly as a location for bomber airfields from which to attack Japan directly. The US Joint Chiefs of Staff decided to take the islands, and preparations began with a heavy air and sea bombardment of Saipan, Tinian, Guam and Rota on 11 June 1944. Adm Marc Mitscher's Task Force 58 launched fighter sweeps from its carriers; these destroyed over 150 Japanese aircraft. This was the beginning of what became known as 'The Great Marianas Turkey Shoot'. US carrier airpower was to inflict huge losses upon the Japanese Army and Naval Air Forces on the islands over the course of the battle. The invasion force landed on 15 June and, despite significant Japanese resistance, which inflicted heavy casualties on the attackers, the beachhead was firmly established by the end of the day. The island was under American control by 9 July.

The arrival of the Japanese fleet in the area forced the Americans to send their ships to fight the battle of the Philippine Sea on 19–20 June. The need to fight this battle delayed the assault on Guam, which was attacked on 21 July, but this delay was the only success for the Japanese, whose aircraft losses reached around 600 machines by the end of the battle. Japanese resistance on Guam was heavy, and casualties significant, but the island was under American control by the end of the month. The last island, Tinian, was assaulted on 24 July. American casualty figures were low in comparison with the attacks on Saipan and Guam and most of the island was under American control in the space of four days, finally being declared secure on 1 August 1944.

■ **Saipan 15 June–9 July 1944**

Capturing the Mariana Islands would provide air bases for long-range air raids on the Japanese homeland by US Boeing B-29 Superfortress bombers. On Saipan, 25,000 troops of MGen Yoshitsugu Saito's 43rd Division and 6000 Japanese naval infantry had fortified the island's caves and cliffs. Cut off from resupply by the American victory in the battle of the Philippine Sea, the defenders made a desperate last stand. After a two-day bombardment, 8000 US Marines of LGen

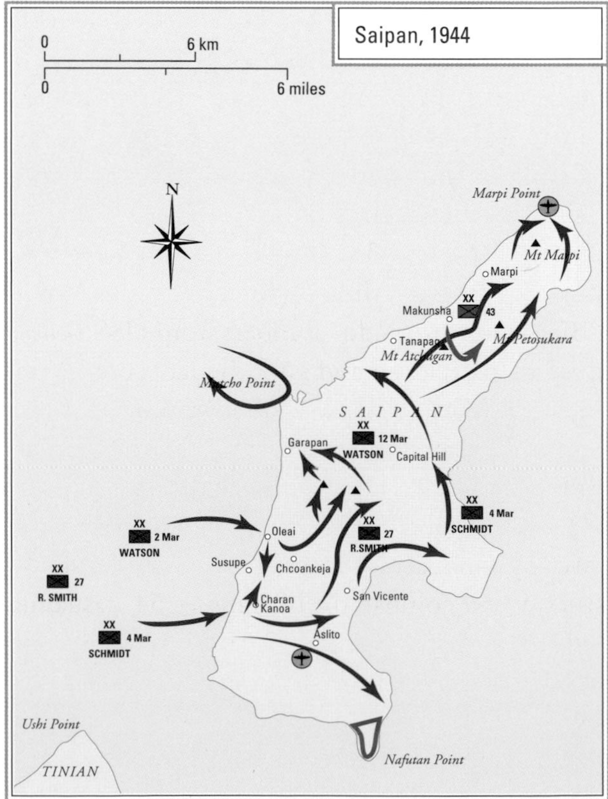

Holland Smith's 2nd and 4th Marine Divisions hit the western beaches. The next day, the US Army's 27th Infantry Division came ashore and drove north to capture Aslito airfield. The Japanese fought tenaciously, with deeply entrenched machine-gun and mortar teams. American 'Satan' tanks (M3 Stuarts, modified to fire the Canadian 'Ronson' Mk 1 vehicle flamethrower) helped burn out the most fanatical defenders. After three weeks of bitter fighting, nearly all of the Japanese defenders were killed. The Americans suffered more than 14,000 casualties.

■ Philippine Sea 19–20 June 1944

VAdm Jisaburo Ozawa's Mobile Fleet, comprising five aircraft carriers and their screen of cruisers and destroyers, sortied from their Philippine bases toward the American invasion force in the Mariana Islands. US intelligence reports indicated that Ozawa had divided his force to draw the American carriers away from the landing at Saipan. Adm Raymond Spruance ordered his Fifth Fleet forces to hold position covering the amphibious squadron and await the Japanese attack.

The action came at 10:00 on 19 June, 966km west of Saipan, as VAdm Marc Mitscher's Task Force 58 intercepted the first wave of Japanese fighters and bombers. The navy's Grumman F6F Hellcat fighters mauled the Mitsubishi A6M Zeros and Aichi D3Val dive-bombers, destroying more than 40 of the first 68 aircraft by 11:00. TBF Avenger torpedo-bombers from USS *Belleau Wood* then attacked and sank the Japanese carrier *Hiyo*. To the Americans, the one-sided fracas became known as 'The Great Marianas Turkey Shoot', in which they downed 385 of Ozawa's 545 planes and sank three Japanese carriers (two by submarine torpedo strikes). American losses were comparatively light – 54 casualties and 26 aircraft. Despite this success, Spruance was criticized for his decision not to close with the Japanese fleet. Both he and Mitscher had wanted to deal the Japanese Navy a decisive blow. However, an offensive sortie could have left the

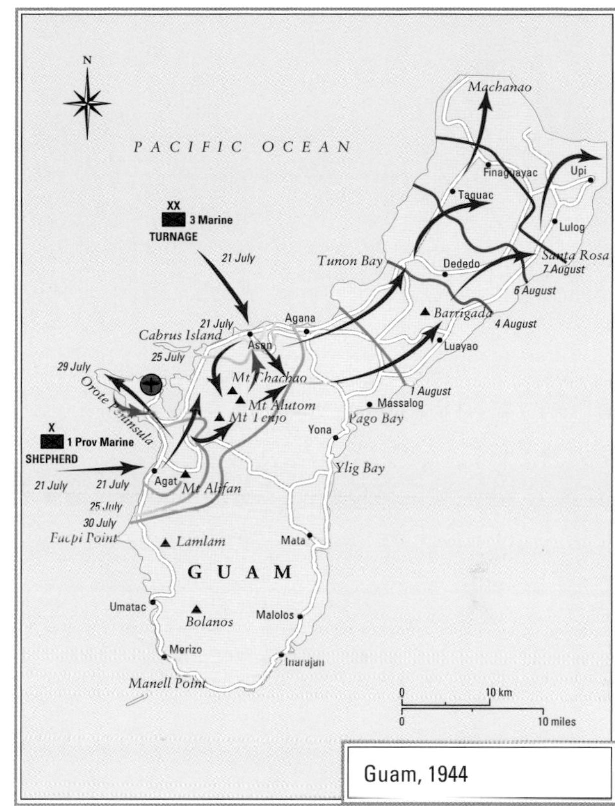

Guam, 1944

amphibious operation at Saipan vulnerable to air and naval attack, had Ozawa divided his force as the Japanese had done at the Aleutians, Midway and in the Solomons. Six of Ozawa's nine 'flat-tops' escaped the battle. However, the Japanese naval air force, already battered after Guadalcanal and the Solomons, never recovered from the crushing blow it suffered over the Philippine Sea.

■ Guam II, 21 July–10 August 1944

From fortified dugouts and caves, the Japanese fought an invasion by MGen Roy Geiger's 3rd Marine Division and US Army's 77th Infantry. US forces recaptured the island after three weeks of intense battle, resulting in the deaths of more than 18,000 Japanese and 10,000 American troops, some from 'friendly fire'.

■ Tinian, 24 July–1 August 1944

For the conquest of Tinian, which lay almost 6km south of Saipan, the US Army and Marine Corps divided their labours: Army soldiers would take the roles of artillery and engineer support, while

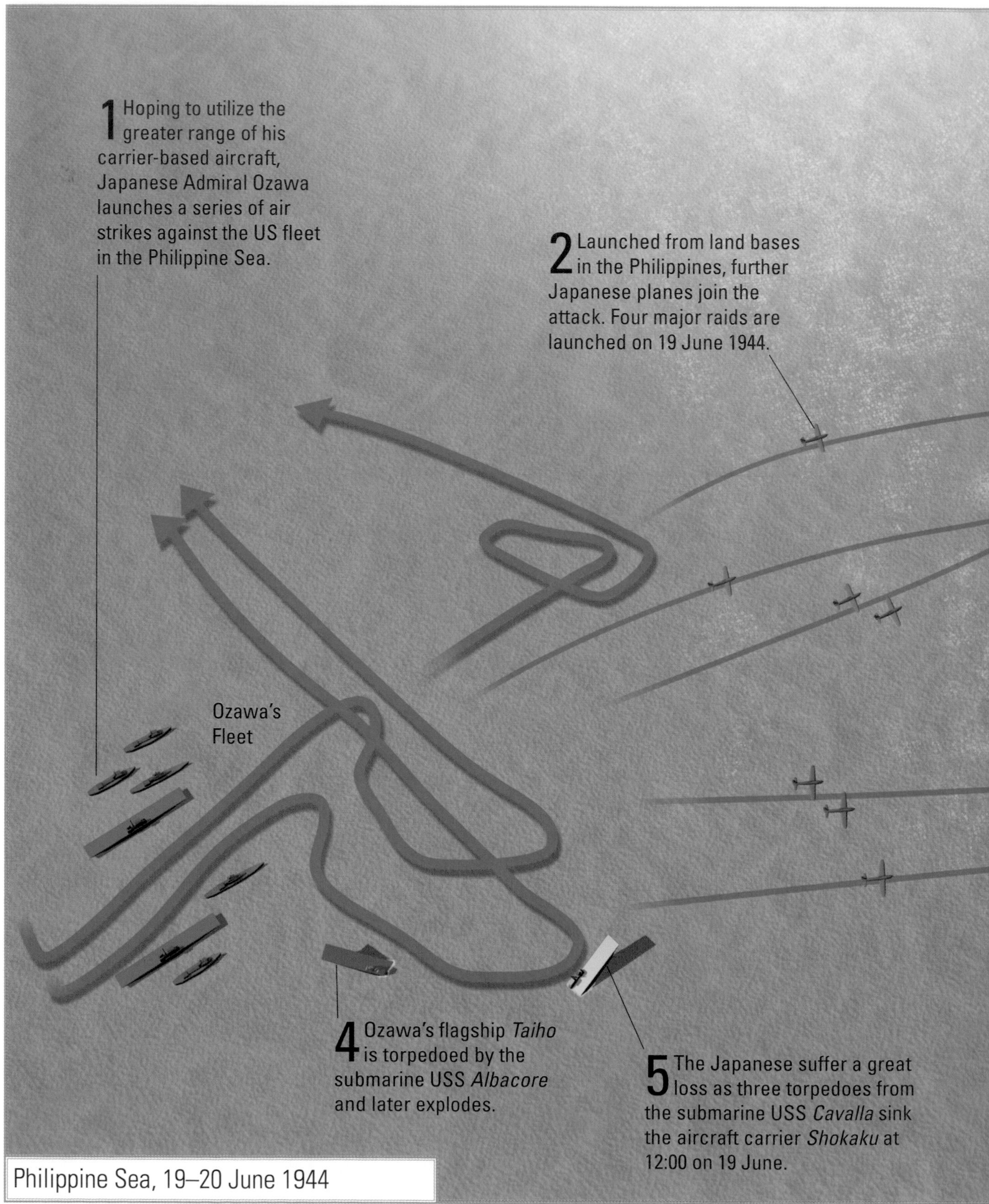

Philippine Sea, 19–20 June 1944

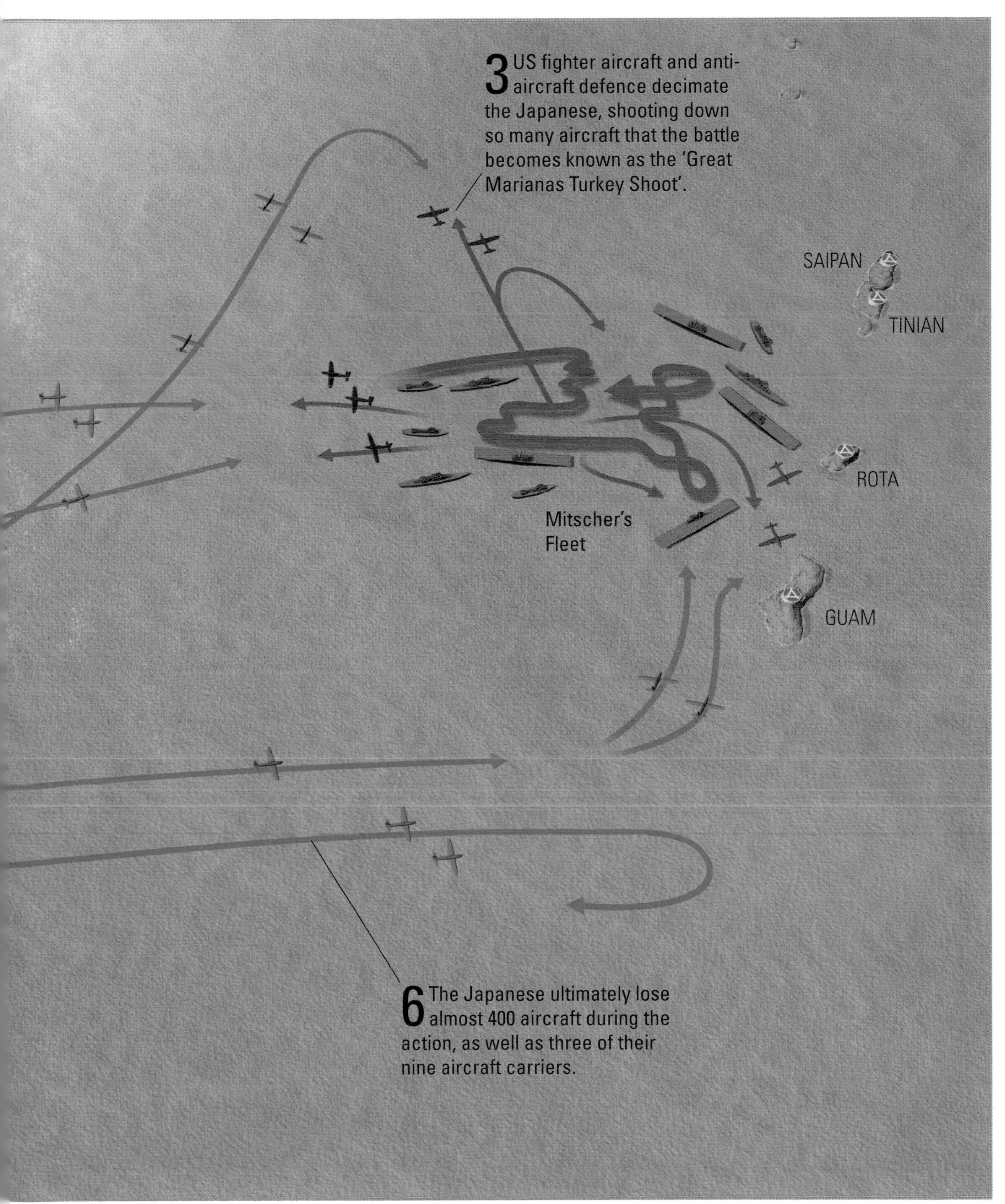
3 US fighter aircraft and anti-aircraft defence decimate the Japanese, shooting down so many aircraft that the battle becomes known as the 'Great Marianas Turkey Shoot'.
SAIPAN
TINIAN
ROTA
Mitscher's Fleet
GUAM
6 The Japanese ultimately lose almost 400 aircraft during the action, as well as three of their nine aircraft carriers.

Marines would be on the point as infantry. Less than one week after Saipan fell, the US Army faced its artillery batteries south and commenced a massive bombardment, during which they had fired thousands of shells by the end of the battle. LGen Harry Schmidt led the 2nd and 4th Marine Divisions, crossing the strait from Saipan in boats and amphibious tractors. The most important objectives were the island's three airfields, which were taken after a nine-day battle that cost more than 8000 Japanese and more than 300 American lives. Tinian became a base for US long-range bombers, including the B-29 'Enola Gay', which on 6 August 1945 famously left the island to carry out the atomic bombing of Hiroshima.

■ Peleliu-Angaur, 15 September–27 November 1944

In their conquest of Peleliu and Angaur islands, the 1st Marine Division, together with the US Army's 81st Infantry, faced bitter opposition. They killed almost all of the Japanese 14th Division's 11,000 men, while suffering 1700 American casualties.

■ Iwo Jima, 19 February–26 March 1945

As 1944 drew to a close, the American High Command concluded that there were strong grounds for seizing the Japanese island of Iwo Jima. The most prevalent operational consideration was the need to provide a suitable base from which USAAF fighter aircraft could reach Japan, thus enabling the provision of escorts for B-29 bombers raiding the enemy homeland. Iwo Jima also had two airfields, one of which was large enough to accommodate B-29s. This offered an ideal emergency landing ground from the outset, as well as a permanent base for the bombers in due course. A final potent factor was that the Japanese viewed Iwo Jima as part of their home territories, and taking it would have a potent psychological effect on the enemy.

The Japanese were aware of the significance of Iwo Jima and set about boosting the defences in late 1944, sending reinforcements and constructing fortified defensive positions. By the end of 1944, a huge network of tunnels had been built, with the aim of sheltering the defenders from the inevitable massive bombardment that would precede an attack. The value of the tunnels was proved from late November, when American air and sea bombardments began.

The invasion itself occurred on 19 February 1945. The American landing forces faced little opposition until they made their way inshore, where they encountered vigorous resistance from fanatically motivated defenders. Hand-to-hand fighting ensued as the US Marines cleared the defensive positions one by one and broke through.

By nightfall, around 30,000 Americans were ashore and surrounding Mount Suribachi, the highest point on Iwo Jima, in the south of the island. Four days of intense fighting then ensued as the US Marines sought to clear the Japanese from Mount Suribachi. The last Japanese positions on Suribachi were cleared by late afternoon of 23

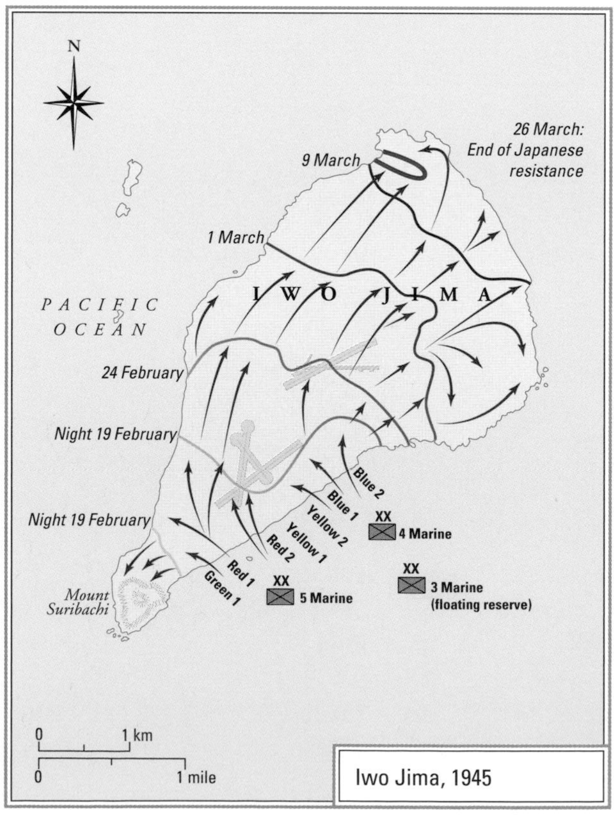

Iwo Jima, 1945

February, accompanied by the raising of the US flag atop the mountain; a flag was, in fact, raised twice, the second occasion being captured by a press photographer and becoming one of the iconic images of the war.

This symbolic moment, however, was far from the end of the battle. A vicious, bunker-to-bunker, attritional clash ensued as the Americans were forced to fight from one defensive position to another, invariably finding that the Japanese defenders would not surrender. The Japanese exploited the tunnel system to the full, often attacking the Americans from behind, and the Americans made ever greater use of close air support, artillery and flamethrowers to clear the defenders from their positions.

The Japanese met the Americans with a *kamikaze* attack on a number of ships during 21 February, and a number of massed frontal assaults on the American positions during the hours of darkness. One such attack on Hill 362 in the north of the island cost the Japanese more than 75 per cent of the attacking force.

Casualties were horrendous for both sides. By the tenth day of the battle, many American units were down to half strength, and the Japanese had sustained even higher casualties. On the night of 25–26 March, the surviving Japanese troops, estimated to number around 300 men, launched a suicidal human-wave charge against the US Marines in the final counter-attack and were wiped out. In total, 23,000 Japanese died, and only 216 survived; the Marines lost 6281 killed and more than 18,000 wounded in what constitutes the bloodiest operation in the US Marine Corps' history.

■ Okinawa, 1 April–21 June 1945

The American attack on Okinawa began on 1 April 1945, the largest amphibious assault in the Pacific during the war. Although the landings met with little opposition to begin with, once the Americans had advanced further into the island,

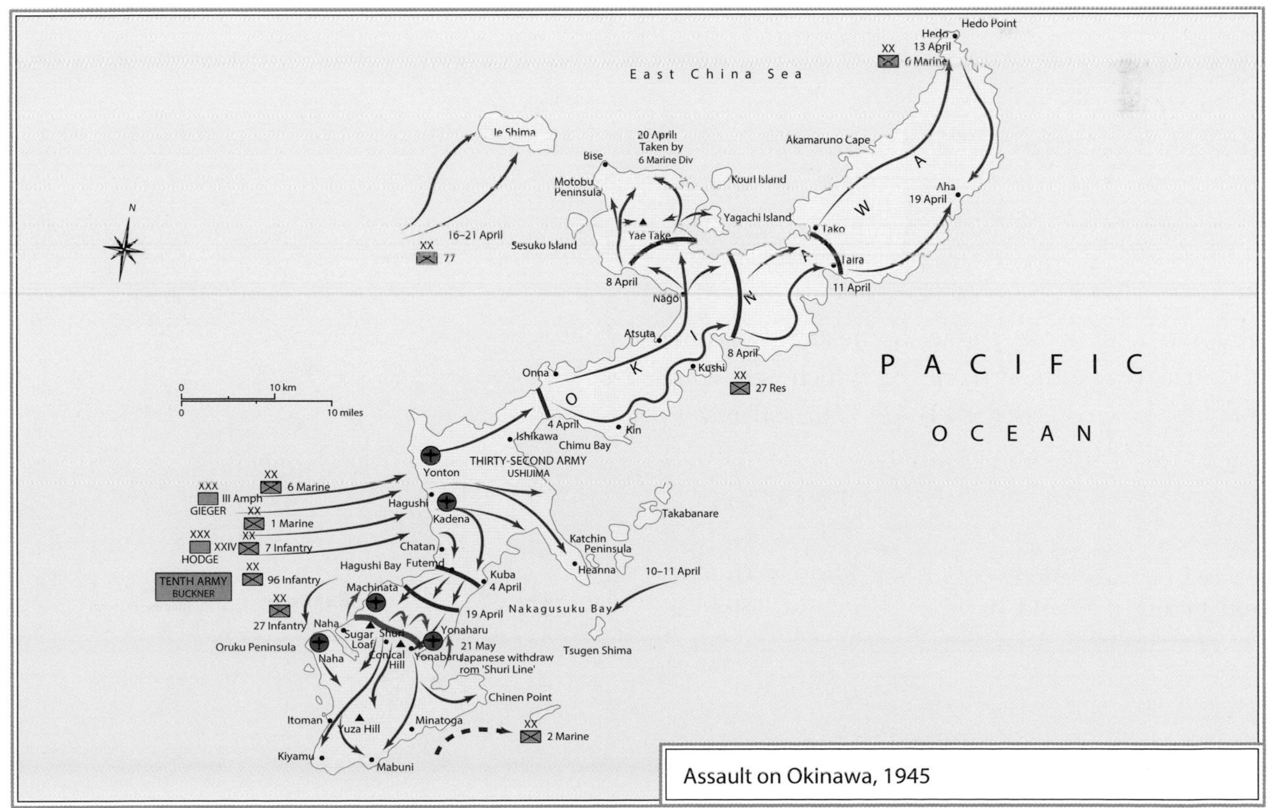

Assault on Okinawa, 1945

A pair of US Marines relax following the capture of Peleliu in November 1944, after a two-month battle to wrest the tiny Pacific atoll from a determined Japanese defence.

resistance was heavy. The Japanese launched a number of *kamikaze* attacks on the American ships, while the abortive *Ten-Go* operation saw the destruction of the Japanese battleship *Yamato*. Tenacious resistance made the American advance slow, and it was not until 21 June that Okinawa finally fell.

The battle had been an enormously bloody one for both sides. There were 62,000 American casualties, 12,000 of whom were fatalities, making this the most costly battle for the Americans in the Pacific campaign. The Japanese lost 94,000 killed, along with a considerable number of civilian fatalities. The casualties on Okinawa, and previously at Iwo Jima, helped influence the decision to use the atomic bomb.

Northern Pacific 1943

Aleutian Islands, 3 June 1942–15 August 1943

Adm Isoroku Yamamoto believed the invasion of the Aleutians would draw the US Navy away from Midway, Japan's primary objective after Pearl Harbor. VAdm Boshiro Hosogaya's Northern Area Fleet landed troops unopposed on 6–7 June 1942. By November, there were 4000 Japanese on Kiska and another 1000 on Attu. Removing this enemy foothold on American soil became a psychologically important US war objective. At the battle of the Komandorski Islands, the US Navy had checked Japan's attempts to resupply their troops on the Aleutians. By January 1943, Alaska Command had 94,000 soldiers and a base on Amchitka Island within 80km of the Japanese occupation force. Anticipating strong resistance on Kiska, the Americans landed 3500 soldiers on Attu. Battling harsh terrain and dangerous weather as much as the Japanese, the Americans drove north to Chichagof Harbor, where Col Yasuyo Yamasaki led his men on a suicidal final assault.

Attu, 11–30 May 1943

In one of the costliest amphibious assaults of the war, the US 7th Division defeated the Japanese 301st Battalion, which had held the island since June 1942. More than 3000 Japanese and American soldiers died, many in the 'banzai' charge at Chichagof Harbor.

Air Campaign Against Japan

Tokyo, 9–10 March 1945

US MGen Curtis LeMay ordered his squadrons to fly low-altitude night attacks with incendiaries against Japan's dispersed wartime industrial base and cities. On the first mission, American bombers burned almost 41.4 square km of Tokyo, killing 85,000 people in history's most destructive conventional air attack.

Hiroshima, 6 August 1945

Nazi Germany had surrendered in May 1945, freeing the Allies to turn their full attention to winning the Pacific War. By mid-summer, the Japanese were militarily defeated in the Philippines, on Iwo Jima and Okinawa. Despite LeMay's relentless aerial bombardment of the Japanese homeland, gutting 68 of its cities and smashing much of the war industry there, the Imperial Government ignored the 26 July Potsdam Declaration demanding its unconditional surrender. The then US President Harry S. Truman, advised by the scientists of the Manhattan Project (America's atomic weapons programme) and War Secretary Henry L. Stimson, authorized the use of atomic bombs to finally break Japan's will to fight. Truman and his War Cabinet hoped to end the conflict without a costly invasion of the Japanese homeland. Although the technology had been successfully demonstrated in July at New Mexico's Alamogordo Bombing and Gunnery Range, many critics inside the US Government questioned the reliability of the project, which only had enough fissile material to produce two weapons that summer.

Initially, the list of possible targets included the military and industrial centres of Kokura,

Hiroshima and Niigata. Kyoto was not on the list, thus sparing the traditional Imperial capital from what Truman warned would call 'a rain of ruin from the air, the like of which has never been seen on this earth'. The first weapon, code-named 'Little Boy', was a gun-type fission device fuelled by 60kg of enriched uranium. Airmen of the 393rd Bombardment Squadron loaded it aboard a B-29 Superfortress called 'Enola Gay', which in the early hours of 6 August launched from Tinian Island with two wingmen. The bombers flew more than six hours to their objective: the naval embarkation port of Hiroshima. 'Enola Gay' released the weapon at 08:15 local time, from just below 9800m altitude. Forty-three seconds later, approximately 600m above the city's centre, the bomb detonated, releasing a force equivalent to 13 kilotons of TNT. Although inefficient (little more than 1 per cent of the weapon's fissile material had released its energy), the blast and the resulting firestorm totally destroyed almost 13 square km, killing as many as 80,000 people.

■ **Nagasaki, 9 August 1945**

Three days after 'Little Boy's' burst etched a human shadow into the stone steps of Hiroshima's Sumitomo Bank, another B-29 bomber, 'Bockscar', released the second atomic bomb over Nagasaki. Codenamed 'Fat Man', Nagasaki's bomb was an implosion-type weapon with a fissile core of 6.1kg of plutonium, similar to the 'gadget' used during the Trinity Site test. On 14 August, Japan surrendered. America's strategic aerial bombardment, including the two atomic bombs, had levelled all of Japan's major cities, causing 800,000 casualties.

Mediterranean Theatre 1942–45

■ **Operation *Torch*, 8th–16th November 1942**

The invasion force of Operation *Torch* comprised 107,000 American, British and Free French troops, who landed in Vichy-held Morocco and Algeria. The Allies were up against a force of 120,000 Vichy troops and their German masters, although whether the French would long resist the Allies was a major unknown. The invasion plan called for the amphibious landing of three task forces at Algiers, Oran and Casablanca. Off the latter target, American naval gunfire and air support sank a French cruiser, six destroyers and six submarines, as well as disabling an unfinished French battleship.

The Vichy troops put up stiff resistance at Oran, until forced to surrender by heavy British naval gunnery and the US 1st Ranger Battalion. The US 509th Parachute Infantry Regiment executed the Americans' first combat airdrop of the war, landing inland to capture airfields south of Oran. At Algiers, a successful coup by the French Resistance, coupled with a swift Allied landing, silenced the Vichy guns.

■ **Tunisia, 17 November 1942–13 May 1943**

Following the American landings in Morocco and Algeria in 1942, the Allies had amassed 253,213 troops with which to conquer North Africa. After a fierce defeat, the Axis suffered 200,000 casualties, with 275,000 captured.

■ **Kasserine Pass, 19–25 February 1943**

During 19–22 February 1943, two Panzer divisions from the German–Italian Panzer Army counter-attacked the 30,000 troops of US II Corps who had occupied the Kasserine Pass through the Atlas Mountains in west-central Tunisia. The Germans inflicted a heavy defeat, pushing the Americans 80km northwest to Tébessa, although the threat to their rear posed by the British Eighth Army's advance led them to withdraw from the pass by the 25th; the Germans suffered 2000 casualties, the Americans/British 10,000.

■ **Sicily, 9 July–17 August 1943**

During 9–10 July 1943, and following victory in North Africa (see below), as part of Operation *Husky*, 140,000 Western Allied troops invaded the Italian island of Sicily. Seventh US Army's three divisions landed at Licata-Scoglitti on the southern coast and the British Eighth Army's one Canadian and three British divisions landed at Pachino-Cassibili on the south-eastern coast, supported by airborne landings. By the 13th, the Allies had driven the defending Italian/German Axis troops back 55km to form a secure lodgement that included the port of Syracuse. Between 14 July and 6 August, American forces cleared western Sicily and the British the central-eastern quadrant, pushing the defenders back to the Etna Line that protected the northeastern peninsula. During 7–17 August, Allied amphibious landings outflanked the Axis defences and during 10–17 August, 130,000 Axis troops evacuated Sicily from Messina at the island's northeastern apex. The Allies suffered 24,500 casualties and the Axis 165,000, including 140,000 Italian prisoners.

■ **Southern Italy, 3–16 September 1943**

US Gen Clark's Fifth Army and British Gen Montgomery's Eighth Army faced 100,000 Germans of GenFM Kesselring's Tenth Army in the contest for Italy. Mussolini capitulated, leaving the Germans to fend for themselves. The invasion began with British landings at Calabria on 3 September. On 9 September, the US Fifth Army came ashore at Salerno. The Germans then withdrew northwards. On 1 October, 190,000 Allied troops liberated Naples, and by 6 October the Allies controlled the Campanian plain.

■ **Salerno, 9 September–6 October 1943**

On 9 September 1943, 55,000 British and American troops of the US Fifth Army landed at Salerno on Italy's western coast south of Naples. During 3–9 September, British forces had invaded the 'toe' and 'heel' of Italy, while on the 8th, the Italians surrendered and the Germans had taken control of the country. During 10–13 September, the Allies consolidated the beachhead as German reserves arrived. German counter-attacks during 14–17 September sorely pressed the Allied line, though it ultimately held. With 160,000 troops in the beachhead on 19 September, the Allies

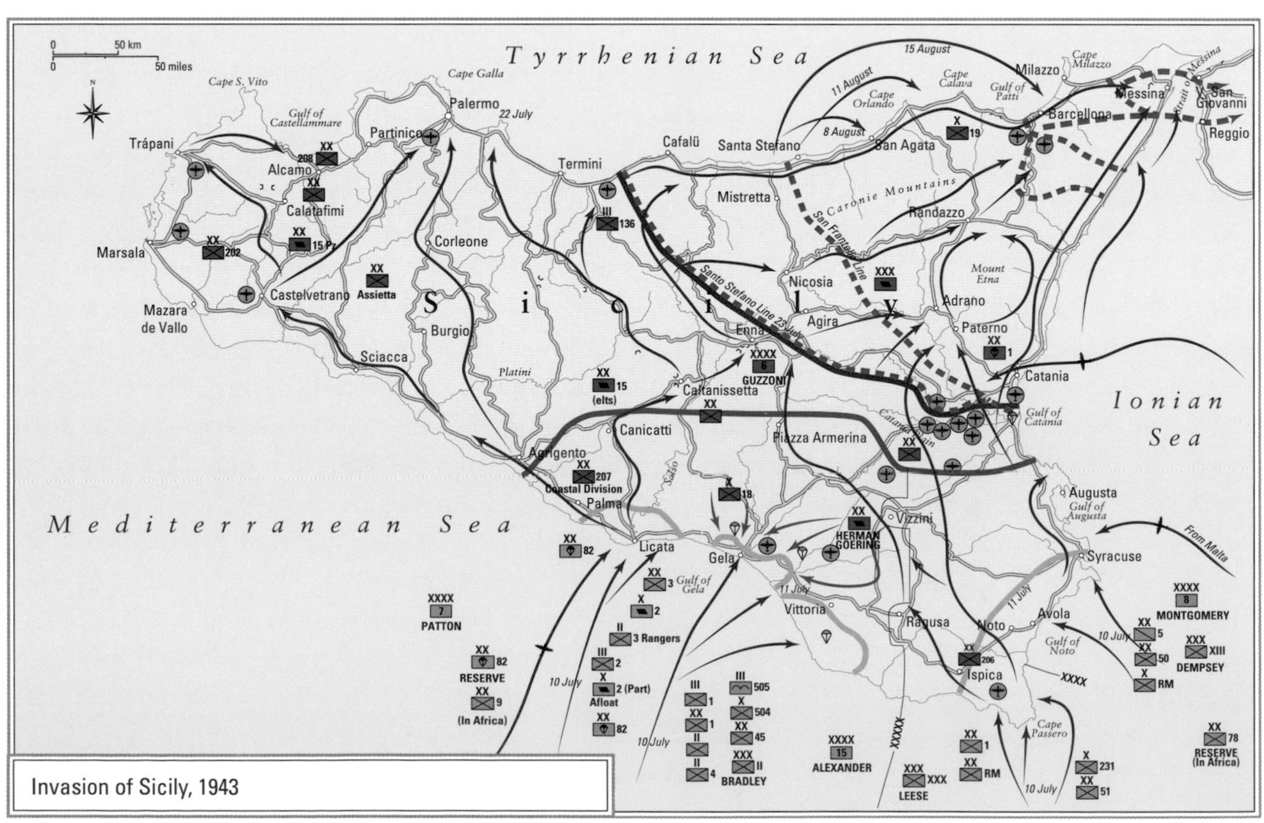

Invasion of Sicily, 1943

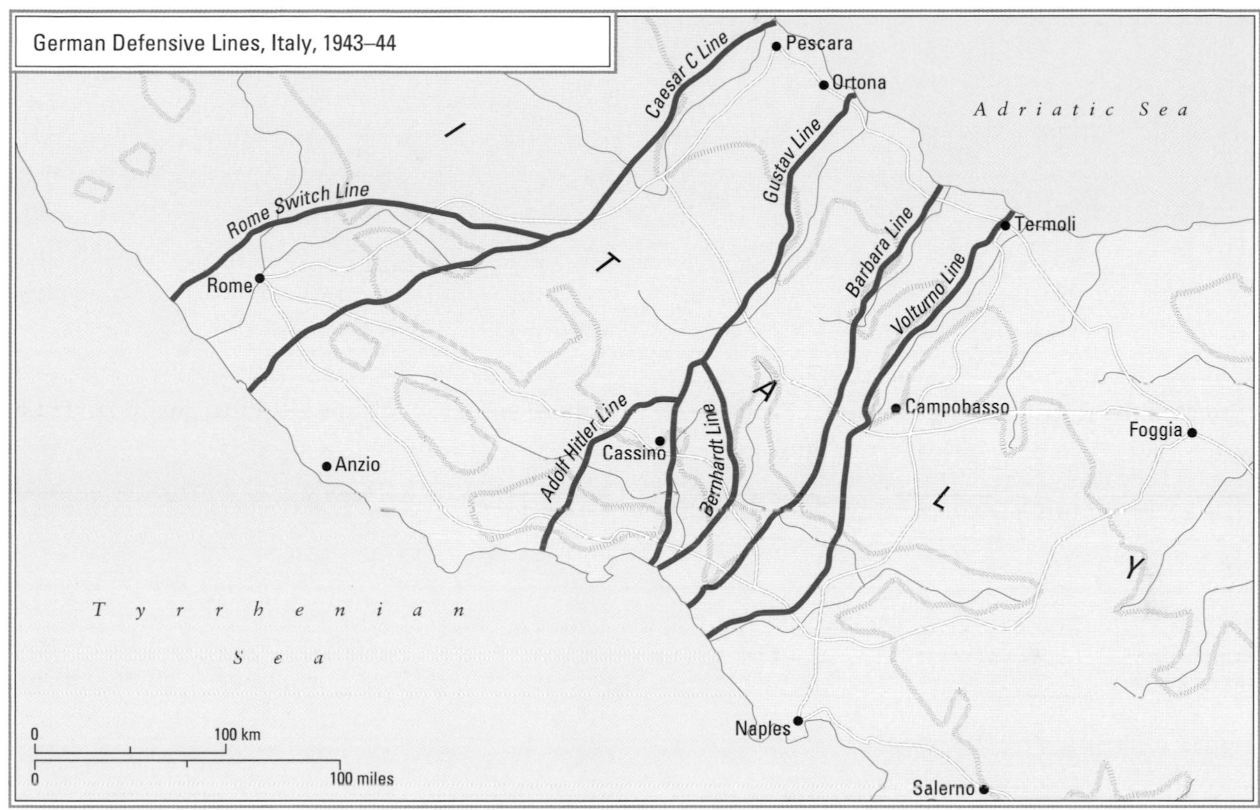

attacked north toward Naples and captured the port on 1 October. By 6 October, the Allies had reached the eastward-running line of the Volturno River, 50km to the north. In the meantime, the British Eighth Army had advanced up Italy's Adriatic coast to the Biferno River, thus linking up with Fifth Army. The latter suffered 5000 casualties and the Germans 7000.

■ **Gustav-Cassino Line, Nov 1943–May 1944** The Gustav (or Winter) Line was a German defensive position constructed in late 1943 across Italy from Gaeta, south of Rome, through Cassino, the Apennine Mountains and onto the Sangro estuary on the eastern coast. It took the Western Allies four offensives to break this position. The optimal Allied route of advance to Rome was through the Liri Valley, but the Gustav defences blocked this route around Cassino, particularly on the Monte Cassino heights, topped by its ancient monastery. In the First Battle of Monte Cassino (17 January–11 February 1944), X Corps' three British divisions attacked across the Garigilano River close to the western coast, while three Fifth US Army divisions attacked Cassino. Subsequently, Allied forces landed behind the Garigliano at Anzio. The Allies closed on the monastery before being halted. During the second battle (15–18 February), one New Zealand and one Indian division attacked the Cassino defences to assist the beleaguered Anzio beachhead. Despite incurring high casualties and destroying the monastery, the Allies again failed to capture Monastery Hill. In the third battle (15–26 March), three Allied divisions attacked Cassino from the northeast, but the Allied advance was again halted short of the monastery. In the fourth battle (11–25 May), Operation *Diadem*, US Fifth Army and British Eighth Army forces attacked the Gustav Line's western sector in a large-scale offensive. While the US II and French I Corps assaulted across the Garigliano and US VI Corps broke out from the Anzio beachhead, Polish II and British XIII Corps assaulted the Cassino

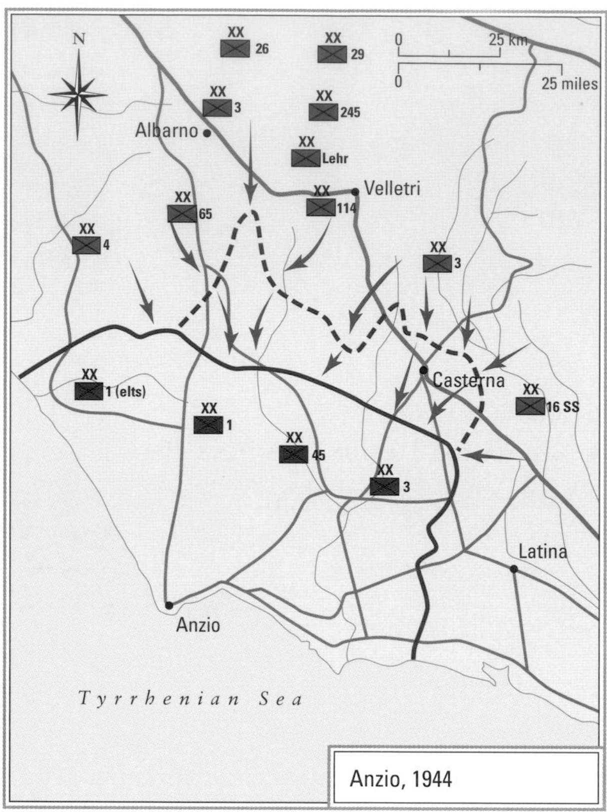

Anzio, 1944

position. This offensive broke through Cassino and, by late May, the German forces were in full retreat north beyond Rome. The Allies suffered 55,000 casualties in these operations, while the Germans took 35,000.

■ **Anzio, 22 January–4 June 1944**
On 22 January 1944, as part of Operation *Shingle*, 36,000 Anglo-American troops of the US VI Corps landed virtually unopposed at Anzio on the western Italian coast, 40km south of Rome and 55km behind the main German Gustav Line defences.The aim was to unhinge the German main line, facilitating an offensive from Cassino north towards Rome. Once ashore, the Allied units dug in instead of advancing, enabling 40,000 German Fourteenth Army troops to rush to the beachhead and seal it off. The 69,000 Allied troops in the beachhead attacked on 28 January, but the ensuing German counter-attacks during 3–20 February (there were now 100,000 German troops in the area) nearly overran the beachhead. By late February, a stalemate had emerged. On 23 May,VI Corps broke out of the beachhead in conjunction with Operation *Diadem* (the Allied offensive against the Gustav Line) and on 4 June Rome fell.

■ **Gothic Line, 25 Aug–17 December 1944**
During August 1944, German forces in Italy retreated north to the Gustav Line defences that stretched from the western coast near Pisa through to Pesaro in the eastern coast.During 25 August–29 September, the British Eighth Army offensive against the line's eastern flank advanced 77km to the River Uso. Concurrently in the centre, during 12 September–15 October, US Fifth Army fought its way 51km forward towards Bologna, before poor weather halted operations.

■ **Po Valley, 6 April–2 May 1945**
During April 1945, 600,000 Western Allied troops smashed through the defensive positions held by 430,000 German/Italian forces, crossed the River Po and pushed 250km north to the Alps by 2 May, when the collapsing Axis forces in Italy surrendered.

Western Front 1942–45

■ **Strategic Air Campaign, March 1942–April 1945**
Before World War I, the Italian Gen Giulio Douhet had championed the role of strategic airpower in war. He had advocated the legitimacy of bombing an enemy's population as well as its military. Nevertheless, by the time World War II broke out, neither the Allies nor the Axis powers fully embraced Douhet's concept. In Nazi Germany, the *Luftwaffe*, under Reichsmarschall Hermann Göring, developed tactical bombing proficiency. The Ju 87 Stuka could carry one 250kg bomb beneath its fuselage and four 50kg bombs beneath its wings. Stukas typically worked in concert with fighters to provide close air support to fast-moving mechanized troops on the ground. Such joint formations swept the *Wehrmacht* to early success in the *Blitzkrieg* of 1939–41 against Poland,

France, Norway and parts of the Soviet Union. During the Battle of Britain, Ju 88s and He 111s, capable of carrying hundreds of kilogrammes of bombs, struck London and other British cities. Yet the Nazis had not developed large fleets of heavy bombers capable of mass attacks deep within enemy territory, as Douhet had envisioned a generation before. This oversight would prove costly, as the Allies, out of reach of the German war machine, built air forces capable of smashing the Third Reich to pieces. In the United Kingdom, under the leadership of AM Sir Arthur Travers Harris, the British Royal Air Force's Bomber Command re-equipped with Halifaxes, Sterlings and Lancasters. These four-engine planes were capable of carrying large payloads (between 5897kg and 6340 kg) on long missions. The Area Bombing Directive of 14 February 1942 gave Harris the authority to unleash his 'heavies' on Axis civilian, as well as military and industrial, targets. At Lübeck on the Baltic, British bombers applied the new strategy, releasing 400 tons of bombs and setting the city ablaze. More than 300 Germans died. Göring responded with air raids on historic British towns. Later in the war, Hitler augmented his bomber force with first-generation ballistic missiles (V-2) and glide bombs (V-1), which were deployed as terror weapons in reprisal for the Allied advance on the Western Front. Meanwhile, the British continued to hone their conventional strategic bombing capabilities. Some Lancasters were modified to carry the massive 10,000kg Grand Slam bomb, which Harris used to 'great effect' against the Third Reich's viaducts, railways and U-boat pens.

Advances in radar and bombsight technologies helped to increase the effectiveness of the joint US 8th Air Force/Bomber Command Combined Bomber Offensive (June 1943–April 1945). American B-17 Flying Fortresses were capable of carrying between 2000kg and 7800kg of bombs; B-24 Liberators could take between 1200kg and 3600kg. Hundreds of these planes participated in mass attacks on Germany's industrial base. In total, the Anglo-American offensive released more than 2.8 million tons of bombs in over 1.4 million bomber sorties. The raids played havoc with Axis industry at target sites like Schweinfurt and Regensburg. But success came at a cost. More than 22,000 Allied bombers were lost and almost 160,000 American and British aircrew were killed. The civilian toll was heavier, with estimates of between 300,000 and 600,000 German deaths. The Nazis' strategic bombing raids killed almost 61,000 in Britain.

■ Normandy Landings, 6 June 1944

The initial British–Canadian–American landings in Normandy (Operation *Neptune,* the first stage of Operation *Overlord*), aimed "to secure a lodgement on the continent from which further offensive operations can be developed". Many preconditions had to be met before the cross-Channel operation could be contemplated: vast American forces had to be transported to Britain, requiring the defeat of the U-boats and the availability of huge amounts of shipping; a high degree of command of the sea and air in the relevant area had to be achieved; enormous amphibious forces had to be built up and trained. Normandy was chosen because of the suitability of its beaches for landings and of the hinterland for the subsequent breakout, and because an assault here, rather than the Pas de Calais, would be unexpected. Careful intelligence preparation went alongside a meticulous campaign of deception to keep the defenders' attention focused on the Pas de Calais and Norway, allowing the Allies to achieve the surprise that was essential for success. The staggering logistical requirements would be guaranteed by two 'Mulberry' artificial harbours, together with undersea oil pipelines and supplies landed over the beaches. Gen Dwight D. Eisenhower was Supreme Allied Commander, with the bulk of the planning being conducted by the naval commander, Adm Sir Bertram Ramsay.

The initial plan envisaged three divisions landing on three beaches over a 48km front, though this

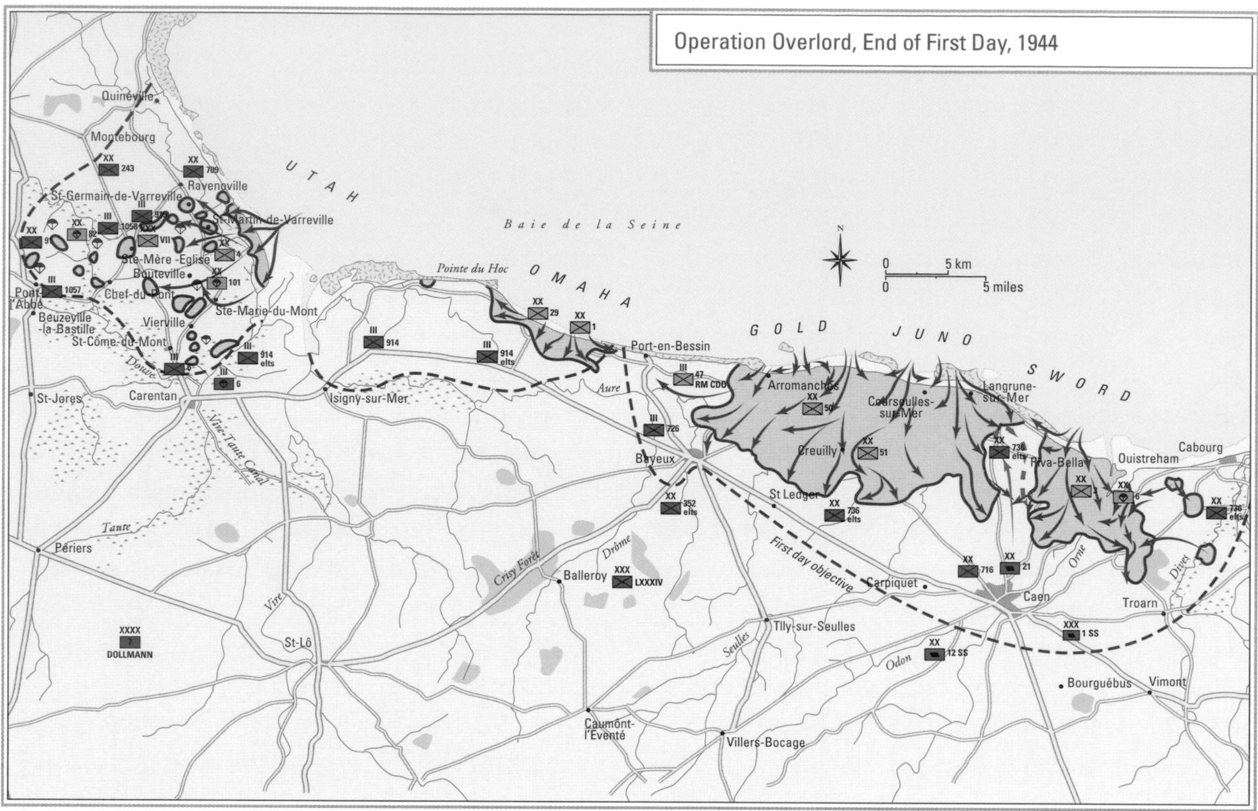

Operation Overlord, End of First Day, 1944

was later revised to five divisions assaulting five beaches along a 96km front. This extended the landings to the Cotentin peninsula, allowing an earlier push for the port of Cherbourg. From the Allied left to right: in the east, British airborne forces took key bridges across the canals and protected the flank, British forces (with one unit of French commandos) landed on Sword Beach, British and Canadian at Juno, British at Gold, and US troops at Omaha and Utah, with US airborne forces dropping on the western flank. The Allied forces conducting the operation included 1213 warships from battleships to midget submarines, some 4125 amphibious ships and craft as well as hundreds of merchant ships, over 11,000 aircraft and 130,000 soldiers with 2000 tanks and 12,000 other vehicles. Atrocious weather caused Eisenhower to take the option of a 24-hour postponement; the decision to go ahead on 6 June was marginal, but while the continuing bad weather caused considerable problems for the airborne and amphibious forces, it also helped the landings to achieve surprise.

German forces had heavily defended the beaches with underwater obstacles, barbed wire and minefields backed by fortified artillery, machine-gun and infantry bunkers, with supporting defensive positions inland. Armoured reserves, with which Germany planned to push the invaders back into the sea, were mainly held back some distance from the beaches. The Allies sought to defeat these defences by heavy preliminary naval bombardment and bombing, airborne and commando assaults against key batteries, then by use of combat engineers, amphibious tanks and – on the British and Canadian beaches – specialist engineering vehicles known as 'Hobart's funnies'. The defensive positions put up stout resistance for a time, especially at Omaha where the landings came closest to failure, but they were eventually isolated and overwhelmed. The Allies suffered 10,300 casualties, but managed to land 132,000 men by the end of D-Day. Although the breakout would take longer than expected, the Allies had successfully breached Germany's Atlantic Wall.

■ Saint-Lô, 2–19 July 1944

A crossroads on the Vere river, Saint-Lô was crucial in wresting Brittany and Normandy from German control. By 19 July, the US First Army had pushed the German Seventh Army out into the Falaise Gap, setting the stage for the liberation of France.

■ Falaise-Argentan Pocket, 25 July–23 August 1944

Between 25 July and 5 August, the US First Army broke the western German front in Normandy, and American forces raced south to the apex of the Normandy peninsula, enabling further advances west into Brittany, south toward the Loire River and east toward the Seine River. The abortive 6–7 August German armoured counter-attack to seal off the American penetration simply pushed German forces west and deeper into an emergent pocket forming in the Condé-Falaise-Argentan area. On 19 August, the Canadian-Polish advance south from Falaise linked up at Trun-Chambois with the northwards American advance from Argentan, trapping 100,000 German troops in a pocket. As II SS-Panzer Corps struck from outside the pocket at the eastern-facing Allied 'plug' of the Trun-Chambois pocket, the desperate forces trapped inside struck the plug's western face. In the ensuing breakout, 40,000 German troops escaped, although they were forced to leave their heavy equipment and many of their vehicles behind.

■ Southern France, 15 August–11 Sept 1944

On 15–16 August 1944, American–French forces landed on France's southeastern Mediterranean coast. With Army Group G's defenders reduced to 90,000 by drafts sent to Normandy, the Allies established an 80km-deep bridgehead by the 18th. During 19 August–11 September, 150,000 Allied troops pursued the withdrawing German forces up the Rhône Valley until the latter linked up with the German front in northeastern France. The Allies incurred 17,000 casualties, the Germans 157,000, including 130,000 trapped in south-western France.

■ Paris, 19–25 August 1944

Beginning with a general strike and an uprising by the French Resistance, the liberation of Paris concluded with Free French armies and the US 4th Infantry Division entering the city to capture 12,800 German troops.

■ Siegfried Line, 12 September 1944–10 March 1945

Between 12 September 1944 and 10 March 1945, Western Allied troops fought their way through the German Siegfried Line defences, which stretched for 635km along Germany's western border near Nijmegen down to the Swiss border at Basle.

■ Hürtgen Forest, 14 September 1944–10 February 1945

Between 14 September 1944 and 10 February 1945, 90,000 US First Army troops were locked in a protracted battle with 80,000 German troops from Army Group B, deployed in the Siegfried Line defences within the 130 square km area of the Hürtgen Forest, which was located close to the German border with Belgium. The main American objective was to reach the German dams astride the Roer River. The Americans suffered 29,000 combat casualties, and the Germans 27,000 casualties.

■ Arnhem, 17–21 September 1944

On 17 September 1944, the Anglo-Canadian 21st Army Group and the First Allied Airborne Army initiated Operation *Market Garden*, an audacious ground offensive augmented by the dropping of three Allied airborne divisions into the German rear. The plan envisaged that as XXX Corps thrust rapidly north, Allied airborne forces would land in the Zon-Veghel, Nijmegen-Groesbeek, and Arnhem-Oosterbeek areas in southern Holland to secure key bridges, including that over the Rhine River at Arnhem. The German Army Group B reacted swiftly to these landings, redeploying numerous battlegroups of garrison troops, backed

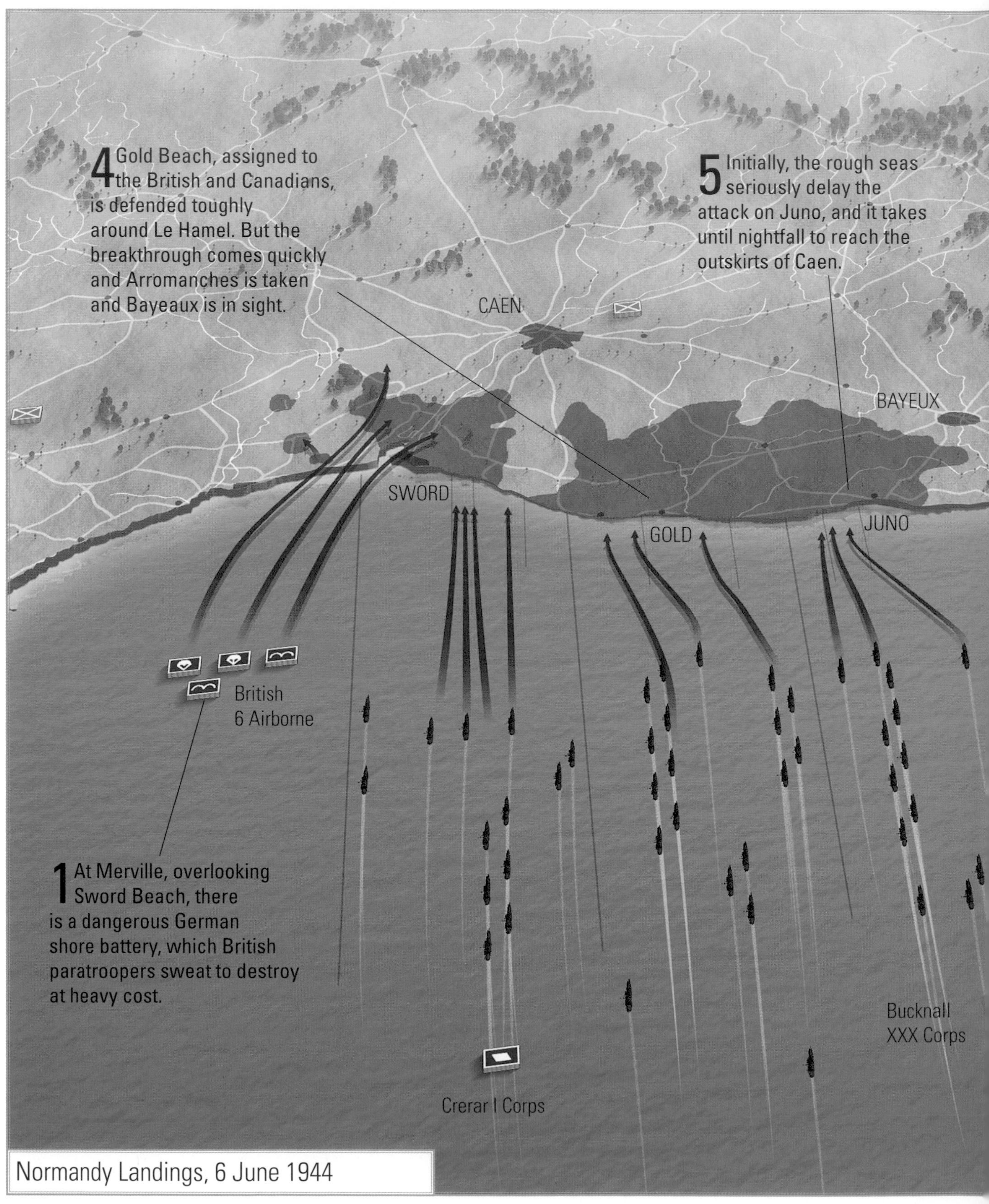

Normandy Landings, 6 June 1944

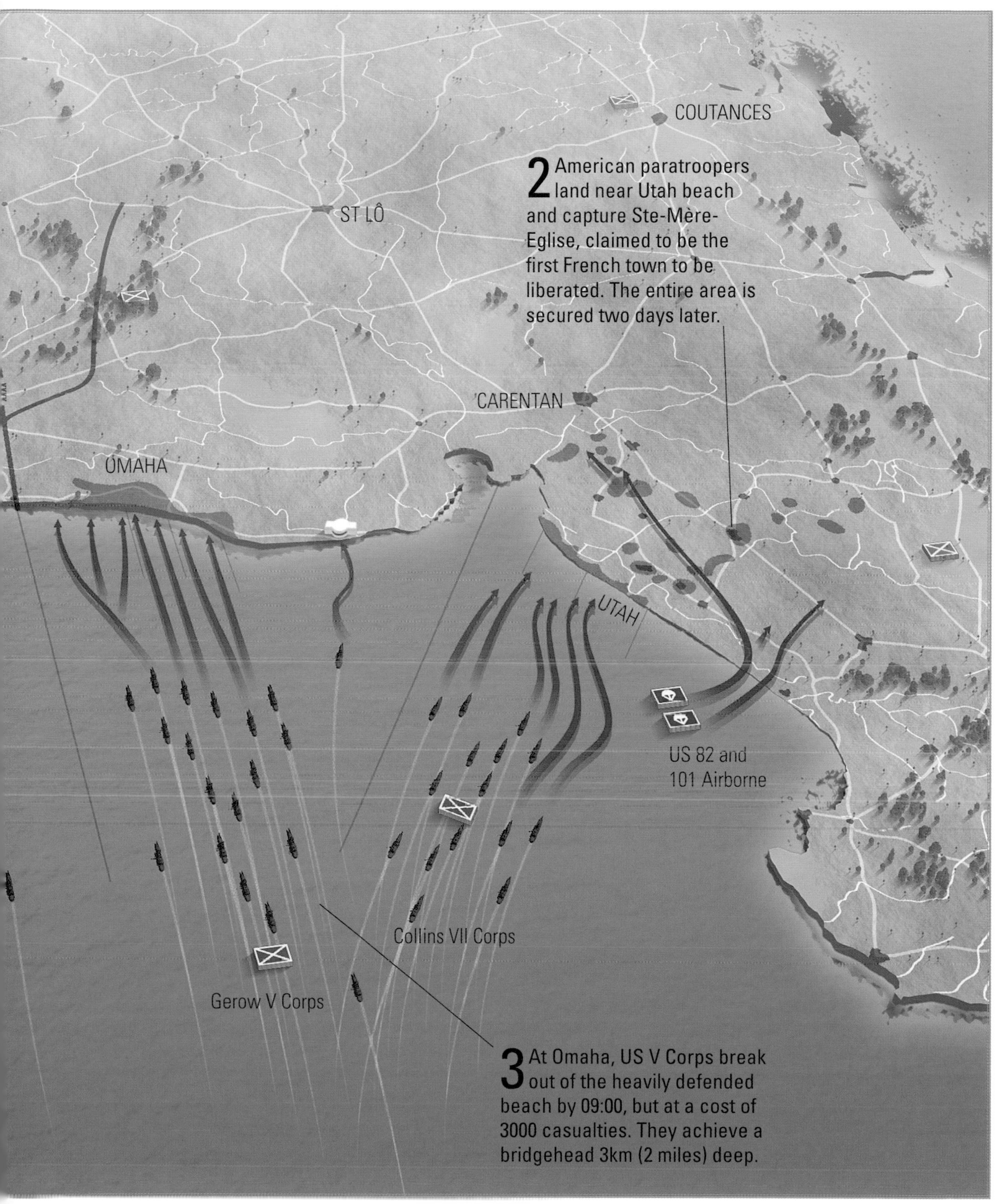

2 American paratroopers land near Utah beach and capture Ste-Mère-Eglise, claimed to be the first French town to be liberated. The entire area is secured two days later.

3 At Omaha, US V Corps break out of the heavily defended beach by 09:00, but at a cost of 3000 casualties. They achieve a bridgehead 3km (2 miles) deep.

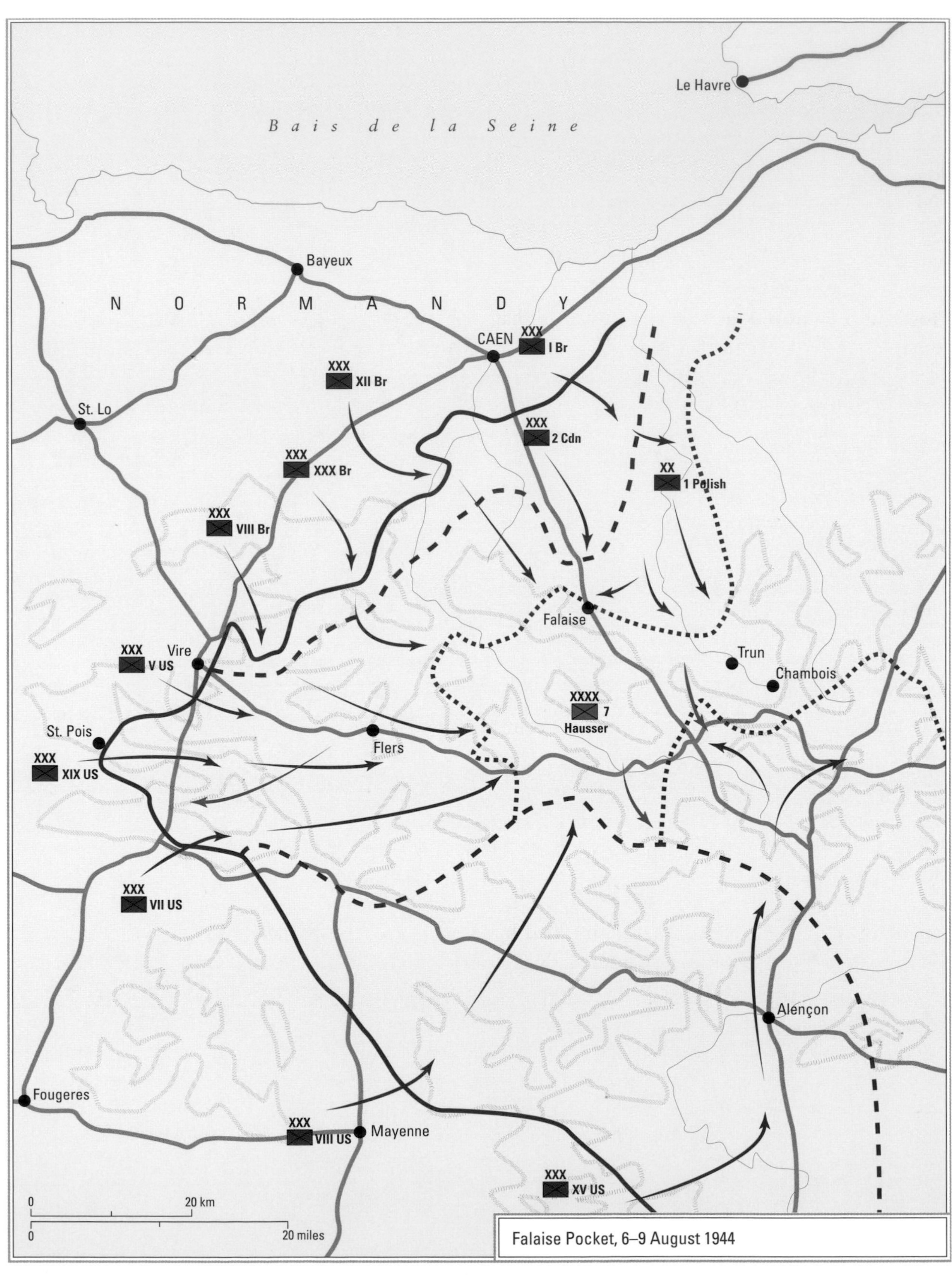

Falaise Pocket, 6–9 August 1944

by the 5000 survivors of the elite II SS-Panzer Corps. That day, the British 1st Airborne Division began landing at Oosterbeek, northwest of Arnhem. Subsequently, the 1st Parachute Brigade advanced on Arnhem, with LCol Frost's 2nd Parachute Battalion pushing south to seize the northern end of the key Rhine road bridge. However, the improvised SS battlegroups *Krafft* and *Spindler* blocked 1st Brigade's advance from reinforcing Frost's positions at the bridge. The next morning, Frost's unit destroyed an SS recce battalion that stormed the bridge, and then dug in, waiting in vain for XXX Corps to arrive. In the meantime, the Germans had rushed another 10 battalions to the Arnhem-Oosterbeek area, and a further 24 to contain the American landings and block XXX Corps' advance. During 19–20 September, II SS-Corps units repeatedly attacked Frost's positions, inflicting severe casualties. Eventually, at noon on 21 September, after four days of heroic resistance, these attacks overwhelmed Frost's few remaining unwounded soldiers; XXX Corps was then still 16km south of Arnhem bridge. Subsequent German attacks forced 1st Airborne Division's remnants at Oosterbeek to withdraw, ending *Market Garden*. The German and British forces suffered 4000 and 7500 casualties respectively in the Arnhem-Oosterbeek area.

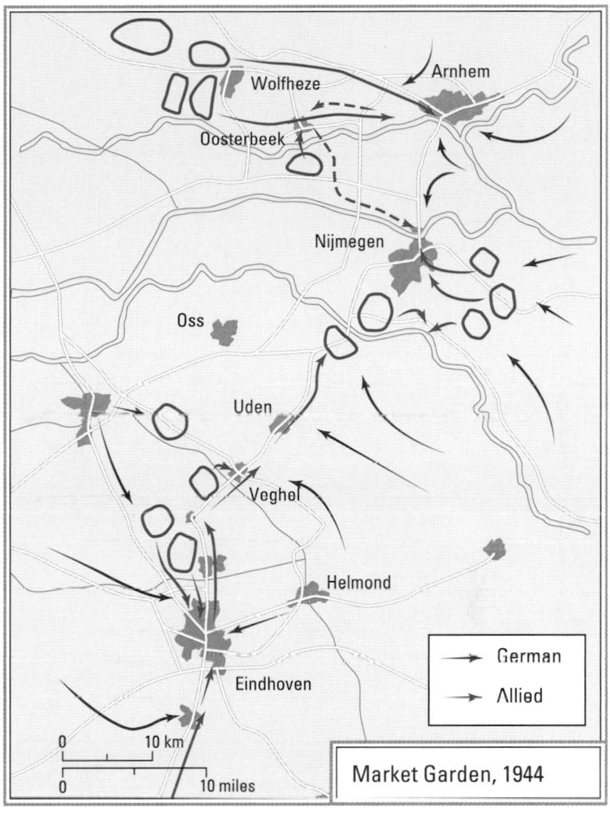

Market Garden, 1944

■ Aachen, 2–21 October 1944

During 2–21 October 1944, 70,000 US First Army troops battered through the German Siegfried Line defences that protected Aachen, manned by 19,000 LXXXI Corps troops. Captured on the 21st, it was the first German city overrun by the Western Allies.

■ Ardennes (Battle of the Bulge), 16 December 1944–15 January 1945

On 16 December 1944, the beleaguered German forces on the Western Front launched a surprise counter-offensive in the hilly and forested Ardennes region; the area's unsuitability for armoured warfare meant that the Americans only deployed four divisions in this sector. At Hitler's insistence, the counter-offensive's objective was to advance 150km to seize the vital port of Antwerp. This was far too ambitious given the limited German resources available (particularly the lack of fuel) and the size of Allied reserves that could be committed to stop the attack. Three armies from GenFM Walther Model's Army Group B commenced the counter-offensive on the 16th amid bad weather that would keep Allied tactical air power grounded. SS-Oberstgruppenführer Dietrich's Sixth Panzer Army attacked in the north, while Panzer Gen Hasso von Manteuffel's Fifth Panzer Army struck in the south. Gen Erich Brandenburger's Seventh Army mounted limited subsidiary attacks to protect Manteuffel's southern flank. In the north, Battlegroup *Peiper* spearheaded the advance of the 1st SS-Panzer Division *Leibstandarte*. During 17–20 December, this battlegroup fought its way 40km forward to Stoumont, but Allied counter-attacks encircled and all but destroyed the unit. With this, Dietrich's

American infantry crouch to avoid enemy fire as their landing craft takes them across the Rhine River at St. Goar, March 1945.

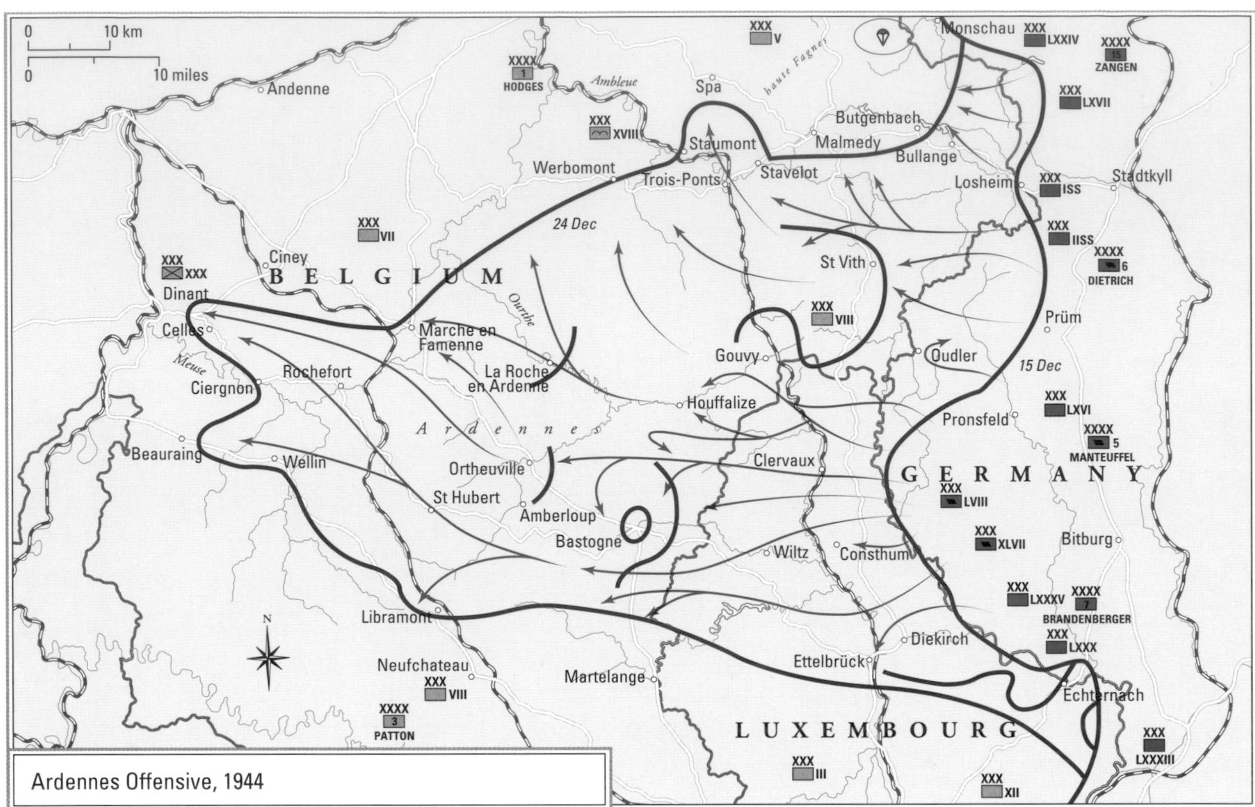

Ardennes Offensive, 1944

advance in the north stalled. In the south, the Fifth Panzer Army enjoyed greater success, with the 2nd Panzer Division advancing by 23 December to within 6km of the Meuse River bridges. By then, its tanks had virtually run out of petrol, having failed to capture Allied fuel dumps. However, later that day, American reinforcements launched large-scale counter-attacks against the German salient or 'Bulge' as it became known. The widening Allied counter-offensive gradually drove the Germans back until, by mid-January 1945, they were back at their 16 December starting positions.

St Vith, 16–24 December 1944

A key objective for the Germans during the Battle of the Bulge in 1944, St Vith fell after several days of hard fighting. This unhinged the German timetable for their offensive. The town was recaptured by the Allies in January 1945.

■ Bastogne, 20–27 December 1944

The site of a major arterial road link in Belgium, Bastogne was a critical initial objective for the Germans during the Ardennes Offensive of 1944. As the Germans converged on Bastogne after overcoming stiff resistance from isolated American formations, Gen Dwight D. Eisenhower dispatched the 82nd and 101st Airborne Divisions to Bastogne to bolster the defences. From 20 December, the Germans besieged Bastogne, outnumbering the encircled paratroopers. On 22 December, a German demand for the Americans to surrender was famously turned down by BGen Anthony McAullife, the acting commander of 101st Airborne, with a single word – 'Nuts'. From 23 December, improved weather conditions enabled aerial resupply of the town as well as attacks on the Germans. On 27 December, lead elements of the American 4th Armored Division broke through German lines and established a corridor to the town, lifting the siege.

■ Celles 1944, 25 December 1944

On Christmas Eve 1944, the German 2nd Panzer Division reached Celles, Belgium. This was the high-water mark of Nazi westwards penetration during the Battle of the Bulge. The US First Army's VII Corps retook Celles and halted the German advance.

■ Rhineland, 8 February–10 March 1945

In early 1945, the 850,000 troops of the Canadian First and US Ninth Armies pushed back the 400,000 troops of the German First Parachute Army from the Maas River to the Rhine at Wesel.

■ Remagen, 8–23 March 1945

On 7 March 1945, American forces reached the sole remaining bridge across the Rhine River, located at Remagen. The defenders detonated demolition charges, but despite a massive explosion the bridge remained obstinately intact. American forces quickly captured the bridge and poured reinforcements across to form a bridgehead. Despite facing fierce counter-attacks, the American forces burst out of the bridgehead on 23 March, crushing the German attempt to halt the Allied advance along the Rhine.

■ West Germany, 8 March–8 May 1945

During March 1945, 3.6 million Western Allied troops smashed the Germans' Rhine River defences. Between late March and early May, the Anglo-Canadian 21st Army Group advanced rapidly north/northeastward to liberate most of the Netherlands and northern Germany up to Schleswig-Holstein.

Meanwhile, two American army groups thrust east to reach the Elbe and link up with the westwards Soviet advance, as well as thrust south/southeast into northern Italy, northern Austria and western Czechoslovakia by 8 May, when Nazi Germany capitulated.

■ Ruhr Pocket, 23 March–18 April 1945

During 23 March–1 April, two American armies surrounded Army Group B's 360,000 troops in a 115km-deep pocket around the key Ruhr industrial zone in the German heartland. The last of the 330,000 Germans to surrender did so on 18 April.

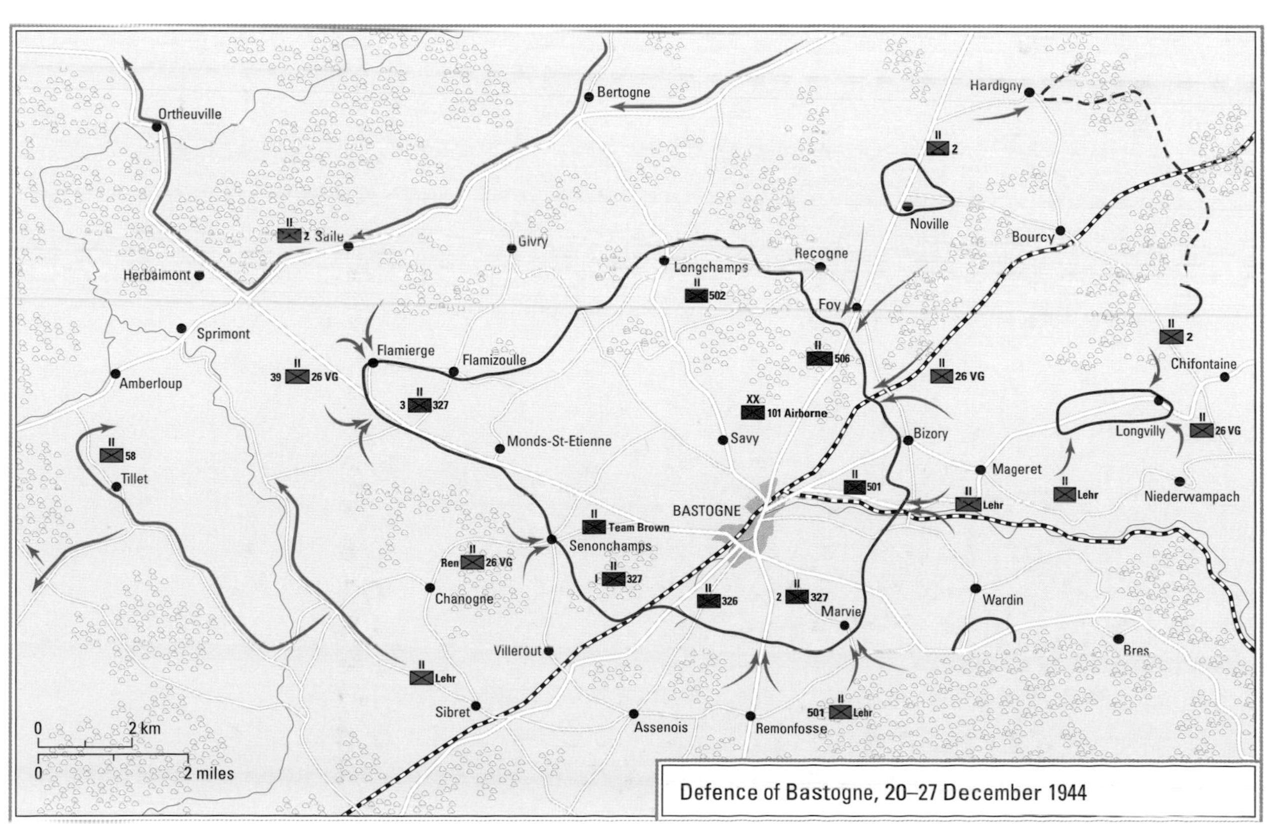

Defence of Bastogne, 20–27 December 1944

Modern Wars

Following the end of World War II, the American military was involved in many conflicts as part of the Cold War stand-off with the Soviet Union, including the Korean War (1950–53), the Vietnam War (1963–75), and wars in Central America. The 1991 Gulf War saw the full power of US war-making technology destroy a Cold War-era Iraqi army. More recently, the invasions of Afghanistan (2001) and Iraq (2003) have involved the wide deployment of cruise missiles, smart bombs and stealth technology against insurgents employing assymetric and terror tactics.

Left: A US Air Force F-15E Strike Eagle multi-role fighter flies a mission over Afghanistan, 2008. Air power has been a crucial element in the United States' ability to carry out recent military operations in the Middle East and South Asia.

Korean War 1950–53

■ North Korean Invasion, 25 June–15 September 1950

In 1950, the North Korean People's Army (NKPA) had built up a fighting force that included approximately 135,000 soldiers in 10 infantry divisions, supported by artillery and an armoured brigade equipped with Soviet-supplied, World War II-vintage T-34/85 tanks. On the eve of the invasion, the Republic of Korea Army (ROKA) comprised 95,000 men, most of whom would be routed within a week of the invasion. On the morning of 25 June, NKPA soldiers and 150 tanks crossed the 38th Parallel and drove south in darkness. Overwhelmed, the South Korean defensive line collapsed on Seoul. ROKA commanders prematurely demolished the bridges north of the capital, stranding much of their army and its equipment. On 28 June, NKPA 3rd and 4th Divisions captured Seoul and prepared for a final push south to destroy what remained of ROKA. As the situation worsened, US President Harry Truman authorized Gen Douglas MacArthur to send combat troops to assist the South Koreans.

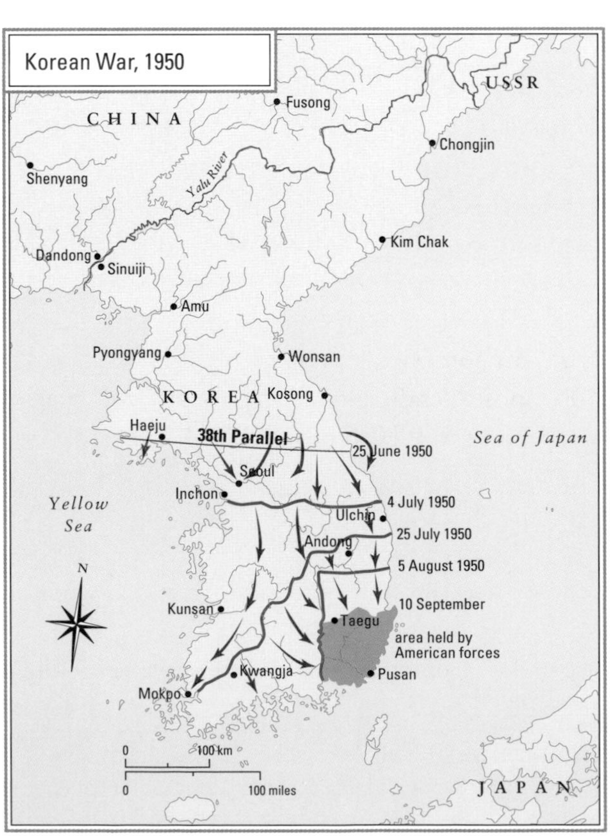

MacArthur ordered MGen William F. Dean of the US 24th Infantry Division (based in Japan) to airlift 500 men into the war zone as a delaying force, while the US Navy brought the rest of the division across in troop ships. LCol Charles B. Smith commanded the 1st Battalion of the 21st Infantry Regiment. On 5 July, Task Force Smith, with artillery support, dug in near Osan. The NKPA 4th Division struck hard, its tanks defeating the Americans' inadequate anti-armour weaponry. The North Koreans successfully flanked the Americans and cut Smith's force in half. By 19 July, Allied troops had withdrawn to fight at Taejon, using new 3.5in rockets to defeat some of the NKPA's T-34s. However, the communists' strong frontal attacks and successful flanking manoeuvres carried the day, driving the defenders back to a 230km defensive line north and west of Pusan on Korea's southern coast. The NKPA captured MGen Dean and inflicted 30 per cent casualties on the 24th Division.

■ Pusan Perimeter, 4 August–15 September 1950

By 1 August, the United Nations' force in South Korea (largely comprised of American and ROKA combat units) numbered 92,000 soldiers, including more than 500 US tanks, the 24th and 25th Divisions, the 1st Cavalry Division, and five ROKA divisions. This force, led by LGen Walton Walker's US Eighth Army, held the vital port at Pusan. Seeking a knockout blow that would drive the UN into the sea, 98,000 NKPA troops attacked unsuccessfully along four axes: Masan, Miryang, Taegu and Kyongju. Allied air power and artillery helped hold the line.

■ Inchon, 15–19 September 1950

With the North Korean invasion halted, the US X Corps, led by MGen Edward M. Almond, had the task of planning an amphibious landing in the rear

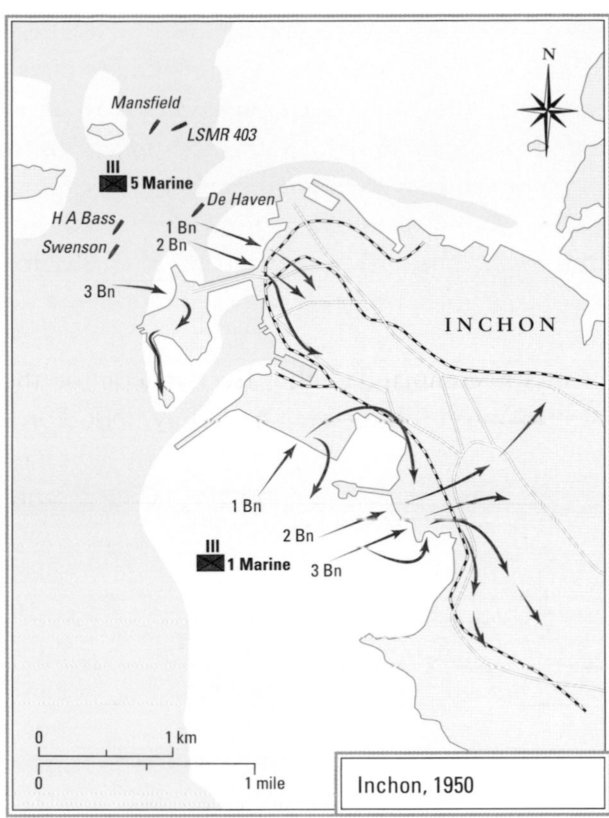

Inchon, 1950

of the NKPA advance. Gen MacArthur wanted to relieve pressure from LGen Walker's Eighth Army, ROKA and UN troops at Pusan. The generals selected Inchon, a Yellow Sea port 41km west of Seoul, and the vital roads and railway hubs that linked the NKPA's troops in the south with their supply lines in the north. MacArthur's strategy was for a surprise landing at Inchon (codenamed Operation *Chromite*) to flank the communists and threaten to cut off their armies, even as the Eighth Army led a breakout from the Pusan Perimeter and pushed north. The landing force included more than 8000 South Korean augmentees, as well as the 1st Marine Division and the US Army's 7th Infantry Division, stationed in Japan. The ROKA 17th Regiment was in reserve, with no other reinforcements available in case the landing was strongly opposed. The gamble was serious, as it required the UN to commit its only combat-ready reserves to an operation fraught with difficulties. McArthur's plan roused the objections of some of his staff, particularly the naval warfare experts of Task Force 77, who noted the Yellow Sea's hazardous 9.1m tides, coastal sandbars and mudflats, and the difficulty of mounting a full-scale amphibious landing into an urban area with a high seawall. Complicating the plan, North Korean attacks had pinned down the Eighth Army's divisions, blunting the strength of the Pusan breakout. Walker was forced to delay his push north until after the landing force had established the Inchon beachhead. Meanwhile, informed by spies on Yonghung Do Island on the Inchon approaches, the UN task force knew it confronted an NKPA force totalling approximately 2000 men. Keystones to the area's defences were the fortifications on Wolmi Do Island (planned site for the landing operation's Green Beach). US Marine Corps' F4U Corsairs attacked with double loads of napalm (43,091kg in total), burning out the western half of the island. On the morning of 15 September, the initial wave of a 70,000-man invasion force completed the first major amphibious assault since the World War II landing at Okinawa (1 April 1945). The Marines of 3rd Battalion, 5th Marine Regiment, 1st Marine Division, supported by nine M26 Pershing tanks, overwhelmed Wolmi Do's garrison of approximately 400 NKPA marines and artillerymen. By 08:00, the UN task force had seized Wolmi Do and the causeway connecting it to Inchon. Two other assault waves, involving 500 landing craft, carried the 1st and 5th Marine Regiments to Red and Blue Beaches on the north and south of the city. Naval artillery from the cruisers HMS *Jamaica* and USS *Rochester* battered the communists as the UN troops hit the beach. At Red Beach, 5th Marines clambered over the seawall and overcame stiff resistance to capture the high ground of Cemetery Hill and Observatory Hill. At Blue Beach, naval rockets silenced an NKPA mortar team that had destroyed one of the landing craft. Subsequently, 1st Marines seized the main road to Seoul.

With the beachhead established, a major logistical operation got underway. By the seventh day, the task force had landed 53,882 people, 6629 vehicles and 25,512 tons of cargo. The battle had cost the UN 222 casualties, including 22 killed. The North Koreans, taken completely by surprise, endured more than 1350 casualties.

■ Breakout from Pusan Perimeter, 16–23 September 1950

With US X Corps at Inchon, LGen Walker's Eighth Army broke out from the 230km Pusan Perimeter. There, 92,000 UN troops faced the 70,000-man North Korean invasion. They attacked north and west, fighting bloody battles for the high ground against a deeply entrenched and determined foe. By 23 September, the NKPA in the south had disintegrated. The fighting cost 790 American and several thousand North Korean lives. UN forces captured 23,000 communist soldiers.

■ Pyongyang, 15–19 October 1950

On 27 September, US Gen Douglas MacArthur had crossed the 38th Parallel to destroy the remnants of the NKPA and unite Korea under President Syngman Rhee. LGen Walker's I Corps, comprising the US 1st Cavalry, 24th Infantry and South Korean 1st Divisions, formed up at Kaesong. Battling through a series of fortified positions en route to the North Korean capital, the 5th Cavalry Regiment and South Korean 1st Division captured the city.

■ First Chinese Offensive, 25 October–30 November 1950

Although Gen MacArthur had not expected Chinese intervention, 200,000 soldiers of the newly re-designated 'Peoples Volunteer Army' (PVA) crossed the Yalu River into North Korea. A dangerous gap had opened between LGen Walker's American troops and allied South Korean units. The Chinese exploited this weakness, driving back the South Korean II Corps and pressuring the US I Corps. At Unsan, PVA attacks broke the South Korean 15th Infantry Regiment and US

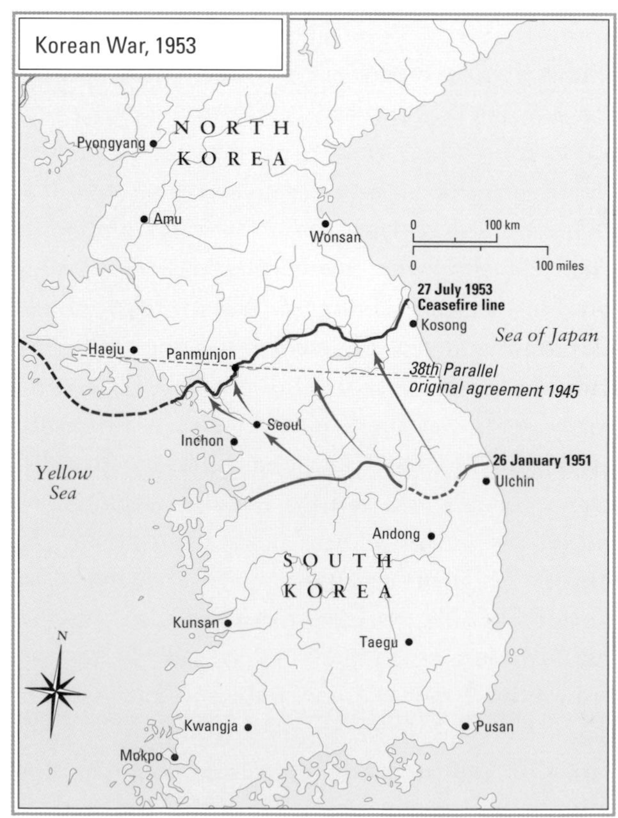

8th Cavalry Regiment. On 1–2 November, the PVA 348th Regiment decimated the 8th Cavalry's 3rd Battalion. The fighting cost more than 1000 American, 500 South Koreans and 600 Chinese lives. As the PVA advance slowed, the US Eighth Army reorganized with the intention of attacking north of the Chongchon River. At that time, UN forces comprised three main bodies of troops, including I Corps (with the US 24th Infantry, South Korean 1st Infantry Divisions and the British 27th Commonwealth Brigade); IX Corps (with the US 2nd and 25th Infantry Divisions and the Turkish Brigade); and the South Korean II Corps (with the 6th, 7th and 8th Infantry Divisions). LGen Walker had placed in reserve the US 1st Cavalry Division, the 187th Regimental Combat Team (Airborne) and the British 29th Infantry Brigade. On 25 November, the Chinese resumed their offensive, crushing the South Korean II Corps and exposing the Eighth Army's right flank. By 28 November, plans for an offensive to the Yalu River had been abandoned and all US and South Korean forces were in retreat. The fighting at the Chongchon turned the tide, costing South Korean and UN forces thousands of dead and wounded, and forcing the Eighth Army to withdraw from North Korea.

■ Chosin Reservoir, 27–29 November 1950

The US X Corps, comprising the 1st Marine Division, the 3rd and 7th Infantry Divisions, and 41 Commando British Royal Marines, together with the South Korean I Corps, were moving north on the east side of the Korean peninsula. At the Chosin Reservoir, the Chinese 79th and 89th Divisions attacked US Marines deployed to the west at Yudam-ni. At the same time, the PVA's 80th Division hit a task force of UN soldiers on the eastern side, effectively splitting X Corps in two. Hand-to-hand night combat in frigid weather ensued. Hundreds of Chinese died in human-wave assaults. Nevertheless, low on ammunition and with hundreds of wounded men to evacuate, the UN task force withdrew south to link up with the other part of X Corps at Hagaru-ri. The Chinese set roadblocks and attacked the retreating column. The task force suffered more than one-third casualties. One Chinese division had been nearly annihilated.

■ Kunu-ri, 28 November 1950

The Chinese 42nd and 38th Armies flanked the US Eighth Army, threatening its retreat. At Kunu-ri, the PVA mauled the US 2nd Infantry Division and the Turkish Brigade, with the Americans suffering 4500 casualties and losing 64 guns and other equipment to the Chinese.

■ Second Chinese Offensive, 26 December 1950–22 January 1951

The Chinese attacked UN and South Korean forces guarding Seoul. Faced with a collapsing front as two of the three South Korean divisions broke, newly arrived Eighth Army commander, LGen Matthew Ridgway, ordered a withdrawal to positions south of the Han River. The British 27th Commonwealth Brigade took casualties in the fighting. On 15–16 January, the 25th Infantry Division conducted a reconnaissance south of Osan, where they made contact with the PVA. The division lost three men and caused 1380 Chinese casualties

■ Operation *Ripper*, 7–22 March 1951

The South Korean 1st Division and US 3rd Division liberated Seoul on 15 March. IX and X Corps pushed north, capturing Hongchon and Chunchon. However, the UN had failed in one of its objectives: to destroy the PVA and North Korean armies in a pitched battle.

Bay of Pigs Invasion 1961

■ Bay of Pigs, 17–19 April 1961

A CIA-backed invasion failed to unseat Fidel Castro's communist regime in Cuba. Preceding the landing, Cuban exile pilots made diversionary attacks near Havana. At the invasion site 150km southeast of the capital, 1400 Cuban exile troops of Brigade 2506 came ashore. Cuban military and

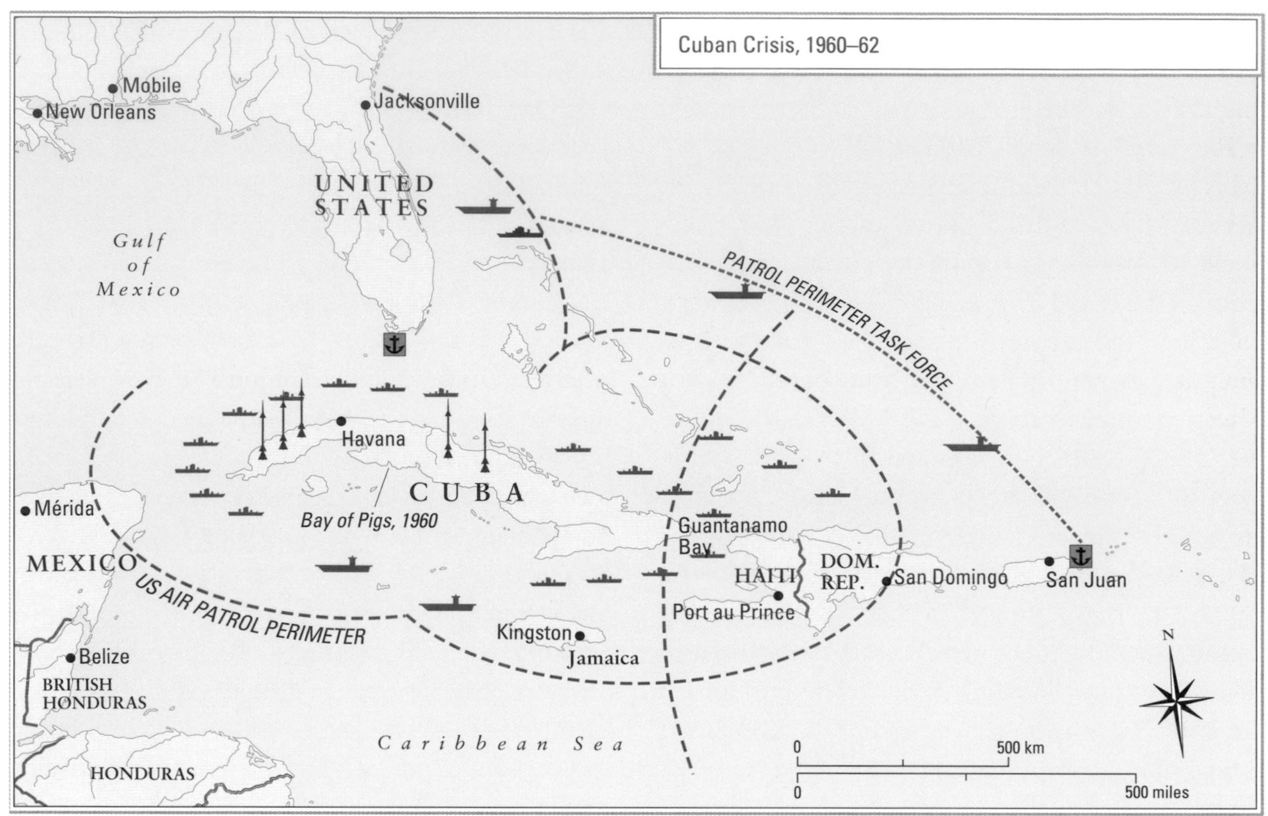

militia units, including tanks and artillery, counter-attacked and crushed the invasion force, killing 118 invaders, capturing more than 1000 and losing 176 of their own.

Vietnam War 1963–75

Gulf of Tonkin, August 1964

On 2 August, three North Vietnamese torpedo boats launched an unsuccessful attack on the USS *Maddux*, which was engaged in surveillance missions off the North Vietnamese coast. On the night of 4 August, Capt John Herrick, of the USS *Turner Joy*, judged a second attack to be under way. President Lyndon Johnson used the incidents to obtain passage of the Gulf of Tonkin Resolution, allowing him a free hand to take military action in Vietnam.

Bien Hoa, 1 November 1964

Viet Cong (VC) forces attacked the American aircraft and crews at the Bien Hoa air base outside Saigon, destroying six B-57s, damaging more than 20 other aircraft, killing five Americans and two South Vietnamese.

US Air War Against Laos, 14 December 1964–29 March 1973

Embroiled in the struggle against North Vietnam's expansion, the US and its regional allies sought to counter sympathetic communist insurgencies, including the Pathet Lao movement, against the Kingdom of Laos. Under a covert programme (Operation *Barrel Roll*), the Central Intelligence Agency (CIA), the US Air Force (USAF) and Navy carried out reconnaissance, forwarded air control, close air support and air mobility missions against Laotian and Vietnamese communists, centred geographically on the Plain of Jars. *Barrel Roll*'s special missions included working with the fiercely anti-communist Hmong tribes to build secret airstrips and install aerial navigation beacons atop Laotian hills. From 1965 to 1968, the Americans also conducted Operations *Steel Tiger* and *Tiger Hound*, which attacked the North Vietnamese supply route through southeastern Laos. These included Arc Light B-52 bombing missions.

■ Rolling Thunder 1965–1968

This US–South Vietnamese bombing campaign against North Vietnam opened on 2 March 1965, designed to intensify military pressure in an effort to persuade the North to stop its support of the VC insurgency. Attacks, emanating from aircraft carriers offshore and from bases in South Vietnam and Thailand, initially focused on North Vietnamese airfields, military bases and storage depots. It was the desire to defend US air bases in South Vietnam that prompted Gen William Westmoreland's initial request for intervention by US combat troops. The slow escalation of bombing proceeded through five phases, reaching a crescendo in 1966 and 1967 with concentration on North Vietnamese petroleum facilities, power generation capability and industrial targets. Bombing targets, however, remained strictly limited, especially in sensitive border areas with China and around Hanoi and the port of Hai Phong, out of fear of escalation of the conflict. Although bombing pauses initially were built into the programme, *Rolling Thunder* had little discernible impact on the war. The North did not choose to negotiate, and traffic down the Ho Chi Minh Trail increased during each year of the bombing. On 31 March 1968, President Lyndon Johnson, in part to spur the beginning of peace talks, limited the area of bombing in North Vietnam to below 19 degrees north latitude, and all bombing was halted on 31 October 1968. In *Rolling Thunder,* US and South Vietnamese aircraft dropped more than 600,000 tons of bombs on North Vietnam, destroying an estimated 65 per cent of the country's petroleum storage capacity and power-generating capabilities. During the campaign, the US lost nearly 900 aircraft, resulting in the capture of more than 300 prisoners of war.

■ Don Xoai, 9 June 1965

Elements of two VC regiments attacked the US Special Forces camp at Dong Xoai on 9 June and ambushed South Vietnamese relief forces. Losses supported the belief that South Vietnam could not survive without greater US commitment.

■ Ia Drang Valley, 14–18 November 1965

After a North Vietnamese attack on the Plei Me Special Forces Camp, on 14 November, 1st Battalion 7th Cavalry air assaulted into Landing Zone X Ray at the Chu Pong Massif near the Cambodian border, resulting in a running series of battles with the North Vietnamese 66th Regiment. US losses of 305 killed against enemy losses of more than 3000 dead helped convince Westmoreland of the wisdom of an attritional strategy.

■ Operation *Market Time*, 1965–1972

Market Time was a US–South Vietnamese naval and air operation to interdict seaborne supplies to communist troops in South Vietnam. Carried out by Task Force 115, under the command of Naval Forces Vietnam (NAVFORV), *Market Time* consisted of three barriers against communist maritime infiltration.

An air barrier consisted of reconnaissance overflights by US Navy aircraft, which reported enemy activity to one of five Coastal Surveillance Centers. An outer ship barrier, stretching from the demilitarized zone (DMZ) on the North/South Vietnam border to the Cambodian border, was made up largely of coast guard cutters and destroyer escorts that operated within 64km of the South Vietnamese coastline to detect and interdict larger communist supply ships.

An inner ship barrier of South Vietnamese junks and US Swift boats operated within 19km of the South Vietnamese coast. This barrier searched the vast amount of Vietnamese coastal traffic and also took part in river raiding operations.

■ Operation *Cedar Falls*, 8–26 January 1967

Two US and one South Vietnamese infantry division swept through the Iron Triangle area north of Saigon from 8 to 26 January 1967. Allied forces lost 83 killed against more than 700 communist deaths, but most VC forces escaped.

An American M50 Ontos (Ancient Greek for 'the thing') prepares for action, Vietnam. Mounting six M40 106mm (4.17in) recoilless guns, the Ontos proved to be excellent at providing close fire support for infantry operations.

■ Operation *Junction City*, 22 February–14 May 1967

Operations from February through May by four South Vietnamese and 22 US battalions to destroy the VC 9th Division in War Zone C. After more than 2000 were killed against 282 US/South Vietnamese losses, the Viet Cong moved their headquarters to Cambodia.

■ Hue, 30 January–3 March 1969

As part of the Tet Offensive of 1968, the VC and North Vietnamese dedicated two regiments to the seizure of the imperial capital of Hue. On the morning of 31 January 1968, the North Vietnamese 6th Regiment attacked the walled citadel north of the Perfume River, while the 4th Regiment attacked the new city south of the river. Hue was defended by minimal South Vietnamese and US forces, who were fixated more on the fighting in the countryside. In the initial fighting, the communists seized most of the city, except for the headquarters of Gen Ngo Quang Truong's 1st ARVN Division in the citadel and a small MACV compound south of the river. Numbering only a few hundred men, both outposts held out against heavy communist assaults. Initially concerned more with the fighting at nearby Khe Sanh, US and South Vietnamese commands were slow to respond to the threat and sent minimal reinforcements.

Once the threat had become clear, troops from the 1st Cavalry and the 101st Airborne worked to cut off communist supply lines outside Hue against elements of three North Vietnamese divisions that US planners had thought were engaged at Khe Sanh. In Hue, three battalions of US Marines made their way to the new city south of the Perfume river and nearly 11 South Vietnamese battalions fought their way into Truong's embattled defences in the citadel. When the situations both south and north of the Perfume River were secure, US and South Vietnamese forces took the offensive in a street-to-street and house-to-house urban battle. Realizing that keeping their flag above the fabled citadel and

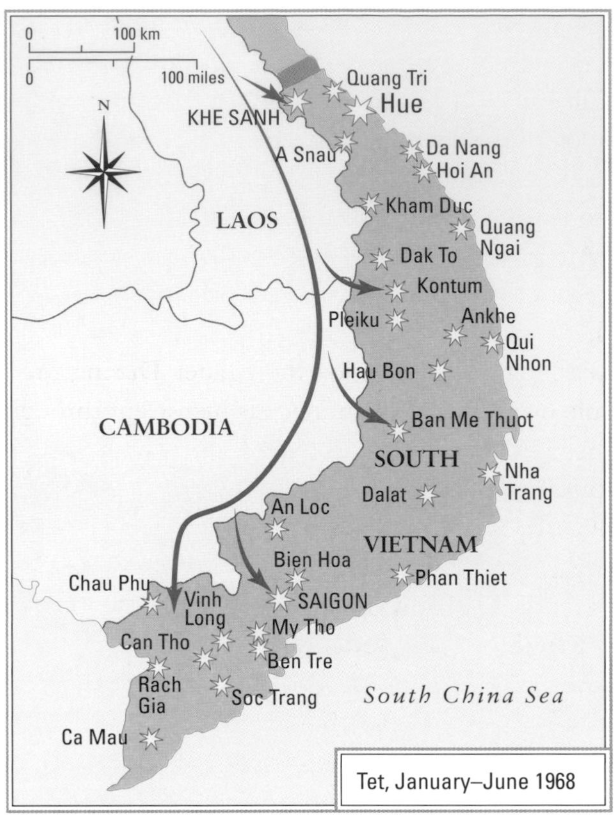

Tet, January–June 1968

imperial palace had immense psychological value, communist forces fought tenaciously. The fighting on both fronts moved very slowly, with very heavy losses until 12 February, when South Vietnamese I Corps commander Gen Hoang Xuon Lam gave permission to use whatever firepower was necessary to clear the city. Communist forces fought with desperation, resulting in artillery and air strikes levelling much of the city and the citadel to blast out communist resistance. With less organic heavy weapon support, South Vietnamese forces in the citadel were augmented by the 1st Battalion, 5th Marines.

On 21 February, the 1st Cavalry Division closed off communist supply lines to Hue after heavy fighting and, on 24 February, the Second Battalion, 3rd ARVN Regiment overran the southern wall of the citadel. They took down the VC flag that had been flying there for nearly a month. The next day, South Vietnamese troops recaptured the imperial palace, heralding an end to the battle. In the fighting, US forces suffered more than 200 dead, while the South Vietnamese lost nearly 400 killed. North Vietnamese and VC losses exceeded 5000 dead. More than half of the city was destroyed in the fighting, leaving 116,000 civilians homeless from a population of 140,000.

After the fighting, US and South Vietnamese began to unearth mass graves in the areas of Hue that the communists had once held, especially the Gia Hoa district outside the citadel. During their rule over Hue, the communists had swept through the city bearing lists of those who had aided the 'puppet government' of South Vietnam. Nearly 3000 bodies were discovered, but some estimates suggest that the communists summarily executed as many as 6000 civilians during the fighting.

■ Khe Sanh, 21 January–8 April 1968

Khe Sanh combat base, built on a hilltop located 10km from the Laotian border, was the westernmost in a line of Allied defences south of the DMZ designed to prevent communist infiltration into South Vietnam. By 1968, Khe Sanh combat base was occupied by 3000 US Marines of the 3rd Marine Division, while a further 3000 Marines were stationed on four nearby hilltop positions surrounding the base, positions that had been the subject of heavy fighting during 1967. That fighting not only had demonstrated a sizable enemy build-up in the area, but also prompted Gen William Westmoreland to believe that Khe Sanh was tenable even in the face of a heavy enemy siege, especially given that it housed a runway capable of landing C-130s.

As part of their planning for the Tet Offensive, North Vietnamese forces began to stream into the area around Khe Sanh in November 1967. They eventually totalled as many as 40,000 troops, especially of the 325th Division and the 320th Division, cutting US ground contact with the Marines at Khe Sanh. Communist planners, led by Gen Vo Nguyen Giap, hoped by attacking Khe Sanh to draw American attention from the cities of South Vietnam, which were the real targets of the coming Tet Offensive. On 21 January 1967, North Vietnamese forces simultaneously attacked two of the outlying US Marine hilltop positions and launched a massive artillery strike on Khe Sanh combat base, opening the siege of Khe Sanh. Fearing a defeat reminiscent of the French at Dien Bien Phu in 1954, President Lyndon Johnson kept a close eye on the fighting at Khe Sanh, receiving hourly reports and even having a mock-up of Khe Sanh constructed in the basement of the White House. Hoping that he had drawn North Vietnamese forces into what might prove to be a climactic battle, Westmoreland ordered the US Marines to hold firm and launched Operation *Niagara*, a series of bombing strikes on the North Vietnamese troop concentrations around Khe Sanh. Tactical bombers flew more than 16,000 sorties in defence of the US Marines, delivering more than 31,000 tons of bombs, while B-52 Arc Light strikes delivered nearly 60,000 tons of bombs, making Operation *Niagara* one of the

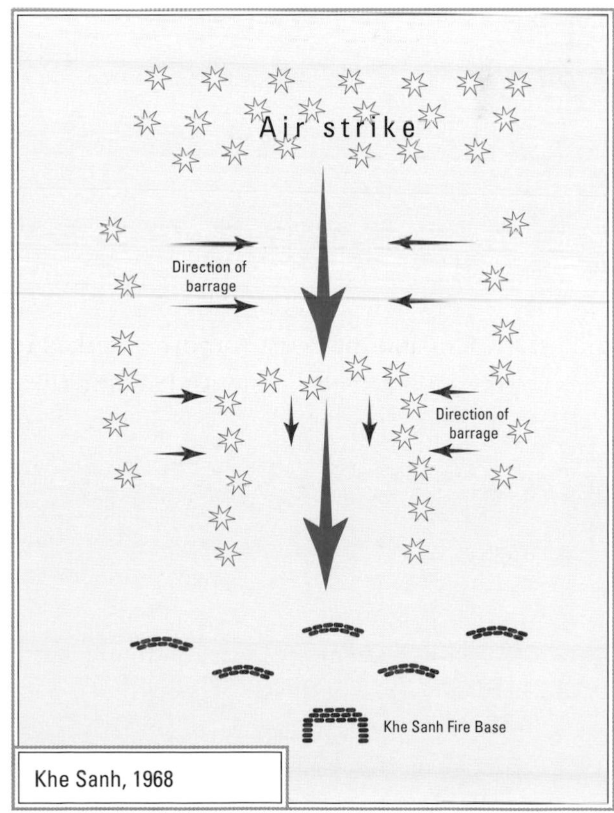

Khe Sanh, 1968

Hue, 30 January–3 March 1969

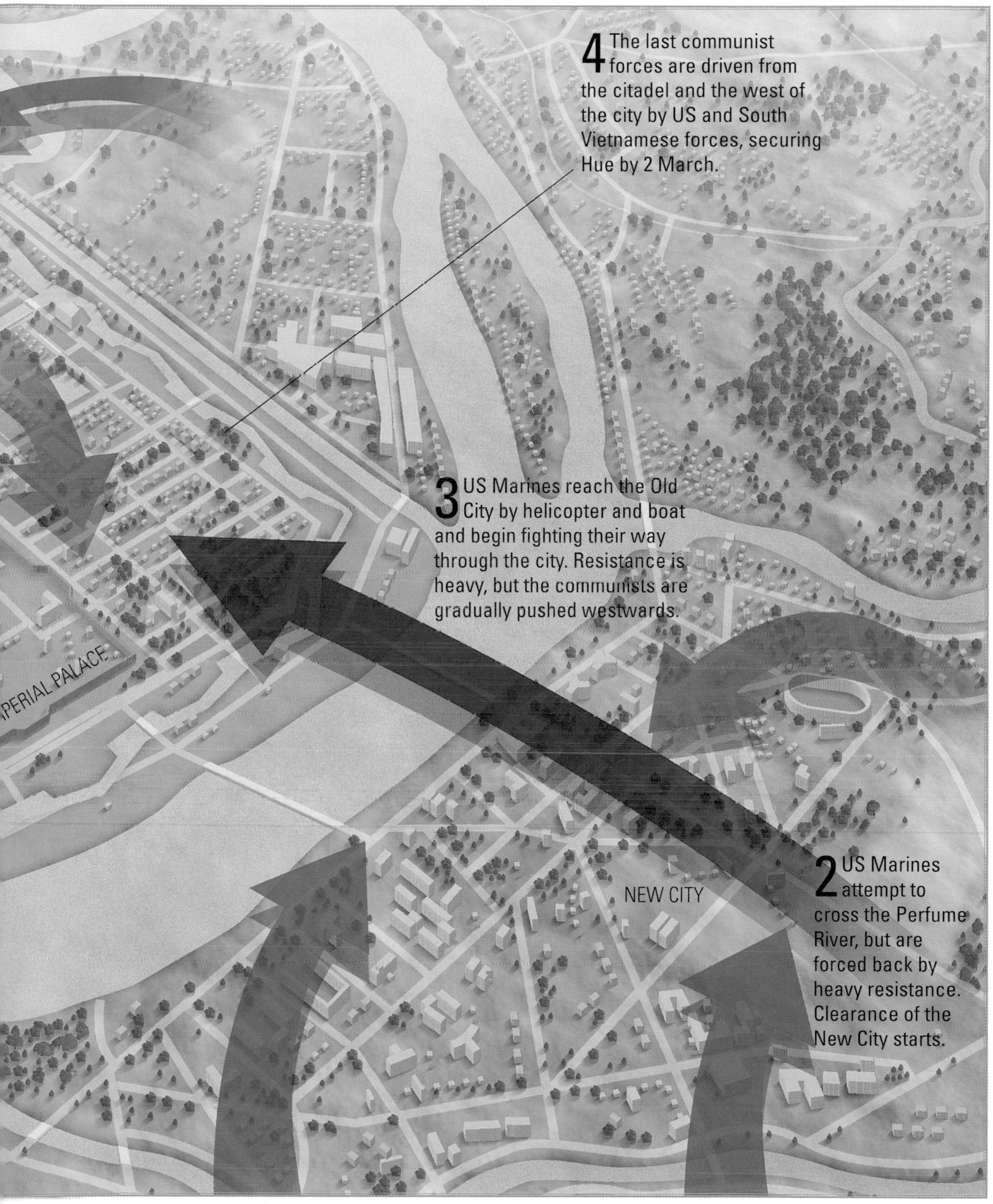
4 The last communist forces are driven from the citadel and the west of the city by US and South Vietnamese forces, securing Hue by 2 March.
3 US Marines reach the Old City by helicopter and boat and begin fighting their way through the city. Resistance is heavy, but the communists are gradually pushed westwards.
PERIAL PALACE
NEW CITY
2 US Marines attempt to cross the Perfume River, but are forced back by heavy resistance. Clearance of the New City starts.

heaviest bombing campaigns in the history of warfare. At the beginning of February 1968, as the Tet Offensive raged throughout South Vietnam, fighting around Khe Sanh combat base intensified.

On 7 February, a North Vietnamese assault involving 12 tanks overran the Special Forces camp at Lang Vei, west of Khe Sanh on Route 9. Bitter fighting also took place on the Marine hilltop outposts surrounding Khe Sanh, with Hill 861 being overrun by mid-February. By late February, the North Vietnamese artillery barrage on Khe Sanh combat base strengthened and, on 29 February elements of the North Vietnamese 304th Division stormed the base, but were driven off with major losses. Under heavy pressure from the air, and with the failure of the wider Tet Offensive, North Vietnamese forces began to withdraw from the Khe Sanh area in early March.

By early April, US forces in Operation *Pegasus* reopened ground communication with Khe Sanh and the siege was at an end. During the fighting, the Marines lost 205 killed and 1600 wounded, while 97 US and 33 South Vietnamese were killed in the relief efforts. The North Vietnamese lost as many as 15,000 casualties during the siege of Khe Sanh.

■ Saigon, 30 January–7 March 1968

On 31 January, a force of more than 35 North Vietnamese and VC battalions attacked targets in Saigon during the Tet Offensive, in efforts designed to seize key military and governmental targets, including the Tan Son Nhut air base and the presidential palace. One platoon of sappers struck the US embassy. In most areas, the communist attacks were repulsed, except for the Cho Lon district, where fighting lingered until early March.

■ Operation *Menu*, 18 March 1969–28 May 1970

Codename for the secret bombing of Cambodia, which dropped more than 100,000 tons of bombs but failed significantly to disrupt the Ho Chi Minh Trail or to destroy the VC command in the South.

■ Operation *Tailwind*, 11–13 September 1970

Hoping to disrupt communist activity in Laos, US and Montagnard special forces made a covert raid that overran a regional headquarters and obtained significant intelligence. The force was then extracted by helicopter.

■ Operation *Lam Son 719*, 8 February–25 March 1971

On 8 February, a South Vietnamese force invaded southern Laos with the goal of severing the Ho Chi Minh Trail at Tchepone. Expecting light resistance, the South Vietnamese, under heavy US air cover, seized hilltop fire support bases to guard an armoured thrust down Route 9. Predicting such an assault, the North Vietnamese gathered as many as 60,000 men to face the 17,000 South Vietnamese attackers. Amid command indecision at the highest levels, the South Vietnamese armoured thrust ground to a halt at A Luoi, not halfway to its objective, as North Vietnamese troops massed to assault the isolated South Vietnamese flanking positions. On 1 March, a South Vietnamese helilborne assault seized Tchepone, but found little of military value. During the withdrawal phase, several of the isolated South Vietnamese fire support bases were overrun and were reliant on US airpower for defence and US helicopters for extraction. More than 100 US aircraft were lost, with over 250 Americans killed. The North Vietnamese lost an estimated 13,000 dead.

■ Quang Tri City, 30 Mar–16 Sep 1972

A South Vietnamese offensive to retake Quang Tri City and citadel, which had been lost during the Easter Offensive. South Vietnamese troops of I Corps, commanded by Gen Ngo Quang Truong, entered Quang Tri in mid-July, fighting against six North Vietnamese divisions. After two months of fighting, Quang Tri fell to the South Vietnamese on 16 September, with the loss of nearly 3000 North Vietnamese killed in action.

■ An Loc, 13 April–20 July 20 1972

The South Vietnamese 5th Division was besieged in An Loc by elements of three North Vietnamese

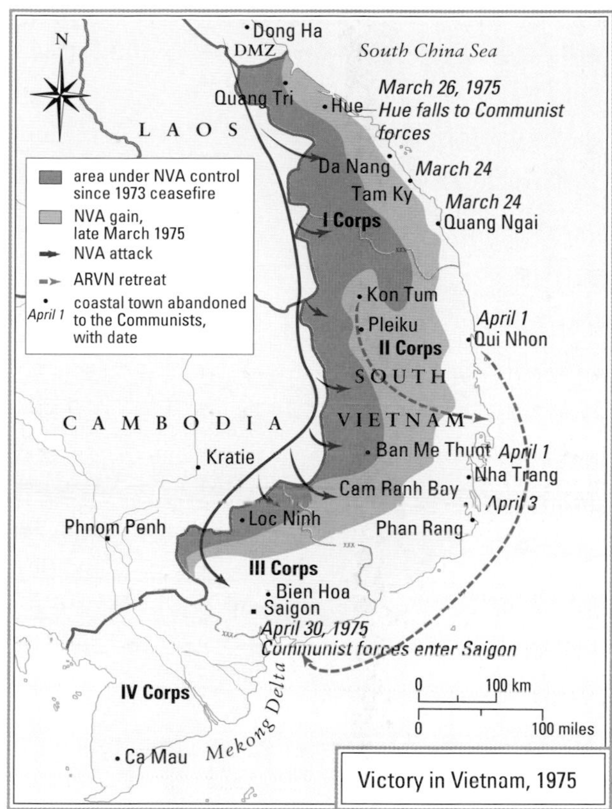

Victory in Vietnam, 1975

divisions from April to June during the Easter Offensive. The South Vietnamese lost 2000 dead, inflicting 10,000 casualties on the North Vietnamese.

■ **Kontum, 26–27 May 1972**

Elements of three North Vietnamese divisions launched failed assaults on the Central Highlands road junction town of Kontum as part of the Easter Offensive. North Vietnamese forces suffered an estimated 15,000 casualties.

■ **Phuoc Binh, 12 Dec 1974–6 Jan 1975**

On 12 December 1974, North Vietnamese forces attacked Phuoc Binh Province in part to discern whether or not US forces would intervene. With no US reaction, the provincial capital fell on 6 January, emboldening the North Vietnamese.

■ **Campaign 275, 10–11 March 1975**

The North Vietnamese launched an assault into South Vietnam through the Central Highlands, commanded by Gen Van Tien Dung. With the fall of Ban Me Thuot, South Vietnamese President Nguyen Van Thieu decided to abandon the Central Highlands.

■ **Xuan Loc, 9–21 April 1975**

Battle at a critical road junction north of Saigon, in which the South Vietnamese 18th Division held for two weeks against the entire North Vietnamese IV Corps. Xuan Loc's fall on 23 April left the road to Saigon clear.

■ **Fall of Saigon, 30 April 1975**

The North Vietnamese unleashed their final offensive against Saigon, the Ho Chi Minh Campaign. By 29 April, North Vietnamese units were pushing into the suburbs of the city before the Americans belatedly launched Operation *Frequent Wind* to evacuate at-risk South Vietnamese personnel. The chaotic evacuations were halted by the fall of Saigon on 30 April, leaving many of the South Vietnamese population that had supported the US behind to face North Vietnamese revolutionary justice.

US Occupation of the Dominican Republic 1965–66

■ **Operation *Power Pack*, 28 April 1965–September 1966**

On 24 April, leftist guerrillas deposed the elected government and began an intense campaign of intimidation against security forces in Santo Domingo. Five hundred US Marines, two battalions from the Army's 82nd Airborne Division, and Special Operations Forces deployed to the island. Their mission was to secure the capital's power station at the Duarte Bridge. Forty-four US soldiers died, but between 6000 and 10,000 Dominicans may have died in the fighting.

Invasion of Grenada 1983

■ **Operation *Urgent Fury*, 25 October–3 November 1983**

In 1983, political instability in the Commonwealth nation of Grenada saw the overthrow and murder of the government of Maurice Bishop by a faction of his revolutionary New Jewel movement. The governor-general, Sir Paul Scoon, was placed under house arrest. The Organization of Eastern Caribbean States appealed to the United States for assistance, which President Ronald Reagan, concerned by the links between the coup plotters and Cuba, was more than willing to provide.

Operation *Urgent Fury* began on 25 October 1983, with several thousand American troops landing at key points on the island, most notably in the form of a parachute assault on Port Salines airfield. Over the course of the next few days, there was notably hard fighting, until on 3 November all US objectives had been taken, and the operation was declared over. US forces suffered 19 killed and 116 wounded.

US Invasion of Panama 1989–90

■ Operation *Just Cause*, 1989–90

Tension between the United States and Panama increased after revelations that the Panamanian dictator, Gen Manuel Noriega, was involved in drug smuggling. In February 1988, he was indicted on drugs charges in the United States. Between 1988 and 1989, Noriega defeated a coup he blamed on the Americans, and overturned the results of elections. In October 1989, a second coup failed. On 15 December 1989, Noriega unwisely declared a state of war with the United States, followed by several provocations. The most serious of these provocations was the killing of a US Marine officer on 16 December, an incident that prompted the US Government into action.

On 20 December, the American President George Bush ordered an invasion, Operation *Just Cause,* to protect American citizens and to capture Noriega. American forces quickly took control of Panama, and Noriega fled to the papal mission in Panama City. After a standoff with American troops, he surrendered on 3 January 1990, effectively bringing Operation *Just Cause* to a conclusion.

First Gulf War 1990–91

■ Gulf War–Air Campaign, 16 January–28 February 1991

In the wake of Iraq's August 1990 invasion of Kuwait, an American-led multinational Coalition deployed to Saudi Arabia. To force an Iraqi withdrawal, the Coalition initiated an aerial campaign on the night of 16–17 January 1991, which lasted for 43 days until the ceasefire on 28 February. The Coalition ground campaign lasted for only 100 hours of this 43-day period.

The Coalition air forces deployed 2330 aircraft, whereas the Iraqis fielded just 820, mostly inferior Soviet-supplied equipment. The overall Coalition air war delivered 88,000 tons of munitions in over 100,000 sorties. The campaign also comprised four overlapping phases: a strategic air campaign, a battle to win air superiority over Kuwait, attacks on the Iraqi ground forces and, from 24 February, attacks supporting the unfolding ground offensive. In the war's first hours, based on the innovative *Instant Thunder* plan, American F-117A Nighthawk Stealth aircraft flew undetected by Iraqi radars to target strategic enemy command facilities in Baghdad. Following this, Coalition aircraft attacked the infrastructures associated with the enemy's sophisticated 'Kari' air defence system to gain control of the skies, so that aerial operations could be mounted without fear of casualties being caused by enemy aircraft attacks or SAM responses. In phase three, Coalition aircraft attacked Iraqi ground forces to inflict casualties and lower their morale, as well as smash their logistical and command capabilities. Finally, once the ground war commenced, Coalition air forces attacked enemy frontline forces, interdicted Iraqi lines of communication and performed reconnaissance missions.

This sophisticated Coalition air war was hugely effective. It degraded overall Iraqi command and control capability by 90 per cent, smashed their ability to move, destroyed literally hundreds of vehicles and inflicted 40 per cent casualties on the enemy's ground forces, making a significant contribution to the Coalition victory.

■ KHAFJI, 29 JANUARY–1 FEBRUARY 1991

Even though Coalition air forces had initiated their aerial campaign against Iraqi forces from mid-January 1991, no significant ground operations materialized until 29 January. On this date, 25,000 Iraqi troops from three mobile divisions mounted a surprise attack from southeastern Kuwait along the coast to the Saudi Arabian town of Al-Khafji. Coalition ground and air forces inflicted heavy casualties as they forced back this incursion. The Coalition suffered 97 casualties, the Iraqis 700.

■ AL BUSAYYAH, 26 FEBRUARY 1991

Fought between American and Iraqi armoured forces, this brief battle saw the Americans take the town with little opposition. The American units involved then moved on to participate in the battle of Medina Ridge the following day, widely regarded as the largest US tank battle in history.

■ PHASE LINE BULLET, 26 FEBRUARY 1991

The battle of Phase Line Bullet was fought on 26 February 1991 by the US 1st and 3rd Armoured Divisions against the Iraqi Tawakalna Republican Guard Division, leading to the latter formation's destruction.

■ WADI AL-BATIN, 16 FEBRUARY 1991

This battle was a successful diversionary operation to convince Iraqi forces that the main weight of the Coalition attack to liberate Kuwait would drive through the wadi, tying down and immobilizing Iraqi troops.

■ 73RD EASTING, 26 FEBRUARY 1991

The battle of 73rd Easting on 26 February 1991 saw the American 2nd Armored Cavalry Regiment destroy more than 250 Iraqi armoured vehicles of the Iraqi 18th Mechanized and 37th Armoured Brigades of the Tawakalna Division.

■ MEDINA RIDGE, 27 FEBRUARY 1991

On 27 February 1991, the US 1st Armored Division engaged the 2nd Brigade of the Medina Luminous Division, Iraqi Republican Guard, on the Medina Ridge just outside the city of Basra. The battle lays claim to being the largest tank battle in the US Army's history and saw the effective integration of tanks, attack helicopters and fixed-wing aircraft as the Republican Guard formation was destroyed.

The Iraqis lost over 180 tanks and at least another 125 armoured vehicles during the course of the two-hour battle, including a number of attacks by AH-64 Apache helicopters and A-10 'tankbuster' aircraft. American casualties were remarkably light: only four M1A1 Abrams tanks were sufficiently badly damaged by return fire to be rendered immobile, and there were no American fatalities. The Iraqis, by contrast, lost over 330 dead.

■ NORFOLK, 27 FEBRUARY 1991

This was the final battle of the 1991 Gulf War before a ceasefire came into effect. Taking its name from the codename for the geographical area in which the fighting occurred, the battle saw elements of the US 1st Infantry and 2nd Armored Divisions engage the remnants of the Tawakalna Division of the Iraqi Republican Guard, and ended with the final destruction of that formation.

Kosovo 1999

■ OPERATION *ALLIED FORCE*, 24 MARCH 1999

After Yugoslavian President Slobodan Milosevic ordered 40,000 of his army and police troops to crack down on the breakaway enclave of ethnic Albanians in Kosovo, NATO warplanes again intervened in the Balkans. The air campaign occurred in three phases, including the destruction of Serbian integrated air defences, strikes against Serbian military targets from the Kosovo border to the 44th Parallel, and strikes against targets north of the 44th Parallel, including Belgrade.

Operation *Desert Fox* 1998

■ *DESERT FOX*, 16–19 DECEMBER 1998

In December 1998, American and British warplanes carried out a series of coordinated

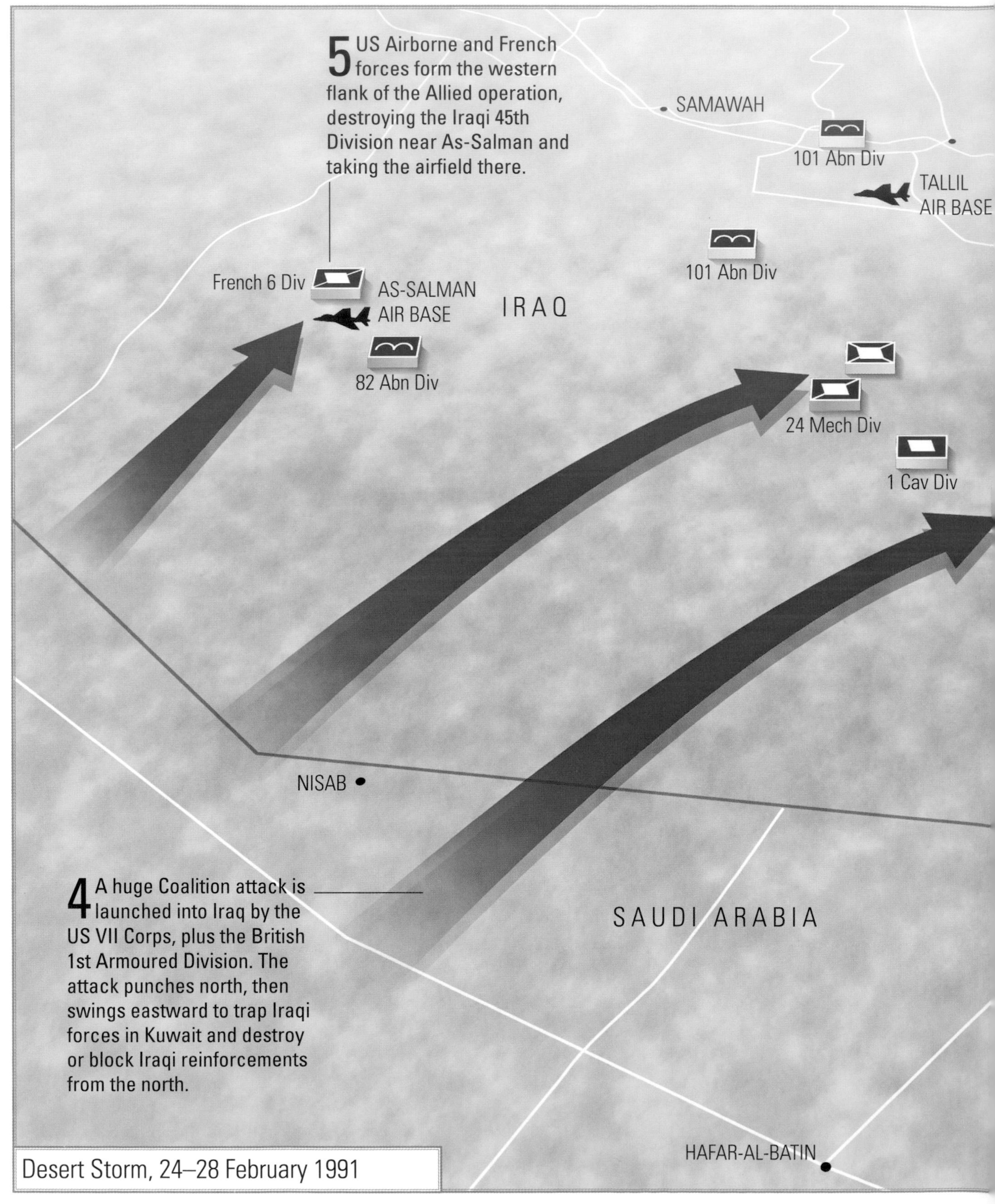

Desert Storm, 24–28 February 1991

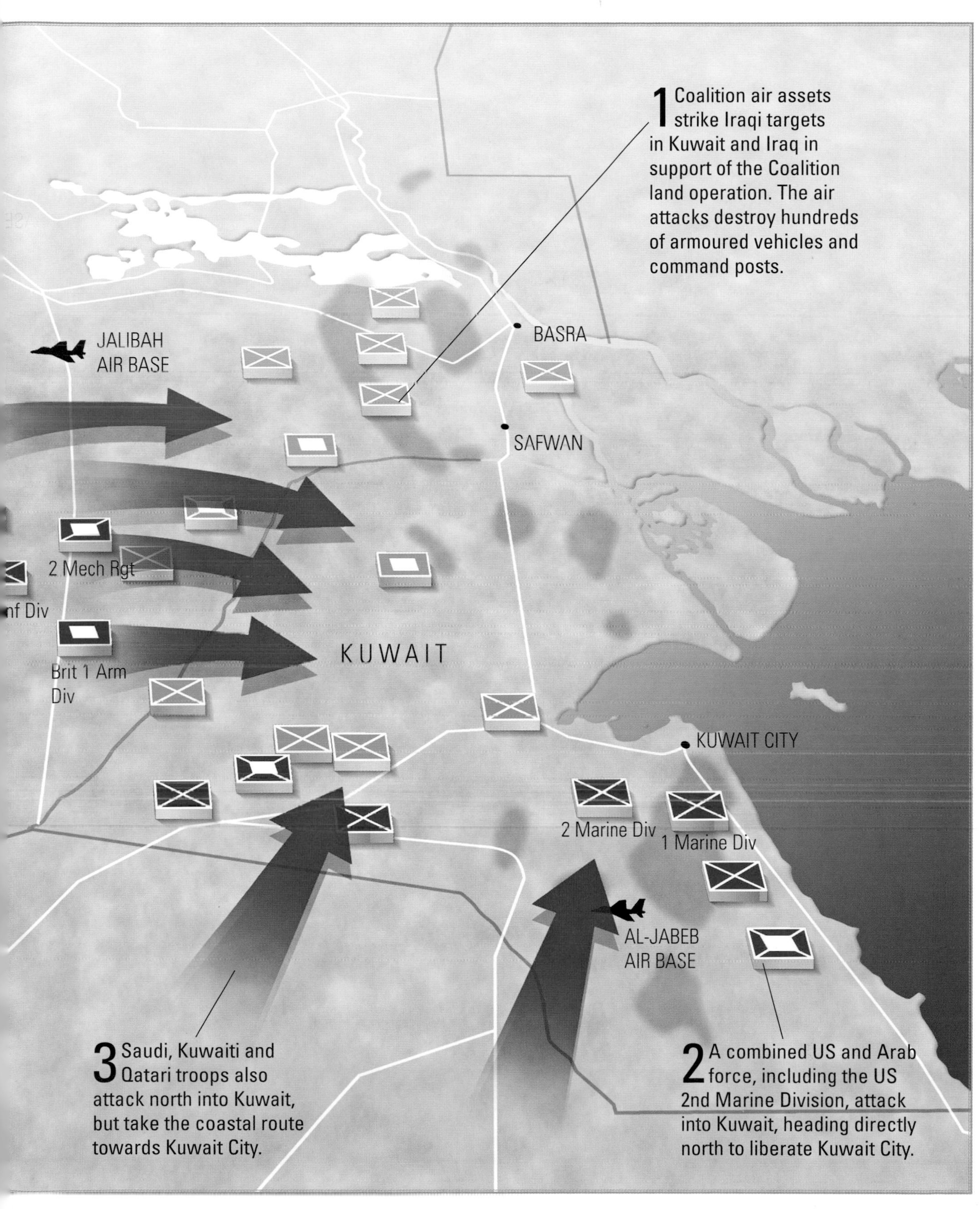

1 Coalition air assets strike Iraqi targets in Kuwait and Iraq in support of the Coalition land operation. The air attacks destroy hundreds of armoured vehicles and command posts.
JALIBAH AIR BASE
BASRA
SAFWAN
2 Mech Rgt
nf Div
KUWAIT
Brit 1 Arm Div
KUWAIT CITY
2 Marine Div
1 Marine Div
AL-JABEB AIR BASE
3 Saudi, Kuwaiti and Qatari troops also attack north into Kuwait, but take the coastal route towards Kuwait City.
2 A combined US and Arab force, including the US 2nd Marine Division, attack into Kuwait, heading directly north to liberate Kuwait City.

strikes designed to destroy Iraq's weapons research and development capabilities. The allies worked through a list of 100 targets that included integrated air defence systems, military command-and-control and other resources. The operation involved as many as 600 combat sorties flown by more than 300 aircraft, including US Air Force B-52 and B-1 Lancer bombers. The US Navy also launched 325 Tomahawk cruise missiles.

Afghanistan 2001–Present

■ Mazar-e Sharif, 19 October–10 November 2001

At the outset of Operation *Enduring Freedom*, US Army Special Operations Forces (SOF) arrived in northern Afghanistan to join Afghan rebels in overthrowing the Taliban. At Mazar-e Sharif, Boeing CH-47 Chinooks of the 160th Special Operations Aviation Regiment (SOAR) airlifted a 12-man SOF unit to a landing zone south of the city. The Americans joined forces with warlord Abdur Dostum's Northern Alliance, calling air strikes against Taliban command posts, armoured vehicles and troops. Dostum moved into Mazar-e Sharif on 10 November.

■ Kunduz, 11–23 November 2001

Northern Alliance fighters, with US SOF support, defeated 13,000 Taliban and al-Qaeda fighters at Kunduz. American aerial bombardment destroyed Taliban vehicles, leaving the insurgents with no choice but surrender on 24 November. The victors claimed 2000 enemy fighters killed and more than 3500 captured.

■ Qala-i-Jangi, 25 November–1 December 2001

At the old fortress of Qala-i-Jangi in Mazar-e Sharif, the Northern Alliance imprisoned 300–500 Taliban and al-Qaeda fighters captured during the siege, as well as those taken at the battles of Taloquon and Kunduz. Northern Alliance soldiers failed to search the prisoners, some of whom had smuggled weapons into the prison. A riot broke out as Central Intelligence Agency (CIA) agents interrogated al-Qaeda militants. Prisoners killed one of the CIA agents and overran the Qala-i-Jangi fort's armoury, seizing more weapons and fighting back.

US and British SOF teams, supported by air strikes, assisted Afghan forces quelling the bloody, week-long uprising. At one point, Northern Alliance troops brought the 100mm gun of a Russian-built T-55 tank to bear against the captured armoury. Only 86 prisoners survived the battle. The Northern Alliance lost 73 Afghan soldiers. An American infantry company from the 10th Mountain Division was deployed from Uzbekistan to help re-secure the prison.

■ Kandahar, 22 November–7 December 2001

Harried by Eastern Alliance fighters and local Afghan militia, the Taliban withdrew from Kandahar. The US Marine Corps' 15th Marine Expeditionary Unit and NATO Special Forces entered the city as Hamid Karzai was named President of Afghanistan.

■ Tora Bora, December 2001

South of Jalalabad, Taliban and al-Qaeda fighters had fortified their positions in the Tora Bora Mountains. US SOF and local Afghan rebels, under warlord Hazrat Ali, launched an offensive to dislodge their enemies. Coalition forces moved cautiously into the broken, high-altitude terrain, using horses and donkeys to bear their heavy equipment.

From ridgeline observation posts, SOF units supported the Northern Alliance advance by calling in air strikes. Night attacks by US AC-130 Spectre gunships poured fire into the Taliban positions. Nevertheless, Ali's forces had difficulty taking and holding ground against determined counter-attacks.

By day, the Afghans would advance under American air cover, only to fall back to more defensible positions as darkness fell. Arab al-Qaeda fighters resisted to the death, resulting in what one SOF soldier reported as a 'very hard gunfight'. By

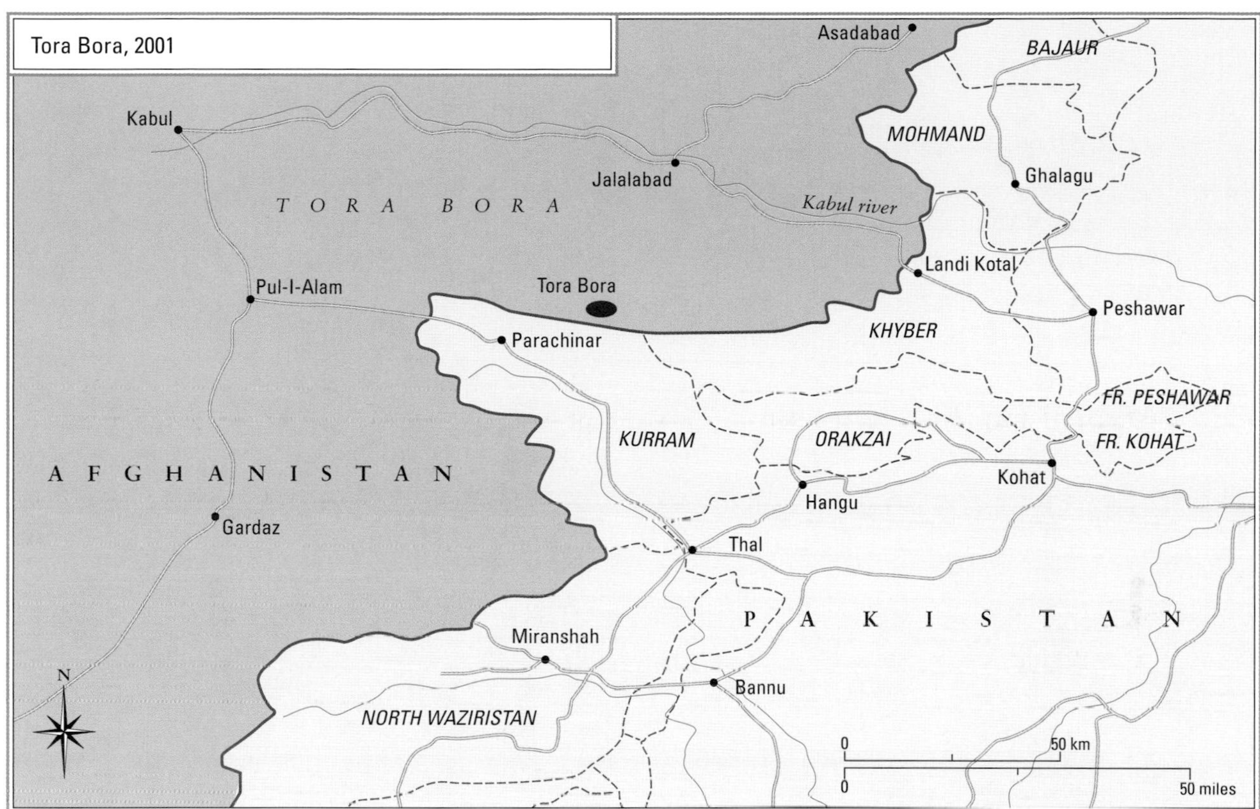

Tora Bora, 2001

mid-December, heavy air strikes on the mountain cave complexes had broken organized Taliban and al-Qaeda resistance.

Operation *Anaconda*, 2–19 March 2002

Operation *Anaconda* was a coordinated attack on Taliban and al-Qaeda positions in the Shahi Kowt Valley. It involved US and Coalition SOF, airborne soldiers and light infantry and 1000 Afghan troops. They faced as many as 1000 Taliban and al-Qaeda fighters. Despite the allies enjoying numerical superiority and powerful close air support assets, much of the combat involved bitter hand-to-hand fighting on the valley's steep slopes.

On the night of 3–4 March, US SOF and Rangers became embroiled with al-Qaeda fighters on Takur Ghar Mountain. During an assault landing, militants shot down one helicopter, killing three Rangers and an aircrewman. The remaining Rangers and SOF fought their way up to join their comrades. An al-Qaeda counter-attack failed to dislodge them. By the end of the operation, 15

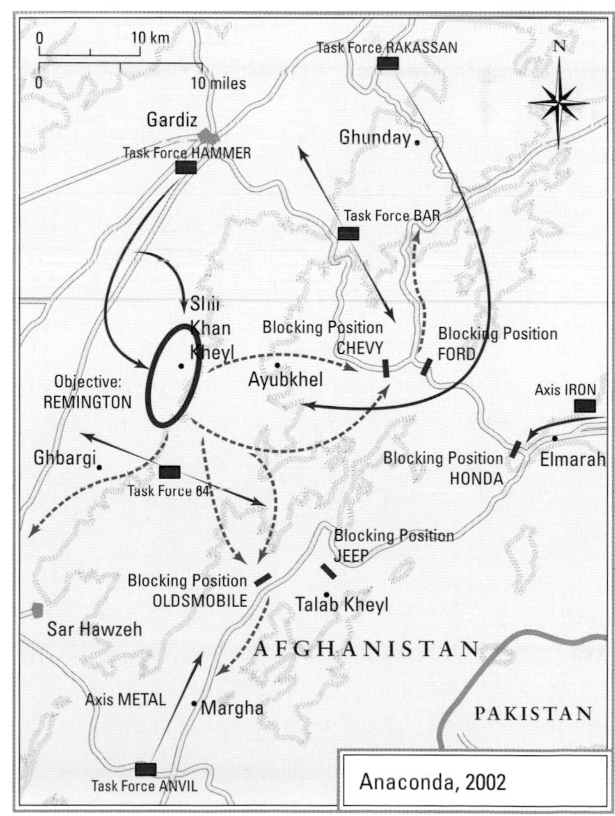

Anaconda, 2002

coalition troops had died along with hundreds of their enemies. Many Taliban and al-Qaeda fighters escaped to Pakistan.

■ Operation *Mongoose*, 27 January–3 February 2003

More than 300 Coalition troops, including elements of the US 82nd Airborne Division, attacked Taliban and al-Qaeda fortifications in the Adi Ghar Mountains, 23km north of Spin Boldak. Operation *Mongoose* followed a battle between soldiers of the International Security Assistance Force (ISAF) and approximately 80 Taliban and al-Qaeda fighters. By the end of the operation, Coalition and Afghan troops cleared 75 caves using explosives as well as precision air strikes to destroy cave complexes that had been used as fighting positions and weapons caches.

■ Operation *Mountain Thrust*, 15 June–31 July 2006

More than 11,000 NATO and Afghan troops attacked Taliban fighters in Uruzgan and Helmand Provinces. US, British, Canadian and Afghan troops sought to establish a permanent NATO presence (via ISAF) in southern Afghanistan, historically a Taliban stronghold. Coalition forces killed more than 1000 Taliban and captured 400, while suffering 155 killed, 106 wounded and 43 of their own captured during the campaign.

■ Operation *Mountain Fury*, 16 September 2006–15 January 2007

NATO sent 3000 ISAF troops and 4000 Afghan National Army (ANA) troops into the central and eastern Afghan provinces of Ghazni, Khost, Logar Paktika and Paktya to root out Taliban safe havens. The US 10th Mountain Division suffered 150 casualties during October and November. In December, British Royal Marines attacked the Taliban near Garmsir. NATO troops inflicted more than 1000 Taliban casualties. The operation built upon the earlier Canadian-led Operation *Medusa* in Kandahar Province (2–17 September 2006).

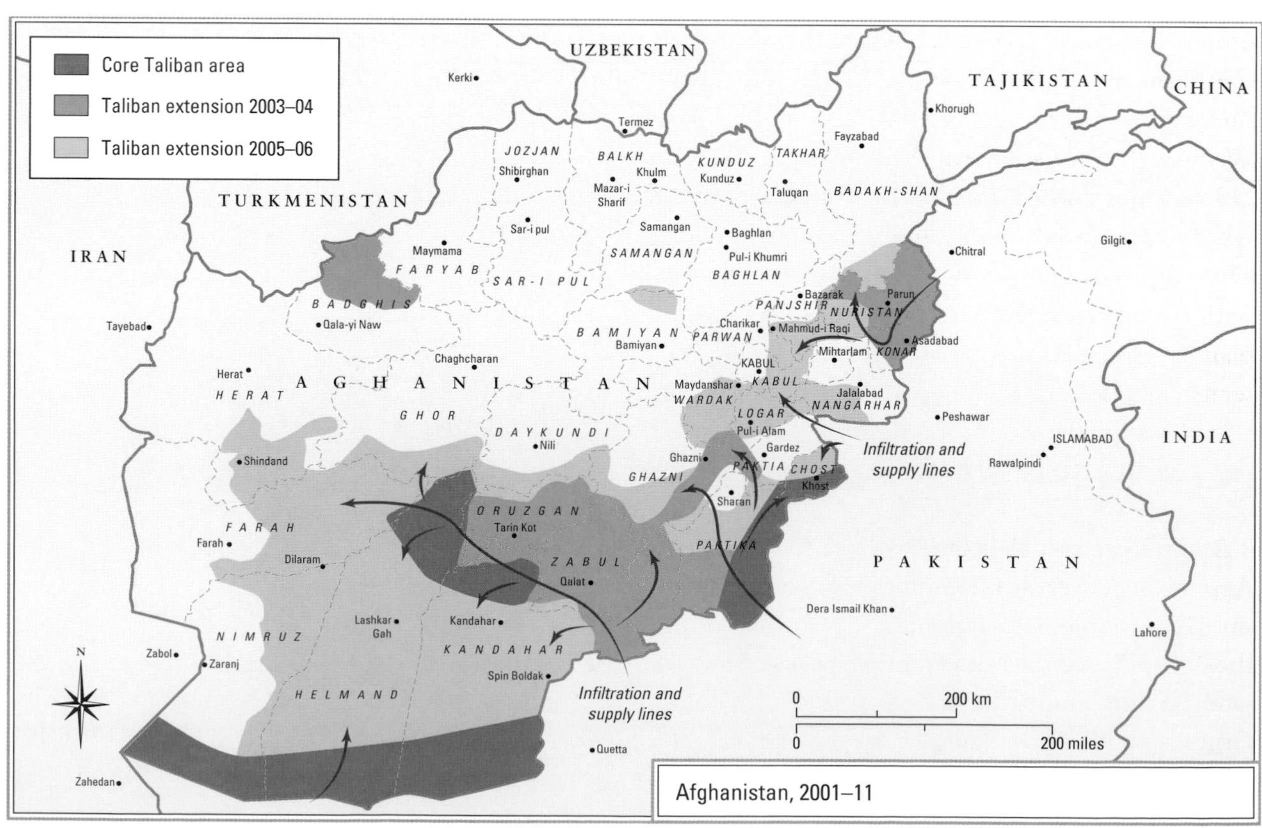

Afghanistan, 2001–11

■ Wanat, 13 July 2008

At Wanat village, in Afghanistan's Waygal Valley, the US 503rd Parachute Infantry Regiment, with 24 ANA troops, defended against a four-hour Taliban attack on their outpost. Nine Americans died in the fighting.

■ Operation *Khanjar*, 2 Jul–20 Aug 2009

In July 2009, the US 2nd Marine Expeditionary Brigade (MEB) sent 4000 Marines and more than 600 ANA troops to clear Taliban forces from Nawa and Garmsir districts in central Helmand Province. As the Coalition and ANA forces moved through the Helmand river valley to several hostile villages south of Lashkar Gah, they encountered improvised explosive devices (IEDs) and skirmished with small units of fighters. US air strikes helped break Taliban resistance, although the Taliban finished the battle still in control of parts of Helmand.

■ Operation *Moshtarak*, 13 February–7 December 2010

More than 15,000 ISAF and Afghan troops successfully ousted the Taliban from Marjah, a major opium-growing district in Helmand Province. Coalition and Afghan SOF helped establish landing sites for Chinooks carrying members of 1st Royal Welsh Battle Group near Showal. Subsequently, US Marines and ANA soldiers landed at Marjah, where they seized a large Taliban weapons cache. Over the next few months, bitter fighting ensued, with daily gun battles interrupting the Coalition's plan to restore Afghan government authority and security to the district.

Iraq 2003–2011

■ Air Campaign, 19 March–1 May 2003

Aerospace power in Operation *Iraqi Freedom* built on the technologies, tactics and lessons learned in the decade since the Gulf War of 1990–91. In 1991 satellites and unmanned aerial vehicles provided target intelligence and navigation support. Airborne command-and-control correlated data and prioritized targets. Forward air controllers on the ground matched weapons loads to targets. Strike planes laser-designated targets and linked targeting information to real time battlespace data. Advanced sensors assessed damage and helped commanders redirect attacks. By the end of April, Coalition air forces had deployed 1801 aircraft and flown more than 41,000 combat sorties.

■ al-Faw Peninsula, 20–24 March 2003

British 3 Commando Brigade Royal Marines led a Coalition force to capture Iraq's al-Faw peninsula at the conjunction of the Tigris and Euphrates rivers. Key objectives of the campaign included seizing Basra, the deepwater port Umm Qasr, and the offshore gas and oil platforms (GOPLATs) Khor al-Amaya and Mina al-Bakr. The 3500-man multinational force included the US 15th Marine Expeditionary Unit (MEU), US Navy SEAL Teams and Polish GROM Special Operations Forces (SOF).

■ Kirkuk, 20 March–10 April 2003

Joint Special Operations Task Force North (known as Task Force 'Viking') supported a Kurdish advance south across the Green Line to capture the oil-rich city of Kirkuk. After a 22-day siege, 2000 Kurdish fighters entered the city, supported by US Special Forces and the 173rd Airborne Division.

■ Umm Qasr, 21–25 March 2003

During the first night of the initial major clash of Operation *Telic* (Britain's reference for the 2003 Iraq War), US and Polish SOF seized the two GOPLATs, Khor al-Amaya and Mina al-Bakr. Ashore, SOF and British 3 Commando Brigade Royal Marines clashed with Iraqi troops, including Fedayeen Saddam internal security forces and Republican Guard units, to secure the port's oil and gas pumping stations.

Meanwhile, air support from RAF GR4 Tornadoes and GR7 Harriers helped destroy Iraqi armoured vehicles, fortified fighting positions and surface-to-air missile (SAM) sites ahead of the invasion. The US 15th MEU, with a platoon of four M1A1 Abrams tanks, helped drive out Iraqi defenders after five days of fighting. With the port secure, Coalition naval minesweepers helped clear the harbours for the imminent arrival of humanitarian aid shipments. As many as 40 Iraqi soldiers died in the fighting. The coalition lost 14 of its own men.

■ AN-NASIRIYAH, 23 MARCH–2 APRIL 2003

The US 2nd Marine Expeditionary Brigade (MEB), comprising 7000 Marines, less its Marine air group and combat service support battalion, formed the core of Task Force 'Tarawa'. This force crossed from Kuwait into Iraq on 21 March with the objective of securing an-Nasiriyah and its two bridges – the Coalition forces' route north to Baghdad led across those bridges.

Prior to the Marines' arrival, the Iraqis ambushed the US Army's 507th Maintenance Company, killing several soldiers and taking six captives. As 'Tarawa' moved through the area on 23 March, they, too, came under attack. Along the Saddam Canal, Iraq's 11th Infantry Division ambushed the Marines, firing RPGs and 100mm T-55 tank shells, destroying eight tracked amphibious assault vehicles and killing 18 Americans. Marine air strikes, including close support by AH-1W Super Cobra helicopters, destroyed 10 Iraqi tanks and blunted the force of their attack.

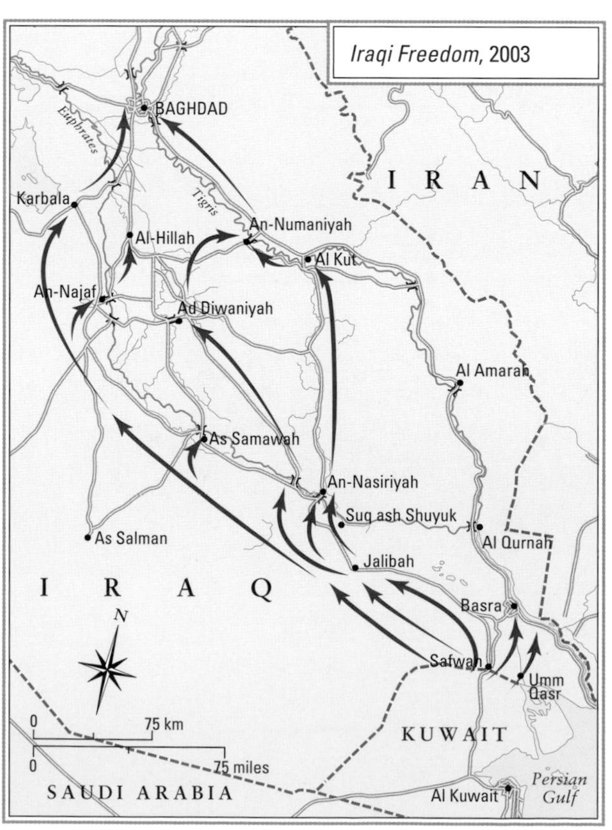

The Marines came to know the area around the Euphrates River and Saddam Canal bridges as 'ambush alley,' a free-fire zone sheltering Ba'athist Fedayeen Saddam fighters. They struck an American convoy, wounding 60 Marines and destroying 15 of their vehicles.

As bitter fighting continued, described by one Marine officer as 'knife fighting in a phone booth', confusion over the location of friend and foe led to some tragic accidents for the Americans. In one instance, two Marine units fired upon one another during a night patrol, resulting in 31 wounded. In another attack, on 23 March, one Marine was killed and more than a dozen others wounded when a US Air Force A-10 Thunderbolt II mistakenly turned its GAU-8 30mm cannon on their light armoured vehicles (LAVs). In the battles to secure an-Nasiriyah's two bridges, 22 Marines and more than 350 Iraqis were killed.

■ AN-NAJAF, 23–25 MARCH 2003

The US Army's 101st Airborne Division, with a brigade of the 82nd Airborne Division, supported by armoured troops from the US 3rd Infantry and 1st Armored Divisions, moved to an-Najaf. Along the route, Fedayeen Saddam paramilitary fighters lay in ambush, fighting tenaciously despite massive US firepower. During a strong sandstorm, the Americans moved north on Highway 28 and east across the Euphrates at Kifal to complete their encirclement of an-Najaf.

■ GREEN LINE, 26 MARCH 2003–FEBRUARY 2004

Task Force 'Viking' held a line demarcating Kurdish-controlled northern Iraq against 13 Ba'athist divisions. Viking's soldiers and Marines helped to occupy a significant portion of Saddam

Hussein's combat power as other American and British units advanced on Baghdad.

■ **BAGHDAD, 3–12 APRIL 2003**

The US Army's 3rd Infantry Division – 18,000 soldiers under MGen Buford Blount – and the 1st Marine Division – 18,000 Marines under MGen James N Mattis – led the attack on the Iraqi capital.The two divisions' M1 Abrams tanks, supported by American and British airpower dropping precision-guided munitions, cut through the defenders, which included 36,000 soldiers of the Iraqi Republican Guard. On 4 April, the 3rd Infantry Division seized the airport while the 1st Marines drove east, completing the city's envelopment. The army sent two armoured columns into Baghdad on so-called 'thunder runs', drawing out the defenders with a provocative attack.

By 7 April, 3rd Infantry Division's tanks had penetrated the city centre, destroying 20 Iraqi armoured fighting vehicles and a host of other materiel. With Baghdad under Coalition control, the commanders counted the cost of the campaign thus far: 42 soldiers killed, 133 wounded, 41 Marines killed, 151 wounded; 19 British troops killed, 36 wounded.

■ **FALLUJAH, 7 NOVEMBER–23 DECEMBER 2004**

Provoked in part by the 31 March murders of four Blackwater Security contractors and a general uprising in April, 2200 US Marines, with US Army and Iraqi Coalition troops in Al Anbar Province, launched Operation *Vigilant Resolve*. The plan marked a failed first attempt, between 5 April and 1 May, to wrest control of Fallujah from an emboldened insurgency, which had approximately 2000 fighters in the city.

The battle proved militarily inconclusive, if deadly: perhaps 600 civilians died in the crossfire along with 200 insurgents and 36 US troops. Coalition forces had gained control of only about 25 per cent of the city. In the autumn, Abu Musab al-Zarqawi's terrorists had re-established themselves in Fallujah, digging into more than 300 prepared fighting positions. The Coalition launched a new campaign called *al Fajr*, literally, Operation *Dawn*. This involved 25,000 troops in six Marine and two army battalions and two Iraqi Army battalions. Coalition aircraft and artillery provided direct and indirect fire support. Anticipating a violent clash, all but 400 civilians evacuated the city.

The joint task force operation bogged down on the night of 8 November as Army units outran the Marines, who were unaccustomed to heavy breach assault operations. Insurgents took advantage of the halt by shelling one of the Marines' trapped bulldozers, inflicting casualties and destroying equipment. Difficult house-to-house fighting followed, with Coalition troops clearing structures in risky searches for insurgents' ambuscades and weapons caches. The Coalition endured 54 US dead and 425 wounded, eight Iraqi soldiers dead and 43 wounded. The soldiers and US Marines killed as many as 2000 insurgents.

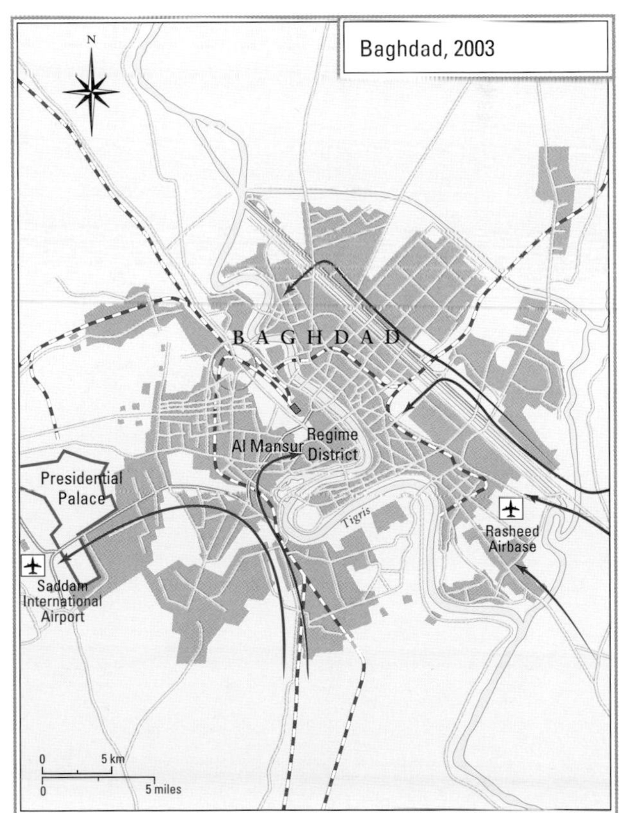

Index

Numbers in *italics* indicate map